Marx at the Movies

Marx at the Movies

Revisiting History, Theory and Practice

Edited by

Ewa Mazierska
University of Central Lancashire, UK

and

Lars Kristensen
University of Skövde, Sweden

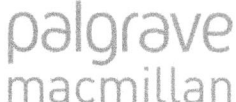

First published 2014 by
PALGRAVE MACMILLAN

Palgrave Macmillan in the UK is an imprint of Macmillan Publishers Limited,
registered in England, company number 785998, of Houndmills, Basingstoke,
Hampshire RG21 6XS.

Palgrave Macmillan in the US is a division of St Martin's Press LLC, 175 Fifth
Avenue, New York, NY 10010.

Palgrave Macmillan is the global academic imprint of the above companies
and has companies and representatives throughout the world.

Palgrave® and Macmillan® are registered trademarks in the United States,
the United Kingdom, Europe and other countries.

ISBN 978–1–137–37860–6

This book is printed on paper suitable for recycling and made from fully
managed and sustained forest sources. Logging, pulping and manufacturing
processes are expected to conform to the environmental regulations of the
country of origin.

A catalogue record for this book is available from the British Library.

A catalog record for this book is available from the Library of Congress.

Typeset by MPS Limited, Chennai, India.

Contents

List of Figures

viii   *List of Figures*

Notes on Contributors

Martin Brady is Lecturer in the German and Film Studies Departments at King's College London. He has published on film (Straub-Huillet, Michael Haneke, Robert Bresson, experimental film, literary adaptation, GDR documentary film, Kafka films, Adorno and cinema, Brechtian cinema, *Heimat 3*, *Downfall*, Ulrich Seidl, Peter Nestler), music (Arnold Schönberg, Paul Dessau), literature (Paul Celan, Elfriede Jelinek), Jewish exile architects, painting (Anselm Kiefer), the portrayal of thalidomide, and foraging in the works of Stifter, Handke and Beuys. He has translated Victor Klemperer's *LTI* and Alexander Kluge's *Cinema Stories* (with Helen Hughes), and works as a freelance translator and interpreter.

William Brown is Senior Lecturer in Film Studies at the University of Roehampton. He is the author of *Supercinema: Film-Philosophy for the Digital Age* (2013) and, with Dina Iordanova and Leshu Torchin, of *Moving People, Moving Images: Cinema and Trafficking in the New Europe* (2010). He is the editor, with David Martin-Jones, of *Deleuze and Film* (2012), and, with Jenna P-S Ng, of a special issue of *Animation: An Interdisciplinary Journal* on *Avatar* (2012). He has published various essays in edited collections and journals. He also makes very low-budget films, including *En Attendant Godard* (2009), *Afterimages* (2010), *Common Ground* (2012), *China: A User's Manual (Films)* (2012) and *Ur: The End of Civilization in 90 Tableaux* (2014). He is currently working on a monograph provisionally entitled *Global Digital Cinema: Non-Cinema and the Multitude*, forthcoming with Berghahn.

Ian Fraser is Senior Lecturer in Politics in the Department of Politics, History and International Relations, Loughborough University, UK. He is the author of *Identity, Politics and the Novel: The Aesthetic Moment* (2013), *Dialectics of the Self: Transcending Charles Taylor* (2007), *Hegel and Marx: The Concept of Need* (1998); co-editor, with Tony Burns, of *The Hegel–Marx Connection* (2001) and co-author, with Lawrence Wilde, of *The Marx Dictionary* (2011). He is currently working on a diverse examination of the relation between political theory and film in selected radical theorists ranging from Adorno to Žižek.

Peter Hames is Visiting Professor in Film Studies at Staffordshire University and a programme advisor to the London Film Festival. His books include *The Czechoslovak New Wave* (second edition, 2005, also translated into Czech and Polish), *Czech and Slovak Cinema: Theme and Tradition* (2010), *Best of Slovak Cinema: Theme and Tradition 1921–91* (Slovak Film Institute, 2013) and as editor, *The Cinema of Central Europe* (2004), *The Cinema of Jan Svankmajer: Dark Alchemy* (2008) and *Cinemas in Transition in Central and Eastern Europe after 1989* (with Catherine Portuges, Temple University Press, 2013). He has also contributed to Marketa Lazarova: *Studie a dokumenty* (2009), *Postcolonial Approaches to Eastern European Cinema* (2014) and *Polish Cinema in a Transnational Context* (2014). His articles have appeared in *Sight and Sound, Vertigo, Studies in Eastern European Cinema, KiniKultura* and *Kinoeye*.

John Hutnyk is author of *The Rumour of Calcutta: Tourism, Charity and the Poverty of Representation* (1996), *Critique of Exotica: Music, Politics and the Culture Industry* (2000), *Bad Marxism: Capitalism and Cultural Studies* (2004) and *Pantomime Terror: Music and Politics* (2014). He co-authored *Diaspora and Hybridity* (2005) with Virinder Kalra and Raminder Kaur and was an editor of several volumes of essays, including *Dis-Orienting Rhythms: The Politics of the New Asian Dance Music* (1996, with Sharma and Sharma), *Travel Worlds: Journeys in Contemporary Cultural Politics* (1998, with Raminder Kaur); editions of the journals *Theory, Culture and Society, Post-Colonial Studies* and *Left Curve*; a festschrift for Klaus Peter Koepping called *Celebrating Transgression* (2006, with Ursula Rao); and the large format book *Beyond Borders* (2012).

Lars Kristensen is Lecturer in Media, Aesthetics and Narration at the University of Skövde, Sweden. His research focuses on representation in cinema, transnational and postcolonial filmmaking and bicycle cinema. After receiving his doctorate at the University of St Andrews, he has held temporary positions at the University of Central Lancashire and University of Glasgow. He has published mainly on cross-cultural issues related to Russian cinema and is the editor of *Postcommunist Film – Russia, Eastern Europe and World Culture* (2012) and co-editor, with Eva Näripea and Ewa Mazierska, of *Postcolonial Approaches to Eastern European Cinema: Portraying Neighbours On-Screen* (2014).

Jakob Ladegaard is Associate Professor in Comparative Literature at Aarhus University, Denmark. Areas of interest include the relations between modern literature, cinema, aesthetic theory and politics. He has previously worked on the relations between Eastern Europe and the West in recent literature and cinema and is currently engaged in a research project about the politics of comedy. Recent publications include 'On the Frontier of Politics – Ideology and the Western in Jerzy

Skolimowski's *Essential Killing* and Jim Jarmusch's *Dead Man'*, *Studies in Eastern European Cinema*, 4:2, 2013 and 'Apple Trees and Barbed Wire: Estonian Memories of Soviet Occupation in *Body Memory'*, *Short Film Studies*, 4.2, 2014.

Iris Luppa is Senior Lecturer in Film Studies in the Department of Culture, Writing and Performance at London South Bank University and the author of *Weimar Cinema* in Wallflower's (now Columbia University Press) 'Close-Up' series. She recently published an article on *M* (Fritz Lang, Germany 1931) in *Movie* (co-authored with Douglas Pye) and has published several articles and reviews of films in Lang's Weimar oeuvre. She specialises in Weimar Cinema, Fritz Lang, epistemic approaches to film and point of view studies.

Ewa Mazierska is Professor in Film Studies at the School of Journalism and Media, University of Central Lancashire. She has published nearly 20 monographs and edited collections. They include *Postcolonial Approaches to Eastern European Cinema: Portraying Neighbours On-Screen*, with Eva Näripea and Lars Kristensen (2014), *Work in Cinema: Labor and the Human Condition* (2013), *European Cinema and Intertextuality: History, Memory, Politics* (2011), *Jerzy Skolimowski: The Cinema of a Nonconformist* (2010), *Masculinities in Polish, Czech and Slovak Cinema* (2008), *Roman Polanski: The Cinema of a Cultural Traveller* (2007), *Women in Polish Cinema* (2006), with Elżbieta Ostrowska, and, with Laura Rascaroli, *Crossing New Europe: The European Road Movie* (2006), *Dreams and Diaries: The Cinema of Nanni Moretti* (2004) and *From Moscow to Madrid: Postmodern Cities, European Cinema* (2003). Mazierska's work has been translated into more than ten languages, including French, Italian, Chinese, Korean, Portuguese, Estonian and Serbian. She is a principal editor of a Routledge journal, *Studies in Eastern European Cinema*.

Silke Panse is Lecturer in Fine Art at the University for the Creative Arts. She has published on documentary moving images in relation to art and continental philosophy in *Third Text* (2006), *Rethinking Documentary* (2008) and *Screening Nature: Cinema beyond the Human* (2013). She is the co-editor of *A Critique of Judgment in Film and Television* (2014), which includes her chapter 'The Judging Spectator in the Image'. Her essay about the documentary protagonist's material labour of aesthetics is forthcoming in *The Blackwell Companion to Contemporary Documentary Cinema* (2015). She wrote 'What Drawings Can Do That Films Can't' for *Blind Movies* (2009) and about materials without motives in *Reading CSI* (2007). Panse is the co-investigator of

The Screening Nature Network (2013–14), which is funded by the Arts and Humanities Research Council (AHRC).

Dennis Rothermel is Emeritus Professor of Philosophy at California State University, Chico. His research lies in the intersection of Continental philosophy and cinema studies. His recent publications include 'Slow Food, Slow Film', 'Heroic Endurance' and a book review appearing in the *Quarterly Review of Film and Video*. Book chapters address Joel and Ethan Coen, Clint Eastwood, John Ford, Bertrand Tavernier, Julie Taymor, *True Blood*, 'Anti-War War Films' and 'Grievability and Precariousness'. He has co-edited a volume of essays on peace studies, and a collection of theoretical essays, *A Critique of Judgment in Film and Television*, which includes his chapter, 'The Tones of Judgment in Local Evening News'. He is working on monographs on Westerns and Gilles Deleuze's cinema books.

Johan Siebers is Reader in Philosophy and Critical Theory at the University of Central Lancashire. He also teaches Religious Studies at Middlesex University, London and is Research Fellow at the Institute of Modern Languages Research, School of Advanced Study, University of London. He is founding editor of *Empedocles: European Journal for the Philosophy of Communication* and a main contributor to the *Ernst Bloch Wörterbuch* (2012). He wrote *The Method of Speculative Philosophy* (1998) and recently published 'Ernst Bloch's Dialectical Anthropology' in S. Žižek and P. Thompson (eds.), *The Privatisation of Hope: Ernst Bloch and the Future of Utopia*. His forthcoming monograph *Transforming Hope: Ernst Bloch and Classical German Philosophy* will be published by Brill.

Mike Wayne is Professor in Screen Media at Brunel University. He is the author of a number of books including *Political Film: the dialectics of Third Cinema* (2001), *Marxism and Media Studies: Key Concepts and Contemporary Trends* (2003) and *Marx's Das Kapital For Beginners* (2012). His forthcoming book *Red Kant: Aesthetics, Marxism and the Third Critique* will be published by Bloomsbury. He is also the co-director (with Deirdre O'Neill) of a feature length documentary, *The Condition of the Working Class* (2012).

Introduction
Marx at the Movies: Revisiting History, Theory and Practice

Ewa Mazierska and Lars Kristensen

The history of the 21st century cannot be told without reference to both cinema and communism. Whilst communism presented itself as the political system entrusted with implementing Marxist ideas and challenging the hegemony of capitalism, cinema became the main tool of social communication and a major cultural institution. However, by the end of the century both had lost their privileged positions. Cinema as an institution became supplanted by other forms of visual communication, such as television and the internet. Its privileged access to reality also became questioned as a result of technological developments, most importantly through a gradual replacement of analogue by digital technologies. Communism, almost everywhere it ruled, gave way to a neoliberal version of capitalism. But neither cinema nor Marxism disappeared from political and artistic debates. On the contrary, in the last decade we observe intensified discussions about their importance, although usually conducted separately. This book intends to bring them together, pointing both to their common fate and differences in relation to culture, social life and politics.

Post-communist Marxism, neoliberal communism

An important task of this book is to reconceptualise and develop Marxism as an analytical framework within the realm of film studies. In this regard, it is necessary to distinguish initially between Marxism as manifested in different spheres – most importantly, politics on the one hand, and philosophy and culture on the other hand, even if this means temporarily departing from the spirit of Marxism, which requires philosophy to be intimately linked to practice. According to

1

Jacques Bidet, two political systems could claim allegiance to Marxism: first, regimes in the communist sphere, where official doctrine claimed to be rooted in Marxism, and second, those in all developed capitalist countries, particularly in Europe, where the Marxist aspect manifested itself through a 'social state' or 'welfare state' (Bidet 2008: 4–5; see also Kouvelakis 2008: 30–38). Both of these systems collapsed, albeit at different speeds, with a welfare state lingering in some parts of Europe, such as Scandinavia. The question worth posing is this: How did their collapse affect the standing of communism as a political alternative to capitalism and Marxism as a world view? It is worth mentioning that the very fact that such a question is posed, suggesting that Marxism might be in crisis, demonstrates that Marxism is not like any other philosophy. As Stathis Kouvelakis points out, it is unlikely that Platonists will speak of 'a crisis of Platonism' or Kantians of a 'crisis of Kantianism' (Kouvelakis 2008: 23).

Regarding the actuality of communism and, by the same token, the validity of Marxism as a political project, there are several distinct positions. According to one, probably the most common, communism is finished and consequently history is finished, reaching its culmination with the victory of the system based on market economy and parliamentary democracy. Such a position is famously attributed to Francis Fukuyama and his term 'the end of history' (1992), but we can also find it among authors such as Fredric Jameson, who famously said that it is easier to imagine the end of the world than the end of capitalism (2003), and Slavoj Žižek, who gave his last book the title *Living in the End Times* (2011). However, the tone of these pronouncements is different. Fukuyama celebrated the end of history, claiming that there is no need to treat communism in different terms to historical ones. Jameson mourned the death of communism and explicitly challenged his readers to change the course of history. In the early 1990s, Fukuyama's capitalist future looked economically prosperous. However, as the decade faded away and the universal prosperity that had been promised through a free labour market and liberal democracy had not been delivered, leading to an increase in international terrorism, urban warfare, nationalism and religious fanaticism, his predictions started to look naive. Žižek's observation, that we live at a time when the global capitalist system is approaching an apocalyptic zero-point, has more currency. Its 'four riders of the apocalypse' comprise the ecological crisis, consequences of the biogenetic revolution, imbalances within the system itself (problems with intellectual property, forthcoming struggles over raw materials, food and water), and the explosive growth of social divisions and exclusions' (Žižek 2011: x). These and other authors argue that even if communism in a certain form was defeated, this does not exclude its chance of resurrection (Groys 2009: 103–127).

The second position regarding the actuality of Marxism and communism pronounces that, although communism was officially abolished in the Soviet Union and Eastern Europe, it survived elsewhere and even colonised the world. Its incarnation is a system known as post-Fordism or neoliberalism, which supplanted a regime known as embedded liberalism in the Western world from the early 1980s and communism from the early 1990s. This opinion is most clearly presented by Paolo Virno in the widely quoted final thesis of his *A Grammar of the Multitude*: 'Post-Fordism is the "communism of capital"' (Virno 2004: 110). Virno comes to such a conclusion by comparing the 1980s and the 1990s in the West with the Western response to the October Revolution and the crisis of 1929. He claims that the first moment consisted of 'the gigantic socialisation (or better, nationalisation) of the means of production', which amounted to 'an abolition of the capitalist private industry on the basis of the capitalist system itself' (110). At that time, to survive, capitalism had to adapt some elements of the communist programme. Then he proceeds to argue that the changes in capitalism which occurred in the 1980s and 1990s, which include the extinction of the state as an industry of coercion and as a monopoly of political decision-making, and the great reduction in wage labour 'guarantee a calm version of realism for the potential communist' (110). In his brief discussion of the history of work in the 20th century, Virno suggests that communism is always a part or aspect of capitalism. Following this line of thought, it is interesting to look at China and Vietnam, because in these countries market capitalism is upheld by a communist party (Harvey 2005: 120–51). Moreover, rather than coercing the population to accept the economic and political *status quo* by appealing to its class consciousness, the ruling elites in these countries are justifying their one party system through calls for national unity (Zhang 2004: 53). In his claim that a neoliberal version of capitalism is 'minimalistic communism' or 'communism for realists', Virno echoes French sociologists Luc Boltanski and Eve Chiapello, who in their influential book *The New Spirit of Capitalism*, published for the first time in France in 1999, argued that neoliberalism is a response to the critique of capitalism, voiced in France and Europe at large in the years 1968–1975. This critique, which they describe as an 'artistic critique' as it was articulated largely by students participating in the events of May '68, consisted of a critique of alienation and decreasing chances for autonomous and creative work, as well as demands for more autonomy, flexibility and scope for creativity. Boltanski and Chiapello claimed that capitalist organisations addressed this critique by changing their structures and mode of operating, becoming open to creativity and flexibility (Boltanski and Chiapello 2005: 184). Creativity and flexibility became not just a privilege of working under neoliberalism, but a basic requirement, as reflected by the demand of workers to participate in continuous training, often at their own expense.

Other thinkers claim that capitalism's positive response to the 'artistic critique' did not make the current system communist or Marxist. This is because neoliberalism destroyed the welfare state and with that deepened class inequalities and consolidated the capitalist class power, eroded social security, atomised the working class, strengthened external surveillance and self-surveillance and homogenised culture, rendering it deadly for the soul (Augé 1995; Harvey 2005, 2006, 2008, 2010a, 2010b; Lash and Urry 1987; Sennett 1998, 2006). In due course it also led to wars and misery, as exemplified by military conflicts in former Yugoslavia, Rwanda, Syria, Somalia, Afghanistan and Iraq. Such an idea is summarised by the French philosopher Jacques Rancière, who wrote that capitalism only produces capitalism. To counteract it, one has to attack it from a distinctly anti-capitalist, egalitarian and emancipatory position. The actuality of communism is thus the actuality of this critique, of rejecting the capitalist *status quo* in the name of egalitarian values. Rancière describes such a position as being 'intempestive', which means:

> that one belongs and yet does not belong to the same time, just as *atopia* means that one belongs and yet does not belong to the same place. An *intempestive* or *atopian* communist thinks and acts so as to enact the unconditional equality of each and everyone in a world where communism has no actuality except for the network framed by communist thoughts and actions. This means that there is no 'objective' communism already at work in the forms of capitalist production, no communism anticipated by the logic of capitalism. Capitalism may produce more and more immateriality, yet this immateriality will never be more than the immateriality of capitalism. Capitalism only produces capitalism. If communism means something, it means something that is radically heterogeneous to the logic of capitalism, entirely heterogeneous to the materiality of the capitalist world. (Rancière 2010: 135)

For Rancière, Marxism and communism are thus alive as long as there are people willing and able to fight in their name, including in the field of cultural production. These people might live in the capitalist world, but at the same time they belong to a different world. But such an attitude raises the question as to whether Rancière's definition of an 'intempestive' communist is not too wide, because if we accept it, then we can argue that almost everybody is a communist of some sort. Even ardent capitalists like Bill Gates dream, at least publicly, about a world without misery or injustice. Slavoj Žižek labels such individuals 'liberal communists' (Žižek 2009: 13–14).

In our view, even if the fall of the 'real' or 'state' socialism weakened the chance of creating a communist society, it helped rather than hindered the revival of Marxism as a worldview. This is because what Hannah Arendt regards as the most formidable charge ever raised against Marx, namely 'that one form of totalitarian domination uses, and apparently developed directly from, Marxism', concerns the past connection rather than the present (Arendt 2002: 276). The fall of the Berlin Wall freed Marx from, or at least weakened his connection with, Bolshevism in a similar way as the end of Nazism freed Nietzsche, Hegel, Luther or Plato from an accusation of being the ancestors of Nazism (276). Instead, the end of this system has allowed us to see with greater clarity that it was in fact a form of capitalism, rather than a dictatorship of the proletariat (Burawoy and Lukács 1992; Groys 2009). Equally its replacement by neoliberalism has demonstrated that capitalism has more in common with the way it was described in *Capital* than with the paradise dreamt of by an average person living behind the Iron Curtain. Thus, those from the East who before were 'instinctive Marxists', but were afraid to act on their views from the fear of being accused of supporting the disgraced authorities, are no longer at risk of such accusations and can find support for their ideas nationally as well as transnationally. It is thus not a surprise that the last decade or so has seen a Marxist revival in countries such as Poland and Ukraine. Neither is it unexpected that philosophers, historians and political activists in the countries of former Yugoslavia continue an interest in Marxist ideas, with Slavoj Žižek serving as a prime example (see, for example, Douzinas and Žižek 2010). Moreover, as a result of the fall of the Berlin Wall, communism is no longer tied to a geographical place or space. It is truly universal, even if only abstract or theoretical, as some authors argue. For authors such as Hardt and Negri, it is a question of transnational or even global phenomena, such as 'Empire' and 'multitude', which can be seen as reconfigured forces of capitalism on the one hand and socialism on the other (Hardt and Negri 2000, 2006).

Marxism, modernism and postmodernism

Even those who regard the 'positive' part of Marx's output as impossible to fulfil, both on practical and moral grounds, believe that it is useful as a superior theorisation and critique of capitalism; hence it can be productively utilised by the apologists of the capitalist system. In particular, Marx's writings on overaccumulation of capital, capitalist crises and internal and external colonisation as the means to overcome these crises (Marx 1965, 1966, 1967, 1973) can be seen as a recipe for avoiding the perennial problems of capitalism and ensure capitalist growth.

But there is more to Marx's actuality than being able to help capitalists avoid economic crises. Marx also had specific views on the future of the material world and human identity. From the first perspective, according to Hannah Arendt and Marshall Berman, he is a model modernist, because he saw the world in terms of dramatic change, of continuous destruction. As they notice, he was not the first to conceive the world in such a way, but followed in the footsteps of earlier German authors, such as Goethe and Hegel (Arendt 2002: 276; Berman 1988: 96). He also predicted that this continuous change will lead to diminishing the world's material dimension, most importantly in his 'fragment on the machines' from *Grundrisse* (Marx 1973: 693–95), which proved a major inspiration to the theorists of immaterial labour. This is captured by these words from *The Communist Manifesto*: 'All that is solid melts into air' (Marx and Engels 2008: 38), which is also a perfect slogan for the age of digital communication, genetic experimentation and obsessive protection of copyrights and patents, rather than material goods.

By the same token, Marx posed a question about the essence and destiny of humanity. If everything melts, does the world and 'man' remain unchanged; should we, perhaps, redefine them? In relation to this issue, there are two distinct answers. According to the prevailing one, Marx was a teleological thinker, who saw the end of the world as paradise on earth, ensured by socialist revolution. In this paradise man will finally reject his identity as labourer and appropriate a new one, that of 'amateur'. According to a second opinion, which is closer to that of the authors of this introduction, even if Marx was a teleological thinker, his work is rich enough to imagine different scenarios of human destiny, including that there is no ultimate destiny or human essence: the world will keep melting, people drift and mutate forever. Such an opinion chimes with Marx's refusal to say much about the shape of future communist society, as if he was assuming that 'man' of the future might be quite different from what we understand by that term today.

Marxist actuality also lies in his approach to the role of an intellectual in social and cultural life. This approach is captured by Maurice Blanchot, who attributed to this thinker three types of speech: 'writer of thoughts', 'political speech' and 'scientific discourse' (Blanchot 2010: 103–5). A similar attitude to Marx is revealed by Eric Hobsbawm, who referring to a recent biography of Marx written by Jacques Attali, maintains that his work 'is not "interdisciplinary" in the conventional sense but integrates all disciplines. [...] Philosophers before him have thought of man in his totality, but he was the first to apprehend the world as a whole which is at once political, economic, scientific and philosophical' (Hobsbawm 2011: 12).

We argue that in his desire to capture man in his/her totality and respond to that totality, Marx is neither a modernist nor postmodernist thinker. He is not a modernist, because the modernist ambition was to divide science into separate compartments and defend specificity and irreducibility of each of the disciplines; an approach epitomised by the rigid division of disciplines in Western academia, archives and museums. Postmodernism, on the other hand, although rejecting such rigid divisions, equally rejects a desire to create an all-encompassing theory. This is conveyed most importantly in its interest in marginality, in local and subjective phenomena and 'small narratives'. Such an approach can be lauded for giving voice to those whose views were previously suppressed, such as women, people of colour, victims of colonial conquest, sexual minorities and children, but also for losing the larger picture, and with that a larger political project (Bertens 1995), and even for supporting the capitalist *status quo*. Such an opinion is expressed by Iain Hamilton-Grant, who describes this situation in such terms: 'Where the political will of a people, a nation or a culture used to be harnessed to long-term general goals, now fragmented groups engage in short-term struggles. The spread of identity politics over the last twenty years is testimony to this, with its emphasis on ethnicity, class, gender and sexuality replacing political credo' (Hamilton-Grant 2001: 30). He further observes that the consequence of engaging in identity and micro-politics is leaving macro-decisions to the enemy: 'By concentrating all the attention on "micro-political" issues, or on short-term single-issue politics, the very real large-scale political structures that govern our everyday lives are disregarded and left uncontested to the enemy, which simply translates into covert support for, or actual complicity with, the *status quo*' (31).

According to Alain Badiou, this shift from modernist to postmodernist politics was to a large extent the consequence of May '68 in France. This seemingly radical event ultimately led to the loss of hierarchy of political agents and causes, and to the downgrading of the proletariat from its special position as the main agent of emancipation (Badiou 2010: 52–3). Hence, it is not an accident that the interest in Marxism both declined and changed its course after the 1970s, when post-structuralism and post-modernism triumphed,[1] with their focus on a decentred and subjective reading of reality. The post-structuralist readings of Marx, if they were at all sympathetic to this thinker,[2] usually attempted to merge him with ideas such as 'minority politics' and changing the world without taking power (Choat 2010; Thoburn 2003). Meaningfully, Slavoj Žižek begins his book on Krzysztof Kieslowski, published in 2001, with the words: 'If this book had been published twenty-five years ago, in the heyday of "structuralist Marxism", its subtitle, undoubtedly, would have been "On Class Struggle in Cinema"' (Žižek 2001: 1). The obvious implication of such a statement is that in 2001 it was no longer the case – class struggle stopped mattering in cinema and elsewhere, giving way to other issues.

However, after dominating the humanities for 30 years or so, post-modernism understood as a period or theory of 'small narratives' is in decline too, as reflected by a widespread sense that it led to unproductive relativism and subjectivism. Mike Wayne, following Georg Lukács and Fredric Jameson, reminds us that 'beneath the appearance of flux, fragmentation and unpredictability lies an ever more integrated and concentrated socioeconomic system' (Wayne 2005: 15). Consequently, there is a search for getting beneath the shattering of narrative worlds of postmodernism, albeit without losing sight of the specific and the marginal, for assessing the state of humanity from an objective vantage point and a new revolutionary subject (Douzinas and Žižek 2010). Marx is an excellent starting point for such a search, because in his works we identify such ambitions. Marx can serve as a matrix for a method of critique and a dialogue about what a post-capitalist future would look like. Not surprisingly, the most discussed interventions in the humanities and social sciences (when humanities also include economy) of the last 20 years or so, continue Marxist thought in one way or another (on this see especially Hutnyk's chapter in this volume). Together with many of the most cited cultural critics of today, the authors of this volume argue that art can play an important role in political and social transformation.

Marxism, art and cinema

It is a well-known fact that economy and politics, rather than art, were at the centre of Marx's work. However, as Maynard Solomon writes in the introduction to his impressive collection (until now the most extensive anthology of Marxist aesthetics), *Marxism and Art*, 'Perhaps it is the very absence of a definitive work by Marx on criticism or aesthetic theory which has opened the door to interpretation, prevented the reduction of Marxist aesthetics to a rigid set of accepted formulas, and made impossible descent into academicism' (Solomon 1979: 8); and elsewhere: 'the Marxist texts on aesthetics are aphorisms pregnant with an aesthetics – an unsystematised aesthetics open to endless analogical and metaphorical development' (9).

Indeed, the field of Marxist aesthetics is very wide and versatile, as demonstrated by the names mentioned in Solomon's anthology, which include William Morris, Franz Mehring, Karl Kautsky, Georgi Plekhanov, Rosa Luxemburg, Vladimir Ilyich Lenin, Leon Trotsky, Maxim Gorki, Mao Tse-Tung, Jean-Paul Sartre, Antonio Gramsci, Béla Balázs, Mikhail Bakhtin, Bertolt Brecht, Theodor Adorno, George Lukács, André Breton, Herbert Marcuse, Walter Benjamin, André Malraux and Ernst Bloch.[3] If somebody were to update such an anthology, they would have to add many more names, such as Raymond Williams, Pierre Macherey, Terry Eagleton, Fredric Jameson, Jean-Luc Nancy, Alain Badiou, Jacques Rancière and Slavoj Žižek. These authors work in different fields, with some interested in literature, others in music and still others in film, and some dealing with general aesthetic questions, such as the relationship between class and taste, art and reality or the genesis and future of art. However, what transpires from studying them is that the vast majority, with the exception of a small group of authors, whom Solomon puts together under the label 'Zhdanovism', proclaim art as a relatively autonomous sphere of human production, whose influence on people's values and behaviour is somewhat mysterious. Art is both social and individual; it tends to convey dominant ideology, but also the idiosyncratic views of the author. It both expresses and represses, as put by the title of the famous essay of Pierre Macherey: 'The Text Says What It Does Not Say' (Macherey 1978). This also means that pre-socialist or even 'bourgeois' art, especially if it is art of high aesthetic value, might serve the purposes of socialist revolution as well as, if not better than, art created specifically for the purpose of subverting the capitalist *status quo*. This point was made by Marx himself, who praised Honoré de Balzac. He did so because Balzac, in spite of being conservative and royalist, was able to reveal the immorality of capitalism and potentially help to fight it (Prawer 1976: 318). After Marx, this point was reiterated by Vladimir Lenin and Leon Trotsky, two of the main architects of the new, socialist art, and in contemporary times by Jacques Rancière. Lenin devoted much of his attention to Tolstoy, writing:

Tolstoy is dead, and the pre-revolutionary Russia whose weakness and impotence found their expression in philosophy and are depicted in the works of the great artist, has become a thing of the past. But the heritage which he has left includes that which has not become a thing of the past, but belongs to the future. [...] The Russian proletariat will explain to the masses of the toilers and the exploited the meaning of Tolstoy's criticism of the state, the church, private property in land [...]. The Russian proletariat will explain to the masses Tolstoy's criticism of capitalism, [...] to create a new society in which the people will not be doomed to poverty, in which there will be no exploitation of man by man (Lenin 1979: 176).

Trotsky argued: 'Works of art developed in a medieval Italian city can, we find, affect us too. What does this require? A small thing: it requires that these feelings and moods shall have received such broad, intense, powerful expression as to have raised them above the limitations of the life of those days' (Trotsky 1979: 197). Jacques Rancière builds on these insights, by drawing attention to the political significance of *Madame Bovary* by Gustave Flaubert. Despite Flaubert's aristocratic situation and political conformity (and, of course, using capitalist channels of communications with his readers, namely profit-oriented publishing houses), he regards *Madame Bovary* as a progressive work of art of great significance, helping in the emancipation of women (Rancière 2004: 12–19).

Marxist aestheticians also point to the fact that art which might help the revolution should inform and move – it should appeal to our brains, including the more hidden layers, and to our hearts. In popular understanding of Marxist aesthetics, however, the opinion prevails that realist styles are closer to Marxism than non-realist styles. Such opinion has some foundation in the fact that Friedrich Engels, who is attributed with a more developed aesthetic theory than Marx, was a proponent of realism, and Balzac, who was Marx's favourite writer, is also seen as a master of realist fiction. However, even if we agree with such an opinion, we have to qualify it by accepting that the criteria of realism change. The realism of Maxim Gorki is different to that of Vladimir Mayakovsky and different still to that of André Breton and other surrealists who also believed that they unearth reality, albeit that of a dream and the unconscious. Nothing is more foreign to the spirit of Marx than a demand to freeze art in one privileged style.[4]

Marxism always looked into the future; hence there is a natural rapport between Marxism and the avant-garde. On the other hand, Marxism was meant to appeal to the most economically and culturally impoverished sections of society. This fact was widely recognised by Gramsci and Trotsky. The former argued: 'Marxism was confronted with two tasks: to combat modern ideologies in their most refined form in order to create its own core of independent intellectuals; and to educate the masses of the people whose level of culture was medieval' (Gramsci 1979: 268). Trotsky asked:

> Does the proletariat of today offer such a cultural-ideological milieu, in which the new artist may obtain, without leaving it in his day-to-day existence, all the inspirations he needs while at the same time mastering the procedures of his craft? No, the working masses are culturally extremely backward; the illiteracy or low level of literacy of the majority of the workers presents in itself a very great obstacle to this. And above all, the proletariat, in so far as it remains a proletariat, is compelled to expand its best forces in political struggle, in restoring the economy, and in meeting elementary cultural needs, fighting against illiteracy, lousiness, syphilis, etc. (Trotsky 1979: 195).

Hence, the challenge for Marxist artists was to create popular masterpieces. Marx himself showed the way by creating in *The Communist Manifesto* a work which is both sophisticated and simple, saturated with metaphors, yet describing capitalist society in vivid images, while also looking into the communist future. In due course it was discovered that cinema can fulfil the above-mentioned requirements perfectly, as noted by Lenin, who pronounced it the most important of all arts (Christie and Taylor 1991: xv).[5] This was because it was avant-garde, even in the most basic sense of being a new art, born out of photography, similar to theatre, music and painting, but irreducible to them. At the same time, it was popular because, at the beginning being silent, it could be understood by the illiterate and later, when it found its 'voice', talk to the people in a language they could understand. In addition, cinema has a dual ability to tell the truth and lie. The first property relies on cinema's mimetic qualities, its ability to show the world as we perceive it with our own eyes, or even better. These qualities are analysed by a long list of authors, from the pioneer Bolesław Matuszewski, through classics of realist film theory, such as Siegfried Kracauer and André Bazin, to Alain Badiou (2009), who proclaims cinema to be an 'ontological art' in an intimate relation with reality, and authors researching the specificity of digital cinema.

The opportunities offered by montage, of connecting distant places and times, and objects seen from different distances and perspectives, render film as a privileged means to link micro- with macro-economy, personal experience with politics, and work's history with its present day and future. Such opportunities were discussed not only by philosophers and film historians, including Walter Benjamin and Theodor Adorno (Hansen 2004: 16), but also by filmmakers, such as Sergei Eisenstein, Alexander Kluge and Jean-Luc Godard. But other authors claim that by the same token cinema can be an arch-manipulator, persuading us into making wrong choices, even coercing us to self-harming actions while showing real things. The examples of cinema at its most 'didactic', Soviet cinema, fascist cinema and Hollywood cinema (although its didacticism comes across as the subtlest of the three), identified by Bazin as being politically manipulative (Bazin 1985), illustrate this tendency very well. Marx himself noticed the potential of realistic art both to reveal and challenge the *status quo* and to naturalise it. He claimed that the world projected for mass consumption by the ruling classes is the world 'upside down', as in a camera obscura (Marx and Engels 1947: 14). Hence the question of whether there is something in the aesthetic of film that makes it a perfect tool for the socialist revolution, yet also 'vulnerable' for totalitarian appropriation. Does it have something to do with the fact that cinema is 'moving', although in reality it is made up of still shots? Such questions will inform many chapters included in this collection.

We mentioned at the beginning that cinema has lost its privileged position as the most important art. However, this does not refer to film, or more specifically to the moving image. On the contrary, this has consolidated its grip on culture and the human mind. The moving image is everywhere; it is a dominant mode of communication in the 21st century, due to the development of digital technologies, which allow, for example, for making and watching films using mobile phones or viewers affecting the course of the watched material as in computer games. The new films often look much more realistic than before the 'digital revolution' and at the same time create worlds which filmmakers of the earlier generations could only imagine (Brown 2009; Manovich 2001; Willemen 2004: 171–190). Moreover, new cinema has largely done away with the camera as a stable point of fixation, thus undermining or at least questioning the role of filmmaker in creating a cinematic world (Brown 2009: 66–85). However, while practically everybody can be a filmmaker these days, the road to a mass audience is more difficult than ever, with fewer, and mostly Hollywood, films occupying privileged sites of mass exhibition. We argue that these transformations in the production, distribution and exhibition of the moving image, and of the world at large, marked by the hegemonic position of neoliberal capitalism, call for a Marxist analysis.

The content and structure of the collection

This book offers a re-evaluation of cinema from the Marxist perspective, by looking at its theory and practice, and past and present examples. The uniqueness of this approach results largely from applying it to the films and phenomena which previously did not lend themselves to such tools and, conversely, paying less attention to the 'usual suspects', namely the films belonging to Russian formalism and socialist realism, seen as a 'natural home' or, less positively, a 'ghetto' of Marxist cinema. This means, in the spirit of Marx, who admired Balzac, Lenin, who was enchanted by Tolstoy and Rancière, who pondered on the progressiveness of Gustave Flaubert, to re-evaluate popular films produced in the capitalist world by large, profit-oriented studios, and even some having no obvious Left-wing message, such as horrors and comedies. There are several essays which deal with cinema produced in the Eastern bloc, but they argue that their relationship with Marxism was far from straightforward. Despite the pressure to produce 'socialist films', including through the use of censorship, socialist filmmakers revealed their enchantment with 'bourgeois art' and often a critical attitude toward 'real socialism'. Indirectly, the chapters concerned with cinema produced in the Eastern bloc confirm our view that Marxist cinema cannot be confined to any period or geographical region.

Secondly, the old disputes about whether Marxist art should be realist or non-realist, style- or content-oriented, are reframed. In this respect the majority of the contributors to this volume, explicitly or implicitly follow in the footsteps of Jacques Rancière, who in his works recognises that there are different types of political art or types of pedagogy attributed to critical art, which he describes as representational mediation, ethical immediacy and aesthetic distance. However, rather than arguing in favour of any of them as the most efficient type of political art, Rancière proposes to define political art as art which disrupts the consensus (introducing dissensus) by 'breaking with the sensory self-evidence of the "natural" order that destines specific individuals and groups to occupy positions of rule or of being ruled, assigning them to private or public lives, pinning them down to a certain time and space, to specific "bodies", that is to specific ways of being, seeing and saying' (Rancière 2013: 139). Authors who refer in this volume to ideas such as Dialectical Image, montage or the Not-Yet-Conscious argue that they are effective means of breaking with the given and introducing dissensus, hence producing political art.

Thirdly, many authors undertake a materialist analysis of films, by drawing attention to the fact that cinema is a collective endeavour and trying to account for the input of artists other than directors, who until recently were privileged in Western film history. This means recognising the role of producers, scriptwriters, cinematographers, actors and composers.

Fourthly, in the spirit of contemporary Marxist thinkers, such as Badiou and Harvey, this collection is preoccupied with moments of hope, as opposed to merely criticising the *status quo*. Hence, it is no accident that two chapters apply to the chosen films the views of the author Ernst Bloch, whose main work has the word 'hope' in its title. In comparison, the authors included in the collection reveal a more critical attitude towards the better known German theorist of cinema and popular art at large, Theodor Adorno, famous for his sour outlook and rants against jazz and Hollywood cinema.

The 'principle of hope' is also expressed in a relatively large part of this collection devoted to the role of laughter in Marxist-oriented art. The authors engaging with this concept admit that laughter can be regressive and progressive. Regressive laughter is, predictably, emphasised by Adorno, who saw fun as a 'medicinal bath which the entertainment industry never ceases to prescribe' (Adorno 2002: 112). Such laughter approves and naturalises the *status quo*. Progressive laughter, by contrast, provokes a break in our perception and discloses some secret connection of things hidden behind the everyday reality' (Rancière, quoted by Ladegaard in the chapter in this collection). By emphasising the importance of laughter in Marxist work we take a cue from Mikhail Bakhtin, who draws attention to its liberating potential and its ability to create a parallel (utopian) universe, where the old hierarchies are overthrown and a more democratic order is introduced, as expressed in such a sentence: 'Laughter liberates not only from external censorship but first of all from the great interior censor; it liberates from the fear that developed in man during thousands of years: fear of the sacred, of prohibitions, of the past, of power. [...] Laughter opened men's eyes on that which is new, on the future' (Bakhtin 1979: 300). The authors engaging with the question 'Marx and laughter' are also picking up film theory where it ended in the early 1990s, as seen in Robert Stam's work *Subversive Pleasures: Bakhtin, Cultural Criticism, and Film* (1992), which used Bakhtin as a remedy for locating the blind spots in the Marxist film theory of Althusser and Lacan (Stam 1989: 53). Claiming superiority of Bakhtin over other Marxist approaches, Stam sees Bakhtin's work as foreshadowing postcolonialism and multiculturalism.

The collection begins with Mike Wayne's discussion of the trajectory of the dialectical image in German philosophy, from Kant through

Marx to the key German cultural philosophers of the 20th century: Adorno, Benjamin and Kracauer. The author observes that among philosophers the image has traditionally had a lower status than the word, largely because comprehending the word (which is symbolic) required education, while understanding the image was not beyond the scope of the masses and even the feeble-minded. The Image (with a capital I, as it refers to all forms of pictorial representation) thus threatened to transfer the property of the ruling class – its cognitive concepts and moral ideas – to the masses in a form *they* could master. This is, as Wayne argues, one reason why Benjamin welcomed the increasing mechanical reproduction of art in the 20th century. In the meantime, the Word (with a capital W, as it designates all forms of discursive communication) also became more democratic, but remained a privileged instrument of the ruling classes. In the course of his argument Wayne refers to the tradition associated with German philosophy that recognises cross-fertilisation between the Word and the Image: the tradition from which the Dialectical Image emerges. He uses the term 'dialectical' to account for the fact that the Dialectical Image overcomes the gap between the conceptual and the perceptual, the universal and the particular, the cognitive and the affective, the elite and the popular. Wayne discusses the input to this idea of Kant, Marx, Adorno and Benjamin (these last two thinkers drawing largely on the moving image). In relation to Adorno, Wayne notices that the Dialectical Image is associated with a non-linear free form, typical of the avant-garde rather than popular cinema, which organises its movements around stories. This fact renders Adorno hostile to popular cinema (as well as other popular forms). However, the concept of natural beauty, to which Adorno returned in the late part of his career, in Wayne's opinion makes it useful to analyse popular films such as horror, which take issue with humans' relationship to nature and to each other. Wayne illustrates this by discussing George Romero's horror, *Land of the Dead* (2005), focusing on the spectacle of fireworks shown in the film. Wayne sees this as an example of a Dialectical Image in all its richness, contradiction and beauty. By extension, he sees the duty of the Marxist film historian as that of somebody who collects and elucidates Dialectical Images in all sorts of films, including those which seem to be made purely for entertainment.

The second chapter, authored by Johan Siebers, is concerned with Ernst Bloch. Siebers argues that Bloch's work was future-oriented and that he largely occupied himself with the means that could be used to transform the unsatisfactory present into a utopian future. Hence, although Bloch was critical of the cinema, which was already by his time becoming a commercial vehicle, especially in Hollywood, he was also aware of the revolutionary and utopian potential of film. For Bloch, film critique should consist of elucidating what he calls the Not-Yet-Conscious. Siebers attempts to identify this utopian core, as seen by Bloch, in one of the most famous creations of early cinema: the figure of the Tramp, created by Charles Chaplin, most famously in his *City Lights* (1931). For Bloch, this utopian potential of film, not unlike for Benjamin, has to do with the montage. Editing, which is seen as an exclusive domain of the moving image, allows films to connect that which exists (in this case extreme economic and social inequality) with that which does not yet exist (equality and its fruits, such as universal welfare and dignity). In this way, it allows us to dream, but not merely in an escapist way, as conveyed by the term Dream Factory, but to envisage and project a different world. Siebers also notes that of all art forms, music is for Bloch the most utopian. It comes closest to expressing the deepest yearnings and hopes, partly due to its pre-semantic nature and partly due to it being a temporal medium. Accordingly, he discusses the similarities between film, especially the silent film, and music and the instances when music expresses the utopian moment, even in commercial Hollywood films. His essay, in common with Mike Wayne's, calls both for rescuing the films, neglected by Marxist historians as 'bourgeois', for Marxist analysis and for creating cinema which would help us to imagine and realise the socialist utopia.

Ian Fraser also uses Bloch's theory, but to discuss a film which on first impression does not lend itself easily to Marxist analysis: Terence Davies' *Distant Voices, Still Lives* (1988). This film can be described as a chamber drama about a working-class family in Liverpool in the 1940s and 1950s, centred on a tyrannical father whose overbearing presence dominates the lives of his wife and three children, Eileen, Tony and Maisie, when he was alive and when he was dead. In a surprising decision, and probably opening himself to a critique from some feminists, Fraser decides to demonstrate that utopian moments, the hope for a better future, can be identified in the episodes where the father shows some goodness and the children reveal their closeness to him despite his usually tyrannical nature. The particular value of Fraser's analysis lies in his concern with those aspects of films which are normally neglected by Marxist historians and which Davies uses with great effect: the appreciation of film through pantomime and the component parts of the technical work of the camera, the gesture of characters, the 'micrological of the incidental', and the affinity of film to painting. He argues that all these aspects of film allow us a glimpse into a better future – of course, if we are able to look. In his discussion he also points to the importance of the family and the local community as a place where one can learn the skill most important in emancipatory struggle – solidarity – yet also learn submissiveness and acceptance of the *status quo*, which make such a struggle difficult.

Shifting the focus from post-war Liverpool to pre-war Hollywood, Iris Luppa examines *You and Me* (1938) by Fritz Lang. Lang's third film made in Hollywood was both a commercial flop and regarded as a critical failure at the time of its release. As a result it was often ignored in Lang scholarship. Luppa seeks to demonstrate that close analysis of the film's narrational strategies, such as camera work, mise-en-scène, editing and performance reveals a complex perspective on the apparent clash between the film's Brechtian methods and its seemingly reactionary politics. Through focusing on three selected moments in the film, she illustrates the tension between style and content in Lang's film, which unsettles the viewing experience. Luppa also argues that the film's overt challenge to the audience's more traditional viewing habits through the use of a more experimental visual style than would have been the norm in classical Hollywood cinema is entirely intentional and that Lang shares with Brecht an interest in addressing the audience in unfamiliar ways. However, despite the film's engagement with epic theatre methods, which Brecht had so clearly intended to be in the service of *explaining* capitalism to people who came to see his plays, the chapter concludes by conceding that the film's Marxist dimension is restricted to subtly drawing the audience's attention to the ideological tensions that pervade the everyday life of a paid worker in capitalism.

The two subsequent chapters assess the role of humour in Marxist analysis and Marxist cinema. Jakob Ladegaard begins the first of two chapters dealing with comedy with an observation that although Karl Marx is barely present in comedy studies, at least two different comic strategies are present in his writings. On the one hand, Marx chastised the revolution of 1848 as a 'farcical' repetition of 1789, thus implying an idea of farce as mass spectacle as opposed to the epic history of revolutionary struggle. On the other hand, Marx used satire to ridicule German idealists as starry-eyed philosophers estranged from everyday reality. By extension, Marxist comedy and Marxist approaches to comedy can take (at least) two directions: the denunciation of comedy *as* ideology, or comedy as a form of ideology critique that reconnects ideas to the material world through humour. The first idea is represented by Theodor Adorno, who denounced ridicule and laughter as central to the culture industry and consigned the vast majority of films produced by the mainstream to the 'regressive comedy' bin. Although this verdict is too hasty, it does remind us, Ladegaard argues, of the inherent ambivalences of comedy. Examples of such ambivalence include the films of Woody Allen, which, while ridiculing the American culture industry, are themselves well integrated in it. Turning to the idea of comedy as ideology critique, Ladegaard discusses three major critical strategies that often work together (or against each other) in comic films, but which can be distinguished for analytical purposes: the celebration of the grotesque body; the use of incongruity and wit; and the comic character. The first is illustrated by the elements of Bakhtinian 'carnival' in Sergei Eisenstein's *The General Line* (1929), which have an uneasy relationship to the dominant ideology, while Dušan Makavejev's *Sweet Movie* (1974) displays a more open-ended and self-critical use of the grotesque. The second approach draws on early films by Jean-Luc Godard. Referring to Bertolt Brecht, Walter Benjamin and Jacques Rancière, the author argues that Godard develops a politics of wit based on the montage of incongruent elements. The last part draws on Slavoj Žižek and Alenka Zupančič, who argue for a link between comic characters and a critique of power. This is illustrated with examples from films like Ernst Lubitsch's *To Be or Not to Be* (1942). In conclusion, Ladegaard argues that comedies at their most progressive can be seen as social experiments that allow us to see the hidden face of ideology, but also imagine a different world.

Dennis Rothermel offers us a Marxist analysis of John Huston's *The Treasure of the Sierra Madre* (1948), which in its classical Hollywood mode tells the story of three gold diggers striking it rich in the Californian mountains and then losing it. The extraordinary thing about this loss of fortune is that these prospectors laugh at it, and it is a laughter that liberates them from their plight as labourers. According to Rothermel, the release of laughter signifies the realisation that there is no true value in the exchange value of the gold, thus coming to the same conclusion as Marx. The source of the story is located in the authorship of B. Traven, a reclusive writer whose identity was never fully revealed, but Rothermel traces Traven's involvement in this smooth Hollywood adaptation, noting how 'a simplistic application of the labour theory of value' turns into a Marxist glimmer of how it could be different. Such 'creative insights', grounded in the film theories of Gilles Deleuze, are found in abundance with workerist humour, where comedy moves beyond its play on stereotype. Rothermel's concept of workerist humour film is also linked to more contemporary film production such as Ken Loach's *The Navigators* (2001) and to a broader theoretical critique of structural dialectics, which, in his opinion, stifle Marxist film analysis. The chapter highlights how watching moving images through Marx's prism of labour value can open passages for spectator liberation in mainstream cinema. While most of the chapters deal with Western filmmakers, Peter Hames looks at the filmmakers in communist Czechoslovakia, tracing the motif of Marxist alienation in the Czechoslovak New Wave cinema of the 1960s. The key question that Hames seeks to answer is to what extent did the films of the 1960s reflect socialist beliefs? It is predominately held that the Czechoslovak New Wave was a critique of Stalinism and neo-Stalinism, but in what way was this critique Marxist? He focuses on the writings of two Marxist philosophers, Ivan Sviták and Karel Kosík, who both struggled with the issue of socialist humanism in art production. In *Dialectics of the Concrete* Karel Kosík viewed humanistic socialism as the negation of both capitalism and Stalinism, while Ivan Sviták saw the problems of alienation as existing within the context of two power blocs that were striving for world hegemony. Ivan Sviták, who was also a film critic, imbued cinema with a special responsibility towards social questions, which was echoed by Karel Kosík, who argued that the dialectics of art production rest on its ability to convey and create reality. The event that triggers this re-evaluation of communist ideology was, according to Hames, a conference on Franz Kafka held at Liblice in 1963, where many of the contributions focused on the subject of alienation. It is this actual communist alienation that Hames locates in the Czechoslovak New Wave films, highlighting films such as Evald Schorm's *Everyday Courage* (1964), Věra Chytilová's *Daisies* (1966), Jiri Menzel's *Closely Observed Trains* (1966), Vojtěch Jasný' s *All My Good Countrymen* (1968) and Jaromil Jireš's *The Joke* (1968).

Silke Panse in the following chapter engages with Marx's and post-Marxist theories of labour, such as 'new' vital materialism and theories of immaterial labour, by seeking an acknowledgment of the contribution of documentary protagonists to their images taken by others. She observes that because the protagonists of documentary images are not supposed to act, they are not paid and cannot even claim that they are working immaterially. In Panse's reading, the artist or filmmaker as the owner of the images becomes the capitalist who appropriates the value the documentary protagonist generates. In order to underscore the dependence of the documentarians on the materiality of their protagonists, she refers to them as 'image-takers'. Because documentary protagonists often cannot claim any rights to the images others took of them, their position is similar to those of workers, as discussed by

Marx. Panse notices that the creative forces of the lives of the documentary protagonists do not result in image rights and recognition of their agency by bestowing authorship. Ultimately, she argues for developing the notion of the documentary protagonist as a worker.

William Brown, in his chapter 'Amateur Digital Filmmaking and Capitalism', suggests that amateur filmmaking may well constitute a form of Marxist progression towards socialism. Discussing amateurism, amateur filmmaking, digital Marxism, and film, Brown explores how it is a commonplace myth that the advent of digital technology involves a 'revolution' that will place all power in the hands of the people, such that the mainstream film industries will come crashing to the ground now that everyone has a camera in their hands and a website on which to distribute their work. This myth, however, seems far from being a reality. Instead, analysing the ways in which websites such as YouTube involve exploitation in the form of what Maurizio Lazzarato would term 'immaterial labour', Brown argues that the revolution is not happening – and that a spectacular revolution as such may not even be workable (since it would only be capitalised immediately). Indeed, this process can be seen in a film such as *¡Ataque de pánico!/Panic Attack!* (Fede Alvarez, 2009), which, far from suggesting that amateur cinema is subversive, in fact suggests that it reinforces the dominance of the mainstream, as witnessed by Alvarez's decision to accept an offer to remake *The Evil Dead* (2013) in Hollywood. However, rather than a revolution, Brown suggests perhaps more simply 'change' – towards socialism. All amateur films – even one like *Panic Attack!* – challenge Hollywood, but some reflect more openly on what it means to be an amateur filmmaker, including Brown's own film, *En Attendant Godard* (2009). Drawing in particular on Jacques Rancière's concept of dissensus, Brown suggests that if there is to be change, it must not be revolutionary in a spectacular sense, but slow. Amateur cinema must be content not to be popular (or not be concerned with popularity, thus being 'apopular'). And amateur cinema must involve an embrace of its own limitations, rather than a replication of the professional standards of mainstream cinema. In this way, progress towards socialism can and will be made.

John Hutnyk's chapter continues the focus on classics of Hollywood, but with an unconventional approach to the film adaptation of Marx's *Capital*. Highlighted as an experiment using the film *Citizen Kane* (1941) as an incitement to read Marx's *Capital* for today, paying attention to structure and characterisation, Hutnyk's argument is that Orson Welles and Karl Marx share traits that can assist our (mutual) comprehension of their work. Welles' 'Kane' is the personification of a class relation, and Rosebud is, according to Hutnyk, not the only fetish object. If the interpretation of *Capital* is a question of scholarship today, then inspired by the work of Gayatri Chakravorty Spivak, this chapter suggests that a provocation from cinema might redirect attention back to critical but patient and insistent engagement. It is Hutnyk's claim that in an old, much discussed film from the 1940s there is something that can bring a book from the 1860s up to the present again. This is not a search for allegory or metaphor, and neither is it a question of cataloguing the monstrous accumulation of things that Kane collects, but, perhaps, the point is to change the way we see and read.

While John Hutnyk compares Marx to Welles and *Das Kapital* to *Citizen Kane*, Ewa Mazierska draws a different parallel – between Marx and Alexander Kluge and *Das Kapital* and Kluge's *News from Ideological Antiquity – Marx/Eisenstein/The Capital* (2008), paying attention both to the content and the formal qualities of both works. She notes that, in common with Marx, Kluge is a renaissance man, who in his life combined theory and political practice and in his films tried to use many languages and broach the divide between high and low culture. Mazierska argues that it is difficult to ascribe Marx's *Das Kapital* to any existing literary genre. Similarly, Kluge's opus magnum, *News from Ideological Antiquity*, bursts the boundaries of a film. Being an adaptation of Marx's work, Kluge's film deals with many themes developed by Marx, but is essentially about the birth and development of capitalist society. However, it also includes different motifs, such as the uses of history and the possibility of translation, most importantly translating complex philosophical ideas and theories, such as those presented in Marx's *Das Kapital*, on screen. Kluge argues that we live in the past if the images, descriptions and theories, created in the past, apply to our current situation. For this reason Marx's description is still valid or is even more pertinent to contemporary times than the period when Marx wrote his book, because the world under the neoliberal regime resembles more the model created by Marx than the one in which he lived himself. Kluge's film provides a strong argument in favour of the possibility and need to translate 'unadaptable' books. We need to translate to bring the masterpieces to the attention of the new generations of readers, and enrich the old works with new insights and even new languages. By and large, in order to save Marx from the fate of the socialist writers, discussed by Marx in *The Communist Manifesto*, whose work lost their political power due to bad translation, we have a duty to put him in the ever-changing context and keep translating his works. It is worth noting that Hutnyk and Mazierska's chapters, which both serve as introductions of sorts to Marx's *Das Kapital*, reflect the heterogeneity of Marx's style. Hutnyk's piece emulates the poetical dimension of Marx's work; Mazierska's is written in a dry prose.

While the other chapters in this volume are rich in Marxist film analysis, historical Marxism and Marxist film theory, none of them deal with actual moving images of Marx himself. This is the object of analysis for Martin Brady and it closes our collection. In his chapter, Brady examines two East German films for children, *Moor and the Ravens of London* (1968), a Marx-biopic in which Marx is portrayed as a nice family man and friend to all children, and *Hans Röckle and the Devil* (1974), a fairy-tale with a strong analogy to Marx as a person. Brady situates these as 'straightforward Marxist pedagogy' aimed at children, but also with the concept of the Gegenwartsfilm, or the so-called 'contemporary film' depicting positive aspects of contemporary German Democratic Republic society. The chapter pays particular attention to issues concerning the production and reception of these two films, tracing their historical origin, context and distribution. Asserting the deep, uncompromisingly didactic combination of the films, Brady views them as a call for action of 'the socialist warrior, the sufferings and triumphs, defeats and victories in his historically inevitable, triumphant victory over the doomed forces of the old capitalist society'. Evoking Ernst Bloch, these portrayals of Karl Marx have a yet-to-be-like quality, like many other East German *Kinderfilme*, depicting the dream of an almost promised land.

To conclude, this collection argues that art and film in particular can play an important role in political and social transformation, but such art has to be at the same time popular and non-conformist, avoiding the traps of a sterile avant-garde and serving the god of capital – what Badiou describes as romantic formalism and *art pompier* (Badiou 2006: 138–39). The role of a Marxist film historian is to discover and rediscover such art, encourage filmmakers to create it and viewers to seek it.

Notes

1. 'Postmodernism' and 'post-structuralism' cover a similar area, but do not have identical meanings (on their comparison see Bertens 1995). For the purpose of our discussion we favour 'postmodernism', because it encompasses ideas conveyed by thinkers not identified with post-structuralism.
2. In relation to the attitude of post-structuralists to Marx, Althusser wrote that it became 'the fashion to sport Gulag buttons in one's lapel' (Althusser 2006: 10). Foucault illustrates this attitude very well, arguing that rather than seeing in Stalinism an error, an aberration of Marxism, one should search in Marx's

texts for an answer to the question: What made its horrors, which Foucault terms 'the Gulag', possible (Foucault 1980: 135)?
3. Solomon clearly privileges the study of literature over cinema. It is meaningful that his anthology does not contain the works of Sergei Eisenstein or Vsevolod Pudovkin.
4. We can derive this from a large number of references to literature in Marx's writings and the versatility of styles used by this author.
5. Lenin's quote about the importance of cinema in the Soviet Union does not come from his writings but is accounted for by Anatoli Lunacharsky, the first Soviet Minister of Education. In a meeting, Lenin should allegedly have told Lunacharsky that '*among our people you* [Lunacharsky] *are reported to be a patron of art so you must remember that of all the arts for us the most important is cinema*' (Lunacharsky 1988: 57). Although the quote is second hand, it is well known and often used in both Western and Soviet film scholarship (for an example of the latter, see Groshev *et al.* 1968: 5).

Bibliography

Adorno, Theodor and Max Horkheimer (2002). *The Dialectics of Enlightenment – Philosophical Fragments*, trans. E. Jephcott (Stanford: Stanford University Press).
Althusser, Louis (2006). *Philosophy of the Encounter: Later Writings, 1978–87*, trans. G. M. Goshgarian (London: Verso).
Arendt, Hannah (2002). 'Karl Marx and the Tradition of Western Political Thought', *Social Research*, 2, pp. 273–319.
Augé, Marc (1995). *Non-Places: Introduction to an Anthropology of Supermodernity* (London: Verso).
Badiou, Alain (2006). *Polemics*, trans. Steve Corcoran (London: Verso).
Badiou, Alain (2007). *The Century*, trans. Alberto Toscano (Cambridge: Polity).
Badiou, Alain (2009) [2005]. 'Cinema as a Democratic Emblem', trans. Alex Ling and Aurélien Mondon, *Parrhesia*, 1.
Badiou, Alain (2010) [2008]. *The Communist Hypothesis*, trans. David Macey and Steve Corcoran (London: Verso).
Badiou, Alain (2012). *The Rebirth of History: Times of Riots and Uprisings* (London: Verso).
Bakhtin, Mikhail (1979). 'Laughter and Freedom', in Maynard Solomon (ed.), *Marxism and Art: Essays Classic and Contemporary* (Sussex: Harvester Press), pp. 295–300.
Bazin, André (1985). 'The Myth of Stalin in Soviet Cinema', in Bill Nichols (ed.), *Movies and Methods*, vol. 2 (Berkeley CA: University of California Press), pp. 31–40.
Berman, Marshall (1988) [1982]. *All That Is Solid Melts Into Air: The Experience of Modernity* (London: Penguin).
Bertens, Hans (1995). *The Idea of the Postmodern* (London: Routledge).
Bidet, Jacques (2008). 'A Key to the *Critical Companion to Contemporary Marxism*', in Jacques Bidet and Stathis Kouvelakis (eds), *Critical Companion to Contemporary Marxism* (Leiden, Boston: Brill), pp. 3–21.
Blanchot, Maurice (2010). *Political Writings*, trans. Zakir Paul (New York: Fordham University Press).

Boltanski, Luc and Eve Chiapello (2005) [1999]. *The New Spirit of Capitalism*, trans. Gregory Elliott (London: Verso).

Brown, William (2009). 'Man without a Movie Camera – Movies without Men: Towards a Posthumanist Cinema', in Warren Buckland (ed.) *Film Theory and Contemporary Hollywood Movies* (New York: Routledge/AFI), pp. 66–85.

Burawoy, Michael and János Lukács (1992). *The Radiant Past: Ideology and Reality in Hungary's Road to Capitalism* (Chicago: The University of Chicago Press).

Choat, Simon (2010). *Marx Through Post-Structuralism: Lyotard, Derrida, Foucault, Deleuze* (London: Continuum).

Christie, Ian and Richard Taylor (eds) (1991). *Inside the Film Factory: New Approaches to Russian and Soviet Cinema* (London and New York: Routledge).

Daly, Macdonald (ed.) (2006). *Karl Marx and Frederick Engels on Literature and Art* (Documents on Marxist Aesthetics).

Douzinas, Costas and Slavoj Žižek (eds) (2010). *The Idea of Communism* (London: Verso).

Foucault, Michel (1980). *Power/Knowledge: Selected Interviews and Other Writings 1972–1977*, trans. Colin Gordon et al. (Brighton: The Harvester Press).

Fukuyama, Francis (1992). *The End of History and the Last Man* (London: Hamish Hamilton).

Gramsci, Antonio (1979). 'Marxism and Modern Culture', in Maynard Solomon (ed.), *Marxism and Art: Essays Classic and Contemporary* (Sussex: Harvester Press), pp. 266–69.

Groshev, A., S. Ginsburg, I. Dolinskii, N. Lebedev, E. Smirnova and N. Tumanova (1968) *Kratkaya istoriya sovetskogo kino* (Moskva: Iskusstvo).

Groys, Boris (2009). *The Communist Postscript* (London: Verso).

Hamilton-Grant, Iain (2001). 'Postmodernism and Politics', in Stuart Sim (ed.), *The Routledge Companion to Postmodernism* (London: Routledge), pp. 28–40.

Hansen, Miriam Bratu (2004). 'Room-for-Play: Benjamin's Gamble with Cinema', *October*, 109, Summer, pp. 3–45.

Haraway, Donna J. (1991). *Simians, Cyborgs and Women: The Reinvention of Nature* (London: Routledge).

Hardt, Michael and Antonio Negri (2000). *Empire* (Cambridge MA: Harvard University Press).

Hardt, Michael and Antonio Negri (2006). *Multitude: War and Democracy in the Age of Empire* (London: Penguin).

Harvey, David (2005). *A Brief History of Neoliberalism* (Oxford: Oxford University Press).

Harvey, David (2006). *The Limits to Capital*, New and fully updated edition (London: Verso).

Harvey, David (2008). 'Introduction' to Karl Marx and Friedrich Engels, *The Communist Manifesto* (London: Pluto), pp. 1–30.

Harvey, David (2010a). *A Companion to Marx's Capital* (London: Verso).

Harvey, David (2010b). *The Enigma of Capital and the Crises of Capitalism* (London: Profile Books).

Hobsbawm, Eric (2011). *How to Change the World: Marx and Marxism 1840–2011* (London: Little, Brown).

Jameson, Fredric (2003). 'Future City', *New Left Review*, 21, http://www.newleftreview .org/?view=2449, accessed 21/09/2011.

Kouvelakis, Stathis (2008). 'The Crises of Marxism and the Transformation of Capitalism', in Jacques Bidet and Stathis Kouvelakis (eds), *Critical Companion to Contemporary Marxism* (Leiden, Boston: Brill), pp. 23–38.

Lash, Scott and John Urry (1987). *The End of Organized Capitalism* (Cambridge: Polity Press).

Lenin, Vladimir Ilyich (1979). 'L. N. Tolstoy', in Maynard Solomon (ed.), *Marxism and Art: Essays Classic and Contemporary* (Sussex: Harvester Press), pp. 174–77.

Lunacharsky, Anatoli (1988). 'Anatoli Lunacharsky: Conversation with Lenin. I. Of all the arts ...' in Ian Christie and Richard Taylor (eds), trans. Richard Taylor, *The Film Factory: Russian and Soviet Cinema in Documents 1896–1939* (London and New York: Routledge), pp. 56–7.

Lyotard, Jean-François (1984). *The Postmodern Condition: A Report on Knowledge*, trans. Geoff Bennington, Brian Massumi (Minneapolis: University of Minnesota Press).

Macherey, Pierre (1978) [1966]. *A Theory of Literary Production* (London: Routledge).

Manovich, Lev (2001). *The Language of New Media* (Cambridge, MA: MIT Press).

Marx, Karl (1965) [1887]. *Capital: A Critical Analysis of Capitalist Production*, vol. 1 (Moscow: Progress Publishers).

Marx, Karl (1967) [1885]. *Capital: A Critique of Political Economy* vol. 2: *The Process of Circulation of Capital* (Moscow: Progress Publishers).

Marx, Karl (1966) [1894]. *Capital: A Critique of Political Economy*, vol. 3: *The Process of Capitalist Production as a Whole* (Moscow: Progress Publishers).

Marx, Karl (1973) [1953]. *Grundrisse: Foundations of the Critique of Political Economy*, trans. Martin Nicolaus (London: Penguin).

Marx, Karl and Frederick Engels (1947). *The German Ideology, Parts I and III* (New York: International Publishers).

Marx, Karl and Friedrich Engels (2008) [1848]. *The Communist Manifesto*, with an introduction by David Harvey (London: Pluto).

Prawer, S. S. (1976). *Karl Marx and World Literature* (Oxford: Clarendon Press).

Rancière, Jacques (2004) [2000]. *The Politics of Aesthetics*, trans. Gabriel Rockhill (London: Continuum).

Rancière, Jacques (2009) [2008]. *The Emancipated Spectator*, trans. Gregory Elliott (London: Verso).

Rancière, Jacques (2010). 'On the Actuality of Communism', in Gal Kirn (ed.), *Post-Fordism and Its Discontents* (Maastricht: Jan van Eyck Academie), pp. 127–37.

Rancière, Jacques (2013) [2010]. *Dissensus: On Politics and Aesthetics*, trans. Steven Corcoran (London; Bloomsbury).

Sennett, Richard (1998). *The Corrosion of Character: The Personal Consequences of Work in the New Capitalism* (New York: W.W. Norton & Company).

Sennett, Richard (2006). *The Culture of New Capitalism* (New Haven: Yale University Press).

Solomon, Maynard (1979). 'General Introduction' to Maynard Solomon (ed.), *Marxism and Art: Essays Classic and Contemporary* (Sussex: Harvester Press), pp. 3–21.

Stam, Robert (1989). *Subversive Pleasure, Bakhtin, Cultural Criticism, and Film* (Baltimore and London: The John Hopkins University Press).

Thoburn, Nicholas (2003). *Deleuze, Marx and Politics* (London: Routledge).
Trotsky, Leon (1979). 'Art and Class', in Maynard Solomon (ed.), *Marxism and Art: Essays Classic and Contemporary* (Sussex: Harvester Press), pp. 196–98.
Virno, Paolo (2004). *A Grammar of the Multitude*, trans. Isabella Bertoletti, James Cascaito, Andrea Casson (Los Angeles: Semiotext(e)).
Wayne, Mike (ed.) (2005). *Understanding Film: Marxist Perspectives* (London: Pluto Press).
Willemen, Paul (2004). 'Eisenstein, the Indexical and the Digital', in Jean Antoine-Dunne, *The Montage Principle: Eisenstein in New Cultural and Critical Contexts* (Amsterdam: Rodopi), pp. 171–190.
Zhang, Yingjin (2004). *Chinese National Cinema* (New York and London: Routledge).
Žižek, Slavoj (2001). *The Fright of Real Life: Krzysztof Kieslowski between Theory and Post-Theory* (London: British Film Institute).
Žižek, Slavoj (2009). *Violence* (London: Profile Books).
Žižek, Slavoj (2011). *Living in the End Times* (London: Verso).

1
The Dialectical Image: Kant, Marx and Adorno

Mike Wayne

For the intellectuals, the philosophers and the priests, the Word has always been favoured over the Image. Since Plato's parable of the cave of shadows helping to enslave the credulous, the Image has been associated with in-authenticity, manipulation, the transient and contingent, the feeble-minded and the masses. There has been a theological dimension to this distaste for the Image. For Thomas Hobbes in *Leviathan*, the Image, which is by definition a finite thing, is singularly ill-equipped to represent something as infinite as God (Hobbes 2006: 34–35); hence the prohibition on Graven Images in the Jewish religion. The Word, by contrast, seemed to belong to the Mind, not matter that could decompose; it was Universal, not particular; its written manifestation belonged for a long time as the exclusive property of the ruling classes. In this context the Image threatened in effect to transfer the property of the ruling class – its cognitive concepts and moral ideas – to the masses in a form *they* could master. For Benjamin, this was one of the implications of the increasing mechanical reproduction of art in the 20th century: 'the technique of reproduction detaches the reproduced object from the domain of tradition [...] in permitting the reproduction to meet the beholder or listener in his own particular situation, it reactivates the object reproduced' (Benjamin 1999a: 215). In the meantime, publishing, mass democracy and mass education changed the Word from a mere instrument of ruling class power to a site of struggle between classes. But it is still an uneven struggle in which the written Word especially continues to exude class conditions. Hans Magnus Enzensberger has given a wonderful summary of the written Word's connection with authority. He notes the rigid body posture writing demands, the taboos associated with writing that are immaterial to communicating, the intimidation with which the written word is drenched, its links with institutionalised authority (for the subject, initially the school and later business and the law) and the way the written word smoothes over contradictions and facilitates rationalisation and unempathetic distanciation (Enzensberger 1982: 70–72). We may add that illiteracy and linguistic divisions amongst the people have made film an attractive medium for radicals in the developing world.

So it is perhaps odd that radical intellectuals have very often gone along with this tradition of valorising the Word over the Image. There are of course reasons for this valorisation, not all of them bad. Writers across the disciplines have found that with the emergence of capitalism we find 'the ubiquity of vision as the master sense of the modern era' (Jay 1988: 3). And the visual, dominated by the model of Cartesian perspectivalism, was hardly innocent. In French philosophical thought in particular, as Martin Jay has shown, the visual field, from Foucault's panopticon, to Debord's Society of the Spectacle, to Althusser and Lacan's specular Imaginary to Metz's cinematic apparatus, was associated with power, domination, illusion and manipulation (Jay 1994).

There is, however, another tradition, one largely associated with German philosophy that breaks down the hierarchical ordering in which the Word is uncritically valorised over the Image. Instead, in this tradition, we can discern a much more productive cross-fertilisation between the Word and the Image, one in which the Word returns to the *aesthetic* Image as a source for revivifying its own formulations, questioning its assumptions or even circumnavigating the aporias in its own philosophical structures (Buck-Morss 1989). This is the tradition from which the Dialectical Image emerges. I want to trace this emergence in the work of Kant, with reference to the *Critique of Pure Reason* and the *Critique of Judgment*. Kant provides the philosophical framework and roots of the Dialectical Image. Then we shall see how Marx takes up the Dialectical Image as cognitive metaphor for the purpose of social scientific critique within political economy. Finally, I want to give some indicators as to how the concept of the Dialectical Image informed the philosophy of cultural critique in the work of Adorno and Benjamin especially. One of the key ways that the Dialectical Image is dialectical is that it overcomes the fissures between the conceptual and the perceptual, the universal and the particular, the cognitive and the affective, the elite and the popular, the given and the ought. The Dialectical Image is much broader than a specific aesthetic strategy, for example, montage. Instead it takes us into a debate about the critical potential of the aesthetic within the visual field.

Kant and the origins of the dialectical image

Kant's *Critique of Pure Reason* is a deeply contradictory text. For Adorno, the profundity of Kant's text is that it brings 'to the surface contradictions that are deeply embedded in the subject of investigation' (Adorno 2001: 82). The *Critique* splits the Word into an antinomy which has its roots in the emerging capitalist order. The Word on the one hand develops the entire field of cognitive rationality by which consciousness maps the world according to the logical relations that concepts and the pure categories of the understanding impose. The pure categories refer to Quantity, Quality, Relation and Modality. For nothing can be thought that does not have some quantity, some qualities, some relations (to itself and other things) and some modality (does it exist objectively or is its status, as with the aesthetic, of a different ontological order from reality?). The problem, however, is that the logical relations that order subjectivity (the transcendental subject) are so pre-given, so *a priori*, that no social and historical consciousness can emerge from the first *Critique*. The self-active consciousness that Kant elucidates in the *Critique of Pure Reason* turns out to be imprisoned within a cage of reified understanding. As a result, the moral-political dimension of the Word is split off and protected from the massive edifice of reification that Kant constructs, but at the cost of consigning Reason to impotence with regard to our actual institutional life. In Kant's *Critique of Practical Reason*, ethical practical activity is locked up in the private individual subject, self-generated, inwardly orientated and uncoupled from 'external' institutional practices that must obey the *a priori* laws of nature mapped out in the *Critique of Pure Reason*. Thus the ethical act, Lukács observed 'collapses as soon as the first concrete content is to be created' (Lukács 1971: 125).

The first *Critique*, however, as well as being structured around such paralyzing antinomies, also displays the pressure of a latent dialectic, as Adorno again noted in his masterful exposition of that work (Adorno 2001: 87). Two key examples of this latent dialectic are particularly relevant for thinking about the Dialectical Image. First, Kant's concept of the noumenon. Kant argued that the subject's mapping of the world was only a mapping of appearance-forms, that is to say only a mapping of those characteristics of the object world that *can* be known according to the logical-empirical limits of our subjectivity. What the object world may be, independent of our way of apprehending the real according to our logical-empirical machinery of consciousness, is to us an unknown object X or what Kant called a noumenon (Kant 1996: 159–160/A109).

Kant's concept of the noumenon, and its distinction from appearances, clearly points forward to Marx's distinction between the phenomenal forms of life under capitalism – how, for example, the market and commodities appear to us in their *immediacy* – and the *essential* relations, that complex network of social relations that mediate and contextualise objects torn from their circumstances and conditions by the ways of seeing and behaving that commodity production imposes on us. The movement from phenomenal forms to essential relations is for Marx a question of critical social scientific research. But the limits and finitude of the image, of the world of appearances, and how the sensuous apprehension of the world might overcome those limits and register something of the domain of the noumenon, was precisely what motivated Kant to take his aesthetic turn and write the *Critique of Judgment*.

The latent dialectic between the empirical and the non-empirical, the immediately given and its mediated conditions, which the concepts of appearances and noumenon register, links to a second latent dialectical pressure pushing against Kant's antinomous philosophical architecture. This is the relationship between the concepts and pure categories of the understanding, where logical relations are secured as universal and necessary, and what Kant calls the Transcendental Aesthetic. Kant recognises that in order for logical relations to have any cognitive power they must actually be applied to sense data coming to the subject from the outside world. This sense data (the world of appearances) can only be mapped conceptually if it is ordered according to principles of temporal and spatial mapping. Time and Space, however, are not derived from concepts, but from the pure forms of intuition that belong to the Transcendental Aesthetic. Before we can apprehend any actual sense data, the subject must have a 'receptivity for being affected by objects' and this 'precedes necessarily all intuitions of these objects' (Kant 1996: 81/B42). The Transcendental Aesthetic makes it possible for us to map objects according to the principles of time and space. Once the subject has assembled objects of sense data according to a process Kant calls synthesis, then these empirical objects can be stamped, as it were, with the objective universality of empirical concepts which are in turn governed by the pure categories. Thus, the empirical concept 'dog' can be stamped on a particular dog *in concreto* that comes to our senses (213–214/A141). A dog, like all things observable, will be a particular instantiation of the pure categories, being a certain quantity (e.g. size), and having certain qualities, relations and modality (a real dog or a representation of a dog). However, crucially, the entire thrust of the *Critique of Pure Reason* is to argue that concepts, whether abstract or empirical, can only be combined into combinations that generate new knowledge because they can be *figured* in pure forms of intuition (time and space). So the Transcendental Aesthetic not only plays a determinate role in relation to actual sense data, it also plays a crucial role in relation to the development of our conceptual and cognitive capacities. This lays the basis for overcoming Kant's dichotomy between concepts and sensuousness.

> [N]o geometric principles – e.g., the principle that in a triangle two sides together are greater than the third – are ever derived from universal concepts of *line* and *triangle*; rather, they are all derived from intuition, and are derived from it moreover *a priori*. (Kant 1996: 79/B40)

Line and triangle are concepts of the understanding, but it is pure intuition of spatial relations that allows us to combine such concepts as 'line', 'length' and 'angle' into geometric principles. Thus, some form of figuration becomes essential for the understanding to *combine* concepts and generate knowledge of principles, and this lays one of the bases for overcoming the otherwise sharp division Kant establishes between the Transcendental Aesthetic and the understanding, and, further, between the pure transcendental conditions of experience and its particular (socially and historically determinate) 'contents'. What will happen with Kant's aesthetic turn in the *Critique of Judgment* is that the aesthetic as an *aid to thinking* will be uncoupled from its role in providing a reified universe of concepts with sense data. Instead, the aesthetic will develop its own relatively autonomous *play with sensuous forms*, a figuring that will relativise universal concepts, call them into question, historicise them and open them up to critique. This in turn provokes the moral-political capacities of reason – hitherto locked up impotently in the private conscience, into re-engaging with the world, because its own principles have been made sensuously palpable in the aesthetic. Thus it is that the aesthetic Image comes to the rescue of the Word, helping it think past the blockages in Kant's philosophical system.

In the *Critique of Judgment* Kant distinguishes between the determinative judgements that subsumed the particular (sense data) under universal concepts and categories in the first *Critique*, and a new mode of judging that he calls *reflective judgment*.

Determinative judgment, [which operates] under universal transcendental laws given by the understanding, is only subsumptive. The law is marked out for it *a priori* [...] reflective judgment [...] is obliged to ascend from the particular in nature to the universal. (Kant 1987: 19)

To *reflect* [...] is to hold given presentations up to, and compare them with, either other presentations or one's cognitive power [itself], in reference to a concept that this [comparison] makes possible. (400)

Reflective judgement thus recognises that the universal is not necessarily given, and this licenses a mode of judging that is far more open and exploratory. Here we have very clearly the origins of a German tradition of thought that mixed the aesthetic with philosophy. Rejecting the universal as given, Kant lays the basis for subjective, aesthetically tinged, 'poetic' juxtapositions that illuminate specific materialist truths of an epoch. Here we have the rationale for a critical procedure (analogy or metaphor) that makes it possible to *think* a concept through perception that it was difficult or not possible to think without that sensible operation. The critical procedure combines induction (starting with the particular) with analogy (comparing particulars in a play of forms) to generate new ways of thinking or thinking about things in new ways, that the reified universe of concepts had blocked (see graph below).

Typically in Kant's third *Critique*, some particular of nature is used to *reflect* on our own cognitive powers, and implicitly, our social relationships. This should be contrasted with the determinative judgement of the first *Critique*, where nature is over-extended to the social world, with the result that our capacities for critical reflective reason atrophy.

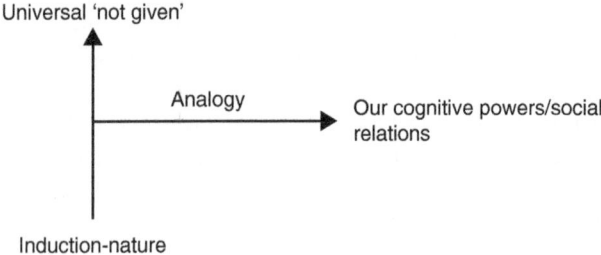

Conceptual metaphors in Marx

Kant's *Critique of Pure Reason* is an attempt to develop a philosophy of consciousness based on the new emerging natural sciences (especially Newton's successes in astronomy). But this led to over-extending the logical and empirically observable laws of nature to the entire terrain of human endeavour. While we are natural creatures, we are by nature also social creatures and it is our social dimension that this over-extension of the natural science framework completely eclipses. This over-extension is of course quite typical, and across the disciplines the social sciences have adapted the models developed in the natural sciences. Economics, sociology, psychology and so forth have been dominated by the problem that first beset Kant in the *Critique of Pure Reason*. Social relations and practices acquire the quality of something given, something *a priori*, constituted, *as if by nature*, without our own participation in their making. Marx tracked the roots of this naturalisation process to the universalisation of commodity production that defines capitalism. The *Critique of Pure Reason* has a dualistic structure which bears the outlines of the commodity form. The commodity form brackets off the wider social relationships which are a condition of commodity exchange because private property is founded on the non-interference of popular control, conscious regulation and oversight of commodity operations. This is what gives the first *Critique* its emphasis on the empirical. Yet of course it is not the case that social imperatives are absent from discrete instances of commodity exchange – whether it is the buying and selling of labour power, the buying and selling of consumer goods, the buying and selling of technology, money and so on. In fact, here what imposes itself on these apparently discrete exchanges is the full force of the capitalist motive to accumulate capital. This abstract power and pressure attempts to subsume everything within its force field and this manifests itself in the first *Critique* as the subsumption of all empirical sense data by the logical rules of determinative judgement. Together, a generalised, abstract, *a priori* capitalist imperative to accumulate and empirical instances of market exchanges torn from their context (the struggle between capital and labour, for example) produce a naturalisation effect.

One cannot combat this naturalisation effect by simply abolishing nature and declaring that everything is a social convention. This has been the default strategy for theories of language and representation for much of the 20th century, starting with structuralism through to postmodernism. A better strategy can be found in Marx's methodology, which attempts to rethink what the categories 'nature' and 'society' mean and how they relate to one another. In the preface to the German edition of *Capital*, Marx, referring to the 'capitalist and the landlord', wrote of how human behaviour within the framework of capitalist social relations and class interests must be viewed 'as a process of natural history' (Marx 1983: 21). What Marx intended by this metaphorical comparison and juxtaposition between the capitalist social system and natural evolution, was *not* to naturalise capitalism, but to suggest that within the context of capitalist society, certain forms of *capitalist* behaviour, certain trends and developments, certain dynamics (such as crises or the tendency towards monopoly) do have a force of nature about them insofar as these patterns pertain to the essentials of capitalism which cannot operate in any other way without violating or at the very least mitigating (through reforms) the nature of capital. Intrinsic to the nature of capital is that it turns itself into (a second) nature, because it is premised on robbing the subject that creates it of collective control over it. Within the mainstream media, for instance, what the 'markets' are doing is discussed as if the 'markets' were not human-made institutions, but instead forces of nature independent of human activity. This naturalisation effect is paradoxically a kind of violation of what is natural to *our* species being – namely that we have differentiated ourselves from nature to a degree and can to a degree that capitalism represses, achieve conscious control over ourselves and our environment.

Marx's metaphorical reference to nature functions as a critique of the way capitalism naturalises itself by making its dynamics and imperatives (such as capital accumulation) 'laws of nature'. From this point of view, the frequent transformation of Marx's concept of 'natural history', which is a critique of the robbing of the object from any mediation by the subject, into a positivistic science of the laws of motion of society that operates exclusively independently of collective intervention is, as Adorno remarks, a perversion. This is why it is important to note that Marx invokes the concept of natural history in relation to the capitalist and the landlord but *not* the proletariat, to whom falls the necessity of *breaking* capital's natural evolution. In the absence of such a break, 'the history of the progressing mastery of nature, continues the unconscious history of nature, of devouring and being devoured' (Adorno 1973: 355). Thus the more the species advances technologically, the more it regresses; where once nature terrorised the species, now it is *our own* powers that we have not brought under our control that does the terrorising. The expansion of the productive forces in the absence of a change in the social relations of production, merely expands our ability to *devour and be devoured*. This transformation of the social into a new kind of nature constitutes the 'law of motion for the unconscious society' (Adorno 1973: 356), which is to say one which escapes democratic collective control. The same point was made by Marx's friend and co-author, Engels:

> Darwin did not know what a bitter satire he wrote on mankind, and especially on his countrymen, when he showed that free competition, the struggle for existence, which the economists celebrate as the highest historical achievement, is the normal state of the *animal kingdom*. Only conscious organization of social production, in which production and distribution are carried on in a planned way, can elevate mankind above the rest of the animal world. (Engels 1977: 349–350)

The dialectical image of nature and history

In a suggestive analogy from his notebooks on dialectics, Leon Trotsky wrote:

> Contrary to a photograph, which is the element of formal logic, the [motion-picture] film is 'dialectical' (badly expressed). (1986: 97)

This should not be taken as the final word on photography, but rather through an analogy between the two mediums Trotsky tries to get at the difference between two antagonistic philosophical traditions: logical positivism or the formal logic that Kant outlined in the first *Critique*, and dialectical thinking, which, I have suggested, Kant's *Critique of Judgment* begins to seed. Trotsky's analogy alights on an element that is crucial to film: namely that it *moves*. The *moving* picture, the *motion* picture emerged from a whole pre-history of technological devices aimed at getting the still image to *move*: dioramas, panoramas, myrioramas, magic lanterns, mutoscopes, kinetescopes and so forth. The moving image moves both the object and the vantage point on the object, and this movement opened up the whole thematics of dialectics: change, development, shifts, altered relationships and the re-evaluation of initial perspectives and identifications. If the naturalisation effect tends to freeze or congeal social nature so that change and the potential for change becomes imperceptible, the *movie*, potentially at least, decongeals social nature by its motion dynamics. The movie realises the potential of the aesthetic as pure intuition (activating the principles of space and time) to not only aid thinking but to critique what we take as given.

It was this thematic of dialectical motion that attracted the Left intelligentsia to film in the 1920s and 1930s. Here's Walter Benjamin for example:

> Our taverns and our metropolitan streets, our offices and furnished rooms, our railroad stations and our factories appeared to have us locked up hopelessly. Then came the film and burst this prison-world asunder by the dynamite of the tenth of a second, so that now, in the midst of its far-flung ruins and debris, we calmly and adventurously go travelling. (1999a: 229)

Here Benjamin stresses the potentialities of the medium as a productive cognitive augmentation of the human eye, which in transforming our relations to material nature is at the same time registering new social meanings, relations and possibilities slumbering within that material nature but unrecognised because we are 'locked up hopelessly' within it. Film explodes this reified world, turning it into 'ruins and debris' – that is, montage elements that can be reconfigured dialectically for cognitive travelling. Now the terms 'ruins' and 'debris' remind us that for Benjamin, the inert qualities which reified material nature acquires under capitalism can be counteracted when that material nature breaks down in some way. A key term that undergirds Benjamin's conception of the dialectical image is *decomposition*. Decomposition refers thematically to death and a dialectic between the living and the dead. Death, mortality, brings nature back into the frame, but not as a support structure for capitalism. Marx's reconfiguring of the concepts of 'nature' and 'history' show us that the conception of nature under capitalism is a thoroughly ideological one. The task is not to reject nature but to recover an authentic understanding of nature and our immersion and relationship to nature which capitalism blocks us from achieving. For capitalism and its commodity consciousness, the mortality of all natural things is a trace of historical change and transformation which it abhors. Consciousness under the sign of the commodity is encouraged to think it will live forever, as if consciousness was not also a material body that will one day die. The hostility towards aging in commodity culture, evident in the cosmetic surgery industry that has spread from film stars to the high street, is symptomatic of this deeply ideological hostility towards nature.

Benjamin's conception of *decomposition* points to a double death. The death which the commodity brings to the living when it dominates them and the potential to in turn bring the living back to a more authentic life once the commodity has aged and been left behind, rendered out of date by the next wave of commodity innovation. Decomposition as death in this double sense and as a methodology is linked, for example, in Benjamin's theory of the collector. The collector lovingly brings back obsolescent commodities whose original uses and exchange values have died, reconstructing their history as a 'magic encyclopedia' that traces the 'fate of his object' (Benjamin 1999a: 62). The collector as a kind of historian has an intense personal relationship with the commodity ambiguously different from the way the commodity interpellates the subject when the commodity is in its full glory as the 'prodigies' of their day (Benjamin 1999b: 203). Death or age makes the commodity more receptive to the living; its powers over the living weaken with its historical displacement into the collector's arrangement of artefacts. The collector then is not only a historian but an artist. Benjamin quotes Marx in the Convolute on The Collector in *The Arcades Project*: 'I can, in practice, relate myself humanly to an object only if the object relates itself humanly to man' (quoted in Benjamin 1999b: 209). The possibility of a human relationship (of the kind found today through Freecycle and using second-hand shops) opens up only with the obsolescence or partial obsolescence of the commodity. At that point the object becomes meaningful, which is to say, through decomposition, the object from history becomes allegorical. As Benjamin cryptically puts it in *The Arcades Project*: 'Broken-down matter: the elevation of the commodity to the status of allegory' (1999b: 207). The genre in which broken-down matter has decomposed to produce an allegory around being alive and being dead under capitalism is, of course, the zombie film.

Adorno and film

Benjamin's thematics of decomposition, ruin, death and so on were linked to his interest in montage of the kind that could be found across the avant-garde arts in the 1920s and 1930s. But like many of the political Left, he was prepared to see a latent culture of avant-garde experimentation and disruption to conventional bourgeois norms in popular and mass culture as well. This was a perspective that Adorno shared rather less than Benjamin or Brecht. Adorno regarded the integration of film into monopoly capital as fateful for the medium, destroying any claim it might have to being an autonomous art. His short essay 'Transparencies on Film' was occasioned by the dispute between the new young German filmmakers who had recently signed the 1962 Oberhausen Manifesto, and the established German cinema which the Oberhauseners described disparagingly as 'Daddy's Cinema'. Although Adorno sided with the young filmmakers of the German New Wave, describing Daddy's Cinema as 'infantile [...] regression manufactured on an industrial scale' (Adorno 1981: 199) and hoped that from the new cinema 'something qualitatively different' might emerge, his thoughts on the ontology of film suggest that the medium had its work cut out if it was to escape its conformist tendencies. Comparing the written word to the iconic medium of film images, he suggests that in the novel, language has an in-built capacity to achieve a distanciation from mere imitation of the empirical world:

> Even when dialogue is used in a novel, the spoken word is not directly spoken but is rather distanced by the act of narration – perhaps even by the typography – and thereby abstracted from the physical presence of living persons. Thus, fictional characters never resemble their empirical counterparts no matter how minutely they are described. In fact, it may be due to the very precision of their presentation that they are removed even further from empirical reality; they become aesthetically autonomous. Such distance is abolished in film: to the extent that a film is realistic, the semblance of immediacy cannot be avoided. (200)

This is a quite conventional privileging of the aesthetic Word over images, especially mass-mediated images. Whereas the novel can make a claim to aesthetic autonomy from empirical reality because language must actively reconstruct its resemblance of the world, so that we are aware that its 'immediacy' has been mediated, the same cannot be said of the cinematic image. For Adorno, the iconic quality of the film image abolishes the sense of mediation and instead leaves us with the 'semblance of immediacy', the direct imitation and copying of the external physical-material world. This immediacy is a *semblance* (Adorno is not arguing that film has an unproblematic 'realist' relationship with the world) because it disguises the *mediation* of the reified social mechanisms that dress the automaticity of the film image's correlation with the real up as natural and inevitable.

The photographic process of film, primarily representational, places a higher intrinsic significance on the object, as foreign to subjectivity, than aesthetically autonomous techniques; this is the retarding aspect of film in the historical process of art. Even where film dissolves and modifies its objects as much as it can, the distintegration is never complete. Consequently, it does not permit absolute construction: its elements, however abstract, always retain something representational; they are never purely aesthetic values. Due to this difference, society projects into films quite differently – far more directly on account of the objects – than into advanced painting or literature. (Adorno 1981: 202)

Adorno seems to come close to suggesting that film is beyond redemption due to the intrinsic nature of its iconic language which appears to transparently inscribe external reality. For Adorno, society 'projects' into film rather more than film itself can 'project' back into society. This, it seems, is questionable to me and indeed the 'intrinsic significance of the object' in film's iconic language means that film is inescapably saturated with the social through and through. But this need not mean that film cannot then acquire enough relative autonomy from the social to encourage the kind of reflective judgements that Kant identified as central to the aesthetic. Adorno, however, does not quite give up on film. In the next passage he evokes a juxtaposition between nature and history (here film technology) that suggests a way out:

Irrespective of the technological origins of the cinema, the aesthetics of film will do better to base itself on a subjective mode of experience which films resemble and which constitutes its artistic character. A person who, after a year in the city, spends a few weeks in the mountains abstaining from all work, may unexpectedly experience colorful images of landscapes consolingly coming over him or her in dreams or daydreams. These images do not merge into one another in a continuous flow, but are rather set off against each other in the course of their appearance, much like the magic lantern slides of our childhood. It is in the discontinuity of their movement that the images of the interior monologue resemble the phenomenon of writing. (201)

This passage is typical of Adorno's writing style and shows how much he worked up his arguments around a collage of images instead of the more traditional modes of logical construction. In a few short lines we find film technology and the city being juxtaposed to the countryside and leisure before the *subjective mediation* of nature in the form of daydreams and dreams that violate traditional continuity rules of the dominant film hark back, not nostalgically, but in the form of a revolutionary constellation, to the pre-cinematic technology of the magic lantern shows. This in turn suggests a model for a radical contemporary cinema attuned to the 'interior monologue' of subjective life which is in turn then made alike, in another analogy, with the discontinuity and mobile, shifting images generated by writing (such as those Adorno has just given us a wonderful demonstration of).

There are two things going on here. First, Adorno's aesthetic prescriptions for film would seem to insist that it moves in the direction of a non-linear, free-form, subjectively associational arrangement of material that would counteract its passive reflection of the reified social world just as it is. But this avant-garde prescriptiveness is problematic insofar as it limits Adorno's receptivity towards popular culture, which instead organises its movements around *stories*. For we can find dialectical images suffusing popular culture rather more routinely than Adorno would admit. In this sense the aesthetic comes to the rescue of Adorno's aesthetic theory (as it did to Kant's philosophy) by demonstrating that his cultural discrimination against popular culture in general and film in particular are non-identical with the general premises of his aesthetic theory. The second thing going on here is that Adorno is mobilising Marx's concept of natural history in his reconfiguring of nature and technology. In Adorno's poetic philosophy nature becomes an inspiration for rethinking how we use a given technology (here film), thus overcoming the division between nature and technology that is typical of dominant modes of thinking.

Adorno's concept of natural beauty, which he developed in his final work *Aesthetic Theory*, does something similar. Here Adorno again returns to the question of nature and culture. The concept of natural beauty has been on the decline ever since the mid-19th century when, under the influence of Hegel, it disappeared from aesthetic theories in favour of a celebration of the autonomy of the artwork as a product made by human design. Ever since, Marxists have been happy to see the back of the concept of natural beauty, seeing in it any number of irredeemable ideological problems. But Adorno is critical of Hegel's dismissal of natural beauty: for nature functions in Adorno's aesthetics as a metaphor for what is denied and disavowed within the social world of men and women – including the denial of nature itself. Now this returns us precisely to Kant's reflective judgement, which as we saw takes a particular image of nature and metaphorically compares it with some aspect of our own relations, including our relations with nature which is always already presumed by the fact that we can find beauty in it.

This strategy of using nature as a way of discussing the social and the cultural is typical of the horror genre for example, although no doubt it is handled with varying degrees of sophistication and cognitive insight. *Monsters* (Gareth Edwards 2010), for example, has the good materialist philosophical basis in the idea that the relationships we strike up with nature, even alien nature, also say something about our social relationships with one another. For Kant, the category of natural beauty was thoroughly historical and social, for we can only find beauty in nature when we are no longer identical with nature but have differentiated ourselves from it. Nature thus poses the question of the terms by which we have differentiated ourselves from it and the relations among ourselves by which we have achieved that differentiation.

Let us take an example of how a popular cultural text may handle the themes of nature, difference, death, decomposition and beauty, and the relations of these terms to our broader social relationships, in George Romero's *Land of the Dead* (2005). Here a brutalised class-divided city, the remnants of civilisation, sends out raids seeking food supplies beyond the electrified fences. Arriving in a small town early on in the film, the raiding party find zombies shuffling around, still dressed in the clothes of their former life and performing, badly, some of the gestures and routines which once made them human. The humans meanwhile have a weapon of *distraction* that allows them to manipulate the zombies, shoot them and grab supplies. This weapon is the spectacle of fireworks that they fire from the militarised vehicle or quasi tank that they travel in. The fireworks – or 'skyflowers' as another significantly simple-minded character calls them – refer to something beautiful which the human characters by and large can no longer appreciate but only use instrumentally (Figure 1.1). The zombies stare at the skyflowers thus indicating that despite their bestial state, they retain, ironically, a trace of human feeling for what they once were that the humans themselves have in many ways inured themselves to because of their brutal conditions of life (Figure 1.2). The eyeline match that takes the viewer to the fireworks/skyflowers, which we ourselves cannot help finding attractive, is from the look of the zombies, a cut that situates the spectator in an ambiguous position which the rest of the film's narrative plays upon.

The fireworks/skyflowers then can be thought of as a dialectical image of our contemporary media whose spectacles distract and manipulate the masses – but even to formulate the allegory in the words of a cliché often associated with Adorno himself is to do an injustice to the richness of the image just elaborated, with its dialectical switching between the zombies and the humans in terms of those who still retain

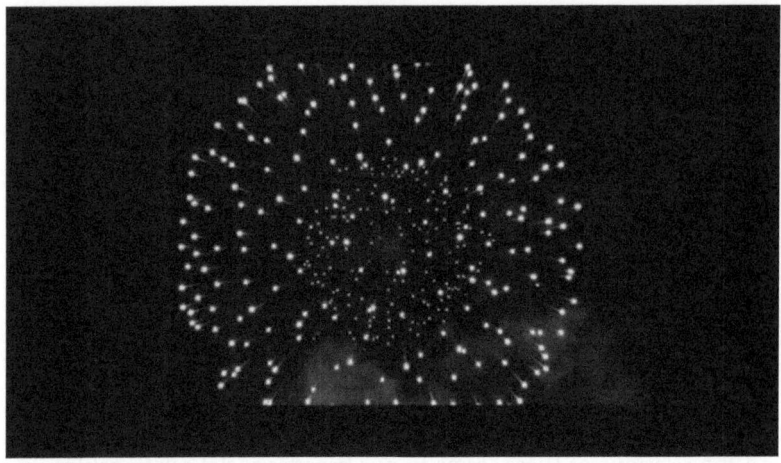

Figure 1.1 Fireworks
Source: Screen capture from *Land of the Dead* (2005), dir. George Romero, Universal Pictures

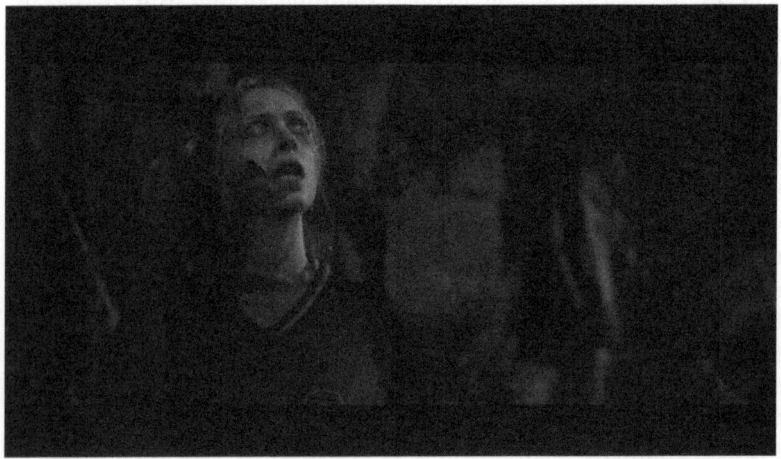

Figure 1.2 The look of zombies
Source: Screen capture from *Land of the Dead* (2005), dir. George Romero, Universal Pictures

a *feeling for beauty* within the mechanism of distraction. The humans are in fact less human than the dead in this regard, a feeling underscored by the reversal of our expectations as to which group – the zombies or the humans – pose a threat to the other. For the humans, with their weapon of distraction, tear through the town shooting it up and taking what they want in an image that self-consciously echoes the US projection of military power around the world. The trace of a feeling for their former life, their former humanity shown by their interest in beauty, is then amplified and developed by the raid, as the zombies begin to organise and march on the city (led by a black working-class zombie, a former garage mechanic). The narrative trajectory of the zombies towards (class?) consciousness of themselves and their interests means that at the end of the film, when the skyflowers are launched once more, the zombies again look up and the trapped humans celebrate a moment of hope, only for the zombies to then turn their heads back to earth and lock their gaze on human flesh. Sensing now the ideological manipulation within the skyflowers, the trace of the feeling of beauty which hinted at their capacity to develop their consciousness, now has to be set aside in a Fanonian moment of necessary violence, at least momentarily, if their liberation is to be achieved. Since we have seen enough of the city to know its corruption and brutality, the spectator has been given every opportunity to feel dialectically ambivalent about its destruction. As in the best horror films, our initial certainties regarding the firm division between the human and the monstrous, precisely the line drawn by those universal concepts that the aesthetic declares is *not given*, are subverted and a more complex dialectic and reconfiguration of the meaning and relations between terms (here zombies and humans, the dead and the living, the civilised and the bestial) is explored.

Conclusion

We have seen that the origins of the Dialectical Image can, philosophically, be discovered in Kant's *Critique of Pure Reason*. The importance of the Transcendental Aesthetic for new concept formation would then be substantively developed in the *Critique of Judgment*, but now the 'concept formation' is uncoupled from the universe of reified concepts that dominated the first *Critique*. Critique through aesthetics becomes possible. Whereas in the first *Critique* Kant insisted on the absolute division between the empirical and the noumenon, in the third *Critique*, the sensible becomes, through the play of aesthetic forms, a way of glimpsing the suprasensible (for example, the real barbarism of modern capitalist 'civilization' in Romero's zombie movies). Marx developed the critical potential of Kant's reflective judgement as conceptual metaphors for social-scientific critique, dialectically reconfiguring the master couplet of nature and history in the concept of natural history. This critique of reification was then taken up by German aesthetic philosophy in the work of Benjamin, Adorno and others. For Kant, what was transcendental about the aesthetic was not the particular judgements that were made – since then they would only reproduce the reified judgements they were critiquing, but the fact that we take these judgements as worth discussing and communicating. Thus the aesthetic opens up the whole dimension of the social and the historical. Evoking Benjamin in his discussion of natural beauty, Adorno poetically conjures up 'illuminated edges of clouds [that] seem to give duration to lightning flashes' (Adorno 1997: 92). The meanings or truths of aesthetic images ought to be given just enough duration before they disappear or are reconfigured into a new pattern. 'Natural beauty is suspended history, a moment of becoming at a standstill' (93) argues Adorno, evoking once again Benjamin's famous definition of the dialectical image. Thus natural beauty or the Dialectical Image is a combination of stasis and transience, where the movement of the dialectic is arrested in a vivid form that illuminates a totality (the condition of the human being under capitalism, for example) but from a position that is a *momentary arrangement* (the aesthetic experience itself) gone before it can congeal into a reified monolith or new universal concept. Yet it leaves traces behind it (in the form of the aesthetic practice and the seeds it has sown in consciousness) that can be reconfigured in future work/future receptions (and also social change) rather than be lost forever.

Bibliography

Adorno, T. W. (1973) *Negative Dialectics*, London: Routledge Kegan Paul.
Adorno, T. W. (1981) 'Transparencies on Film', *New German Critique*, no.24/45.
Adorno, T. W. (1997) *Aesthetic Theory*, London: Continuum Press.
Adorno, T. W. (2001) *Kant's Critique of Pure Reason*, Oxford: Polity Press.
Benjamin, W. (1999a) *Illuminations*, London: Pimlico.
Benjamin, W. (1999b) *The Arcades Project*, Translated by Howard Eiland and Kevin McLaughlin, Cambridge Massachusetts: Harvard University Press.
Buck-Morss, S. (1989) *The Dialectics of Seeing*, Cambridge Massachusetts: MIT Press.
Engels, F. (1977) 'Introduction to Dialectics of Nature' in *Karl Marx and Frederick Engels, Selected Works, Vol. 1*, London: Lawrence and Wishart.
Enzensberger, H. M. (1982) *Critical Essays*, New York: Continuum.
Hobbes, T. (2006) 'Image and Idolatry' in *Images: A Reader* (eds) Sunil Manghani, Arthur Piper and Jon Simons, London: Sage.
Jay, M. (1988) 'Scopic Regimes of Modernity' in *Vision & Visuality* (ed.) Hal Foster, San Franscisco: Bay Press.

Jay, M. (1994) *The Denigration of Vision in Twentieth-Century French Thought*, Berkeley: University of California Press.

Lukács, G. (1971) *History and Class Consciousness: Studies in Marxist dialectics*, Translated by Rodney Livingstone, London: Merlin Press.

Kant, I. (1987) *Critique of Judgment*, Translated by Werner S. Pluhar, Indianapolis/ Cambridge: Hackett Publishing Company, Inc.

Kant, I. (1996) *Critique of Pure Reason*, Translated by Werner S. Pluhar, Indianapolis/Cambridge: Hackett Publishing Company, Inc.

Marx, K. (1983) *Capital, A Critique of Political Economy*, London: Lawrence and Wishart.

Trotsky, L. (1986) *Trotsky's Notebooks, 1933–1935*, Translated by Philip Pomper, New York: Columbia University Text.

2
The Utopian Function of Film Music

Johan Siebers

Ernst Bloch, the utopian Marxist thinker born in 1885, before cinema existed, wrote, on and off, about film from the early years of the 20th century until the end of his life in 1977. He was concerned with the meaning of film as a new medium, its capacity for social transformation and critique, its status as an art form and its role in the process of modernisation of society. As a Marxist, Bloch was critical of a cinema which was already by his time becoming a commercial vehicle, but arguably it is his ability to see the revolutionary and utopian potential of film that is most important and that can offer us insights regarding the nature of film which are relevant today. Supportive of Lenin's statement that film was the most important form of contemporary art because it could reach the people and directly engage with their consciousness, Bloch added, implicitly, an aesthetical understanding of cinema which emphasised the way in which cinema can take apart the integrated experience of reality and distort, fragment or transform it by virtue of its technical affordances – zooming in and out, panning, slow motion and fast forward, but also the use of music, which I will explore in this chapter. We know these ideas also from Benjamin's remarks on film as the art form commensurate to a fragmented, shattered modernity. But for Bloch they are part of a utopian aesthetic of cinema; the parameters of montage are different for Bloch than they are for Benjamin.

Montage for Benjamin expresses a shattered history in which the light of redemption reflects, as it were, between the shards of history. What Benjamin called the *dialectical image* is the estranged experience of the fact *that there is history* in the confrontation of realities belonging to different times, as when we find an old object at the back of a cupboard for which we no longer have any use. In those, essentially passive, apprehensive, moments we experience that there is time, and a time that is not moving towards an all-encompassing totality. The redemptive totality is, as it were, equally far removed from each point in time. That, in my view, itself still, or again, theological interpretation of history, is reflected in Benjamin's understanding of montage. For Bloch montage also expresses modernity that had become a *'Hohlraummit Funken'*, a cavity with sparks as opposed to a world filled with the presence of the divine (Bloch 1998). But the relation of the sparks to the redemptive totality is a different one. For Bloch, the old object has an unredeemed future within it. Understanding Blochian montage will give us a better appreciation of the potential of Bloch's philosophy for film theory today. For Bloch, film critique can be seen to consist primarily in elucidating what he calls the Not-Yet-Conscious in this cultural form: how the medium channels and articulates human hopes, aspirations, longings and desires, how the fragmented world in which we live is not only the shattered ruin of a false, ideological sense of unity and purpose, but the possibility for a truer relation to unity and identity as yet to come, as a self-realising, precarious but not yet thwarted possibility. A world without a recognition, schooling and critique of the human potential for hope is a 'world without why' as Raymond Geuss once called it. The commoditisation of desire and the disappearance (or re-theologisation) of the big questions regarding the meaning of human existence go hand in hand and have dominated cultural theory for decades. Now that the climate is changing, looking again at Bloch, who had no doubts about the importance of asking the big questions of life and did so from within historical materialism, can help us in the task of putting cultural theory once again in a position in which it can provide a critical voice and active resistance with respect to the nihilism of contemporary culture. This is not just an academic undertaking. It reflects and can reinforce the attempts to formulate positive alternatives to the socio-political realities created by neoliberalism: the increasing gap between rich and poor, the privatisation of all aspects of life, the lack of felt significance in the lives of many people, the exploitation of the social and natural environment, the still continuing totalisation of the subservience of the state to the economy, the withering away of freedom. We are experiencing more than before the devastation of the human and natural life-world that has been brought about, and are more and more losing faith in the ability of existing systems to correct themselves.

With Bloch's philosophy we can see that these realities have something to do with the absence of a vision, or if you prefer, a discourse, of the ultimate questions of human life: 'Who are we? Where do we come from? Where are we going? What are we waiting for? What awaits us?' (Bloch 1986: 3). Asking these questions, which means exposing ourselves to them, makes us human because it is the recognition of the fact that we are not known to ourselves and that we are, in essence, incognito and therefore we create above ourselves, go out of ourselves and are underway. This is a central idea for critical theory, expressed by Adorno several years later: '(N)othing can be even experienced as living if it does not contain a promise of something transcending life. This transcendence therefore is, and at the same time is not – and beyond that contradiction it is no doubt very difficult, and probably impossible, for thought to go' (Adorno 2001: 145). It has been one of the motivations of Western Marxism (at least up to Habermas) to insist on this need for transcendence; the analysis of the commoditisation or functionalisation of the life world and of reason acquires its significance in the light of this underlying idea. Adorno, in his aesthetics, sought not to go beyond the contradiction. He thought no more could be done than to perpetually seek reminders of it, reminders that 'there can be no true life in falseness'. Bloch does try to go beyond it. For him, the ontology of not-yet-being is the vehicle with which to move beyond the joint 'is' and 'is not' of the promise that animates all life, the vehicle with which to perceive that promise for what it is and what it asks of us in the first place. We must be careful not to misread Bloch on this point.

His marginal position owes much to the subtlety of his thought: it is easily mistaken as an attempt to put religion into historical materialism and Marxism, or vice versa. It has indeed been taken as such by Marxists, for whom Bloch often retained the atmosphere of bourgeois thought, but also for the theologians, for whom Bloch mostly seemed too much of a materialist. The ontology of the not-yet, however, gives us the means by which to understand what the religious interpretation of the transcendence of life really amounts to, just as it gives us the means by which to understand why mechanical, positivist materialism is itself an ideological formation and not a philosophical position. Both the religious and the positivist stance reify the transcending function of life into a transcendent realm, pre-given destiny or pre-given normativity, which one then affirms, the other denies. Both lead to a worldview that ignores the constant movement beyond itself in which all that exists is enveloped; both, from Adorno's point of view as we just introduced it, miss what gives life meaning: process as the immanent movement of life. With that we have reached the standpoint of cinema, or at least of a certain form of cinema.

Bloch's philosophy has been applied to film as a cultural phenomenon by Douglas Kellner and Fredric Jameson, but has not found any
widespread application so far (Jameson 2007; Kellner 1997). Kellner and
Jameson have, above all, referred to Bloch's understanding of ideology.[1]
For Bloch, ideology is effective because it has a utopian core. Ideological
formations are forms of false consciousness, but they arise around a core
human desire for truth from which they draw much of their life force.
In what may appear to us as an irrational dialectic, the distortion of the
utopian core does not diminish the efficacy of the ideology – on the
contrary, the falseness of the ideology seems to always be known, in
some sense, by those who subscribe to it – and yet they act in accordance with the ideology. This point has also been made by Žižek (Žižek
2009): an ideology works precisely because it distorts that from which
it lives, because those who are under the sway of it do not really believe
it. For, as Žižek argues in many places, someone who were to fully subscribe, let us say to limitless capitalism as the colonisation of all use
value by exchange value, would soon lose all will to do anything at all.
For Žižek it is only because the ideology of value is not accepted fully
as belief – some value remains irreducible to exchange value – that the
rule of exchange value can become total.

This negative belief that makes ideology possible shoves itself in
between the 'official' ideological rationalisation and the – always
ineffable – utopian core of human existence, the incognito that is in the
process of becoming. Thus, ideology is a double colonisation: it encap-
sulates the potentially shattering, and at any rate, uncanny, experience
of the incognito of existence in the form of a rationalising ideological
neutralisation of it, which is then reinforced, paradoxically, by negating
it, thereby giving the subject a sense of a certain distance towards it.
But the utopian core, the incognito, has become doubly invisible: first
it is neutralised by rationalisation, then the rationalisation, by refus-
ing its totalisation, strengthens its hold. If ideology insisted on being
accepted as complete truth, it would quickly show its irrationality and
would lose its grip on us. The ideological neutralisation is effective
precisely because it is not fully believed, and so the experience of the
incognito remains effective as well, but it is co-opted because it now
only functions to sustain the ideology. Ideology is utopia's vampire.
The operation of ideology distorts the incognito twice: first, ideology
neutralises it; second, ideology can do this because it still takes its
energy from the negative of the incognito. To our conscious lives, the
result is an attitude of congratulating ourselves with the fact that we
do not fully believe what we are told to believe or what we in fact – or

better, in our actions – manifest as subscribing to. The good sense of reserving judgement is mobilised for the totalising rule of ideology as the enjoyment we get from being allowed to transgress the ideological framework to which we yet subscribe. 'I know all is said to be, and made to be, exchange value, but I also know that that is not really true, so I can go ahead and, with approval of the economic system, enjoy this particular product as being there just for myself' – and in this way I reinforce and help the totalisation of the rule of exchange value. This is the perversion inherent in all ideological formations, all forms of 'law' (in the Lacanian sense of law that Žižek uses) or patriarchy. The law says 'you shall not', but looks away knowingly as you transgress it, as long as you do so in its name and this experience is the experience of enjoyment. The small favour ideology extends to its subjects and keeps them in its grip (hence Žižek can say that ideology today, in fact, orders us to 'enjoy!'; Žižek 2002).The outcome of this situation is that the critique of ideology can only be effective if it brings out the utopian core in the way the subject relates to ideology, and rescues that core from its perversion: false consciousness remains mostly unaffected, and is sometimes even strengthened, by its mere unmasking as such without something else, namely an experimental relation to its opposite, being put into action in the same gesture. At this point, we need to move beyond Žižek's perceptive analysis, and for that purpose we have to turn to Bloch. The critique of ideology requires a positive alternative, a creative and experimental relation to the incognito of existence. Bloch sometimes expresses this by saying that a utopia that remains abstract is itself ideological; a real utopia exists only as a concrete utopia.

In Žižek's thought, the incognito of existence is conceptualised as the Lacanian subject, which is always a lack. It cannot be encountered, formulated or be held in view unambiguously, but only as the incommensurability of different discourses and practices that all circle around it as a vanishing point – culture, politics, economics, psychoanalysis, ethics, love and so on. Žižek's name for this state of affairs is 'the parallax view', the skewed position that appears to be there when we view an object from different positions. There is a large overlap between the Lacanian lack and the Blochian incognito, for which much of this holds true, too. But there is also a difference. Žižek sees philosophy (as a cultural construct) as the mistaken attempt to reach closure with respect to this subjectivity, to encapsulate it in a systematic, ordered totality. This is for him, as we can understand, an ideological operation. It is the ideological operation par excellence, we might say. Theory, as opposed to philosophy, does not fall into this trap but, in accepting the parallax view, and hence the incompleteness of anything theory can do, is able to give space to subjectivity (Žižek 2006). However, as Fredric Jameson has noted, while there is in theory, as opposed to philosophy, 'no master code', 'the provisional terms in which it does its work inevitably over time [...] get reified [...] and eventually turn into systems in their own right [...], the anti-philosophy becomes a philosophy' (Jameson 2006).

So, precisely by treating incompleteness, the lack, as final, theory closes in on itself and achieves the opposite of what it sets out to do. It becomes ideology, following exactly the pattern of ideological colonisation that Žižek himself described so persuasively. It is only by keeping open the question of completeness that the practice of theory can avoid becoming ideological. But this means that there cannot be just a negative utopian element, the permanent non-place that theory circles; theory has to understand itself dialectically as standing in the movement towards something there is no guarantee of ever reaching. It can only remain true to itself if it gives up control in this ultimate dimension; stating the finality of incompleteness is, as it were, its last temptation. This is what Bloch means by the 'principle of hope' and the 'spirit of utopia', and what, later, inspired Adorno to write that the 'only philosophy which can be responsibly practised in face of despair is the attempt to contemplate all things as they would present themselves from the standpoint of redemption' (Adorno 2005: 247). Philosophy, understood in this way, is a struggle with the impossible in the name of possibility. It is the difficult position between having and not-having that is, in the last instance, the incognito itself, the 'darkness of the lived moment' (Bloch 2000). At this point, Bloch concludes that psychoanalysis is one-sided. There is not just the repressed unconscious (the 'night dream'), but also, on the other side of consciousness as it were, the not-yet-conscious, where we are in touch with the utopian in desires, wishes, inspiration and creativity (the 'day dream'; Bloch 1986: 86–88). For Bloch, philosophy as ideology critique deals with this not-yet-conscious dimension. A new language and a new conceptuality are necessary to express it.

Bloch analysed the rise of fascism as the double-bind of ideology in his *Heritage of our Times* (1935) and we can see how Hollywood cinema is open to a similar analysis. Bloch had, indeed, started this analysis himself in *The Principle of Hope* (1959). For Hollywood cinema the perversely enjoyed, distorted, utopian core can be summarised as 'happy end within a completely unchanged world' (Bloch 1986: 410).The medium of film created the technical possibility of an artistic expression of the immediacy of what Bloch called the 'darkness of the lived moment', our subjective existence in its moving, double, *claire-obscure* nature of partial illumination and partial incognito, as at once a spatio-temporal and a narrative reality: 'the technique of film shows actions through quite different bodies to those of painting, namely through moved, not stationary bodies; so that the borders between descriptive space-form, narrative time-form, disappear' (Bloch 1986: 411–12). Moreover, film affords possibilities neither theatre nor opera, the other movement- or time-based arts, provide, which in the time of 'cracking' capitalism bring close the ironical result of showing the possibility of another world through the cracks exposed by the technical affordances of the cinematographic medium:

> [N]o distance, no peep-show, rather the spectator walking alongside; chamber-music pantomime, not entirely lost even in the mass produced commodity, predominant in good films; opening up of the wide world, especially nearby, in the incidental, in pantomimic detail. In addition there is the maneuverability of detail, of groupings which have become fixed themselves, made possible by the techniques of film and so closely related to the waking dream. Now, given this so good, if also thwarted technical How, as far as the What of the film is concerned, namely the *subject-materials specific to it*, the period in which the development of film falls not only had a capitalistically devastating, but in a limited sense also – we may say: ironically usable effect. For as a period of bourgeois decay it is also a period of cracked surface, of the previous groupings and identities decaying; consequently it is, as in painting, so in film, the time of a not only subjectively, but objectively possible montage. Because this became objectively possible it is in no way necessarily arbitrary and completely unreal (with regard to the objective events); it is much rather in a position to correspond to changes in the external relation of appearance and essence itself. Here is the field of new hints and genuine authorities, the field of discovered-real separations between objects which previously appeared to be closely adjoining, of discovered-real attachment between apparently very remote ones in the bourgeois order of relations; good films correspondingly made constant use of such maneuverability which has become realistically possible even in terms of subject-materials. (Bloch 1986: 410–411)

Precisely because of its technical possibilities, even commercial film comes to tell the tale, *à contrecoeur*, on the fragmenting world in which we live, exposing the nakedness of even the happy end without changing the world. As an example of the spatiotemporal montage Bloch speaks about, we could think of the scene in *City Lights* in which the tramp, on the run from the police, jumps into the car of the millionaire on one side, to step out of it on the other. That montage of rich and poor, which would be unconvincing if staged in a theatre or opera because it requires a hint at a rupture of the unity of action, time and place, sets off the action in which the blind girl mistakes the tramp for a millionaire. The tramp's jump through the car is the leap of the imagination which founds the theme of the film. Then the dialectic of rich and poor can unfold, the open question of the possibility of a happy end in an unchanged world of tramps and millionaires can be prepared, and the moment of recognition, which remains also a moment of incognito, can occur.

Chaplin's tramp is a fairy-tale figure. Fairy-tales have a utopian form because they typically express wishes and dreams in a magical way and the narratives develop by actions of 'ordinary' people without power who, by cleverness, perseverance and a dose of luck succeed in dethroning power. Bloch contrasts the fairy-tale to the myth and the saga, which, in contrast, serve to preserve power relations and dominant ideologies:

> To speak in a modern way, most fairy-tales have something Chaplinesque about them. They are not 'mini-myths' as the reactionary interpretation would have it; nor are they crudely disenchanted myths. The fairy-tale is a genre that has tried to avoid falling into the feudalism of the saga and the despotism of the myth, and has managed to save the mythical element in a different form – a form which suits its own proper spirit. (Bloch 2009: 25; translation amended)

In a short essay from 1932, *Significant Change in Cinematic Fables* (Bloch 1998: 59–62), Bloch writes about the changes film makes to traditional narratives. He emphasises that motifs of failure, of passing-by, of missing each other are often foregrounded in movie adaptations of traditional tales and fairy-tales. He sees in this a feature of modernity. In this context he again mentions Chaplin, in a remark that addresses the incognito in film directly:

> [T]he gentle tale of missed opportunity, resurfacing on occasion in the work of Chaplin, [...] offers an insight into the nature of things. Into the nature of time, where the old vanishes away while the new

has not yet become clearly evident; and where that which is best is not a tale, but is likewise traveling, passing us by, unrecognised. (Bloch 1998: 62)

Art, for Bloch, expresses what is yet to come. It creates premonitions, pre-figurations, pre-appearances of what might be; art has a utopian core. This view of the function of the work of art has its roots in Schopenhauer's aesthetics and its distinction between will and representation, but Bloch turns Schopenhauer's philosophy inside-out. In art we come to know and come to be part of the creative process that is reality itself; Bloch sees the artist as the avant-gardist who lives at the front of realisation. Of all art forms, music is for Bloch the most utopian one. It comes closest to expressing the deepest strivings and hopes, the tendency that is latent in being, just as, for Schopenhauer, music was the art form which most directly makes the life-will itself accessible to experience. For Bloch, the reasons for the special place of music have to do, on the one hand, with the pre-semantic nature of music; on the other it is because of the fact that music is a temporalising, moving art form. This makes the relation between cinema and music particularly interesting. Indeed, some of Bloch's earliest writings (from 1913) on film deal with the question of music in film. In the silent movie, Bloch argues, the isolated visual image opens up a pantomimic space and the music, which runs like a tapestry underneath the moving image, has the task of compensating for all the other senses, establishing the connection between the image on the screen and lived reality. Music creates the whole sensorium within the art form, without which the moving image cannot become expressive. In the silent movie, *the material world becomes music*, and so we experience the utopian tone of reality itself in film. The fact that film puts all weight on the optical and renders the rest of the sensorium peripheral heightens this utopian potential even more, because the utopian, the absolute, is given to us only in the indirect experience, at the periphery of our field of experience and in the gaps in the field of experience, in the irreducible gap between foreground and background.

The material world becoming music – that had happened before, Bloch suggests, in the 'musical drama' of Wagner. In *Spirit of Utopia* (1918) Bloch had devoted a long section to a discussion of Wagner's musicological innovations, and had stated that Wagner breaks with the closed form of the symphony in retrieving the 'endless melody' of song. In a similar way, Bloch argues, film music uses essentially open, often improvised, compositional (melodic and rhythmic) patterns. Like the

Wagnerian motif, film music uses scores that can easily be recognised and that allow for easy variation. Thus a contrast emerges between the open, improvised form of music in film, and the closed form of music in symphony and opera before Wagner. It will be clear that this way of approaching the role of music, not just in film, but also in opera, sets us off on quite a different footing than the perspective Adorno elaborates from the viewpoint that the Wagnerian *Leitmotif* prefigures the jingle as commoditised form of identity or a manifestation of the repetitiveness of the death drive (Adorno 1952).Yet, one does not exclude the other – just as the technique of film can be corrupted, but even within its corruption give a voice to the 'not-yet'.

In his earliest texts on music in silent cinema (Bloch 1998: 156–162) it is precisely the fact that film is 'silent' that makes it a truly utopian art form. Not just subjective emotion, but the whole of reality becomes music and is expressed from its musical, read utopian, core as a longing and a hope for an identity between subject and object, the human and the world – a longing for the world at home. Music points in the direction of what is not yet in this ultimate sense. The particular mediality that results from the combination of music and the silent movie gives cinema, this type of cinema, an unchartered potential for expressing the immanent utopianism, the hope that is central to Bloch's understanding of Marxism. As an avant-garde medium, film becomes itself an instance of the front of realisation. Between the silent image and the sounding music a pre-appearance can open up, fleeting and ungraspable, of a utopian world. Not a utopian world with a specific form, not a programmatic utopia, but as the symbolic intention that captures an always identical if inexpressible expectation: this is what it would have to sound like and look like. I am not thinking here only of a lyrical moment in the silent movie, but about the gap that opens up between the possibilities intimated by music, even by a comical fanfare, certainly by a swing beat or blues, and the pantomimic act on the screen, whether it is comical or tragic, epical or lyrical. Utopian sensibility lives in the gaze askance or awry. The utopian is encountered in the gap between image and sound, or in the fragment, in the surplus, in that which escapes order.

In Marxist terms we could say that this gap is a factor of the 'use value' of art that is resistant to being reduced to exchange value. It is, as Bloch insists throughout his writing, encountered in a movement of transgression. In the silent movie, Chaplin's figure of the tramp, which stands for the one who is 'too much in any situation', the one who 'should not be there' (Žižek and Fiennes 2006) is such a transgressive, and hence *latently utopian* image. Chaplin uses this figure to mutely point to a goal that can only be raised into consciousness negatively, via the act of failure, slapstick, and its concomitant affect, laughter: something was attempted, against the odds, and it fails. In this way the missing something becomes conscious. Positively speaking, as Žižek formulates the position of the tramp, the subject desires recognition, but for the situation where recognition could occur, he is always too much, 'an obscene and excessive surplus' (Žižek and Fiennes 2006). In his analysis of the ending of Chaplin's *City Lights*, Žižek points out that the moment of recognition between the tramp and the girl, the moment the girl realises the person who helped her to cure her blindness, is the moment where false love, treating the loved person as having to conform to your own ideal, can turn into true love, which is a recognition of the real other: 'here I am as what I really am'. But the happy end is not guaranteed. The music, Žižek says, goes on while the screen fades to black, and the words 'The End' appear and disappear again, leaving only the imageless movement of the music behind. What has opened up is too strong for anything but music; the music (Žižek says 'singing', although the score is entirely instrumental) exceeds the frame.

This moment of recognition is a classical example of anagnorisis, the plot-turning moment in which the true nature of the situation is recognised – one of the most centrally utopian moments to which Bloch returns time and again. Oedipus, Joseph, Saul's experience on the road to Damascus – these are all examples where the truth comes to light and creates a transgression, as much as the awareness of a previous transgression: a retroactive light thrown upon a crime. In *City Lights* the psychological complexity of erotic desire, as Plato says the son of poverty and riches, is personified in the tramp who becomes a millionaire in the eyes of the blind girl. He suffers for it, and we are left to wonder what his own blindness was or if the girl will be blinded once again by the truth that she discovers at the end. Žižek reads the tramp's poverty as his nakedness, that for which he must be ashamed, once his love can see who he really is, while at the same time the only thing he wants is to be seen for who he is. We can contrast Žižek's psychoanalytical reading with a Blochian one, which is not so much in contradiction with it, but which emphasises another aspect, the one that is implied in the music which goes on and which puts the whole world in the light of the love between the two protagonists, without identifying what that love is, can or will be. It is as if the film follows the prohibition, or better the impossibility, of making an image of what happens when we 'behold face to face', when the darkness at the heart of subjectivity is illuminated by adequate objectivity. This limit-moment of recognition comes after the thunder of anagnorisis has died away. We can, as yet, only be taken there by a return to a form of darkness, to a mere, but nevertheless real, pre-appearance of identity. That is why the screen goes black and the music remains. The music pulls us along as it migrates into the other world – *'der schwingende Ton zieht fort'*. 'The vibration of sound fades away' is the translation used in the English edition of *Literary Essays* (Bloch 1998: 290). It fails to capture the deliberate ambiguity of *'fortzie- hen'*: to move away, to disappear, but also to migrate, to go elsewhere, or even, transitively, to pull something away or along. The vibrating tone also pulls us away, goads us on towards the new, to what was not yet.

But let us be clear: film persists predominantly as a site of reproduc- tion of ideology. Why? Is all that is left for film criticism ideology cri- tique? Is there anything more utopian to be discerned? Can we discern a utopian, subversive'not-yet' in film today by which this medium can escape its function of enacting the double colonisation of ideology? Can film music still be 'the swinging tone that pulls us away and along'? Is the temporal nature of the medium still able to embody the exodus of utopian, transgressive thinking, feeling and acting, or has the time of cinema become the time of the succession of now-moments, unrelated or only related in an a-historical messianic longing for redemption that is equally strong, or weak, at each moment? Film has to seek the limits of narrativity and, because of the fragmenting and re-combining nature of the medium, it has always done that. But how are exodus and narrativ- ity related? How can one become the salvaging of the other, giving hope back to film, and vice versa? Can that connection be a credible principle for a cinematographic aesthetic? Such are the challenges a Marxist film aesthetic faces today.

Kellner and Jameson both used Bloch's utopian analysis of ideology to show up the utopian elements in Hollywood cinema (e.g. in *Jaws* (1975), as it were, despite the ideology. With a more accurate under- standing of Bloch, we can now say that at the heart of the ideological formation lies a utopian motivation, which is expressed and distorted, often beyond recognition, by its ideological articulation. Moments where film is not (just) the articulation of ideology, but becomes aware of the utopian silent core in all expression as the source and goal of artistic expression, as well as of the necessity to use forms that are liable to ideological distortion to bring the utopian into the world, are not plentiful. But they are there and they resist all forms of sentimental reading. A Blochian-Marxist film criticism would look for the point at which all films are yet silent movies, manifestations of the not-yet con- scious and even the not-yet-real.

Wagnerian reprisals abound: the shark theme in *Jaws*, Darth Vader's motif, the unbearable tremolos and violins in blockbuster cinema (*Titanic* (1997), *Lord of the Rings* (2001–2003)). Iconic moments in which film music, also in spoken film, is utopian, not-yet, exodus can be seen in the opening sequence of *Once upon a Time in the West* (1968), where the music enters the action of the film and in the same vein the sounds of the image, the beating of the locomotive engine, the whistle and the rhythm of the train on the tracks, become musical. We can see utopia also in the theme, now comical, of *The Pink Panther* (1963), which crosses out the Wagnerian *Leitmotif* in the self-ironisation of the expectation-laden melody. The self-assured crescendo of the theme builds up an anticipation which is subverted, almost in slapstick fashion, by the sudden decrescendo. This is the comical element. But it opens up onto a surplus in the theme, the lightly syncopic, rhythmically fading coda of swing that, much in Bloch's sense, is the swinging tone that moves on and that pulls us along with it, into an open possibility, having overcome the earlier lapse. The panther, like the tramp, is a fairy-tale figure.

Far from being usurped by the logic of capital, the exodus motif still abounds in film. In its commoditised, less commoditised and authentic forms, film is the art form of exodus. At all levels of its materialisation it is a transformative and transforming medium: technology, reception, the way it has transformed the art world itself and other art forms such as painting, theatre and literature (the novel), the development of narrative, the change to the sensorium itself such that we now live in an image culture, but also one in which music, equally double-faced, is ubiquitous and endless. As Lars von Trier showed in *Melancholia*, frankly in a reactionary fashion (in other words from a depressive position), we will go down to the sound of Wagner's strings and their endless melody – a metonym of music's ubiquitous presence in contemporary culture. Here, the preciousness of life can only be experienced under the threat of its imminent and total negation. This is the situation Adorno called the administered world (*Die verwaltete Welt*, Adorno 1970), and it is what Žižek means by ideology (Žižek and Fiennes 2013).

The utopian, whether in music or in other aspects of film, remains, and this is the great advance brought by Bloch's philosophy, a matter of the askance and awry, of what does not fit and transgresses, what transports us. No direct, literal utopian aesthetic can be anything but inadequate. The fragmentation, isolation, micrological gaze that film has allowed with respect to our sensory consciousness has opened up the possibility of a creative culture after the death of God, after the deconstruction of the grand narrative – a process already in full swing when Bloch started to write about film. But – and this is important – the montage that becomes possible now and that shows the utopian as it lights up and dies away and yet retains its validity, like the music in the silent movie (and, the same thing, the dialectical image in Benjamin's work), is no less committed to an idea of the necessary, universal nature of that which cannot be expressed in any single way but always needs juxtaposition and movement from one to another to appear: the promise of fulfilment. Film still has the capacity to give a form to this promise of something transcending life, and is exposed to doing just that all the time, even if only in the commoditised expectations of the movie-going audience, as in Woody Allen's *The Purple Rose of Cairo* (1985) where these expectations unsettle the medium, and its place in transforming life, itself. In the montage of music's transformative efficacy and narratives of personal or collective liberation, the utopian, the no-place of longing can shine up dramatically as being all around us – ungraspable, uncolonisable, but there. We can see this for example in the montage of the Ulysses motif, the exodus motif of the escape from Egypt and the dialectical sound-image of the American folk and rock tradition in *O Brother Where Art Thou?* (2000), or in the hopeful and yet disillusioned exploration of the light that 'shines into the childhood of all and in which no one has yet been' (Bloch 1986: 1376) of Bergman's *Fanny and Alexander* (1982).These films are not only social or ideology critiques, they also activate a utopian image, a hope for a better world and the direction in which it may lie.

Bloch's no less existential than Marxist film aesthetic allows us to enrich the sometimes worn schematism of Marxist ideology critique, and its sighing under the image prohibition regarding the communist society which it inherited from its religious roots. It allows us to enrich utopian consciousness with the open creativity, the montage, the fractal and moving imagery of the cinematographic experience; it allows us to salvage the fairy-tale and make it meaningful for social and cultural transformation. Conversely, cinema can come to play a vital role in the renewal of Marxist thought itself, so that, as Bloch already wrote in the 1940s: 'Marxism therefore is not a non-utopia, but the genuine, concretely-mediated and processually open one'. We can say that cinema, correctly understood, by coordinating the utopian not-yet of imagination, the field of sensory perception and the ideational space, has the ability to open up radical futurity for us. But radical futurity is not the pure contingency of the absolute ability to be surprised – a notion that flips over into its opposite, the ever-sameness of mere nextness. No, the radical futurity that cinema can teach us to see and take hold of, is one in which we learn to understand our night-dreams, the realm of the unconscious, and learn to take hold of our day-dreams, the realm of the not-yet conscious. Film can be, as Bloch calls it, a medium for concrete utopia. Film is often a dream factory, the denial of the very thing that makes the dream what it is, but it can be a critique, in the Benjaminian sense of a reflective consideration of the truth content of a work of art, a schooling and a material realisation of our capacity to dream beyond our expectations, to actively hope for a different world. To reclaim the radical purport and potential of the (day-)dream work of film today is the task of a cinematographic aesthetics that takes its cues from Marxism. In ways that have not been made explicit up until now, Bloch's thought can provide a starting point for that work.

Note

1. In this chapter I will use the term ideology as referring to dominant forms of normative and naturalised false consciousness, not in the more descriptive sense of any belief system not based on the nature of the material means of production and shared by a group, which serves to create and reproduce social structure and cohesion (See Geuss 1981: 9–13).

Bibliography

Adorno, Theodor W. (1952). *Versuch über Wagner* (Frankfurt: Suhrkamp).
Adorno, Theodor W. (1970). *Negative Dialektik* (Frankfurt: Suhrkamp).
Adorno, Theodor W. (2001) [1998]. *Metaphysics. Concept and Problems* (Cambridge: Polity Press)
Adorno, Theodor W. (2005) [1951]. *Minima Moralia. Reflections on a Damaged Life* (London: Verso).
Bloch, Ernst (1986) [1959]. *The Principle of Hope*, 3 vols. (Cambridge, Mass.: MIT Press).
Bloch, Ernst (1998) [1965]. *Literary Essays* (Stanford: Stanford University Press).
Bloch, Ernst (2000) [1918]. *The Spirit of Utopia* (Stanford: Stanford University Press).
Bloch, Ernst (2009) [1935]. *The Heritage of our Times* (Cambridge: Polity Press)
Geuss, Raymond (1981). *The Idea of a Critical Theory: Habermas and the Frankfurt School* (Cambridge: Cambridge University Press).
Jameson, Fredric (2006). 'First Impressions' (Review of S. Žižek, *The Parallax View*), *London Review of Books*, 28 (17), pp. 7–8.
Jameson, Frederic (2007). *Archaeologies of the Future: The Desire Called Utopia and Other Science-Fictions* (London: Verso).

Kellner, Douglas (1997). 'Ernst Bloch, Utopia, and Ideology Critique', in J. Owen and T. Moyland (eds.), *Not Yet: Reconsidering Ernst Bloch* (London: Verso), pp. 80–95.

Žižek, Slavoj (2009) [1989]. *The Sublime Object of Ideology* (London: Verso).

Žižek, Slavoj (2006). *The Parallax View* (Cambridge, Mass.: MIT Press).

Žižek, Slavoj (2002). *For They Know Not What They Do: Enjoyment as a Political Factor* (London: Verso).

Žižek, Slavoj and Sophie Fiennes (2006). *The Pervert's Guide to Cinema* (ICA Projects).

Žižek, Slavoj and Sophie Fiennes (2013). *The Pervert's Guide to Ideology* (Film 4).

3
Bloch on Film as Utopia: Terence Davies' *Distant Voices, Still Lives*

Ian Fraser

Distant Voices, Still Lives focuses on a working-class family in Liverpool in the 1940s and 1950s and centres on a tyrannical father and how the mother and three children, Eileen, Maisie and Tony respond to his overbearing presence both when he is alive and when he is dead. The first half of the film, *Distant Voices*, moves back and forth in time as the characters remember incidents, or memories are portrayed of their family life, both happy and sad. The second half, *Still Lives*, focuses on the developing lives of the family without the father as they experience births and marriages. The story is told in such a way by Davies that it offers us a picture of a lost world of the working class that has now been aesthetically preserved forever.

I analyse this film by utilising the potent theories of the Marxist philosopher and cultural critic Ernst Bloch. For Bloch, film is part of his utopian project that attempts to make us yearn for a principle of hope through moments of the 'Not-Yet'. Bloch understands hope as both subjective and objective (Bloch 1995: 7; cf. Geoghegan 1996: 34). Subjective hope refers to the 'intention towards possibility that has still not become', which is a 'basic feature of human consciousness' (Bloch 1995: 7). Objective hope arises when subjective hope is 'concretely corrected and grasped' and both form the 'hope-contents of the world'. On this basis, Bloch's Marxism is typified by uniting the 'cold stream of analysis' with the 'warm stream' that fires the imagination and passion in the consciousness of millions of people (1369). It is therefore *'humanity actively comprehending itself'*, an 'addressed humanity, one which is directed towards those alone who need it' (Bloch 1995: 1357). Moreover, since it is a 'concrete humanity', it 'also contains an embittered streak' because it depends on which path it will take, 'anger' or 'exhortation', until it 'seeks, finds, and communicates objective salvation'. So even in misery there is a 'revolting element', which is an 'active force' against what is causing such misery in the first place. Once misery realises its causes, it 'becomes the revolutionary lever itself' (Bloch 1995: 1357–1358). Hence, 'Bloch's thought is rooted in a humanist anthropology which grounds his critique of oppression and emancipatory perspectives' (Kellner 2014). Consequently, Bloch begins with the real needs and desires of people in terms of their hopes and dreams; he analyses what stops them being realised and he identifies capitalism as the main culprit.

Film, as part of this Marxist project of emancipation, is the 'movement of wishful dream'. It uses what is real to show another reality, and so displays how another society or world is circulating, even if it is hindered, in the present one, offering a 'wishful action' or a 'wishful landscape'. Film in its positive usage is like a 'powerful mirror – and distortion' – in which there are images that are concentrated to display a wish for the fullness of life and as information rich in imagery. It is as though the film can climb into the stalls and make the audience part of the experience. Bloch states that this is why Lenin could declare film 'one of the most important forms of art' (Bloch 1995: 410). So in contrast to what he sees as the bad dream factory of Hollywood, Bloch argues for the '*good* dream factory' or a 'camera of dreams', which critically inspires and is based on having a humanistic plan (410). For Bloch, this is why Marxism is not simply 'contemplative but an instruction for action' and hence part of an emancipatory aesthetics in relation to film.

The key themes from Bloch's understanding of film that I want to focus on and relate to *Distant Voices, Still Lives* centre on his appreciation of film through pantomime and its component parts. These are the technical work of the camera, gesture and the 'micrological of the incidental' and film as a mirror image of painting. All of these aspects will be shown to support Bloch's desire for film to offer us the wish for the fullness of life, employing a humanistic plan that uses what is real to display a different reality and show how another society is circulating in the present one in moments of the 'Not-Yet'. As we shall see, hope is present in the film predominantly in its subjective mode as something which seems to be absent, but the possibility of it being concretely grasped emerges as we analyse some key scenes. There is certainly misery in the film but there is a revolting aspect to this misery in the complex relations of the family members in response to the dominance of the father, suggesting that a more emancipatory world may be possible.

We must also remember that the film is deeply autobiographical in its depiction of working-class life and operates very much on the micro level. The scenes from the Second World War have no particular political import and the post-war consensus is merely implicit in that there is full employment. Capitalism, as the world of work and the power relations it engenders, remains relatively hidden. Hence, the film is somewhat dislocated from capital. However, larger themes do emerge from these microcosmic examinations of the human condition that can show us that the emancipatory hope for a different society and a greater humanity in our relations with each other is possible.

Pantomime

Bloch praises the early silent films for the ways in which they could express what could not be said in words, and so carried on the greatness of the art of pantomime (Bloch 1995: 405). He considers Asta Nielsen (1881–1972) to be the first great film actress of the silent screen because she could, with the mere flicker of an eyelid or movement of her shoulder, express more than a myriad of average poets put together (405 and 407). Bloch contends that in the context of silent film, gesture was to become incredibly potent in the expression of feeling and meaning (406). In this regard, Bloch endorses the American film director D. W. Griffith's (1875–1948) technique of changing the viewpoints of the spectator, and for his use of close-ups, which revealed in the facial muscles of the actor moments of 'suffering, joy' and 'hope' (406–407).[1] Silent film therefore offers the 'movement of wishful dream' (407).

Bloch then considers sound film and although it appeared that its arrival would imply the end of pantomime, the latter in fact survives it where the dialogue in a film falls silent (408). The sound films he approvingly mentions here are René Clair's 'masterpiece' *Un Chapeau de Paille d'Italie* (*An Italian Straw Hat*, 1928) and George Cukor's *Gaslight* (1943). Mimic expression also continues in that sound film needs audible pantomime using noises, such as a pair of scissors cutting a canvas, or the drumming of raindrops on a window. All this produces what Bloch calls a 'micrological world of sensory perception and expression' where the sound film presents 'thing-like gestures'. Photography and microphone reveal the 'whole of real experience in a streamlike mime' and film is like a 'powerful mirror' in which there are images that are concentrated to display a wish for the fullness of life and as information rich in imagery (408).

Bloch also venerates the way silent film deals with the 'micrology of the incidental', which is not incidental at all, that is, it appears incidental but is actually showing something that is significant (Bloch 1995: 407). He offers as an example the Soviet director Sergei Eisenstein's work *The Battleship Potemkin* (1925) about the mutiny in Odessa during the failed 1905 Russian Revolution. Not only does Eisenstein depict such 'incidental' moments with people, as in the stamping boots sequence on the Odessa steps, but he also does it with things, as in the cooking pots swaying with the ship, all of which increases the suspense and tension for the audience. Similarly, in his film *October: Ten Days that Shook the World* (1927) Eisenstein uses the firstly gentle, then violent, shaking of the giant chandelier in the Winter Palace, as a symbol for the wavering of the defenders of the Tsar (407–408). What is interesting for Bloch's utopian Marxism here is that he includes seemingly apolitical films such as *Gaslight* along with more overtly political ones as is the case with Eisenstein's above. Bloch's Marxism is an expansive understanding of the many moments of the 'Not-Yet' in all its various forms that can impact on our consciousness to make us question the world and begin the process of emancipation in creating a better one. I now want to consider these aspects of pantomime in relation to *Distant Voices, Still Lives*.

One aspect of pantomime, for Bloch, is the technical use of camera, and Davies' use of tracking is of note here. He describes tracking as being 'incredibly powerful and intimate' because 'it draws you into the film emotionally' and changes the relationship 'between the space and you' (quoted in Farley 2006: 52). This is evident at the start of the film as the camera follows the mother into the hallway and shows her exit right to the kitchen after calling her children to come down for breakfast. The camera stays fixed on the stairs as we hear but do not see the children descend, their shoes clipping the wood and then their greetings as they enter the kitchen and see their mother. The camera then continues its slow movement and makes a 180 degree turn to face the door which it has just entered. In a Blochian sense, the film has climbed into the stalls and pulled us into the house as though we will be part of this family for the next 85 minutes, creating an intense intimacy and intensifying the film's affective power. Moreover, by not showing the children yet we are being confronted with what we now assume is a present and a past, what was and what might be, and thereby an aesthetic representation of the 'Not-Yet' through memory and dreaming, which the audience will be part of. Such long tracking shots and the 180 degree cutting permeate the film, drawing the audience in and, as Bloch says, climbing into the stalls and making us part of the experience. Davies uses this technique to move forward towards the subject to frame it aesthetically and so preserve instances of working-class life that we can compare and contrast with our own class identities in contemporary capitalism today.

In the front parlour of the house in the middle of the wall is a photograph of the father standing next to his horse framed on a mirror (Figure 3.1).

The positing of this photograph seems incidental on first watching the film but with repeated viewing it looms as a symbolic presence of the father, both in his life and in his death. However, it seems to me that the other members of the family are all reacting to him in different ways, so in the Blochian sense the photograph is incidental but really substantial as a representation of his dominance over their lives. This seems to undermine Paul Farley's contention that as the film does not have a central character there is a 'hole' in the film because although the father is a 'brutal patriarch', he 'doesn't hold' it (Farley 2006: 34). Instead, Farley argues that it is as though the 'whole film shows a family as if caught in a whirlpool'. In contrast, I will show that the whirlpool they are caught in emanates from the centrality of the father's influence.

Wendy Everett, in her study of the film, proposes that the photograph of the father 'is not a consolation but a menace' (Everett 2004: 74), but

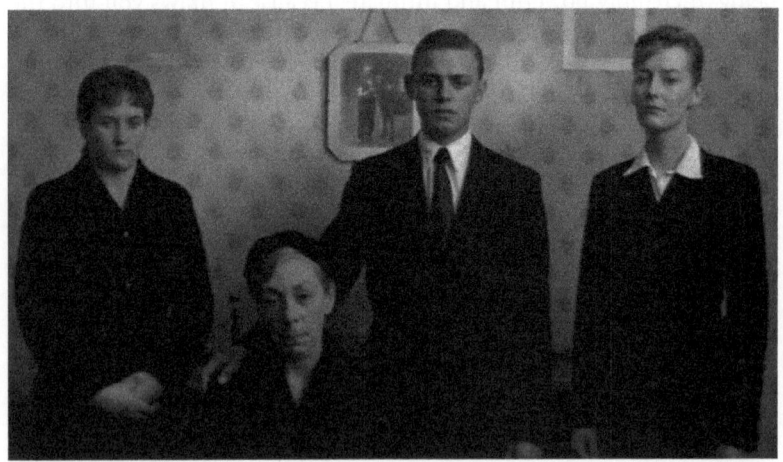

Figure 3.1   The photograph of the father symbolically dominating the family
Source: Screen capture from *Distant Voices, Still Lives* (1988), dir. Terence Davies, BFI/Channel Four Films

I contend that she misunderstands its role in relation to the moments of hope and aspects of the 'Not-Yet' that occur in the film. There are a number of juxtapositions that display the sweet and tender moments of the father's character against the more dominant narrative of his brutality. So this should alert us to the aspects of objective hope that are present in the film, even in its darkest portrayals of the misery of family life, and in the memories that are evoked in the mother and children about the father where subjective hope predominates. As such, an emancipatory ethics is possible here because the dialectical contradictions of our interpersonal relations point to the patriarchal power of the father that is symbolic of the patriarchal power of capitalism that has to be overcome for Bloch's utopian Marxism to succeed. I now want to explore this by examining some illustrative scenes.

Tracking is also related to memory because as we read from left to right 'a camera track left to right indicates forward movement', whereas a 'track in the opposite direction suggests a journey back in time' (quoted in Farley 2006: 52). There is a right to left track that introduces a previous Christmas, which begins by panning along a row of houses showing their front parlours with various decorations. Eventually the camera stops on the father, who is carefully decorating a small Christmas tree that is on the sideboard. The mother brings the three young children to say goodnight to him before they go to bed and he reciprocates by gently uttering, 'Goodnight kids'. The father is certainly not the ogre that he is meant to be here and the incident gains added poignancy when in the next scene he goes into their bedroom and places their Christmas stockings on the end of the bed. The three children are sleeping peacefully and a close-up of the father shows that he is deeply moved and almost in tears as he whispers 'God bless' before he leaves the room.

In his commentary on the film, Davies explains how people have suggested that this scene makes the father more human and that they feel a certain amount of sympathy for him. Davies' response is dismissive because he contends that like all tyrants, the father shows sentimentality rather than real emotion. Moreover, if he wanted to show emotion, he should have done so while they were awake and not when they were asleep. Davies is also amazed how people reinterpret this scene as being sympathetic to the father when it was not his original intention. Yet, perhaps as a patriarch it is difficult for the father to express his more caring emotions, and whether it was Davies' intention or not the artwork does have an autonomous life of its own in which resides its power. Moreover, Davies is ignoring the reasons why Tony and Eileen have a more ambiguous and nuanced relationship with the father, which the film exposes so beautifully. Instead, Davies is aligning himself with the more one-dimensional viewpoint of Maisie, although this is understandable considering how she seemed to suffer more at her father's hands as we shall see shortly. So there is a moment of objective hope emerging here from within the misery that the father causes within the family, and the 'revolting element' takes two forms: outright rejection or a compromise of sorts in the hope that relations can improve. The father, lest we forget, is also a victim of capitalism and we can surmise from his age that he lived through the harshness and brutality of the Depression. This, again, is not to excuse his actions, but we can at least understand them and hopefully try to change them to create a more emancipated world.

Nevertheless, the following scene has him again at his worst as, with the three children in terrified attendance, he drags a tablecloth laden with Christmas food off the table in a furious rage and shouts, 'Nellie, clean it up!' This is followed by him banishing Tony from the house, who when he knocks at the door and asks why he cannot come in, is told there is no place for him there and that he should 'frigg off'. The camera pans up to the front bedroom window to show that the mother has witnessed the awful scene and is in tears but totally helpless because of the prevailing power of her husband. Such juxtapositions, displaying sweet and tender moments of the father's character against the more dominant narrative of his brutality, should alert us to the aspects of objective hope that are present in the film. This is based on a subjective hope that is being denied, even in its darkest portrayals of family life, and in the memories that are evoked in the mother and children about the father.

The micrological of the incidental is present in the use of shadow, as in the scene when the mother is falling asleep in an armchair by the fire and lighting shows her illuminated in a radiant glow but behind her is a dark shadow to suggest the lingering and ghostly presence of her husband. Similarly, a shot of the light penetrating an open window, with the wind gently caressing the net curtain, has a voice-over by the mother, who expresses delight at the light nights only for one of the daughters to say that the nights are drawing in now. Thunder is then heard along with the voice of the father aggressively shouting their names. Nonetheless, another memorable shot is more positive and indicative of objective hope as it depicts the mother sitting in a white, hazy frame with the photograph of the father to the right showing him in a more positive light – perhaps a reflection of why she married him in the first place.

Similarly, the implicit continuity with one shot leading to another is used imaginatively even when it appears to be in juxtaposition. For example, there is the eerie scene when the children are with the grandmother in the dark, illuminated only by candles as they are looking into a mirror. She tells them that if you look in the mirror after midnight then you will see the devil. The next shot is of the father singing 'When Irish Eyes Are Smiling' as he brushes the horse in a moment of care and affection while also doing a professional job. The implication from the previous scene is that he is the devil and it also links back to the photograph on the parlour wall as a symbol of his patriarchy, but the contradictory nature of his character is to challenge this by showing him doing such a caring act. Moreover, unbeknown to him, the children have sneaked up into the loft to observe him from above and are no doubt also surprised to see their normally tyrannical father in this benign light. One possibility is that he cares more about the horse than his family, but we see enough instances of his kind moments to problematise that.

At the end of the film the mother is the one who has the last song after her son's wedding and she sings 'Thanks For Everything' while Tony stands outside the house crying his heart out. There has been disagreement among commentators on why he does so (see Everett 2004: 77–78) but I want to suggest that this links back to the micrological incidental moment of the dominance of the photograph that framed the beginning of his wedding day because Tony is thinking about his father. Indeed, the trumpet song that is played while he is sobbing is Eddie Calvert's 'Oh Mein Papa'. The lyrics, unsung here, are instructive on further understanding Tony's relationship with his father because they say how wonderful he is and how much he is missed today, which strengthens my interpretation. In his commentary, Davies says there is an 'unintended irony there' but, unintended or not, it captures perfectly Tony's real love for his father despite the way he and the family suffered at his hands. Tony's subjective hope that his father could be different manifests itself objectively in his own consciousness and the possibility that such a moment of emancipation will translate positively if and when he becomes a father.

To support this further, I want to refer to two pivotal scenes that the micrologically incidental moment of the photograph forces Tony to remember and that also contain Bloch's emphasis on gesture. In an early scene, Tony goes to the hospital to see his dying father who can barely speak. The scene prior to this has Tony at home with his mother, who thanks him for coming to see his ill father; but Tony tells her that he got compassionate leave from the army, which implies that he would not be there otherwise. He then looks at her, sees how upset she is and lowers his head almost shamefully for making such an admission. This gesture is then repeated when the film cuts to the hospital and shows the father lying in bed and having difficulty breathing. The camera portrays Tony staring down at his father, now in a state of power over him at last. To his surprise, the father then says, 'I was wrong, lad'. There is a slight tension because Tony pauses, apparently in a state of shock at the confession and he is trying to keep his emotions in check, and then he gulps before softly and soothingly replying: 'OK, Dad. OK'. The shot lingers on Tony as he bows his head in a similar manner to the previous scene with his mother and is close to tears. The gesture of the bowing head is important here and shows a more complex attitude to the father from Tony than one of just 'menace' as Everett suggests. It is also the moment of reconciliation between Tony and his father and a further instance of the 'Not-Yet' that Tony can relate to his own children should he have any. In his commentary on the film, Davies says this admission was a bit late in the day, given all the damage the father inflicted. Tony, though, is more magnanimous than Davies.

A reciprocal scene that contains this gesture occurs with his mother when she is cleaning the hall floor. She shouts to Tony to tell him that his tea is in the oven. The camera frames him looking down at her as he had been looking down on his father in the hospital bed. He asks her if she is coming to have her tea as well and she says she will do but in a minute, that is, once she has finished her cleaning. The camera stays on him and he is almost in tears as he recognises the courageous and caring nature of this woman on her hands and knees before him and utters, 'OK, Mam', completing the symmetry of this gesture with his response to his less than courageous father but whose apology he accepted. Tony's figure then dissolves as the screen turns white and in the next scene he is in the pub alongside his fiancée, singing 'I Want A Girl, Just Like The Girl That Married Dear Old Dad', which reinforces the appreciation and love he has for his mother but also his father.

Further support for this interpretation of the father occurs in a scene before Tony goes off in the car to get married. Eileen walks towards him in the parlour and the two of them are framed looking at each other in a single shot. However, in the centre of the frame is the micrological incidental photograph of their father with the horse. He holds centre stage even in death, and part of their faces are reflected in the area of mirror outside the photograph suggesting, as if it could be denied, that part of their identity is shared with him and the powerful influence he has had on their lives, for good or bad. They both move out of shot to go into the hall but the camera stays still with the father's photograph now dominating the frame for about a further eight seconds before cutting back to the stairs to show a coat hanging on the newel-post – again, perhaps symbolic of the father, who is not there in body but certainly in spirit.

So the micrologically incidental presence of the photograph and the gesture of understanding and forgiveness encapsulated in the bowing of Tony's head and the phrases 'OK, Dad' and 'OK, Mam' reinforce a more enlightened appreciation of the role of the father within the family. This is a moment of objective hope even in the most painful moments that we can experience within a family as an institution. It also shows us that things do not need to be this way and that we can make informed choices and actions as we constitute our own identities. Bloch's utopian Marxism encourages us to do this with its focus on the everyday and the seemingly incidental for moments of the 'Not-Yet' on the path to a more emancipatory world.

Eileen also has a contradictory attitude towards her father as he produces both positive and negative emotions in her. After the initial scene where we have been shown the father's coffin in the hearse, the next scene is her wedding day. They are all framed in the shot with the father's photograph behind them but central. Then the camera zooms in slowly for a close-up of Tony and Eileen with the photograph still prominent behind but between them. Eileen is contemplative and then says suddenly, 'I wish my dad was here'. It is at this point that the differing responses to the father come to the fore because the camera pans right on to Maisie who, with a slight grimace, says to herself, 'I don't. He was a bastard and I bleedin' hated him!' The subsequent scene of her cleaning the cellar floor to get money from him for the dance shows why, as he beats her repeatedly with a broom even as she screams out in pain. Maisie sees no redemptive qualities in her father and this is expressed in the shot after the hearse has pulled up outside the front door. Maisie is the furthest away from the photograph. The mother, Tony and Eileen are in far greater proximity, indicating their own closeness to their father. When they are viewing their father's body, the photograph is positioned close to Maisie's head but she suddenly moves forward and puts a comforting arm around her mother. Tony and Eileen are now on the outskirts of the shot, suggesting that they are the ones who have lost something and Maisie is claiming her mum for herself.

The next scene has Eileen say again that she wishes her dad was here as she looks at Tony, who then has his more contradictory memories of his relationship with him as we have seen above. Davies then cleverly juxtaposes the next scene where the family go to the hospital to see the father, who is lying in bed and barely able to breathe. There is then a voice-over of Micky saying to Eileen, 'He was alright your dad'. Eileen responds by telling Micky that she was the only one that could get round him and we then see her charm the father to get money so she and Eileen can go to the dance. The more human side of the father as an expression of objective hope is presented here as he smiles at the way he is being coaxed and utters affectionately that they are 'bleedin dance mad'. His darker side expressing the subjective absence of hope is never far away though, and as they return from the dance and are having a last cigarette outside before going to bed, the father warns Eileen to hurry up and come in. He agrees to her having a few more minutes but within a few seconds he screams, 'Eileen, what bleedin' time do you call this!' and has her scurrying inside as quickly as she can to appease him. Yet the counterpoint to this is a few scenes later on her wedding night, when we see Eileen outside the pub, sobbing hysterically as she is comforted by Tony. She cries out twice 'I want my dad!', so there is a real longing that she has for him even after he is dead.

A few scenes later, bad memories are evoked for Eileen. During the war, the children have been pulling a cart laden with wood and the air raid siren goes off. They have become separated from their parents and at Eileen's initiative they hide under the cart and eventually take the chance to run to the shelter. As she goes towards her father he slaps her across the face and angrily asks her where she has been. She stands there, her face covered in soot, and seemingly in a state of shock, staring at the camera as her father puts his arms around her. The noise of the bombs landing can be heard and the father looks frightened and asks Eileen to sing, which she does while looking vacant and lost straight at the camera. The scene perfectly captures the contradictory nature of the father changing from aggression to touching concern within an instant, and the almost helpless look from Eileen as she stares into the camera seems to be saying to us, 'Look at how difficult this man is to deal with'. Hostility one minute and concern the next.

In another scene, Eileen is waiting for her date and there is a knock at the door. She expects it to be him and is smiling as she opens the door but her smile disappears and the camera cuts to show her dishevelled father crumpled and sweating, standing outside almost on the point of passing out. He tells her he has signed himself out of hospital and that he has walked home. Exhausted, he then slumps sideways onto the door frame. The following scene shows his dead body, which is then followed by Eileen tenderly asking him to say goodbye to her as she is going away to work. The photograph is posited above and to the left of her head in the corner of the shot as though she is between the dead and the living father, which in memory she will of course always be. She remonstrates with him saying she is only going for the season but he sits there staring into space uttering nothing. There is then a close-up of Eileen as she stares down at him and says, 'Do you know what? If I ever get a gun, I'll blow your bleedin' brains out'. She is angry but her face reveals that she is also upset, which is confirmed a few scenes later when she is on the train.

Jingles tells her to have a cigarette, which she smokes, and despite Micky's attempts at song to cheer her up, her hands shake and she begins to cry as she stares out of the window and into space just like her father had. The screeching sound of the train wheels also captures the inner emotional turmoil of Eileen. We then see shots of her working frantically as a waitress in a seaside hotel in Pwllheli; the mother's voice-over tells her to come home as her father is seriously ill, so she cuts short her work and he gets his own way as she returns to the house. So why does the father not want Eileen to go? In his commentary on the film, Davies explains that it is because the father was very possessive, a trait present in all tyrants who want to keep their subjects close at hand. However, it might also be that the father does have real affection for her. It is worth mentioning here the power of the actor, Pete Postlethwaite, to suggest some ambiguity and how this relates to Bloch's appreciation of the pantomimic actions of actors. The father says nothing but he sighs deeply and turns his head to one side to look away from her. Why the sigh? A sigh can be an expression of many things and a sense of loss can certainly be one of them. Again this is not to deny the overriding negative understanding of his character but to appreciate that we are complex beings that can be open to acts of kindness as well as evil and which Postlethwaite's acting exposes so potently in its subtlety.

On a more macro level, the father's dialectical movement between despotic and more enlightened rule seems to mirror the harshness of pre-Second-World-War capitalism and its more caring face after 1945 with the post-war consensus. Both, of course, are still forms of capitalist control that have emerged out of class struggle, just as the father's domination has taken these two forms in relation to his children. Bloch's Marxism as a critique of both forms of oppression means that his utopian solution is to transcend them on the emancipatory path to affirm objective hope in a better world.

Yet Eileen also has to face an admittedly milder but still powerful form of patriarchy and possessiveness with her own husband, Dave, who also seems to replicate these forms of capitalist rule. She often expresses her own unhappiness by perceiving what she interprets as the unhappiness of others but which is a reflection of her own sense of misery in her marriage. This is highlighted in a scene after her wedding where she is sitting back to camera with the fire glowing before her framed in the right side of the shot. What should be a comforting feeling of warmth from the fire is instead its opposite as a fire that can burn, and Dave's voice, off camera, shouts, 'You're married now. I'm your husband. Your duty's to me, frigg everyone else. Monica, Jingles, that's all ancient history now'. Eileen begins to shake and sob inconsolably as the fire burns away in front of her; but because of the way the shot is composed, it is as if the fire is very close to her face, indicating that she may be about to be consumed by it as a symbol of Dave's patriarchal control.

On the way back from the pub, Dave urinates outside the house before entering and begins singing while the grandmother is also shouting at Eileen to get in, as her father had done when she was younger when having a final cigarette with Micky outside. Eileen says after he has finished urinating, 'I'm sure I was put on this earth to be tormented'. Similarly, when Eileen and Dave are eating their tea while listening to the radio, Eileen is annoyed and disgusted with the noise Dave makes while he eats, which he is oblivious to when she points it out to him. The confining nature of her life is expressed by her exasperated plea as she asks if this is what she has got to endure for the next 25 years.

Eileen also reveals her unhappiness by her interactions with her friends. She is often asking them if something is wrong in their relationship or expressing her own anger and frustrations vicariously. At one point she asks Micky if her husband Red ever hits her and Micky laughs such a suggestion off. Yet it is even more risible because the love that Micky and Red display is clear for everyone to see. They do so by mocking and making fun of each other but this is a couple that are so affirmed in their love that they can afford to do that. Indeed, the way that they show their love is by denying it through humour. For Eileen, Dave is anything but funny, and that something darker is taking place within their relationship is intimated further when Micky says she will pop round to visit Eileen as they do not see enough of each other. Eileen recoils and tells her that Dave would not like that. Micky senses something is wrong but knows not to interfere and makes her excuses and leaves. Of course, one other reason why they have not seen enough of each other is that, as we know, Dave has already said her friends are 'ancient history' and her loyalty must be to him first. This tension is further exposed in the scene when Jingles and her aggressive husband Les come to the pub after the christening of Maisie's baby.

Jingles is first seen outside the pub with her husband belligerently telling her that they are not staying long. He is an obvious brute and Jingles is evidently scared of him. She joins Eileen and Micky and sings along with one of their songs until she cannot bear the pressure any longer and begins to cry. Her husband is in the doorway shouting at her and Eileen is becoming increasingly furious and suggests she might go up and tell him how badly he is behaving. Jingles can see the danger and what would await her if Eileen did so and quickly decides to obey him and leaves. Eileen cannot help commenting on what has happened and attempts to show a sisterly solidarity with Jingles' plight but Dave intervenes and tells her it is none of her business. At first it seems that Eileen is again showing her unhappiness vicariously through Jingles but she is also defiant in relation to Dave here. She points out that Jingles is her friend, calls Dave a 'callous bleeder' and says that like all men they only think of themselves. Dave starts to get angry and tells Eileen not to tell him what he should think and adds that no one knows what is going on in his mind. Eileen wittily, but still angrily, retorts, 'Including you'. Dave tries to justify himself by stating that women are different from men and that it is impossible to have an argument with Eileen because she 'flies off the handle at the least thing'. Eileen will not relent and denies this, saying that given what has happened to Jingles she has 'good cause to'. They are near to having a full argument and the tension between them is palpable when the mother intercedes, tells them not to fall out with each other and asks Micky to sing to divert matters. After this, there is then a close-up of Eileen as she sings a song on her own called 'I Want To Be Around', which is about having your heart broken and is clearly linked to her increasing dissatisfaction with her husband. She is close to tears when she finishes and the poignancy of shattered dreams and lost hope is clearly evident as an example of subjective hope. Nevertheless, that she is attempting to stand up to Dave and assert the rights of women against male dominance and aggression suggests a moment of the 'Not-Yet' and an objective hope that perhaps is a portent of the liberation that awaits such women with the second wave of feminism that was to develop from the 1960s.

Again, Davies approaches these issues very much on the micro level, but if we follow Bloch's Marxism through, we must venture beyond to the macro level and how the patriarchy present is symbolic of the nature of the power relations in capitalism. The repetition of the patriarchy from the father and then on to Dave in Eileen's life almost reflects the structural constraints of capital on subjects seeking their emancipation. Yet for Bloch, it is 'precisely in the Nothing of this point zero' that 'Marx teaches us to find our All' and 'struggle against the dehumanisation which culminates in capitalism until it is completely cancelled out' (Bloch 1995: 1358). In this way, Marxism's 'goal-content is, can be, will be nothing but the promotion of humanity'.

These pantomimic moments at the micrological level have put us in touch with major themes that give instances of a 'Not-Yet' when patriarchy and capitalist domination can be overcome and women and men can treat each other fairly and equally and so achieve objective hope. The affective power of the film in showing how patriarchy operates can fulfil Bloch's Marxist edict to fire the imagination and consciousness of millions of people, an addressed humanity that comprehends itself to overcome such oppression and achieve the 'hope-contents of the world'.

Painting

Bloch also compares film's images to being like a painting (411–412). He admits that the 'art of film-illusion' is not painting or poetry, even in its most potent forms, but maintains that it 'still gives an *image* which allows *movement*, and a *narration*' that can demand the 'descriptive *standstill* of a close-up' (411). Bloch argues that cinema cannot become a 'mixed creation' in the way that 'Lessing's "Laocoon" defined narrative painting, descriptive poetry' (411). Bloch is referring to Lessing's 1776 work on philosophical aesthetics (Lessing 2005) that took its title from the famous marble statue depicting the Trojan priest Laocoon (Osborne 1993: 641). Both he and his two sons are being squeezed to death by snakes as punishment for alerting the Trojans not to trust the wooden horse being offered by the Greeks. For Bloch, Lessing denoted that painting illustrates 'only actions through bodies' whereas poetry represents 'only bodies through actions'. Film 'shows actions [...] through moved, not stationary bodies; so that the borders between descriptive space-form, narrative time-form disappear, according to Bloch (Bloch 1995: 411–412). Bloch suggests that because film can represent every object it 'has at least become as broad as a painting, and the image is always the primary thing even in the sound-film' (412). Film is a 'soi-disant painting' that has 'become a succession of actions, a soi-disant poetry itself a juxtaposition of bodies: and the Laocoon of the film, in contrast to that of the statue, screams'. What Bloch is alluding to here, although he does not explain so himself, is Lessing's thesis that the statue does not depict Laocoon in a fully realistic light. He is meant to be suffering extreme pain but this is not completely expressed as it would negate the beauty of the artwork. For Bloch, Laocoon has a 'rigid grimace' whereas in a film, even in the standstill of a close-up, this grimace would be only transient rather than rigid, so 'every background turns towards the foreground here, and the wishful action or wishful landscape so essential to the film climbs, although only photographed, into the stalls'.

Interestingly, Bloch also has a discussion of painting as a 'wishful landscape' of utopian moments (Bloch 1995: 794–820). In a short section entitled *Still life composed of human beings*, he focuses on the Dutch artists Johannes Vermeer (1632–1675), Gabriel Metsu (1629–1667) and Pieter de Hooch (1629–1683) (796–797), generally referred to as the Delft school of painters. He notes how in their paintings of interiors 'everything becomes a parlour here, even in the street, a stove is always burning, even outside in the spring' (796). For Bloch, all three painters 'portrayed such cosy living, a home sweet home still without any mustiness' as 'sunbeams pour through the small silent scene' and the interior is 'structured by light falling in at various angles'. As Bloch explains further, 'nothing but domestic everyday life is painted in the Dutch genre picture, but for all its nearness it is also presented in just the same way as a sailor may see it from a distance when he thinks of home: as the small, sharp painting which bears homesickness within it'. Bloch explains how within these paintings there are maps of the world hanging on the walls to indicate a larger theme of what surrounds this 'domestic comfort' and how the 'rooms and windows looking out on to the street are painted as if there were no disruption in the world' and where 'nothing is in a hurry' (797).

Paul Farley relates how Davies has repeatedly referred to Vermeer as an 'inspiration and exemplar' in his work (Farley 2006: 58). Farley identifies the framing of the mother when she is cleaning the windows and the hall as examples of this, and there are a number of other incidences that also fall into Bloch's appreciation of the Dutch painters of this period in general.

Bloch mentions the use of the stove that is always burning and within the *Distant Voices* part of the film this is evident with the open fire. It is used on a number of occasions to portray the cosiness of living at home, through the numerous shots of the mother sitting beside it to the final camera track into it as we move from *Distant Voices* into *Still Lives*. Yet, as a depiction of the reality of a complex ordinary life the fire also has negative connotations, as when Eileen is berated by Dave as we saw earlier. Tony also throws the last few pennies he has into the fire rather than give them to his father, who then belligerently pokes them further into the flames to melt. Even these negative scenes are framed like paintings, and so they should be, as even the horrors and miseries of life deserve to be depicted aesthetically as a pictorial rendition of the reality of our complex existence and are the 'screams' that the Laocoon of the film allows.

The use of light by these painters, 'sunbeams' pouring through 'the small scene' is another feature that Bloch draws attention to, and in the scenes with the mother the analogies are lucid. Additionally, these painters captured servants in their everyday activities and similarities persist as the mother and children in a patriarchal household also acted as servants. Maisie in particular is singled out for domestic chores, as in the scene in the cellar and when she is shovelling coal. She stands under the coalhole with the shaft of light illuminating her in the darkness as she looks upwards and declares that she will kill her father if anything happens to her mother. The servant theme is also continued when Eileen and her friends go to Pwllheli to work as waitresses in a hotel; a shot frames the three of them side by side in their black and white uniforms nervously anticipating the work they will do (Figure 3.2).

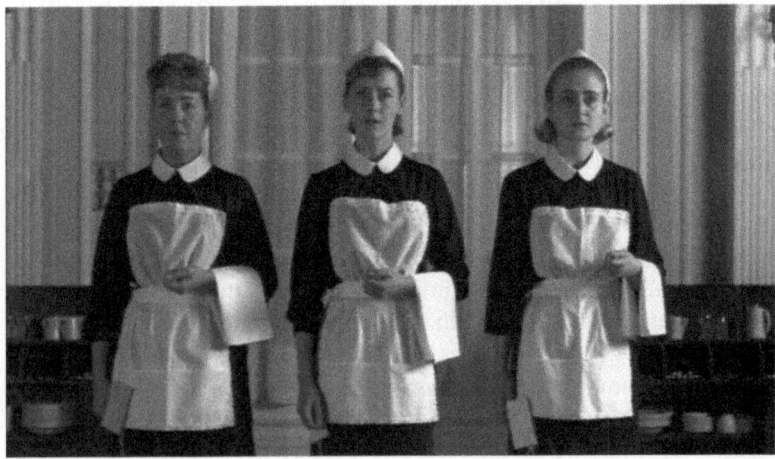

Figure 3.2   Ready for work?
Source: Screen capture from *Distant Voices, Still Lives* (1988), dir. Terence Davies, BFI/Channel Four Films

Similarly, the real world of work enters in the scene where George and Tony fall from the scaffolding and crash into the glass windows beneath them. These are the few scenes that present the world of work but they do indicate certain aspects of labour within capitalism at that time. Work in the house is assumed to be done by women rather than men. The work in the hotel is indicative of the impending increase in the tertiary sector of the economy as the century progresses. The accident at work evokes dangerous conditions within which such labour is performed. That Davies can depict such scenes so aesthetically illustrates how the Laocoon of the film can act as a painting and so preserve moments of the labours of everyday life just as the Dutch painters accomplished.

The framing of women throughout the film also draws strong links with the Delft Dutch style with the compositional shots of Eileen and Micky as they stand outside the open front door having one last cigarette before bed. Or there is the shot of them and Jingles at the kitchen table composed around a bottle of perfume that an admirer has bought for Eileen. Kitchen utensils sit on the mantelpiece behind them and stockings hang from a rail above their heads to relay the 'domestic everyday life of the scene' but indicate a larger world outside as the perfume is Chanel No. 5. The three of them are wide-eyed, staring in awe at the bottle, which we can see is symbolic of the development of consumer capitalism, the increase in living standards for the working class that will occur in the decade ahead and their subsequent absorption into the capitalist system. Yet from a Blochian perspective, there is also a longing for the 'Not-Yet' in such moments in terms of 'wishful images in the mirror' where we want ourselves to look and feel nice and where there is evidence of our genuine needs and desires (Bloch 1995: 340). The problem is when such wishing occurs within an ideological world and so becomes passive and unthreatening, with the end placed on increasing social mobility rather than enacting social revolution. The key, then, is to turn subjective hope into objective hope and make these moments of the 'Not-Yet', these wishful images, into a reality and live a more authentic existence within, but eventually beyond, the confines of capitalism.

There is also a scene after Eileen, Tony and Maisie have been standing outside after Eileen's wedding. The shot dissolves and they have now gone, but the camera stays on the door and now also includes part of the front parlour window in the frame. A shaft of light emanates from the parlour onto the inside of the hall, so structuring the interior at various angles, and outlines of the wedding guests and family are barely visible through the vibrant whiteness of the light reflected on the net curtains. We are outside looking in, but the power of the picture presented using light gives its nearness and also its distance, just as Bloch specifies it does for a sailor who sees the image from far away. The shot is so extraordinary in its ordinariness and this is enhanced further as another dissolve now shows us that the door is shut and the lights are off. It is as though the inner lives are hermetically sealed in their everyday domesticity until the camera pans up to the top window and a dissolve takes us through it bathed in the morning light.

These aesthetic portraits of everyday life fulfil Bloch's Marxist desire for film to be like painting and so create an affective power in the consciousness of the audience. What we see here are encapsulations of working-class life at a particular period in history that future generations can look back at and imaginatively share in. These are pictorial moments of subjective and objective hope that show how working-class life was and how it might be in a different world once emancipation from capitalism has been achieved.

Conclusion

Bloch's utopian Marxism that begins with the needs and desires of people translates into a movement from subjective to objective hope through moments of the 'Not-Yet' and offers an emancipatory political project to defeat oppression and ultimately transcend capitalism. Film is one important part of such an aim and it is through his focus on pantomime with the technical work of the camera, gesture and the 'micrological of the incidental' and film as a mirror image of painting that he illustrates this. Bloch's is an expansive Marxism that marauds across cultural forms in the search for instances of the 'Not-Yet' wherever they may be. As applied to *Distant Voices, Still Lives*, across the above themes, the film shows us on a micro level the interpersonal relations of working-class life in a particular historical period in all its misery but also in moments of hope. Although largely dislocated from capital, Bloch's Marxism allows us to draw the wider implications of the patriarchal power relations that operate in the film, particularly with the father, and the attempts by people to develop a 'revolting element' against these relations in various ways. We, as viewers, have through the sheer aesthetic power of the film, been pulled out of the stalls and entered its world with the Blochian hope being that we too can create a better society and so act as a *'humanity actively comprehending itself'*.

Note

I would like to thank Lars Kristensen, Ewa Mazierska and Lawrence Wilde for their helpful comments and suggestions. The usual disclaimers apply. A version of this paper was presented at Utopian Studies Society 13th International Conference, New Lanark, 1–4 July, 2013 so thanks to all the participants there, especially Richard Howells and Dan Smith.

1. Griffith's major film was *Birth of a Nation* (1914) which, controversially, was about the American Civil War and the rise of the Klu Klux Klan based on Thomas Dixon's novel and play, *The Clansman*. The film was interpreted as being sympathetic to the Klan. Bloch doesn't mention the film or its subject matter, but does explicitly attack the Klan for being fascists (347–349).

Bibliography

Bloch, Ernst (1995), *The Principle of Hope*, 3 Volumes (Cambridge, Mass: MIT Press)

Davies, Terence (1992), *A Modest Pageant* (London: Faber and Faber).

Everett, Wendy (2004), *Terence Davies* (Manchester and New York: Manchester University Press).

Farley, Paul (2006), *Distant Voices, Still Lives* (London: British Film Institute).

Geoghegan, Vincent (1996), *Ernst Bloch* (London: Routledge).

Kellner, Douglas, (2014), 'Ernst Bloch, Utopia and Ideology Critique'. Available at http://pages.gseis.ucla.edu/faculty/kellner/Illumina%20Folder/kell1.htm (accessed 16 January, 2014).

Lessing, Gotthold Ephraim (2005), *Laocoon: An Essay upon the Limits of Painting and Poetry* (New York: Dover).

Osborne, Harold (1993) (ed.), *The Oxford Companion to Art* (Oxford: Clarendon).

4

'But Joe, it's "Hour of Ecstasy"': A Materialist Re-evaluation of Fritz Lang's *You and Me*

Iris Luppa

You and Me (1938) was Fritz Lang's third film made in Hollywood, after *Fury* (1936) and *You Only Live Once* (1937), which are generally categorised as a trilogy of 'social problem/consciousness' films because of their shared interest in the relationship between criminality and the Law and – significantly – the focus in each film on individuals caught up in the wheels of the American judicial system. Tom Gunning attributes the discernible political commentary in these early Hollywood films to Lang's own status as 'refuge' (albeit a welcome and cosseted one upon his arrival in the United States in June 1934) and Lang's 'revulsion at the Nazi takeover' (Gunning 2000: 213). Although there is certainly no doubt about Lang's resolute anti-Nazi stance,[1] Lang's broader political views are harder to define, despite his friendship with intellectuals on the Far Left, such as Theodor Adorno, and his great admiration for Brecht; yet any partisan political readings of his films remain by definition partial, as they ignore the often kaleidoscopic treatment of various – often opposed – political viewpoints and ideologies in his films.[2]

Robin Wood expresses an uneasiness about *You and Me* precisely because of its explicit use of Brechtian elements 'in the service of a safely capitalist moral', leading Wood to speculate – with mild vexation – as to whether there is a 'level of irony' he as a critic could have missed, making *You and Me* a film accessible only to 'the most intellectually sophisticated of viewers' (Wood 2000: 4). In another publication on Lang in the same year Tom Gunning also grapples with the issue of the film's 'explicit', yet 'muddled' politics: 'As a *Lehrstuck* [sic], *You and Me* states a more explicit political message than any other Lang film, and this stated message, 'Crime does not pay', stays mainly within the vaguely reformist conventional politics of most Hollywood message films' (Gunning 2000: 263).[3]

Both Wood and Gunning's remarks imply that the analysis of the film's politics is a deeply unsatisfactory task as the film's ultimately reactionary politics are embedded in an experimental modernist tradition championed by political artists such as Brecht. Robin Wood comments:

> The aims – the *essence* of Brecht – should be familiar enough [...] [t] heir basic premise is the hatred of capitalism and the denunciation of the manifold miseries it has produced: its emphasis on competition (rather than cooperation); its elevation of wealth as the dominant human need, the resulting implicit endorsement and encouragement of greed and possessiveness as the essence of human desire; the setting not merely of class against class but of individual against individual, resulting in the massive exaggeration of the drive to dominate, hence in the destruction of positive human relations. (Wood 2000: 5)

Arguably, *You and Me* does engage with some of these issues, in particular the consequences for individuals such as Helen Roberts (Sylvia Sidney) and Joe Dennis (George Raft), who have fallen foul of the Law surrounding the ownership of capital in one way or another (we learn that Joe was involved in a criminal racket but Helen's past misdemeanours are not elaborated on). As will be shown in the following analysis the film goes to great length to illustrate the extent to which Helen's parole rules restrict her personal freedom in a country that prides itself on its claims to liberty, an irony the exile Lang draws attention to several times in the film, through characters referring to the 'Statue of Liberty' at moments of entrapment.[4]

The question arises as to what could be gained from attempting a Marxist reading of a film that in terms of its politics presents the viewer with more questions than answers. However, I hope to be able to demonstrate that the film's concerns with issues surrounding not only life on parole, but the wider, equally palpable social and economic constraints of the urban salaried/white collar workers of 1930s America offer themselves to a reading that focuses on the characters' socio-economic circumstances. (These white collar workers share with their comrades of the traditional industrial working class the same subjugation under a political and economic system which, in the name of democracy, binds them into a social contract that is not designed to meet their needs, or work in their interest, but to maximise profit.) By the same token, the critical revaluation in recent years of several of Lang's other films made in Hollywood that *equally* present, on the surface, social messages that are at best ambiguous will be crucial to my analysis of key moments in the film in order to demonstrate the need for close textual analysis to gain greater understanding of their fundamental concerns.

American Lang scholarship over the last 30 years, with its intense scrutiny of films such as *You Only Live Once* (1936) – which precedes *You and Me* as well as starring Sylvia Sidney – and *Beyond a Reasonable Doubt* (1956) has revealed that the perceived *ambiguity* of these films' social message *regarding* crime and punishment, innocence and guilt, the judiciary process and the Law, is closely bound up with wider questions surrounding film narration's ability to conceal, as much as reveal, narrative information.[5] This epistemological conceptual approach centring on the film's cognitive and ideological positioning of the spectator will help to bring clarity of understanding to the meaning of several of the film's more opaque scenes.

Modernist experimentation – 'You cannot get something for nothing'

The film's opening sequence is divided into two distinct parts: first, an opening song immediately following on from the opening credits; and second, an arguably more conventional introduction to the film's fictional reality, depicting a woman attempting to steal a satin blouse in the department store where Helen, the ex-convict now on parole, works as a shop-floor assistant. Naturally, it is the film's opening song which, being stylistically most conscious of modernist trends, has attracted the greatest critical attention by scholars attempting to read it as a kind of particularly Brechtian experimentation with song form. This is hardly surprising considering that Lang, in his role as producer as well as director, had hired Kurt Weill to write the music. (Their collaboration was nonetheless fraught with problems and Weill left the production before it was finished.)

A montage of stylised images of unrelated objects and things that 'money can buy' is accompanied by the song 'You Cannot Get Something for Nothing', with music written by Kurt Weill. Its harsh tone and disharmonious melody, which includes the use of '*Sprechstimme*' – the use of stylised speech in the song, abruptly breaking the flow of the melody – is typical of Weill's compositions of his late 1920s musical collaborations with Brecht in Weimar Germany, and both Gunning and Wood cite Brecht and Weill's *The Threepenny Opera* (1928) as a direct influence on the film. However, surprisingly, neither Wood, nor Gunning, mention Brecht and Weill's opera *The Rise and Fall of the City of Mahagonny* (1931), which is considerably more closely linked to the content and fundamental concerns of *You and Me*, the irony being perhaps that *The Threepenny Opera* – undoubtedly Brecht's most popular play – has become a kind of shorthand to acknowledge the presence of a 'Brechtian' aesthetics in a given film. The following analysis of the scene will focus on the similarities in political commentary between the opening sequence of the film and selected moments from Brecht and Weill's *The Rise and Fall of the City of Mahagonny* in order to offer a tentative interpretation to the logic of the song's consistently noted and critiqued confused and confusing political message.

In order to understand how vexing it can be to make sense of 'You Cannot Get Something for Nothing', one needs to look closely at the strategies put in place to convey the film's political message during the first few minutes of narration. Above all, *every* aspect of the film's opening montage sequence is intended to withhold from the viewer a more conventional access to the film's fictional reality – an establishing shot and opening scene to familiarise us with its setting, characters and action to get the plot underway. Although we do get a brief glimpse of the setting, the Morris department store, inside which much of the action will take place, the remainder of a long series of shots accompanying the song is made up of entirely self-contained images, depicting commodities in such a way that they seem simultaneously on display for the audience to admire and desire and yet strangely unobtainable, as they are put on screen and whisked away from our gaze in an increasingly rapid succession.

Each shot is carefully composed, whereby even a pile of bricks is purposefully arranged and each object on display is harshly lit and tightly framed, not with any naturalistic background but on a blank canvas, or, in the case of shots depicting things that 'money cannot buy' in strangely stylised settings, so that 'knowledge' is depicted as anonymous figures browsing a table laden with books, and with an owl perched on a post – as a symbol of wisdom – also in the frame.

These abstract compositions clearly signal that at this point the film is resisting the more conventional option of depicting these goods within a narrative context, such as a naturalistic depiction of the department store, with the commodities on show in display cases, or inside the store's shop windows. Although it may be taking the interpretation too far by suggesting a 'Brechtian' distanciation through a separation of the elements that make up the world of the film, one can certainly argue that the aesthetic style of the shots illustrating the opening song is decidedly non-naturalistic, echoing instead the sober and detached still-life character of paintings in the modernist style of *Neue Sachlichkeit* (New Objectivity), foregrounding each thing's shiny surface materiality. Above all, within a few seconds of the beginning, the film undeniably signals its interest in stylistic experimentation, rather than the construction of a 'tangible' fictional reality. Significantly, our perception of these images is tied to the lyrics of the song, which consistently refer to their *exchange* value – 'remember they can only belong to you/if you can *pay* for them'. The song evokes Marx's concept of the commodity as having two factors: use-value and [exchange] value. Marx notices, however, that for a capitalist (and capitalism at large), only exchange value matters. During the process of exchange, the exchange value becomes abstracted from the commodity – the thing becomes reduced to money paid for it (Marx 1976: 125–244). Equally, taken out of a narrative context, such as the department store, or Helen and Joe's apartment, these goods presented in *You and Me* become abstracted from any natural environment and are placed in *one* relationship only – namely that of the cash register, which gives them their entirely abstract value measured in bank notes and coins.

The first line of the song 'You Cannot Get Something for Nothing' is spoken in a declamatory manner over a black screen by a disembodied voice, addressing the audience directly, thus calling to mind not only the opening of *M* (1931), with its address to the audience over a black screen to 'wait, just wait a little while, (soon the man in black will come)', but also replicating the effect of the direct address to the auditorium in *The Threepenny Opera*, 'Tonight, you are going to see an opera for beggars', Brecht's emphatic signalling of his radical break with the Aristotelian model of a theatre of identification. The impact of the direct address in *You and Me* also momentarily prevents the audience from settling into the movie in more habitual ways.

The voice continues in a rhythmic recitation '[...] and only a chump would try it/Whatever you see that you really want you may have/Provided you *buy* it', which exactly mirrors Marx's discussion of commodities. On the word 'buy' there's a cut to a static shot (in the abstract and harshly lit style remarked on above) of a cash register, its heavy bulk filling the screen entirely (Figure 4.1).

In subsequent depictions, the cash register continues to dominate the frame (suggesting that under capitalism exchange value takes over use value), its black shiny buttons denominating various amounts of cash value in US dollars and cents. In a subsequent shot a disembodied female hand is seen pressing the buttons, thus finalising an unseen transaction of money in exchange for goods. In another, a close-up of a

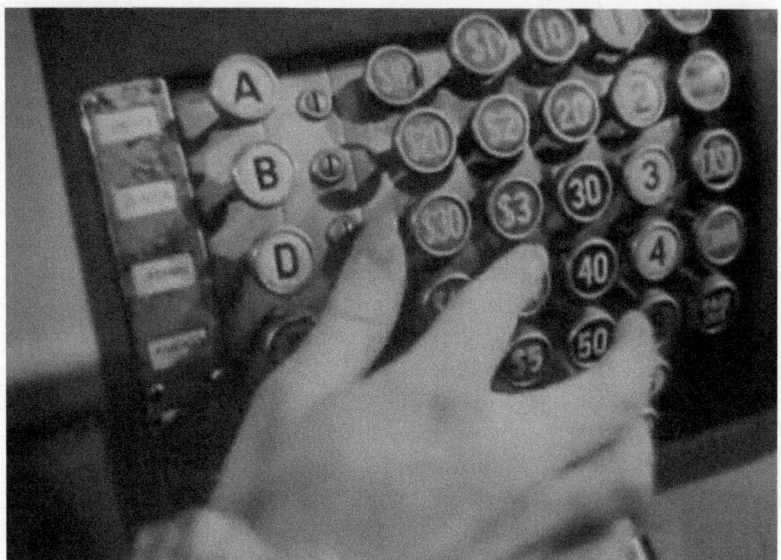

Figure 4.1   'You Cannot Get Something For Nothing' – cash register in the opening song
Source: Screen capture from *You and Me* (1938), dir. Fritz Lang, Paramount Pictures

finger pressing a 'cash' button opens the till to reveal the money inside. Each shot of the cash register is followed by a dissolve to a commodity, varying from luxury goods such as furs and jewels to essentials such as fruit, vegetables and meat, unremittingly establishing the abstract yet brutally inescapable exchange of cash for goods. Every single item shown in the montage of shots is enticingly placed on offer and yet can only be enjoyed or owned if money changes hands via the immovable, almost oppressive presence of the cash register. In this respect, the opening provides a damning Marxist critique of the relationship between shop windows that may be full and needs that can only be met if money changes hands.

The singing voice challenges the listener to name 'a few things' that 'money cannot buy', but then coolly asserts that *everything* has its price, from beauty 'to attract the man you love (you have to buy)', to education, leisure and health. These words bring to mind the passage from *The Communist Manifesto*, which defines the bourgeoisie as a class which 'has pitilessly torn asunder the motley feudal ties that bound man to his "natural superiors", and has left remaining no other nexus between man and man than naked self-interest, than callous "cash payment".

It has drowned the most heavenly ecstasies of religious fervour, of chivalrous enthusiasm, of philistine sentimentalism, in the icy water of egotistical calculation. It has resolved personal worth into exchange value, and in place of numberless indefeasible chartered freedom – Free Trade' (Marx and Engels 2008: 37).

With the seemingly endless stream of all the things one could need, or might desire, whereby even 'sunny skies and mother nature's wealth you have to buy', the rhythm of the *Sprechstimme* becomes more frantic, as is the pace of editing, ending in a quick succession of objects ranging from 'perfume and pistols/piccolos and dynamos' to 'silver chests and movie sets/aeroplanes and streamline trains/[...] Let's see the colour of your dough!'. The resolute tone of the *Sprechstimme* does not, however, dictate that we should not treat the lyrics *uncritically* – instead it invites us to contemplate the merits of a (capitalist) ideology which worships money as the highest value whilst simultaneously making sure that there's never enough of it going round, thus placing anyone depending on *paid* work for their survival in a permanently precarious position. By punctuating the flow of images depicting both materialist objects of desire *and* 'greater goods' such as health and happiness with the over-determined presence of the cash register, as well as the singing voice's repeated reminder that none of these things on display 'can belong to you/until you pay for them' the opening song is indeed, as Tom Gunning observes, a 'quite remarkable [...] demystifying of the cash nexus and exchange value in a Hollywood comedy' (Gunning 2000: 274). I would like to go further and suggest that in the emphatic fore-grounding of the starring role – in the opening sequence – of money as the *barrier* which separates a person's needs and the goods that would *meet* those needs, the film's opening number addresses rarely debated issues surrounding the function of money in capitalism as well as the bourgeois individual's relationship to money and wealth.

Thus the cash register is a constant reminder that even the satisfaction of a person's most basic needs, 'the food we live on/you have to buy', is subject to our *ability to pay* for this satisfaction. As mentioned above, the scene immediately following the song depicts Helen Roberts catching a female shopper (Margaret Randall) stealing a satin blouse, before deciding not to turn her over to the authorities, underscoring – now in a more conventional action-based narrative and tangible fictional reality – the point made in the opening song: namely, that anything one wishes to enjoy or own has to be paid for with money – because it is already owned by someone else. 'Morals' and laws demand that we can only take what we can turn into our own property, and the woman's desperate plea to Helen not to report the theft serves as a concrete example of the sanctions that await anyone breaking the social contract stipulating the exchange of money for goods into which they are inescapably bound in capitalism.

Money itself, in the form of neatly stacked notes and coins, is on display in the montage sequence as the melody reaches a climactic crescendo and the singer demands 'Let's see the colour of your dough'; the *accumulation* of money is clearly identified as the means which grants the individual a slice of private power over the wealth society produces, an astute observation which closely aligns the film with Marx's own explanation of how capitalism works (Marx 1976).The remainder of the film illustrates how the majority of characters in the world of the film, the salaried workers at Morris's department store, surrounded by a wealth of desirable goods, from satin blouses to the perfume Helen so desires, have to pay for the odd occasion of splashing out with impending abstinence and moderation. When later on in the film Joe asks Helen to choose a honeymoon from a stack of travel brochures the day after their impromptu wedding, she rightly asks: 'Where are you going to get the money for a honeymoon?' on account that it is a person's wealth that stipulates their degree of freedom in an economic system that guarantees ownership of capital.

Seen in this light, little separates the world of Morris's department store from Mahagonny, Brecht's imaginary American city where money not only becomes the measure for everything but, above all, turns needs, desire and social relations into commodities that deny their owner genuine satisfaction. Most disturbingly, as the city goes up in flames due to the self-destructive excesses of a society governed by the principle that everything that pleases is allowed (as long as one can pay for it), the survivors walk around the ruins of Mahagonny in a noisy procession paradoxically demanding the continuation of this 'golden age' of exploitation. The line which closes the play in a direct address, 'Nothing will save us or you or anyone now', proves to be a final provocation to the audience already faced with a scenario of utter chaos and devastation. Brecht's break with any form of culinary theatre experience herewith became final and was replaced with a new aesthetics – one that aimed to have a political impact.

The opera's devastating finale led to some confusion in the audience as to *how* to respond to this apparent perspective of hopelessness. Brecht's dialectical approach of presenting the audience, at the end of *The Rise and Fall of the City of Mahagonny*, with a situation of having to find themselves either uncritically accepting, or vehemently opposing what is shown on stage, formed part of his wider interest in developing methods of staging his plays that aimed to raise political consciousness, leading to the theatrical practice and, by the early 1930s, fully formed theoretical concept of the epic theatre.

It may at first seem like a long stretch to compare the provocative ending of *The Rise and Fall of the City of Mahagonny* with the equally fatalistic and revisionist lyrics 'You cannot rearrange the plan/made by man/since the world began/You cannot get something for nothing/And only a chump would think he can' on which the opening song and montage sequence end. From a political perspective, the meaning conveyed by these lines – the collapsing into one and the same of, on the one hand, the historical exchange of goods of different origin (presumably what is meant by the 'plan made by man since the world began') and, on the other, the private power the accumulation of money guarantees its owner over the wealth society produces in a capitalist society – is of course disappointing. However, to therefore interpret the song as a whole as reactionary means to disregard the impact of its striking imagery, particularly the overpowering dominance of the cash register in the flow of images that signify that in an economic system rooted in the private ownership of the means of production, virtually every aspect of life is ultimately reduced purely to its exchange value. Although stylistically the film never returns to the degree of experimentation it displays in the opening sequence, it nonetheless puts into play an invitation to the audience to engage with what is shown on screen in a complex manner, registering the discrepancy between what is heard and what can be seen and subsequently be required to decide whether the image should function at a lower level than the spoken word. The degree of directing the audience to first cognitively, then politically, take sides at the beginning of *You and Me* is of course a lot less developed than at the end of *Mahagonny*, or any other of Brecht's plays at the time; nonetheless, it is a narrational strategy that – subsequent analysis will reveal – is consistently applied throughout the film to open up the possibility of complex perspectives on the action, not least to create – in the juxtaposition of dialogue and *mise-en-scène* – a novel space for political commentary.

The commodification of love and 'liberty' on parole – 'But Joe, it's "Hour of Ecstasy"'

After our introduction to Helen we now observe several of the other shop assistants at work in various sections of the store and witness a conversation between Mr Morris (Harry Carey), the department store owner and his wife (Cecile Cunningham), who laments his 'hobby' of employing ex-convicts as sales people. Referring to Patsy Mason's (George E. Stone) skilful usage of a can opener in the store's hardware section, she observes, 'The man practically admitted he was a safe robber', to which Morris retorts, 'Well, who but the next safe cracker could handle one of those new-fangled kitchen gadgets?'. The humorous tone and play on *double entendre* continues in a scene introducing Joe selling a tennis racket by claiming that he *would* know a good racket 'because there isn't a racket that I haven't tried'. The flirtatious conversation between Joe and his female customer makes it plain that the young woman is interested more in Joe than the racket, and a deft inquiry into his sexual prowess ('you look like you'd be pretty good') is thinly veiled ostensibly in their small talk about tennis. Not diminishing the emancipatory outlook of this scene, which enables increasingly independent women to enjoy casual sexual relations in the anonymity of the modern city, the emphasis is nonetheless on the increasing commodification of *all* areas of life, where even romance becomes an act of consumption based on performance ('How are you?' – 'Well, I've never had any complaints') and supply and demand ('Who have you played with?' – 'Ooh, a lot of good players').

Significantly, during Joe's conversation with the female shopper he passes Helen on the shop escalator and a close-up depicts their hands touching briefly as they move in opposite directions. Although the dialogue at this point deals with the topic of the ready and plentiful availability of casual sex in the city ('a lot of good players'), the imagery emphasises the very opposite: the constraint demonstrated by Joe and Helen as they both enjoy the briefest moment of touch illustrates the opposite of the casual consumption and gratification of love and romance that dominates the conversation. Once again, the film invites the audience to scrutinise the image in juxtaposition with the spoken word and – as the *double entendre* of introducing each sales person by their criminal proficiency illustrates – the (in this case) rather comical ambiguity of what is said and what it means. It is therefore with increased awareness of the film's tacit insistence that we pay attention to every aspect of the performance and every detail of the *mise-en-scène* that we move into a moment in the film that proves to be highly significant in the development of Joe and Helen's personal relationship with each other. I want to argue that the construction of point of view in these subsequent scenes, although they *appear* to be the most conventionally realised moments stylistically – instantly recognisable as rooted in romantic comedy territory – also enables the film to provide its most scathing critique of the hypocrisy of liberty in American society.

After Joe and Helen's tender moment on the escalator we learn that Joe has quit his job and is preparing to leave the city. The paradox of his obvious fondness for Helen and yet his decision to depart is explained as we witness the couple's final meeting on the pavement outside the Morris department store as passers-by make their hurried way home after work. As an ex-convict, though now no longer subject to parole conditions, Joe feels unable to ask Helen to marry him and there is no sign that Helen will put the question to him, presumably in accordance with the more traditional – albeit at this point already outdated – social code that puts the onus of popping the question on the male.

Although clearly pleased to see Joe, we witness Helen nervously rubbing her handbag, and after initial hellos – as if uncomfortable with the sudden intimacy of the meeting – she quickly draws his attention to a display of perfume bottles in the shop window behind them, thus averting his gaze from her and fixing it onto the display. It seems that even in the anonymity of an urban evening rush hour Helen is very conscious of her closeness to Joe, unable to enjoy the freedom of the city's distractions in public spaces after working hours. At this point in the narrative we may interpret her nervousness and the slightly hysterical edge to her behaviour – her facial expression alternating between unease and enjoyment throughout the scene – as lover's nerves, conscious that the next few hours will be Joe's final opportunity to ask her to marry him before he leaves for California for good. The following dialogue between the couple ensues:

HELEN   I've been looking at that [*a selection of perfume bottles fashion-ably arranged in the shop window*] again. See, just imagine, some girls go in there and buy it and think nothing of it.
JOE   Just a smell, isn't it?
HELEN   But, Joe, it's 'Hour of Ecstasy'!
JOE   Is it?
HELEN   Joe! You just don't understand I guess. There isn't anything in the world that can build a girl up like perfume. Does something to her soul, kind of. See?

We first see Helen from Joe's optical point of view as he approaches her on the pavement (Figure 4.2). Helen casts a small figure in front of the tall window, which frames and places her in front of a curtain that forms part of the display inside. A large heart-shaped placard with the caption 'Hour of Ecstasy' can be seen hanging overhead slightly to the left of Helen, and an arrangement of draped veils completes the elegant display. However, the display seems fairly stark, as only a small selection of perfume bottles is on display in the big space behind the glass in order to allude to the object's status as an exclusive luxury item.

As Joe enters the frame, the camera dollies forward and reframes to depict the couple in a medium shot with the heart-shaped placard now to their left and the curtain behind them, making the background look more like a faux romantic stage setting than the pavement of an urban boulevard. Reverse field editing reveals Joe's blank expression at the allure the perfume holds for Helen, but the visual strategy of the reverse field edit also spatially separates the couple. They are reframed once more in a two-shot as Helen finishes describing the perfume's effect of 'building up a girl'.

There is a wonderful complexity to this scene which appeals to our understanding and interpretation of the action on various levels. It would be hard not to notice the irony the inscription 'Hour of Ecstasy' holds on a purely narrative level as social conventions and moral codes inhibit the couple at this stage from taking their relationship further to a level of romantic union (and possibly an 'Hour of Ecstasy').

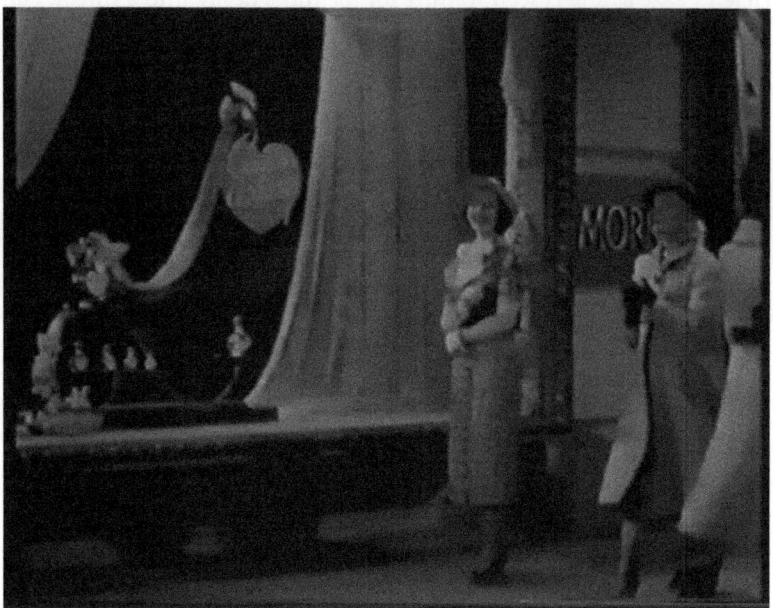

Figure 4.2   Helen waiting for Joe outside Morris's Department Store
Source: Screen capture from *You and Me* (1938), dir. Fritz Lang, Paramount Pictures

Although we may suspect that there is something secretive about Helen in the way she behaves, we have no knowledge at this point that Helen is of course also an ex-convict. A visual clue hinting that she shares with Joe more than the same work place is the identical style of hat both Helen and Joe and Mickey (a gangster who we see in conversation with Joe earlier on in the film) wear. Helen's reference to other women who – unlike her – can simply purchase a bottle of 'Hour of Ecstasy' if they can afford the expense reflects more than Helen's own lower income status: she can't 'afford' an 'Hour of Ecstasy' with Joe as it would mean breaking her parole rules, which forbid her to form relationships or get married at the threat of being returned to jail. Her comment that Joe 'doesn't understand' refers to both his limited knowledge on perfume and his complete lack of understanding of her dilemma.

But there is an even greater cynicism discernible in the scene. Like Paul Ackermann, the protagonist in Brecht's *The Rise and Fall of the City of Mahagonny* condemned to death because he committed the biggest crime possible in the city, namely, not being *able to pay* for whiskey he has bought, both Helen and Joe have in the past taken things they couldn't afford. The alluring display of 'Hour of Ecstasy' which entices Helen's gaze as she is seen waiting for Joe turns desire into a threat. Full shop windows and goods on shelves, which were regarded – especially in Europe during the 1920s and 1930s – as evidence of the high standard of living and degree of personal freedom (to consume) under American capitalism (Hermand 1994: 63) in this scene signal the very opposite, namely the cynical demonstration that for a low-salaried worker like Helen, many of the goods she herself sells would most certainly also be out of her reach financially.

Finally, the scene once more draws attention to the already noticed increased commodification of all areas of social life. Helen's attempt at explaining the allure of owning a bottle of 'Hour of Ecstasy' (because 'there isn't anything in the world that can build a girl up like perfume') shows that she uncritically believes that owning the perfume will give her some gratification she is not at liberty to enjoy in her daily life. Even the couple's subsequent visit to a dance hall – attracted by a sign of alternately flashing neon lights mimicking the twirling movement of a dancing couple advertising the venue – is not represented as a unique experience but as a highly standardised form of mass entertainment, as we observe Helen and Joe among dozens of couples sweeping the dance floor and a big band belting out a popular tune. A dissolve from Helen and Joe entering 'Danceland' to the dancing neon couple of the entrance sign underscores this point. However, even their brief stay at the dance hall is breaking Helen's parole rules and we witness her anxiety throughout the scene.

The sequence draws to a close with Joe boarding the coach and Helen blurting out her wish to be married to Joe. Joe hops off and a whirlwind wedding at a 24-hour registry called 'The Lightning Marriage Bureau' ensues, its offer of 'reasonable rates' again pointing to the fact that a consumer mentality suffuses all areas of social life, including getting married. A short period of marital bliss and harmony ensues, but is ultimately frustrated by Helen's untenable position of hiding her secret past from Joe as well as her newfound marital status to her parole officer. Helen's increasingly agitated behaviour raises Joe's suspicion, the couple argue and Joe, at a reunion with former gang members at Thanksgiving, is told by Mickey (Barton MacLane) of Helen's own criminal record. Deeply hurt by what he regards as her betrayal, Joe is persuaded alongside ex-con Morris employees Patsy, Cuffy (Roscoe Karns) and Gimpy (Warren Hymer) to join Mickey in a raid on Morris's department store. My analysis of the depiction of the (failed) break-in and Helen's lesson to Joe and the gang that 'crime doesn't pay' once more returns to the film's use of Brechtian methods, although I will argue that, again, the film's stylistic experimentation with Brecht's *Lehrstück* model falls short of reflecting Brechtian political thought.

'Crime doesn't pay' – Brechtian *Lehrstück* Hollywood style

The gang's break in at Morris's department store via – ironically – the employee's entrance is accompanied by dramatic music and the use of *chiaroscuro* lighting, with a single torch beam dancing across the floor as the gang silently make their way up the stairs of the otherwise dark building. On entering the toy shop section, the opening chords of 'You Cannot Get Something for Nothing' can be heard on the soundtrack, now distorted in a minor key; and as the tune plays 'and only a chump would try', the lights go on and the gang – caught red-handed – comes face to face with Mr Morris and Helen standing in the now brightly lit space. The store's security guards disarm the criminals but, significantly, Morris promises not to turn the men over to the police if they listen to a lecture delivered by Helen and return back to work the following day in return. Morris's justification, 'You gonna work for your living the same as I do', is another example of the chasm between what is said and the economic circumstances depicted in the world of the film; in Mr Morris's case, *his* 'work' consists of simply being the master over the goods the ex-cons sell for him and it is his money – the very fact that he has so much of it – that enables him to spend it in such a way that he keeps making forever more of it.

Standing in front of a blackboard with a piece of chalk in her hand, Helen performs a calculation to demonstrate how 'crime doesn't pay'– showing that after paying off any expenses incurred in the run-up to the raid, during and after (passing the stolen goods on to an even 'bigger' gangster boss in return for a fraction of their actual worth), barely a pittance is left for each gang member at the end of the day (Figure 4.3).

Although the sequence is interspersed with many humorous moments, showing the men awkwardly wedged between the store's assortment of toys, with Patsy squeezing into a child-size toy sports car, it darkens in tone when Joe confronts Helen about being a 'jailbird' and a liar. The painful rift between the couple now seems irreconcilable and Helen runs off distraught. However, after everyone has left the building – with Gimpy subserviently turning off all the lights as instructed to do so by Mr Morris – Joe, now alone in the store, has a sudden change of heart and can be seen searching for the perfume Helen fancies with the beam

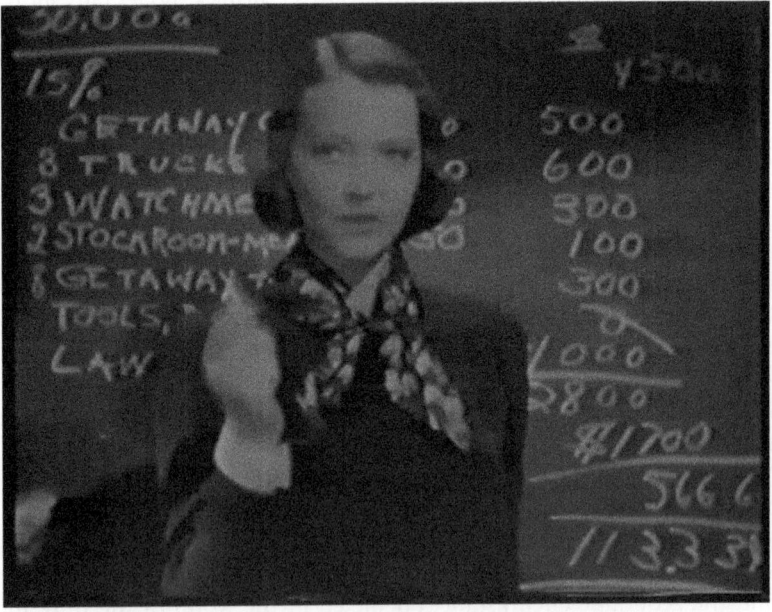

Figure 4.3   Helen gives a lecture on the topic of 'Crime doesn't pay'
Source: Screen capture from *You and Me* (1938), dir. Fritz Lang, Paramount Pictures

of his torch. He takes a small bottle of 'Hour of Ecstasy' out of a display case, evidently confirming the assumption that Joe, who didn't seem convinced by Helen's lecture, is still out to rob the store, boldly ripping off the bottle's price tag and discarding it on the store floor as he makes his getaway. However, passing the cash register on his way out Joe changes his mind, retrieves his steps to find the price tag and after paying the exact amount into the till he, too, finally leaves the store, only to return to their rented flat to find Helen gone. Joe pressing the 'cash' button on the cash register mirrors the shot of a (female) hand pressing the button in the opening sequence (Figure 4.4).

The cash register, which measures everything in terms of its exchange value, thus bookends the narrative, emphasising its dominance over every aspect of social behaviour under capitalism.

The literally didactic tone of the sequence, with Helen in the role of a school teacher, doing sums on the blackboard, has led critics to repeat unquestioningly Lang's own assertion that *You and Me* was made in the Brechtian *Lehrstück* style: 'I made it [the film] probably a little under

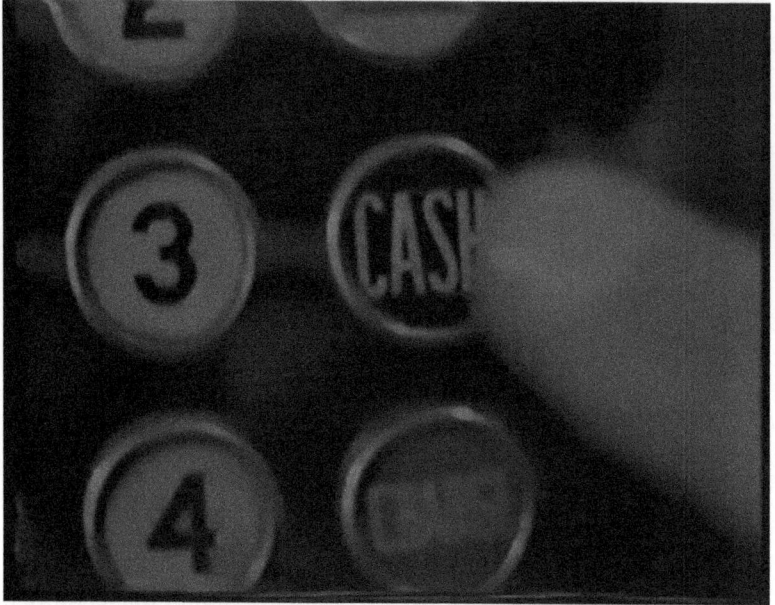

Figure 4.4 Joe pays for a bottle of 'Hour of Ecstasy'
Source: Screen capture from *You and Me* (1938), dir. Fritz Lang, Paramount Pictures

the influence of my friend Bertolt Brecht, who had created a style in the theatre which he called *Lehrstück*, meaning a play that teaches you something. And I wanted to make a didactic picture teaching the audience that crime doesn't pay – which is a lie, because crime pays very well' (Higham and Greenberg 1969: 108).

Lang's paradox statement about making a film with a faux moral cautioning needs disentangling to make any sense. First, Lang's evidently rudimentary and superficial understanding of the concept of the *Lehrstück* as a 'play that teaches you something' is problematic. In fact, Brecht's model of the *Lehrstück* is rooted in a thoroughly dynamic relationship between play and audience: 'its task is to show the world as it changes (and also how it may be changed)' (Brecht in Willett 1992: 79). Brecht clearly envisaged the audience's active participation in the *Lehrstück*, and several of his *Lehrstücke* were written specifically for schools.[6] The didacticism of the *Lehrstücke* is therefore based on active participation, not a passive acceptance of what is played out on stage. Thus, Helen's lecture on why 'crime doesn't pay' and both the gang's passive acceptance of her sums and Gimpy's deferential compliance with Mr Morris's request to 'turn off all the lights' (on leaving the store) epitomise the exact opposite of Brecht's critical intentions.

Equally, Lang's assertion that 'crime pays very well' seems rooted more in intellectual cynicism than in the Marxist political thought on which Brecht's rationale for the epic theatre and the *Lehrstück* is based. The bourgeois moral that 'crime doesn't pay' rests on the idea of working as the only permissible way for a worker to 'earn a living' in capitalism (stealing, a much quicker route to success, is not); Karl Held notes that non-politicised workers, rather than questioning their absolute dependency on employment in order to survive, often *perceive* their exploitation as a motivational challenge and opportunity to demonstrate their productivity, a false belief in the entitlement to an income on account of their very own usefulness (Held 1985: 61).[7]

That so many workers unquestioningly submit to the conditions of a system that decidedly does not have their interest at heart but subjugates all social and economic processes to the doctrine of ownership of capital is perhaps one of the most puzzling contradictions. Brecht recognised that in order to change this unthinking acceptance of their social and economic circumstances, in the first instance a person's thinking about the reasons why things are the way they are had to change. To challenge those habitual ways of seeing and explaining the world that kept the *status quo* in place became the rationale for Brecht's development of a new set of aesthetics for political, no longer culinary, effect.

For Brecht, both the *Lehrstück* and the epic theatre offered new ways of addressing the audience in such a way that a conscious noticing of these clear-as-day and yet seemingly invisible contradictions would become possible by means of *making* them visible – through demonstrational acting, social gestus (the use of gests to emphasise how economic circumstances dominate social processes between people), stage design and distancing effects such as the use of songs, placards and parable to comment on the action on stage. It is in this aspect, that I want to argue that – despite its nauseating politics on a surface level – Brecht's use of narrational strategies in *You and Me* has the fundamental principle of challenging habitual viewing in common with the rationale of the epic theatre.

The greatest difficulty in making sense of the raid/Helen's lecture sequence lies in the tensions created by the film drawing on different genres stylistically, whereby *noir* elements at the beginning give way to comedy once the gang is trapped in the store's toy section by Morris's security men. The obvious visual clash of men holding tommy guns surrounded by children's toys is underscored by the comical treatment of what could be perceived as the film's dramatic climax of the ex-cons turning once more to crime and Joe coming face to face with Helen, their spatial separation now signalling an ideological division that firmly places Joe back with his gang and shows Helen aligned with the boss. The seriousness of the situation is moderated by moments of comedy, mostly through the clownish behaviour of Gimpy, who blames his suppressed chuckles on being searched for weapons by Morris's men on being 'too ticklish' and whose weapon is an antiquated musket ('It's an heirloom'). Although we are not supposed to question the mathematical accuracy of Helen's calculation that crime doesn't pay, reverse field shots of Helen doing her sums and the criminals' half bored, half bemused attention allows for the possibility of aligning ourselves with either point of view – crime may pay, or it may not.

Above all, the jarring effect of setting Helen's lecture in the toy section of the store brings to mind the earlier use of *mise-en-scène* to comment on the action and emphasises the film's concern with creating complex perspectives on the action. In the end, returning to work on a low-paid wage still doesn't allow the ex-convicts to own, or take a share in the goods they sell, and Patsy squeezing into a car in the toy section illustrates as absurdly 'childish' any notion that they could. Frieda Grafe, in her seminal study on Lang, observes that both Lang and Brecht 'for similar reasons preferred using objects and things to expose, with the help of non-linguistic means, the false claims of generally

held ideas' (Grafe 1987: 17). Grafe also criticises Brecht for failing to recognise that Lang 'expressed through the cinema that which he [Brecht]
explored in the theatre: that ideology is hidden in forms in which it
survives and operates unnoticed' (19). In this respect, both the opening
sequence and the shop window scene in *You and Me* can be regarded as
perfect examples of Lang's awareness of the ideology hidden in objects.
By creating these complex perspectives that encourage the audience to
scrutinise what is shown on screen, Lang demonstrates an understanding of Brechtian methods that may not extend to sharing Brecht's politics, but help to create a vigilant audience nonetheless, without offering
any political solutions beyond the ability to start noticing (ideological)
contradiction. Seen in this light, Robin Wood's intuitive musing as to
whether *You and Me* could only be accessible to 'the most intellectually
sophisticated of viewers' seems entirely plausible.

Note

I would like to dedicate this essay to the memory of the film critic Robin
Wood.

1. See McGilligan (1997) and Gandert (2003) *Filmexil*, 17 *Adressat Fritz Lang,
   Hollywood* about Lang's activism in the Hollywood Anti-Nazi League and
   increased political interest in the US.
2. Most notably perhaps, *Metropolis* (1926) and *M* (1931), which were both at
   the time of their release heavily criticised for the apparent lack of any clear
   political message. See Luppa (2009) and Pye and Luppa (2011).
3. Italicisation by Gunning; further, the correct German spelling of the word
   should be with an 'umlaut', *Lehrstück*. I will stick to Tom Gunning's own
   spelling of the term in quotations and use the accurate spelling in my
   own writing.
4. The two moments occur as the newly-weds Helen and Joe return to Helen's
   lodgings to begin their life together. Ascending a dark staircase (Helen's land-
   lady has already turned off the lights), Joe lights a match and, holding it up
   above his head, exclaims 'Statue of Liberty', much to Helen's bemusement
   and giggles. Carrying his new bride over the threshold of Helen's bedsit, Joe
   drops the match and, once again in darkness, Joe stumbles and they fall,
   breaking a table lamp in the process. Helen flicks on a light switch and we see
   Joe entangled in wires, and this time it is Helen – holding the broken lamp
   above her head – who imitates Joe with an excited cry of 'Statue of Liberty'.
   Considering the extent to which Helen's parole rules curtail her personal
   freedom – including, significantly, a clause that forbids marriage whilst still
   on parole – the reference to the 'liberty' the Statute of Liberty is meant to
   represent is as brittle as a broken light bulb. Although it is Joe who we see tied
   up in cables, it is Helen who is trapped by oppressive parole rules and whose
   liberty is now at stake.
5. See in particular George Wilson's seminal piece on *You Only Live Once* and
   Douglas Pye's analysis of *Beyond A Reasonable Doubt* for in-depth analyses of

each film's narrational strategies and the construction of point of view, which subsequently led to completely new interpretations of Lang's critical intentions and each film's fundamental concerns with seeing and blindness.

6. For instance, in *Der Jasager und Der Neinsager* the issue of consent (*'Einverständnis'*) is acted out twice with two different endings in order to show how different circumstances affect one's decision making. By actively taking part in the play, rather than by merely watching it, the spectator will, according to Brecht, learn something.

7. See Held (1985) for an in-depth analysis of ideas surrounding competition and false beliefs in a right to employment.

Bibliography

Brecht, Bertolt (1992) 'The German Drama: pre-Hitler', in John Willett (ed. and trans.) *Brecht on Theatre: The Development of an Aesthetic* (London: Methuen), pp. 77–81.

Gandert, Gero (2003) *Filmexil: Adressat Fritz Lang, Hollywood*. 17. Berlin. Edition text+kritik

Grafe, Frieda (1987) 'Für Fritz Lang: Einen Platz, kein Denkmal' in Frieda Grafe, Enno Patalas and Hans Helmut Prinzler (eds) *Fritz Lang: Reihe Film 7* (Munich: Hanser Verlag).

Gunning, Tom (2000) *The Films of Fritz Lang: Allegories of Vision and Modernity* (London: *Bfi* Publishing).

Held, Karl (1985) *Die Psychologie des bürgerlichen Individuums* (Munich: Resultate Verlag).

Hermand, Jost (1994) 'Neue Sachlichkeit: Ideology, Lifestyle or Artistic Movement' in Thomas Kniesche and Stephen Brockmann (eds) *Dancing on the Volcano: Essays on the Culture of the Weimar Republic* (Columbia, Sc: Camden House), pp 57–67.

Higham, Charles and Greenberg, Joel (1969) *The Celluloid Muse* (Chicago: Henry Regnery).

Luppa, Iris (2009) 'Weimar Cinema', in John Gibbs and Douglas Pye (eds) *Close-Up 2* (London: Wallflower).

Marx, Karl (1976) [1887]. *Capital. A Critique of Political Economy*, Volume One, transl. Ben Fowkes (London: Penguin).

Marx, Karl and Friedrich Engels (2008) [1848]. *The Communist Manifesto*, with an introduction by David Harvey (London: Pluto).

McGilligan, Patrick (1997) *Fritz Lang: The Nature of the Beast* (London: Faber and Faber)

Möhl, Wolfgang and Wentzke, Theo (2007) *Das Geld: Von den vielgepriesenen Leistungen des schnöden Mammons* (Munich: GegenStandpunkt Verlag).

Pye, Douglas (1992) '*Film Noir* and Suppressive Narrative: *Beyond a Reasonable Doubt*' in Ian Cameron (ed.) *The Movie Book of Film Noir* (London: Studio Vista), pp. 98–109.

Pye, Douglas and Luppa, Iris (2011) '*M*: Leading the Blind' in *Movie*, 2, pp.1–13.

Wilson, George M. (1986) *Narration in Light: Studies in Cinematic Point of View*(Baltimore and London: John Hopkins University Press).

Wood, Robin (2000) 'Lang and Brecht', *CineAction*, 52, pp. 4–11.

5
Laughing Matters: Four Marxist Takes on Film Comedy

Jakob Ladegaard

At first sight, Karl is not the most obvious Marx to mention in the context of film comedy. The analytical prose and careful argumentation of *Das Capital* appear as the near opposites of Groucho's volleys of verbal humour, and the philosopher's stern view of society as determined by economic laws and class struggle does not seem easily compatible with the lighthearted universe of comedy, where the Marx brothers are able to transgress all social barriers without effort and reprisals – as if the rules of the social field were as easily changed as the rules of American football in *Horse Feathers* (1932). Although Marx did imagine that history would eventually reach the happy ending proper to comedy as a narrative genre, he generally thought of history in terms of heroic struggle associated with the epic or tragedy. This is evident in his famous remark in the beginning of *The Eighteenth Brumaire* that 'all facts and personages of great importance in world history occur, so to speak, twice [...]: the first time as tragedy, the second as farce' (Marx 2010: 103). Tragedy here stands for the true mode of 'serious' revolutionary struggle, while farce designates its empty, formal repetition in the revolution of 1848–1851, the mocking 'caricature' or 'parody' as Marx proceeds to call it, of a revolution carried out by reactionaries. The implied view is that farce is a spectacle that enthralls the audience (here, the French people) by an outward show that perverts the truth of the historical situation. As we shall see, this view is echoed in later denunciations of film comedy by some critics in the Marxist tradition.

But if revolutionary struggle was not a joking matter for Marx, comic strategies entered his writings in another way; in the shape of polemics and satire. This is especially palpable in his early writings on ideology, not least *The German Ideology* which explicitly aims to 'ridicule and discredit' the 'bleating' of the philosophical 'sheep' of German idealism, 'who take themselves and are taken for wolves' (Marx and Engels 2010: 23). The aim of Marx's ridicule, of course, is the reverence in contemporary German philosophy for the Hegelian assumption that the historical process is essentially the history of Spirit. Marx's satirical tone models the proponents of this view – especially Bruno Bauer and Max Stirner, irreverently dubbed St Bruno and St Max to emphasise their estrangement from worldly matters – after the absent-minded, starry-eyed philosopher who has been a stock-figure of Western comedy since Aristophanes' ridicule of Socrates in *The Clouds*. And just like the Athenian comedy writer and so many after him, Marx takes obvious joy in leading these unworldly idealists head-first into the solid wall of materialism. This indicates an inherent affinity between the world of comedy and that of ideology with all its self-conceit, mistaken identities, misrecognitions and illusions. It additionally points to a similarity between the clash of such follies with materiality, bodily life and communal laughter in comedy and the endeavour to reconnect ideas to the material conditions of social life in Marxist ideology critique.

From Marx himself we can thus take (at least) two opposing views on the politics of comedy. The false, affirmative spectacle of distracting entertainment (or, comedy *as* ideology) and the ridiculing laughter of materialist ideology critique. In what follows, I will trace some of the ways in which these ideas have lived on in cinema and the writings of important Marxist film critics of the 20th and 21st centuries. I will start with a section about the first view and subsequently zoom in on dominant features in three strands of comical filmic ideology critique: the grotesque body; montage as wit; and the comical character. I should add that of the two accepted uses of the term comedy – as a specific genre and as a mode, tone or element that can be present in art works that need not be exclusively comic (Stott 2010: 2) – I follow the latter, which means that my examples are not all taken from genre comedies.

'Make 'em Laugh': the culture industry and the discipline of laughter

In the well-known chapter on the culture industry in Adorno and Horkheimer's *The Dialectics of Enlightenment*, Adorno (the main author of this part) criticises the American film industry for its significant contribution to a market-based mass culture, whose banal, constantly reproduced formulas for entertainment effect a deadening uniformisation and a liquidation of critical thinking. According to Adorno, comedy is central to the functioning of the culture industry: 'Fun is a medicinal bath which the

104 Marx at the Movies

entertainment industry never ceases to prescribe' (Adorno & Horkheimer 2002: 112) As Donald O'Connor sang in his spectacular performance in *Singin' in the Rain* (1952) a few years later, 'Make 'em Laugh' (Figure 5.1).

According to Adorno, laughter 'always accompanies the moment when a fear is ended. It indicates a release, whether from physical danger or from the grip of logic' (112). This release can have two forms: It can be aligned with a critical self-reflection that promises a 'suspension of law' and a 'passage to the homeland' (60) defined in purely negative terms as 'a state of having escaped' (61) – in a word, emancipation. But laughter can also be aligned with the opposite principle: 'a sign of violence, an outbreak of blind, obdurate nature' (60). The fun prescribed by the entertainment industry is in league with the latter. For instead of marking an escape from power, mainstream cinematic comedy in Adorno's view identifies with power. It serves to externalise the fear and pain arising from man's alienation by transferring it to an object of sadistic ridicule: 'In wrong society [...] Laughter [*Lachen*] about something is always

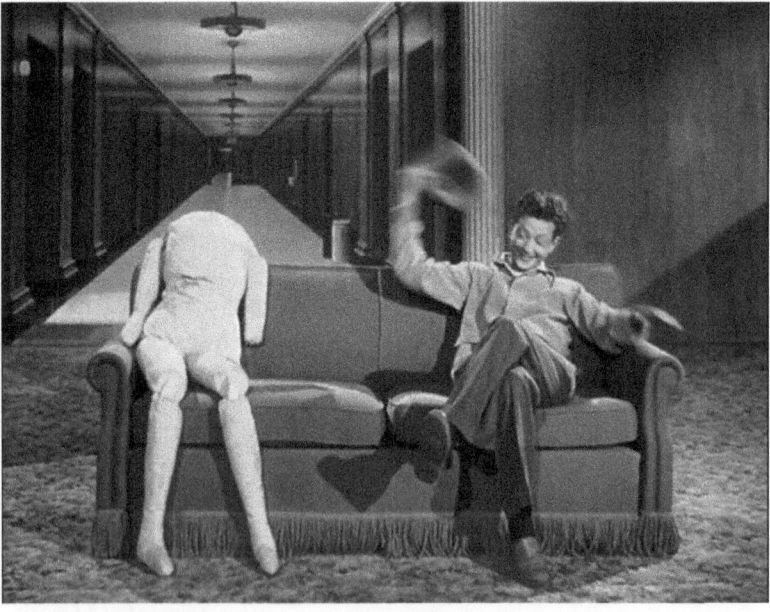

Figure 5.1 Donald O'Connor singing 'Make 'em Laugh'
Source: Screen capture from *Singin' in the Rain* (1952), dir. Stanley Donen and Gene Kelly, Metro-Goldwin-Mayer

laughing at it [*Verlachen*: ridicule]' (Adorno & Horkheimer 2002: 112). In this respect Adorno follows Henri Bergson's idea about laughter as a disciplinary punishment of behaviour that departs from the sanctioned codes of social life. But he argues against the French philosopher (and in line with Hobbes) that what manifests itself in this laughter is not the vital spirit, but simple 'self-assertion which, in convivial settings, dares to celebrate its liberation from scruple' (112). For Adorno, then, the laughter arising in the movie theatres of his time is that of the alienated masses overcoming their fear by identifying with power and violently ridiculing deviations from the social norm in a way that resembles the imaginary logic of fascism.[1] Thus,

> The collectivity of those who laugh parodies humanity. They are monads, each abandoning himself to the pleasure – at the expense of everyone else and with the majority in support – of being ready to shrink from nothing. Their harmony presents a caricature of solidarity. (112)

One recognises in these lines the echo of Marx' denunciation of the revolution of 1848–1851 as a 'parody' and 'caricature' of 1789. For Adorno, the calculated laughter of the movie audience overcoming its individual fears in the darkness of the projection room is a farcical repetition of the true laughter of emancipation, creating a parody of humanity and a caricature of solidarity. At a distance, this sombre diagnosis might seem exaggerated. But reversely, of course, one could argue that it is a testimony to the pervasive internalisation of the entertainment industry's imperative of fun even in academic circles, that a commonly heard casual objection to Adorno's thinking is its 'seriousness' and elitist lack of humour. In any case, comedy and humour remain a major factor in today's dominant Western culture – not only in Hollywood films,[2] but also in popular media, increasingly characterised 'by a continual tone of irreverence' (Billig 2005: 240), in public debates, where a joke rates higher than an argument, not to mention corporate culture. As Anca Parvalescu writes in *Laughter – Notes on a Passion*, extending Adorno's analysis to today's corporate capitalism:

> We are told to laugh from all directions. There is an industry of laughter. Corporations organize laughing events on the threshold that marks the nondistinction between 'working hours' and the rapidly disappearing 'leisure time'. There are laughter clubs, where one goes to 'exercise' for one hour at a time. There are laughter therapists,

who preach the benefits of laughter as 'stress-reducing'. There are medical practices which recommend at least one session of laughter a week. It is Adorno and Horkheimer's worst nightmare: the world is a nightmarish Emerald City, laughing the day – and Horkheimer and Adorno's hope for our happiness – away. (Parvulescu 2010: 149–150)

All this must make us wary of that which Michael Billig describes as the 'widespread belief in the self-evident desirability of humour' (Billig 2005: 236). Instead of automatically assuming that humour, irony, parody and comedy are linked to a progressive politics, as is too often the case, one must recognise that they also play a twofold role in the current ideological landscape; as an instrument in the policing of the dominant social order through ridicule and as a vital grease in the smooth 'creative' and 'network-based' rather than hierarchical corporate culture of late modern capitalism.

The problematic role of comedy in media and mainstream film culture has not only been analysed in critical theory, but also reflected in films such as Preston Sturges' *Sullivan's Travels* (1941), Woody Allen's *Annie Hall* (1977) and Martin Scorsese's *King of Comedy* (1983). Allen's comedy in particular, although more oriented towards existential than political issues, shares some of Adorno's critical observations about laughter, but also points to a difficulty in distinguishing progressive and regressive comedy. Not unlike Adorno, the film portrays two opposing ways in which laughter can function as a release from fear. The first is the lifeless laughter of the entertainment industry emblematically 'embodied' in the canned laughter that Rob (Tony Roberts) uses in his sitcom production to the chagrin of the comedian Alvy Singer (Woody Allen). The mechanical laughter is closely associated with the hip circle of the Californian entertainment industry that Rob frequents. The dominating principle of this milieu is a continuous effort to deny death through new technology (Rob's space suit that allegedly protects him from alpha rays and thus prevents aging, New Age religion, diets and drugs). Canned laughter functions as one of the film's central symbols of a culture that represses its fear of death through entertainment.

The second type of laughter is associated with Alvy, who has a distanced, reflective approach to himself and others, and whose thoughts revolve around death. The emblematic expression of this critical attitude is his constant stream of verbal humour. There is a certain emancipatory power in his comical scrutiny of every established wisdom or personal motive as well as a potential to create more vital communities than the 'mellow' Californian New Agers – the genuine amusement at

Alvy's stand-up shows and, especially, the love relationship with Annie (Diane Keaton), the couple's shared joy in the face of fear emblematically expressed in the famous lobster scene. But the other side of Alvy's critical and comic autonomy is self-absorption and a growing personal isolation. He has become like Manhattan, an island, Annie notes towards the end. His increasing inability to commit himself to women confirms this verdict. His short-lived relationships mirror the form of the joke: It must constantly be renewed or told to a different audience to incite laughter. There is thus something compulsive, even mechanical about his constant attempts to temporarily defeat death through humour. His jokes are born from fear and return to it as soon as they are told: Ideally, they would be pearls on a never-ending string of laughter confirming the vitality of the joker, but not allowing a passage from the critical negation of his humour to positive political action. This is where the laughter of the critical comedian approximates and perhaps even mingles with the sound of the Californian can.

We might say from an Adornian perspective that this aspect of Allen's film (and even his oeuvre in general) testify to the powers of the cultural industry to integrate and exploit critical gestures. But perhaps there is also a lesson about the ambiguity of laughter to be learned. For although Allen's film does not confront the issue with Adorno's philosophical rigour, *Annie Hall* reminds us of the difficulties in neatly separating – as Adorno does – regressive and progressive forms of comedy. For as most of us know from experience, it is not always easy to decide the exact cause of our mirth. In the following presentation of three different Marxist perspectives on filmic comedy, one should not forget this, for one reason why comedy continues to hold a fascination and a promise – however evasive – for critical thinking is that it cannot be fully controlled by either philosophical categorisation or political motivation; at least, not without running a serious risk of ceasing to be funny.

Laughing matter: comic materiality

'Is it true that the Bolsheviks have killed off laughter?' Faced with this question at a lecture in Paris in 1930, Sergei Eisenstein tells us that he 'burst out laughing'. He then added: 'There will be even more laughter in the Soviet Union when I tell them your ridiculous question!' (Eisenstein 1996: 68–69). This anecdote, which opens Eisenstein's essay 'Bolsheviks Do Laugh (Thoughts on Soviet Comedy)' (1935), perfectly illustrates the idea he then develops about the function of comedy in Soviet cinema.

The object of Soviet laughter, he claims, is 'social infantility, caught up in an age of social adulthood, socialist adulthood' (Eisenstein 1996: 70). Just as the ridiculous question of the ignorant Frenchman will make the Soviet public laugh, Soviet film should provoke laughter through its ridicule of the childish class enemy. 'Laughter', he concludes, 'is simply a light weapon whose strike is just as deadly and which can be deployed where there is no sense in bringing in the all-crushing tanks of social wrath' (72). Belonging to 'the tradition of black humour', Eisenstein thus embraces for political purposes 'the laughter of destruction' (71), which Adorno later identified with the culture industry. As such, Eisenstein is faithful to the satirical wit of Marx and Engels in their exposure of the illusions of German idealism.

The Russian director exemplifies his claim by a reference to the comic moments in the film, which brought him to the lecture hall in Paris in the first place, *Staroyeinovoye* (*The General Line*, aka *Old and New*, 1929). And certainly, the film contains great moments of satire, for example in the depiction of the indolent, decadent bureaucrats opposing the progress of the heroine Marfa and her farming collective; or the ridicule of religious superstition in the scene where a procession ends with unanswered prayers for rain. However, there is nothing satirical about the film's comical highpoint: the wedding between Fomka the bull and a cow dressed up as the bride with garlands of flowers (Figure 5.2). After a hilarious build-up with several shots from the eager bull's perspective of the heifer's hindquarters, Eisenstein illustrates the moment of consummation with images of explosions and shots of foaming milk and swirling cream from the famous scene with the cream separator earlier in the film. This allusion in turn impregnates that earlier scene, retrospectively enhancing the festive mirth in the images of Marfa covered with spurts of cream and the laughing peasants witnessing the secular miracle of the cream separator, the first acquisition of the dairy collective. In the same vein, the comic vitality of the bovine wedding spills over into the related images of Marfa's 'dream' of a giant bull towering over herds of cattle and a sea of milk later bottled in a modern factory. As David Bordwell notes, the common theme of these scenes is fecundity (Bordwell 1993: 105) – the fecundity of sexuality that links human and animal world, the fecundity of the earth through the marriage of agriculture and new technology, and the socio-economic fecundity of collective farming promoted by Soviet ideology (the medallion of Lenin at the harvest festivity replacing the religious icons of the miscarried drought procession).

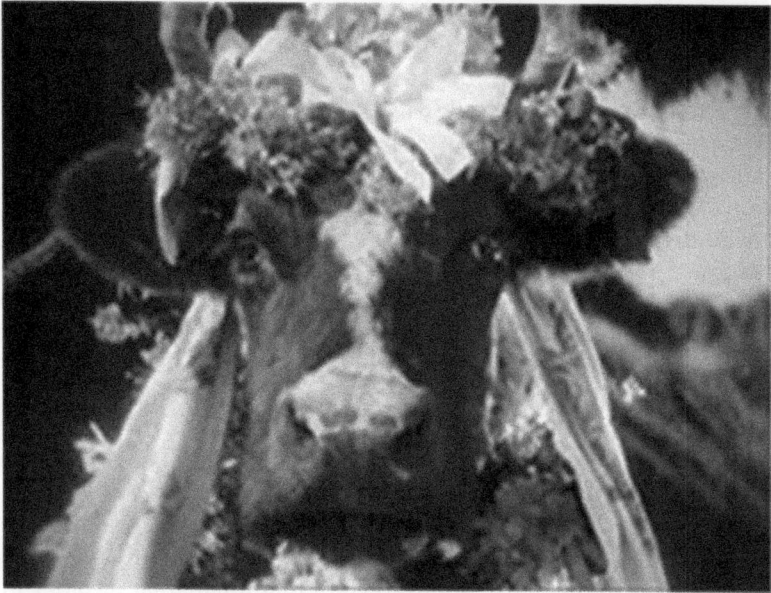

Figure 5.2 Carnivalesque materialism: The bride of Fomka the bull
Source: Screen capture from *The General Line (Old and New)* (1929), dir. Sergei Eisenstein, Sovkino

The festive imagery of these scenes is reminiscent of Mikhail Bakhtin's conception of carnival and grotesque realism developed in *Rabelais and his World* (1965). According to Bakhtin, medieval carnivals were celebrations of the fecundity of the material world, the powers of regeneration common to nature and the human body's 'lower stratum' expressed in the grotesque imagination of the popular mind and a holiday spirit of laughter. By appropriating the imagery of such ancient festive folk culture in his depiction of collectivised and industrialised farming, Eisenstein sought to bestow on it the legitimacy of popular tradition and replace orthodox religion with Soviet doctrine (and the new icons of cinema) as the guarantee of the fecundity of nature. For Bakhtin, the celebration of vitality that periodically suspended the order of medieval society also had a critical, destructive side: the degrading ridicule and parody of the clerical and worldly authorities and their supporting ideologies. As we have seen, this dimension of carnivalesque laughter is also present in Eisenstein's film. The reason why he focuses exclusively on this in his essay on comedy from 1935 might have to do with the communist party's embrace of socialist realism as the official art form in 1934. For although Bakhtin and Eisenstein's celebrations of the vital powers of body and nature are surely 'materialist', there is a long way from the original festive spirit of comedy to the heroic virtuousness and sacrifice propagated by socialist realism – a distance already visible in Eisenstein's own film in the uneasily bridged incongruence between the virginal purity of Marfa's commitment to the communist ideal and the carnality of Fomka's nuptials.

This disparity between the imagery of folkloric comedy and the stern doctrines of early socialist realism might seem to confirm the often repeated notion that genuine laughter is anti-totalitarian and liberating. But one should not forget the effort Eisenstein makes to fit both sides of the carnivalesque laughter with official Soviet ideology, thereby glossing over the systematic violence of forced collectivisation. This illustrates the possibility of an intimate connection between official ideology and 'subversive' carnival that Bakhtin (like many of his followers) brackets, when he claims that the idiom of laughter is 'never used by violence and authority' (Bakhtin 1984: 90). As Slavoj Žižek has observed, the underlying premise of such an assertion – that genuine laughter is anti-totalitarian – fails to grasp that totalitarian ideology in order to function needs a certain carnivalesque suspension of the rule of law, wherefore 'cynical distance, laughter, irony are, so to speak, part of the game' (Žižek 2008: 24).[3]

This political ambivalence of grotesque comic materiality finds one of its most direct and provocative expressions in Dušan Makavejev's *Sweet Movie* (1974). The human (and particularly female) body is at the centre of two parallel stories about the political and economic investment in erotic desire common to capitalism and totalitarianism. In one scene, the heroine of the 'capitalist story', Miss World (Carole Laure), is bathed in melted chocolate and then sensually caresses her naked body, while the cameraman who is filming the spectacle for a television commercial explains that 'I want them to feel as if they are eating you'. The scene's controlled carnival thus literalises the exploitation of sexual desire by capitalist consumer fetishism. In a parallel scene, the protagonist of the 'communist' story, Anna Planeta (Anna Prucnal), the captain of a boat sporting a sculpture of Marx at its bow, performs a striptease for a group of young boys lured onto the boat with promises of candy. The boys later end up wrapped in plastic, apparently as dead as the revolutionary seaman Anna stabs when they lie naked in a giant bowl of sugar. In this way, the film denounces the discrepancy between the sweet promises of communist ideology and the violence of the regimes allegedly committed to it. However, the film also provides its audience

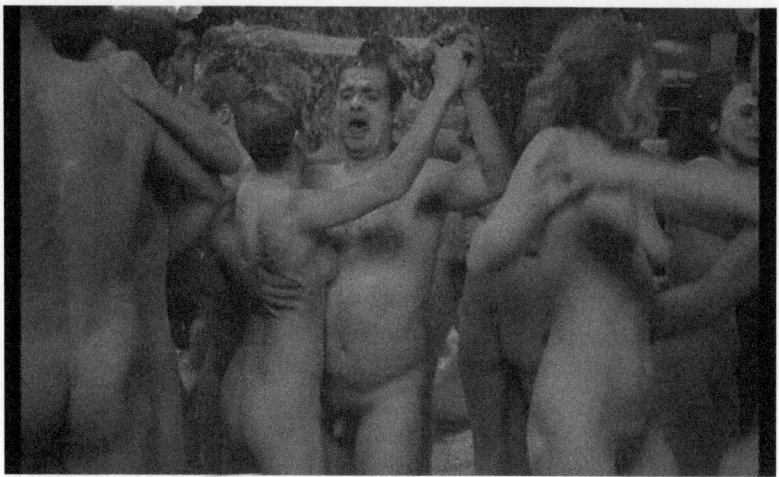

Figure 5.3 Emancipation?
Source: Screen capture from *Sweet Movie* (1974), dir. Dušan Makavejev, Maran Films

with (at least seemingly) more positive images of bodily transgression in
the carnivalesque orgies of the Viennese Actionists inspired by Wilhelm
Reich's ideas of emancipatory sexuality (which Makavejev had already
celebrated in *W. R. – Mysteries of the Organism* (1971)) (Figure 5.3). But
as Lorraine Mortimer notes, there is something deeply disturbing about
the collective's attempt to liberate themselves from all social norms and
regress to a stage of pre-symbolic – and therefore also pre-political –
infancy (Mortimer 2008). Thus, Makavejev not only satirises the
biopolitical power in both capitalist and totalitarian societies, but also
illustrates some of the problems of 'subversive' art projects that equate
social emancipation with bodily transgression. In this sense, *Sweet
Movie* opens new ways for the analysis of the ambivalent politics of the
grotesque body beyond the dichotomies of Bakhtin and Eisenstein's
agricultural ideology, while avoiding the folkloric stereotypes of recent
directors such as Emir Kusturica.

Incongruity and ideology: critical wit

The ambivalent humour and politics of *Sweet Movie* rely to a large degree
on its shocking montage of seemingly incongruent images (for example, Miss World drowning in chocolate next to documentary footage
of the unearthed remains of the victims of the Katyn massacre). In the

modern history of humour theories, the notion of incongruity plays a prominent role. In particular, the concept was at the centre of the definitions of wit that were developed in 18th-century Britain and continue to inform such prominent 20th-century theorists of humour as Henri Bergson and Arthur Koestler. Broadly speaking, this tradition sees wit as a primarily verbal form of humour (the joke is its clearest expression) that relies on the ability to construct and perceive similarities between otherwise incongruent ideas. Wit deals in double meanings, in sudden shifts between narrative patterns and playful short circuits of cognitive categories (Billig 2005: 57–70). Thus, if the theories and practices of grotesque carnival underline the physical side of the comic emblematised in laughter, the tradition of quick wit aligns humour with intellectual reflection, creativity and cognitive agility.

Comic incongruity is not necessarily political, but it can be, when the reflection it provokes is directed towards social issues. This, according to Walter Benjamin, is the case in Berthold Brecht's epic theatre. For Benjamin, the essential thing about Brecht's theatre is its intention to cause critical reflection on the social meaning of the stage characters rather than emotional identification. Brecht pursues this aim through constant interruptions of the narrative and any illusions of verisimilitude in ways that remind Benjamin of the montage of cinema (Benjamin 1967: 112), but which might also bring to mind the structure of a joke: the sudden disruption of the expected course of a story by an incongruent element which forces the listener to reflect. In fact, Benjamin proceeds to link Brecht's strategy of reflective interruption and estrangement to comedy, contending that 'there is no better starting point for thought than laughter' and adding 'Epic theatre is lavish only in its occasions for laughter' (113).[4] Through Benjamin we can thus return from the epic theatre to our present context with an idea of a formal strategy for politically committed film comedy: the idea of disruptive, incongruous montage – the clash of heterogeneous images and/or sounds – as a way to provoke social reflection and laughter.

Few directors have exploited this principle with the same creative and critical imagination as Jean-Luc Godard. However, if Godard's debt to Brecht is often noted by critics, it is surprisingly difficult to find extended writings about the comic dimension of his work, not to mention its relation to the political dimension. Nicole Brenez comes close in her essay 'Jean-Luc Godard, *Witz* et invention formelle', where she traces a link between Godard's formal inventiveness and the conception of *Witz* (wit) in Early German Romanticism. *Witz* for romantics such as

Friedrich Schlegel and Novalis was not as in the 18th century a leisurely exercise in verbal finesse among gentlemen, but a name for the flash of insight into a fragment of the world's hidden relations at the core of artistic creativity. In the words of Brenez: '*Witz* is a praxis of thought as montage and as spiritual deflagration'. She adds, 'From the verbal find to visual collage, from explosive fragmentation to creative excess, its principle irrigates Godard's formal inventiveness' (Brenez 2005: 29).[5]

In this light, it does not, as Brenez notes (16–17), appear coincidental that Novalis' portrait hangs on the wall behind the cameraman in *La Chinoise* (1967), when the young Maoist, Guillaume (Jean-Pierre Léaud) is interviewed about socialist theatre. But Brenez fails to note the connotations of humour and irony, which the notion of *Witz* continued to hold for the Romantics (particularly Schlegel) – and, perhaps, for Godard. In so far as we are permitted to regard the scene in *La Chinoise* (4:44–9:55) as a reflection on the film's own formal and critical practice – with its self-conscious shots of the film crew, its montage of incongruent images and sound, insertion of text on the screen, and so on – then we should take seriously the fact that Guillaume's first choice to illustrates his ideas about socialist theatre is a comic anecdote (Figure 5.4). It goes something like this: A group of Chinese students demonstrates in Moscow and they are beaten up by Russian police. The next day, they meet with a host of Western journalists. A young Chinese turns up, his head wrapped in bandages, and starts screaming about police abuse. He takes the bandage off, surrounded by expectant journalists, and reveals an unharmed face. The reporters yell insults, but they do not understand, Guillaume explains in conclusion, that it was all theatre – 'real theatre, like Shakespeare or Brecht'. The untouched face here functions as an anti-climatic punch line that punctures narrative expectations. The Chinese student plays the part of a victim of Russian state violence desired by the Western reporters, but then steps out of the role – not in order to deny the event, but to reveal in a truly dialectical turn the desire of the 'impartial' observers and thereby invite them to reflect on their own part in shaping the spectacle of global politics. Their inability to accept this invitation makes them the real butts of this burst of Brechtian wit. In the words of Jacques Rancière – to whom *La Chinoise* is not a film *about* Marxism, but a film 'with Marxism', that is, a film whose main principle of representation is Marxist dialectics (Rancière 2006: 143) – the anecdote ultimately demonstrates that 'the political militant and the actor are alike: their work is to show us not visible horrors, but what cannot be seen' (150). For what is mirrored in the smooth face of the Chinese student, unseen by the

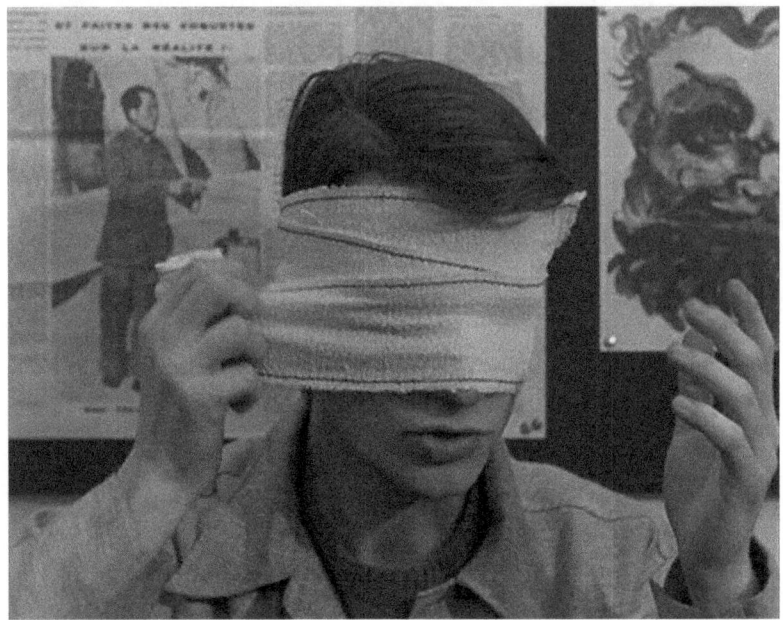

Figure 5.4   Guillaume (Jean-Pierre Léaud) recounts the story about the Chinese student
Source: Screen capture from *La Chinoise* (1967), dir. Jean-Luc Godard, Anouchka Films

reporters, is their own blindness towards the ideological structures that interpellate them as subjects in the social field, like characters in a play blind to their own meaning.[6]

Many further examples from Godard's work could be offered, but one more will have to do: The scene at the beginning of *Pierrot le Fou* (1965), where Pierre (Jean-Paul Belmondo) reads aloud an advertisement about the 'freedom' offered by his wife's Scandal girdle as a prelude to a scene showing people at a party speaking like commercials about their cars and make-up. The comic incongruity between the relaxed poses and voices of the guests seemingly engaged in small talk and the 'scripted' advertisements flowing from their mouths is yet another illustration of the powers of ideology speaking through subjects performing their social roles. For Rancière, this scene is emblematic of the dialectical procedure of Godard's early political films that rely on a 'clash' of heterogeneous elements (we might also say, on incongruity), in 'staging a strangeness of the familiar and testifying to a reality marked by antagonism' (Rancière 2004: 224–225). This procedure is in turn exemplary of the politics of that which Rancière calls the aesthetic regime of art. This regime, which first came to prominence in the era of Romanticism, not least through the influence of Schlegel and Novalis, identifies art as a paradoxical knot of autonomy and heteronomy, art and non-art (Rancière 2002: 137). Its political potential lies in the possibility of playing out one side of this paradox against the other: 'The main procedure of political or critical art consists in setting out the encounter and possibly the clash of heterogeneous elements [...] to provoke a break in our perception, to disclose some secret connection of things hidden behind the everyday reality' (Rancière 2014: 5). The idea of politics behind this definition of political art is Marxist or communist in so far as it designates emancipatory practices animated by a principle of radical equality that aim to expose the hidden antagonisms and alter the inequalities of the social order (Rancière 2010: 167). Rancière mentions Brecht as an 'archetype' of art committed to such a politics, but the 'work' of the Chinese student playing on the ambivalence of the bandage as a theatrical mask signalling aesthetic autonomy and a medical remedy testifying to the heteronomous powers of history also illustrates the idea.

According to Rancière, Godard's later works, most notably *Histoire(s) du Cinéma* (1988–1998), replace this dialectical clash with a symbolist montage that stages instead the hidden co-existence of all things and a mystical 'familiarity of the strange' (Rancière 2004: 225). In Rancière's view, this development is part of a general movement in recent decades from the aesthetic to an ethical regime of art, where concerns about political antagonism are overshadowed by questions of humanity and 'the inhuman' (231) accompanied by ethical musings on mourning, victimhood, sacrifice and unthinkable otherness (Rancière 1999: 125–136). A proper discussion of Rancière's arguments for this verdict lies beyond the scope of this article. It is thus at the risk of speculation that I suggest that one characteristic of the passage from the aesthetic to the ethical regime of art – in the case of Godard and perhaps more generally – is a trend to move from a political logic of comic incongruence towards a post-political, ethical logic of tragedy. This does not mean that comedies are no longer made, but it seems telling that those that have generated most public debate in recent years are films such as Roberto Benigni's *La Vita è Bella* (1997) or Sacha Baron Cohen's *Borat* (2006), which have primarily been discussed from an ethical perspective of 'proper' representation of historical catastrophes and cultural 'otherness'. Rancière does not himself consider the possible link between the politics of aesthetics and comic incongruity, and of course,

Godard's politics cannot be summed up in such a formulaic statement. Even so, it might be a link worth investigating further from a Marxist perspective on film comedy.

The comic character: identity and power

In her recent book, *The Odd One In – On Comedy*, Alenka Zupančič offers an investigation of comedy and the comical character in particular from a philosophical point of view similar to that of her Slovenian compatriot Slavoj Žižek – that is to say, inspired by Hegel, Lacan and Marxist ideology critique. Zupančič's definition of comedy is decidedly formal. Taking her cue from Hegel's treatment of comedy in *The Phenomenology of the Spirit*, she argues that the comic character is defined by a particular integration of a universal in a concrete individuality. Contrary to a Bakhtinian view, it is not a question of living materiality subverting abstract ideas, but the manifestation of the universal *in* the material:

> Comedy is not the undermining of the universal, but its (own) reversal into the concrete; it is not an objection to the universal, but the concrete labor or work of the universal itself. Or to put it in a single slogan: comedy is the universal at work. (Zupančič 2008: 27)

This would explain why comedies and comic figures are often named after abstract concepts or character traits (think of Shakespeare's *Measure for Measure* and *The Taming of the Shrew*; Molière's *Miser* and *Misanthrope*; or Chaplin's 'Tramp' and 'Worker') instead of individual names (as in classical tragedies, where the individual is often set *against* the universality of law and destiny: *Antigone, Oedipus, Hamlet* and so on). As an embodiment of an abstract universal concept in a concrete individual, the comic hero introduces the moment of self-consciousness which the abstract universal lacks in itself (Zupančič 2008: 38). The stuff of comedy is thus the relation of the universal to itself in and through the concrete individual.

To illustrate this abstract definition, Zupančič revisits the archetypical comic episode: a self-important baron who slips on a banana peel and falls into a puddle only to get up and continue his walk unaffected. What we are laughing at here, according to Zupančič, is not an abstract-universal idea (the elevated nature of aristocracy), undermined by a slip into the materiality of common human existence. Rather than the slip itself, the funny thing is that the baron continues his walk unperturbedly, for this demonstrates his 'unshakeable belief in himself and his own importance: that is to say, his presumptuousness' (Zupančič 2008: 29) – and much more than his fall it is this belief manifested in his behaviour that constitutes his basic, laughable humanity. The puddle, then, is not the site of concrete reality, but a prop or device – and such props can be highly unrealistic – through which 'the very concreteness or humanity of the concept itself – in our case, the concept of baronage or aristocracy – is processed, crystalized, and concretized' (Zupančič 2008: 30). Or, to cite Zupančič's paraphrase of Lacan, 'It is not some poor chap who believes himself to be a king who is comical, but a king who believes that he really is a king' (32).

There is a link between Zupančič's definition of comedy and the theory of ideology developed by Slavoj Žižek. In *The Sublime Object of Ideology*, Žižek argues against the idea of ideology as 'false consciousness' – an illusion covering social reality – and instead promotes an idea of ideology as 'a fantasy-construction which serves as support for our "reality" itself: an "illusion" which structures our effective, real social relations and thereby masks some insupportable, real, impossible kernel' (Žižek 2008: 45). In our previous example, such a fantasy is involved in the baron's belief in his aristocratic nature (while the 'impossible kernel' masked by this belief is the real contingency of social identities). In other words, the object of laughter in Zupančič is the ideological fantasy that acts in and through the subject – a fantasy that often in comedies seems to drag the subject along involuntarily but irresistibly.

This formal description allows Zupančič to draw a distinction between 'true and false comedies', which 'broadly corresponds to the distinction between subversive and conservative' (Žižek 2008: 30). The formula of the latter is the following: 'the aristocrat [...] is also a man (who snores, farts, slips, and is subject to the same physical laws as other mortals' (Žižek 2008: 30). This kind of comedy relies on the peaceful co-existence of the abstract and the concrete in its attempt to remind us that even the elites are only human. But as Zupančič notes, this separation of the abstract aristocrat and the concrete man is itself utterly abstract, and while this type of comedy invites sympathetic identification with the human weakness of the man ('we are all fallible'), it leaves the ego-ideal of the aristocrat and the social hierarchy it supports untouched. A 'true' comedy, on the contrary, exposes the fundamental incongruity between men and their fantasies in all its concrete materiality. While this kind of comedy extracts laughter from the over-investment in social identities, the desire to *be* somebody, it is also always – and precisely at the point when a character identifies the most with his social role, when he or she *is* somebody – involved in disidentification, offering a glimpse of the contingency of the social order in the exposure of the gap between the desiring subject and its ego-ideal (Žižek 2008: 31–32).

One can find a number of examples of this idea of true comedy in films that deal with authoritarian rulers and power. An often used emblematic visual illustration of the identification/disidentification of the comic character is the scene in which a powerful person is seen next to his own idealised portrait. One could think here of Chaplin's dictator, who has a bust of himself on his desk; Mr. Dickinson, the steelwork owner in the town of Machine in Jarmusch's *Dead Man* (1995), who has a giant portrait of himself carrying a gun behind his desk; or Baron Cohen's Middle-Eastern dictator, who is repeatedly portrayed in front of propaganda posters with his own idealised visage. A perfect verbal version of this visual representation is Hitler's salute in Ernst Lubitsch's *To Have or Not to Have* (1942): 'Heil myself!' (Figure 5.5). One can, of course, discuss if all these films are 'true' comedies all the way through: Chaplin's speech at the end of *The Great Dictator (1940)* could be interpreted as a concession to 'false' comedy; and the love story in Cohen's *The Dictator* (2012) balances between acting out and parodying the conservative conventions of romantic comedies in the Jane Austen tradition of rich-guy-meets-clever-girl (both are prejudiced, but learn that the other is *also* just a human being). In that light, rather than providing us with clear-cut distinctions between conservative and progressive comedies, Zupančič's terms seem more apt at detecting and conceptualising the often conflicting political tendencies within filmic comedies Figure 5.5.

That said, Zupančič's formal definition of 'true' comedy can hardly stand alone. As we can see from her example of the presumptuous baron, the laughter of this type of comedy is close to ridicule. Now, this can easily be understood as 'progressive' in the particular case of the aristocrat. But what if the comic character was a member of an oppressed minority (say, in different epochs of Western history, a Jew, an Afro-American or homosexual), embodying the entire stereotypical 'essence' of such a person? In other words, could 'true' comedy not as easily ridicule the powerless as the powerful and thus serve a demonising, oppressing politics rather than a progressive one? Zupančič's confidence that a definition of comedy can dispense with any consideration of its content seems to rely on the widespread Leftist presumption that the conservative Right is fundamentally humourless. But as Michael Billig observes, this is hardly the case in an age where even the former President of the United States can joke about his own illiteracy to the applause of the rich and powerful, while Right-wing commentators

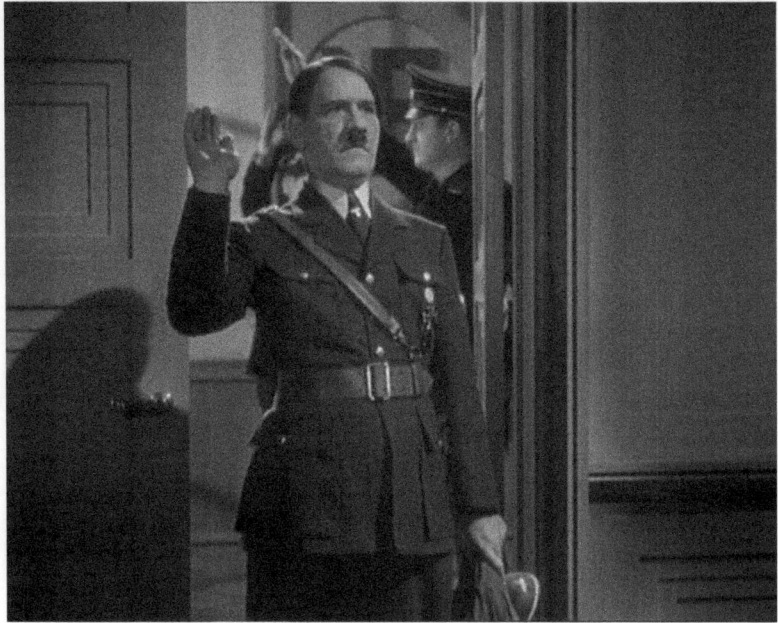

Figure 5.5   'Heil myself!' – Tom Dugan as Hitler
Source: Screen capture from *To Be or Not to Be* (1942), dir. Ernst Lubitsch, United Artists

and radio hosts compete about jokes that transgress the boundaries of the 'political correctness' associated with the Centre Left (Billig 2005: 241). Challenging political correctness and its humanist underpinnings is also an obvious task for true comedy in Zupančič's sense, but from a formal perspective, the line between a progressive transgression and the sadistic ridicule denounced by Adorno, cannot be drawn easily. To do that, one would have to complement Zupančič's Hegelianism with a Marxist historical analysis of the specific content and context of a particular comedy. For to cause laughter, comedy always depends on a socio-cultural framework with its internal and external power relations – and no other critical tradition has contributed more to the understanding of such relations than that inaugurated by Karl Marx.

The last laugh

Comedy is a contested genre that seems particularly resistant to theoretical conceptualisation. Any serious, abstract definition of the comical might itself soon become an object of laughter – like the idealist philosophers ridiculed by Marx in *The German Ideology*. One reason why comedy is so slippery is that it draws life from the ability to shift perspective, to perceive the structures and norms of society from a different side – not least their material 'underside'. Marxist ideology critique has the same aim, and shares with traditional comedy the hope for a happy ending – that the oppressed will have the last laugh. Even so, Marxist approaches are not abundant in film comedy studies. In this article, I have sketched out four different takes on film comedy from a Marxist perspective in the hope that it might serve as inspiration for further studies in this field. For as the examples have illustrated, comedies are able to both powerfully expose social conflicts and defend the *status quo* – and Marxist theories are particularly well equipped to articulate and qualify both sides of comedies.

The four perspectives, I have presented, are only separated for the purpose of conceptual clarity, and hardly even that. The notion of incongruity, for example, is not only central for the definition of wit, but could also be said to be at the heart of Zupančič's idea of comic characters as concrete universals. In many films, a variety of comic techniques and tendencies is at work, sometimes mixed with other genres, so the critic must thus be able combine different analytical perspectives, developing the theoretical approach in continuous dialogue with the objects of investigation. True comedy is always moving, ever on the lookout for the overlooked perspective. In the spirit of comic couples from Don Quixote and Sancho Panza to Laurel and Hardy and beyond, it invites the Marxist critic to come along.

Notes

1. Although Adorno's critique of comedy in *The Dialectics of Enlightenment* also targets Chaplin's *The Great Dictator*, his two brief essays on Chaplin written on other occasions present a positive evaluation of the comedian (Adorno 1996). Shea Coulson includes these essays as evidence for the existence of a little-studied relation between progressive art and laughter in Adorno's work (Coulson 2007).
2. Each year between 1991 and 2010, comedy films have accounted for approximately twenty percent of the top 50 grossing Hollywood productions (Redfern 2012: 150).
3. Another entry point to this complicity between totalitarian regimes and 'rebellious' laughter is provided by Hans Speier, who observes that 'whispered jokes' told by citizens in authoritarian societies about their rulers can ease 'the adaptation to the discipline and regimen of a strict regime' and thus serve as alibies for those who dare not rebel rather than offer any real resistance (Speier 1998: 1395).
4. My translation.

5. My translation.
6. The reference to Althusser's term here is not accidental. Guillaume ends his interview by quoting the last lines of the chapter on Brecht in *Pour Marx* about an 'unfamiliar play [...] pursuing in me its incomplete meaning, searching in me, despite myself, now that all the actors and sets have been cleared away, for the advent of its silent discourse' (Althusser 2005: 151). For Guillaume, the act of the Chinese student is precisely such an 'unfamiliar play'.

Bibliography

Adorno, Theodor W. (1996) [1930/1964] 'Chaplin Times Two', *The Yale Journal of Criticism*, Vol. 9, no. 1, pp. 57–61.

Adorno, Theodor W. & Max Horkheimer (2002) [1944] *The Dialectics of Enlightenment – Philosophical Fragments*, trans. Edmund Jephcott (Stanford: Stanford University Press).

Althusser, Louis (2005) [1965] *For Marx*, trans. Ben Brewster (London & New York: Verso).

Bakhtin, Mikhail (1984) [1965] *Rabelais and His World*, trans. HélèneIswolsky (Bloomington: Indiana University Press).

Benjamin, Walter (1967) [1934] 'Der Autorals Produzent', *Versucheüber Brecht* (Frankfurt a.M.: Suhrkamp Verlag), pp. 95–116.

Billig, Michael (2005) *Laughter and Ridicule – Towards a Social Critique of Humour* (London: Sage Publications).

Bordwell, David (1993) *The Cinema of Eisenstein* (Cambridge, Mass. & London: Harvard University Press).

Brenez, Nicole (2005) 'Jean-Luc Godard, *Witz* et invention formelle (notes préparatoiressur les rapports entre critique et pouvoirsymbolique)' *Cinémas – Revue d'étudescinématographiques/Cinémas – Journal of Film Studies*, vol. 15, no. 2–3, pp. 15–43.

Coulson, Shea (2007) 'Funnier than Unhappiness: Adorno and the Art of Laughter', *New German Critique*, Vol. 34, no. 1, pp. 141–163.

Eisenstein, Sergei M. (1996) [1935] 'Bolsheviks Do Laugh (Thoughts on Soviet Comedy)', in Richard Taylor (ed.) *Selected Works*, vol. 3 (London: BFI Publishing), pp. 68–72.

Marx, Karl (2010) [1852] 'The Eighteenth Brumaire of Louis Bonaparte', in Karl Marx and Friedrich Engels *Collected Works*, Vol. 11 (London: Lawrence &Wishart with Electric Book).

Marx, Karl & Friedrich Engels,(2010) [1845–1846] 'The German Ideology', in Karl Marx and Friedrich Engels *Collected Works*, vol. 5 (London: Lawrence &Wishart with Electric Book).

Mortimer, Lorraine (2008) 'The World Tasted: Dušan Makavejev'sSweet Movie', *Senses of Cinema*, vol. 47 (http://sensesofcinema.com/2008/feature-articles/sweet-movie-mortimer/).

Parvulescu, Anca (2010) *Laughter – Notes on a Passion* (London & Cambridge, Mass.: MIT Press).

Rancière, Jacques (2002) 'The Aesthetic Revolution and its Outcomes – Emplotments of Autonomy and Heteronomy', *New Left Review*, Vol. 14 pp. 133–151.

Rancière, Jacques (1999) [1995] *Dis-agreement – Politics and Philosophy*, trans. Julie Rose (Minneapolis and London: University of Minnesota Press).

Rancière, Jacques (2004) 'Godard, Hitchcock, and the Cinematographic Image', in Michael Temple, James S. Williams, Michael Witt (eds) *For Ever Godard* (London: Black Dog Publishing), pp. 214–231.

Rancière, Jacques (2006) [2001] *Film Fables*, trans. Emilio Battista (Oxford, New York: Berg).

Rancière, Jacques (2010) 'Communists Without Communism?', in Costas Douzinas & Slavoj Žižek (eds) *The Idea of Communism* (London & New York: Verso), pp. 167–177.

Rancière, Jacques (2014) 'Politics of Aesthetics', http://theater.kein.org/node/93 (10.1 2014).

Redfern, Nick (2012) 'Genre Trends at the US Box Office', *European Journal of American Culture*, vol. 31, no. 2, pp. 145–167.

Speier, Hans (1998) 'Wit and Politics – An Essay on Power and Laughter', *American Journal of Sociology*, vol. 103, no. 5, pp. 1352–1401.

Stott, Andrew (2010) *Comedy* (New York & London: Routledge).

Žižek, Slavoj (2008) *The Sublime Object of Ideology* (London: Verso).

Zupančič, Alenka (2008) *The Odd One In – On Comedy* (Cambridge & London: MIT Press).

6
Workerist Film Humour

Dennis Rothermel

> *Grau, teurer Freund, ist alle Theorie...*
> Karl Marx to Friedrich Engels, 20 August 1862
> (Marx and Engels 1987: 74)

Singularly meaningful laughter

Humour isn't a simple thing, and it is not always the same. Humour can say more than can be expressed in grey statements of theory. Unusual laughter means something unusual.

Walter Huston, as Howard the gold prospector, laughs at the end of John Huston's *The Treasure of the Sierra Madre* (1948). He laughs, and laughs, and laughs some more. He stops to catch his breath, and then laughs some more. He explains to Curtain (Tim Holt), why it's funny, gets him to laugh, and they both laugh. They stop, go sit down, and burst into laughter again. Howard laughs for all of a minute and 20 seconds, which is a long time for a film to show someone just laugh. It's unusual.

Howard's laughter marks the climax of the story, which had not evoked much mirth at all. Howard's is not sarcastic laughter, nor farcical laughter, nor laughter at someone, nor resentful laughter, nor desperate laughter, nor hysterical laughter. It is joyous laughter, laughter that Walter Huston sustains concertedly, boisterously, and unreservedly – as if it were the laughter that resolved all worldly ailments, failures, needs, hopes, troubles and desires. But it is not the joy of finding love, nor the joy of finding redemption, nor the joy of finding vocation, nor the joy of finding success. Quite specifically, it is *not* the joy of finding fortune. It is from having *lost* a fortune that Howard laughs, and laughs, and laughs some more. Losing a fortune does not automatically inspire joy.

123

Curtain is perplexed at first, until Howard beseeches him to see the humour in fate or the deity or whatever it is that is having fun at their expense, for the wind has blown the gold dust back up into the mountains where they got it. Having been at first puzzled at Howard's mirth, Curtain then takes the cue and laughs as well – laughing long, hard and as freely exuberantly as does Howard.

Howard, Curtain and Dobbs (Humphrey Bogart) endured the tortuous labour of mining gold for ten months in an unforgiving, mountainous desert wilderness. There would be no easy reason for this laughter coming so easily. They survived their own growing suspicion of each other, fended off an attack by bandits and once came to the point of deciding that they needed to murder an innocent stranger rather than let him muscle in on or even learn about their prospecting diggings. Curtain and Dobbs learned from Howard the hard work and expertise it takes to mine gold. The gold dust that they had gathered was enough to make all three men comfortably rich for the rest of their lives. So what's so funny about losing all that hard-earned fortune?

Dobbs and Curtain had met Howard in a boarding house in Tampico and listened with rapt attention to the tales he told of prospecting. Howard also told them of the dangers of finding gold. Partners become ruthless rivals who could be tempted to murder just by the logic of the situation of having fortunes at hand in isolated wilderness locales beyond the rule of law. Dobbs and Curtain proclaimed they would never succumb to that kind of greed, but Howard notes carefully how Dobbs talks lasciviously of becoming rich. The diminution of humanity that comes from affliction with gold fever will be the greater risk of their expedition. Curtain and Howard will each have an avenue to happiness in the end, even without wealth. But even if Dobbs had not perished, his life would surely always have been miserable once he became committed to pursuing wealth single-mindedly, to protecting that wealth, and to using it to impose his will and vanity upon whomever. Howard will count Dobbs as a partner even though he observes Dobbs' predisposition for greed and domination. There is both hope and cautious pragmatism in Howard accepting Curtain and Dobbs as partners.

During that first encounter in the Tampico boarding house, Howard explained that it is not because it is scarce that gold is worth what it is. A thousand prospectors go out into the mountains and only one of them strikes it rich. The value of the gold the lucky one brings back is equal to the cost of the labour of all one thousand prospectors. That labour is hard, indeed. It is when Dobbs and Curtain are ready to quit the expedition, too exhausted just from the ascent into the mountains, that

Howard bursts into one of just a few moments of laughter in the film. For where they have flopped down dejected and exhausted is precisely on the ground where there are the first traces of gold dust. Howard laughs hard here, too, leaping spontaneously into gleeful dance. His laughter is at their expense, but just because it's so funny – two would-be prospectors capitulate exactly when they have the clues of striking it rich literally right before their noses on the ground where they lie. Only they can't see it.

Howard enjoys a reflective distance upon the circumstance of gold prospecting. We see this in his exuberant dance, his finding humour in the human drama of two men close enough to taste what they crave but who cannot recognise it, his careful perception of Dobbs' fixation upon wealth, and his acquisition of a perspective to understand the labour of gold prospectors as a combined economic force. It is Howard's reflective distance that allows him such inestimable mirth at the end. What the wind does to the gold dust is funny beyond comprehension, but only if one could appreciate a larger standpoint beyond one's own immediate predicament. A wizened prospector such as Howard may come to that distanced perspective, and he might be able to impart it to Curtain, just as readily as he was able to teach Curtain and Dobbs the techniques for mining gold. But Dobbs will never have that perspective. Hence we have a small set of possibilities for gold prospectors coming to comprehend the broader context of their labour. Howard attains that wisdom, Curtain can learn it and Dobbs probably never will. For Dobbs, wisdom remains grey and remote.

Sneaky Marxism

John Huston adapted the screenplay for *The Treasure of the Sierra Madre* from the novel by the writer known as B. Traven (Grobel 1989: 283–285; Huston 1979). Huston had first planned to make this film several years before World War II but Huston's wartime documentary work intervened (235). He was able to commence work on it after the war, casting his father, Walter, as Howard, who is the major protagonist of the film. Walter agreed to play the role without his dentures, giving his character the toothless diction of an older man (282–286). Traven was famously reclusive. He wrote under a pseudonym. The generally held hypothesis is that he was a German who emigrated to Mexico. Details about his origins and early years remain speculative (Guthke 1991: 63–105). Traven's novel explores national politics, military adventurism, the plight of labourers working at the margins of industrial economy, and the organisation of labour in the business of oil drilling. Those themes corroborate a sophisticated Marxist world-view, consistent with Traven's novels generally. Traven's stories are spectacularly dramatic though episodic, and edifying though entirely without jargon or didacticism. There is enough in the film's narrative from the much longer and more detailed novel to show how especially in the marginal elements of global economy the advantage in the competition of capital investments even on a small scale goes to the labour contractor who can reduce costs and maintain the difference between labour-power contracted and wages paid (or not paid) by play-ing upon the desperation and naivety of transient workers. The lessons imparted derive from particulars such as people who labour can come to understand as elemental to the conditions of their labour. So steeped is Traven's narrative just in the facts of the conditions of labour that the novel's third person narrative rarely needs to impart what characters think privately. Insights into how they cope with these conditions are evident in what they do and say, which makes for a smooth adaptation into cinema narrative. So the clue we get that Howard understands Dobbs' frailty about wealth from the outset is one that encompasses the broader arc of character development of the story (Traven 2010: 51, 68). John Huston shows this simply, though there is no direct correlate to this moment of perspicacity in the novel. Huston positions Howard sitting down with Curtain and Dobbs standing before him. Their faces are just barely off the top edge of the frame, so that it is just Howard's reaction that we see. As the two younger men fantasise about their pros-pects for wealth, we see Howard's surreptitious glance at Dobbs from below and thus understand how Howard is apprised at the outset of the danger that Dobbs might eventually pose.

Walter Huston's exuberant dance on the mountainside is another emendation of the story without exact derivation from the source text (78), nor is it indicated in John Huston's script (Huston 1979: 86). The elder Huston improvised the laughter and dance, surprising son John. The laughter reprised what Walter had devised for his performance in the lead role in a 1934 Broadway production of *Othello*, and the dance was a jig that Eugene O'Neill had taught him (Grobel 1989: 170–171, 292). John loved the improvisation, and one guesses that the extended laughter in the last scene was at the instigation of the elder and junior Hustons. Howard's culminating laughter comprises only a sentence in the source text (Traven 2010: 306), and it is hardly indicated as longer than that in Huston's script (Huston 1979: 194). Decades later, and dec-ades after Walter Huston's death, John Huston named this exuberant dance when prompted for a single image 'in a time capsule and label it John Huston, director' (Long 2001, 47). Even without needing to articulate the meaning of the unusual duration of laughter that comes at the end of the film, its significance was implanted upon John Huston, certainly enough to indulge it.

The most interesting change from novel to film is the speech about gold that Howard delivers in the boarding house in Tampico. In the novel, Howard talks about the allure of the glitter of gold as a source of its power and valuation, and how dreams of riches skew perceptions of gold's real value (Traven 2010: 51–55). Explication of the worth of gold *in terms of the labour theory of value* appears in the screenplay and in the film, but not in the novel (Huston 1979: 61). In the novel, Howard also tells how 'one prospector out of ten thousand would make a hundred thousand dollars inside of six months', but the connection he then makes is not to how this establishes the value of gold but to how singular reports of even extremely rare success fuel the fever among twenty thousand more (Traven 2010: 65). Howard also extols the necessity for hard work to win the gold, warning Dobbs and Curtain, 'Gold means hard work, and very hard work at that ... There are very few men in the world, or in all history, who have actually made millions by digging for gold' (77). But this, too, isn't the same point as the labours of thousands creating the value of the gold retrieved by the one lucky prospector. The labour theory of value provided Marx with the means to elucidate capitalism's dependency upon extracting surplus value from the labourer's sale of labour-power for wages. That a simple rendition of the labour theory of value arises seamlessly in the context of a mainstream Hollywood film is unusual indeed in 1948, on the brink of government and industry campaigns to repress radical voices in Hollywood. *And yet that no one notices* is as much good cause for prolonged boisterous laughter as Howard's mirth at the end of the film. (See Agee 1958: 290–293, 329–333, 398–401; Brill 1997: 20–21, 24–25; Crowther 1948; Ebert 2003; Engell 1993: 83–87; Grobel 2000: 291; Naremore 1979: 14).

Applying the labour theory of value to the price of gold posed Karl Marx with a compelling issue to resolve. There would be no commodity with a value seemingly independent of the cost of labour in its production other than gold. So, either this would reveal a telltale weakness in the theory, or an opportunity to demonstrate its explanatory robustness. Marx divided the issue: The metallic value of gold is a function of the labour expended in mining and processing it. But the value of gold as money or a repository of wealth no longer pertains to gold as a commodity but rather as the economic means of exchange (Marx 1992a: 184–186; see Steedman 1985: 562–564).

So how did this Marxist mini-discourse on the value of gold get into the film? John Huston was initially convinced that Hal Croves, the individual who participated on Traven's behalf in the production of the film in Mexico, was indeed Traven himself, and not as he presented himself, namely as Traven's representative. Traven had composed a script for the film adaptation, which Huston possessed before he began writing his screenplay (Guthke 1991: 331). Perhaps the injection of the labour theory of value applied to gold arose in Traven's consultation during production in Mexico through his proxy or through him posing as his proxy. Perhaps it was entirely the input of the man who was indeed just his representative. Huston felt disabused of the assumption of the identity of author and author's representative due to Croves' persistent nagging interference, which Huston thought improbable to attribute to the author of the brilliantly nuanced novel (Grobel 1989: 286–287). Initially, Traven had praised Huston's script, specifically for leaving Curtin and Howard penniless in the end (285). After filming had finished, Traven announced he would have nothing further to do with Huston (290, 310–311). So, in the end, the two men came to agreement in their mutual regard just as they had been at the outset, though both having reversed their initial impressions.

Traven envisioned a future cinema, one where 'the plot is superseded by the idea, by the basic argument which led up to the plot, and the plot will be used merely to make visible the tendency the writer had in mind and wanted to drive home' (Guthke 1991: 330). The episodic story *The Treasure of the Sierra Madre* – in both novel and film – and the anti-dramatic conclusion amplified by the prolonged laughter in the concluding scene of the film would be emblematic of cinema in which the plot recedes from the film's impact. John Huston forged the film as anti-Hollywood as was then possible: movie star appeal undermined by scruffy appearances and petty behaviour, the main protagonist's toothless diction, no romance and no women, non-exoticism in the Mexican locale, nothing remotely beautiful in the desert mountain wilderness, anti-climatic, and an absurdly dramatic reversal that counts as upbeat only ironically.

Huston's resolute iconoclastic naturalism did get noticed in contemporary reception of the film (Naremore 1979: 31). Huston chose to shoot on location far from the direct control of the studio just in order to get away from all the usual studio interference (Grobel 1989: 293). Warner Brothers marketed the film with emphasis on the treasure hunt.

Poster images show of the three prospectors on horseback, a voluptuous woman, Mexican *banditos* in sombreros charging en masse on horseback and so on – none of which appears in the film (Naremore 1979: 22). Just as startling, though, is how the radical political content is missed, both in contemporary reception and in the legacy of scholarship on the film. As noted, Howard's exposition in the screenplay and in the film of the morally degrading magical appeal of the glitter of gold and the seductive illusions about sudden wealth does derive from the text, as does much of the screenplay. But these points resonate in apolitical religious and secular teachings generally, and are not central to Marxist thought. But the labour theory of value *is* – though in itself hardly enough to adumbrate the whole of Marxist economic theory. And so, this odd ingredient of Howard's speech in the boarding house in Tampico, which is in the film but not in the book, *still doesn't get noticed*, and it is the most important point of the political thrust of the story.

Intellectuals and academics typically comprehend Marxism as within the domain of debates about distribution of goods and welfare for the working poor. Situating Marxist thought as one point at one far end of a continuum of contemporary political sentiment misses the fundamental challenge Marx posed to the organisation of labour and the exploitation of the means of production that define capitalism. Aside from missing the vital clue of Howard's explication of the value of gold, the critical focus on how well the film imparts a properly socialist attitude, worldview or ideology reverts to the kind of intellectual posturing that derives more from traditions of philosophy still in the throes of theology that Marx thoroughly disdained. Rather famously, Marx associated radical thought with 'grasping things by the root'. That makes radicalness a qualitative conceptual distinction, and not a matter of being more radical, or most radical or extremely radical within the extant spectrum of relative positions in bourgeois political thought (Marx 1975: 251; Marx 1977b, 1977c; see Brill 1997: 22–23, 30; Engell 1993; Naremore 1979: 16–17). Somehow, in this serendipitous collaboration of two singular but headstrong creative individuals – John Huston and B. Traven – who did not get along with each other, was the cooperative instigation nevertheless of something utterly unique in the history of Hollywood cinema, *and yet no one notices*, particularly not even those who explore the film in terms of its perceived Leftist sympathies.

The loss of the gold back to the mountain is funny, though funny only from a certain perspective. But that wouldn't be enough to inspire that deep, exuberant and prolonged laughter. It is precisely that injection of the labour theory of value applied simplistically to the worth of gold that informs the profound exuberance of Howard's laughter at the end of the film. The laughter comes at the point of realisation of release from the domain of labour governed by the material conditions of labour, where all economic value devolves to labour provided, or, more properly in capitalism, to a significant quantum more than the wages paid for the labour provided. Howard's laughter is deep and gleeful because the gold no longer has value for him. The conditions whereby the wages for his labour translate to wealth – be it meagre or large – no longer govern his life. Howard's realisation that this could be so for him comes from his adoption by a local village as its doctor and designated wise elder. It is this transformation in his life, where he no longer has need of gold or wealth, that makes Howard's prolonged, exuberant outburst of laughter possible and gleeful. It is the laughter of release from how the world structures our lives, work and endeavours to conform to absurd and debilitating rules that are in force just because they happen to maximise profits. Howard's laughter grasps things by the root.

Comedy in mainstream cinema has become predominantly a matter of endless successions of snappy one-liners, come-back lines, and puerile gags. The political or intellectual perspective of the whole of it amounts to nothing, subject to an ambiguous mealy-mouthed 'message' that anyone can associate with whatever beliefs they may harbour about values and purpose. Slapstick toilet jokes are *de rigeur* for movies intended for children, and kicks to the crotch for older audiences. Moreover, it is the easy reliance upon common stereotypes that directs the dramatic continuity away from anything approaching depth. Playing upon stereotypes also figures heavily in comedy in contemporary mainstream cinema. Hollywood movie characters affect exaggerated vocal intonation, dialect or telltale outlook that is automatically associated with ethnicity, gender, sexual orientation, race, age or economic class. The induced laughter celebrates the invocation of difference, but in the sense of acceptance of safely circumscribed stereotypes. Where the character who delivers the funny line shows the upper hand in the exchange, then the stereotype is positive, and negative if it shows the character up as boorish, buffoonish, oafish or offish. But it is stereotype either way. The comedy of stereotypes will always play into a conservative political outlook – one that solidifies the way things are, one that encourages seeing people as set in their existing identities. Howard's laughter at the end of *The Treasure of the Sierra Madre* is not comedy of this sort. It is inventive laughter, amusement suddenly and deeply drawn at the peculiar circumstances – the irony of the fate of the gold dust arising precisely when Howard's release from the dominion of labour where his work always plays into the advantage of someone else. Hence the freely exuberant, actively sustained joyousness that Howard has realised accrues to what has happened *to* him or, better, what has happened *for* him. So Howard's sustained exuberant laughter constitutes an unusual humour – not humour of clichés, gags, stereotypes, and not the humour of farce or satire, either. None of these comedic tropes could sustain more than two seconds of laughter, much less Howard's one minute and 20 seconds. At the core of this humour is *a glimmer of how things could be different from how they are seemingly intransigently determined to be.* This will be an important humour for the sake of understanding Marxist cinema if it is to avoid the dreary trap of socialist realism, which is compelled to include grey theoretical points and which, as well, plays predominantly upon class stereotypes. Howard's laughter is innovative, liberating and inspirational – and hence he can laugh, and laugh, and laugh some more.

Marxian humour

Though amiably wry and ironic in personal correspondence, Marx was reputably so 'unemotional' and 'frigid' by nature that he was even unable to take delight in being young and living in Paris (Berlin 1978: 63). Exile, though, is likely to temper thrills of adventures abroad. Marx exercised little constraint in his proclivity for biting ridicule of theorists he considered not just profoundly wrong but negligently so. Marx's own humour is sardonic and unrestrained, such as befits the urgency that Marx saw in the endeavour to understand the material conditions of labour and how that constrained revolutionary praxis. Consistently, Marx disdained theoretical abstraction that showed no comprehension of those conditions and which thus reified utopian extrapolations of the prevailing rule of bourgeois legal and political structures. Given the urgency and magnitude of the possible outcomes, it's no wonder that Marx's acidic dismissiveness hardly assimilates the genteel, collegial discourse expected of contemporary academic theoreticians (Bimbach 1987: 193–211). When, thus, Marx invokes 'the *categorical imperative* to overthrow *all those conditions* in which man is an abased, enslaved, abandoned, contemptible being', it is with implied disdain for the ludicrously effete Kantian moral standpoint taken as a response to the dominance of oppression under capitalism (Marx 1978: 60). That these conditions call for the categorical imperative to overthrow them is *the very least* one could say.

Marx's sardonic humour shows again in the well-known passage in *The German Ideology*, where Marx and Engels echo utopian accounts of a socialist ideal in which one could 'hunt in the morning, fish in the afternoon, rear cattle in the evening, criticise after dinner' (Marx and Engels 1970: 53). Consistent with his mode of analysis and focus, Marx was theoretically loath to say anything about what a communist society would look like, and one could hardly take this depiction of an exhausting and haphazardly composed typical day seriously (Avineri 1970: 202–224). There is sufficient complexity in what Marx has to say about labour to adumbrate how labour can be meaningful or degrading, imaginative or rote, liberating or enslaving (Harvey 2010: 111–120). How the varieties of labour might be determined differently in some projected socialist organisation of labour does not address the root issue.

The passage in *The German Ideology* projecting freely chosen roles of endeavour is one of very few in the extant writings where Marx offers some hint as to what he might think a future communist society might look like. But of course it isn't that at all, so long as one pays attention to context. Marx's focus upon understanding the material conditions of labour separated his thinking from the legacy of political theorising and philosophy that he wished to jettison. The philosophical endeavour to understand political change in terms of abstract utopianism prevails in contemporary philosophy. In reverse perspective, Marx is 'not ... a philosopher but ... a revolutionary communist', 'who refused to speculate in detail about the nature of communism' – 'which [, however,] was not the realisation of a pre-determined moral ideal' – and who showed 'no interest in locating his criticism of capitalism in any of the traditions of moral philosophy, or explaining how he was generating a new tradition' (Wolff 2011). Thus one could not better misconstrue Marxian thought more severely than to find its place in the contemporary discourse of moral and political philosophy. To update the famous eleventh thesis on Feurbach, the philosophers have long since given up on interpreting the world variously, and now are absorbed in laboriously explicating the arcane intricacies of meta-theoretical arguments pertaining to social good. The point, however, is to change the world (Marx 1997b). Changing the world, for Marx, means first of all understanding it without the hindrance of mystifying conceptual structures that assimilate what is normal into what is necessary and normative. Just to understand what's at stake in the topical struggle of the length of the working day already poses the need to challenge how readily a discourse of 'rights' may seem to ground any feasible solution. Rather, understanding the conflict in terms of rights only obscures the real struggle, and also obscures how the struggle is a matter of force on both sides. The capitalist acts on his rights as a purchaser of labour, and the worker acts on his rights as a seller. So rights and law will not decide it. Force will decide it, and that is the underlying importance of where the struggle lies (Marx 1992a: 344).

It is not without inviting some measure of Marxian mirth that it is the remark about spending the day hunting, fishing, herding cattle and finally doing critique that is taken as the sole part of the corpus worth taking seriously as his own foundational philosophical principle, and, indeed, understood as a utopian projection (Rawls 1999: 460n). Consistent with that barrier of incomprehensibility is the citation of Marx's *Critique of the Gotha Program* as undertaking principles of determining fairness in the allocation of benefits. It was Marx's intent, ever so briefly, to demonstrate how the Gotha experiment had naively presumed that that problem could be easily sorted out, which, however, does not make that issue decisive for radical praxis (268n). But, of course, for Marx the fixation on the issue of fairness only capitulates to the prevailing rule of bourgeois social and legal structures (Marx 1977a: 564–570). Again, what Marx had disdainfully touched upon in passing, as something only absurdly necessary by context to discuss, is taken as the inner core of his thought. He would have had to have found it amusing – exasperating, perhaps, but worth a good laugh.

Workerism

An important element of 20th-century Italian Leftist political activity and discourse has fallen under the nomenclature of *workerism* (*operaismo*) (Wright 2002: 63–88). Although initially strongly reliant upon a classical definition of the working class as connected with factory labourers, the theoretical expansion into a broader definition of work capable of revolutionary action arose eventually, particularly with the theoretical writings and personal activism of Antonio Hardt and Negri, 2002b: 138–139. Aside from reference to Italian progressive political activity, and with direct reference to essential points in Volume 1 of Marx's *Das Capital*, we can best understand the underlying notion first simply as the assertion of need for action on the part of the working class, in response to which capitalist forces are reactive, rather than vice versa (Marx 1992a: 408–409; Wright 2002: 3–5). Workers lose out if they are continually reactive to how capital dictates the conditions of labour. Second, capitalist leadership implements machinery and automation in response to gains that workers win in the class struggle (Marx 1992a: 561–564). It is, thus, the extant outlook of how workers – in solidarity – comprehend their situation that establishes the starting point for political tactics, rather than a theoretically remote conceptualisation imposed upon that situation. Michael Hardt and Antonio Negri have shown how this element of radical political thought still has efficacy in the context of globalisation (Hardt and Negri 2002a).

Action will be difficult to initiate if its purpose and rationale do not have a clear connection with immanent circumstances as well as the class-consciousness of workers. Comedy that plays upon cheap stereotypes served up in capsule portions is inherently capitalist, because it presumes amenability to the predictable but conditioned reaction to the ways the social context preserves prevalent identities. The humour that takes in the viewpoint of the whole, that is timely and innovative and hence active rather than reactive, and also without delusion, but yet inventively visionary and thus contrary to immanent circumstances, such as Howard's, is humour in a particularly workerist manner. Howard's laughter in joyous elation seeing how the gold has blown back up into the mountain revels in that *glimmer of how things could be different from how they are seemingly intransigently determined to be*, which is to say, exactly Marx's point in *The German Ideology*, that labour for those who labour can be something not inexorably determined. It is a glimmer, and a humour, that only those who labour can experience genuinely. And so it is the *workerist* sense of humour that entertains this specific kind of laughter.

In addition to *The Treasure of the Sierra Madre*, four films – Ugo Gregoretti's *Omicron* (1964), Ermanno Olmi's *Il Posto* (*The Job*, 1961), Ken Loach's *The Navigators* (2001), and Želimir Žilnik's *The Old School of Capitalism* (2009) – demonstrate humour that is active rather than reactive and also aligned to the viewpoint comprehending a mindset not wholly, or at least not thoroughly, moulded by the conditions of labour. These films exhibit a humour that provides a glimmer into the negation of those conditions. We don't see Howard's boisterous laughter repeated in any of these films – but a sympathetic humour presides. These films feature protagonists who are painfully aware, at least for a moment, of how they don't belong to how their lives, their work and their identities have been defined for them by the conditions of labour to which they are neither happily nor wilfully committed. By posing challenges to dominant socialising influences, these cinematic efforts demonstrate progressive humour. By striking at the core of alienation, they are radical. By creating a context of humour sustained without reliance upon cheap gags, come-back lines and stereotypes, they attain contextual depth, while avoiding tendentious polemic. Howard's mirth is not that of a belly-laugh, a smirk, a guffaw, a chuckle – it is an exuberant burst of liberating laughing out loud upon release from how the world structures life stupidly. Workerist humour offers us a taste of that same kind of mirth.

Working on the Railroad

In a letter to an acquaintance, Marx wrote that he tried to get a job on the railroad, but wasn't hired because of his notoriously poor penmanship. Lucky or not?, Marx wondered. But he was joking, of course (Marx and Engels 1987: 72).

In an early scene in *The Navigators*, a supervisor addresses a meeting of a group of 15 British railway workers. He talks of the importance of this morning's briefing, which already inspires the men's jokes in response. The supervisor is clearly one from their own ranks who has been promoted into low-level management. One senses, nevertheless, that until this moment he had held the respect of the gathered men as the person who served as their representative liaison with middle management of the national rail. But his tone already suggests something new in that relationship, especially the fact of him insisting upon an authoritarian tone that ostensibly has never before been a pretence that he ventured to put on. The national institution has been privatised and divided into competitive segments. So the three men who had been on loan from another contingent must leave since they are now employees of a competitor and hence their presence cannot be allowed in this briefing. All guffaw at the thought that three friends and co-workers are now industry spies. And the ridiculing joking intensifies.

The supervisor reads hesitantly from a printed loose-leaf handbook, stumbling on every point. One guesses he acquired the handbook at a management-led workshop where he was schooled in the rhetoric of structural change, which he has been instructed to impart to the workforce that he supervises. But the jargon rings false and strange and he is obviously still finding it difficult to recite this rhetoric naturally, to use it as if it were his own and as if it made sense. Increasingly he stumbles over the jargon that he's only vaguely assimilated, and the men's spontaneous jovial heckling continues. He explains that they will need to compose a mission statement. None of the men have any idea of what that is or why they should want one. What's a mission statement? The supervisor abandons all pretence of understanding what he is supposed to impart at this point and puts it into his own words.

'A mission statement', he says, 'says what we are going to do. And then we have to do it'. Great guffawing and joking explode at this point. What actually happens with mission statements is to have on record, with the force of mandate, an established norm for performance and outcomes that is impossible to realise, and thus to create a context that guarantees the critical ascertainment of inevitable failure to meet lofty goals. Management wants the workers to write their own mission statement that management can use as the basis for diminishing wages and finding redundancies in personnel. All of this will happen by the end of the story in *The Navigators*, though the task of composing a mission statement will have long been forgotten.

We see workerist humour at full throttle in the opening scenes of *The Navigators*. The railway workers will at this point have little inkling what sort of transformations they are facing and, truly, the battle is already lost by the time of that initial briefing and their humorous flights. There is no hint in that early scene set in the familiar confines of where they can feel most in control of their place in the institution, where there is some sense of the space belonging to them, just as they will have had no inkling of how one of their own could have become – ineptly as it is – so easily co-opted into becoming the messenger of the rhetoric and the mandate of privatisation. The ultimate outcome is to pit each worker against all others, whereby competition rules production at all levels. Far from gaining efficiency or quality of work, the results inspire shoddy work. Workers lose security, see their net income reduced radically, lose any sense of ownership in their work, sacrifice collaborative practices, abandon procedures designed to maintain safety and find their frustrations impacting their relationships with their wives and children. Management and the political environment pit their welfare as against the paying public.

The irony of the film's title lies in how the railway workers imagine themselves to be in command of their work, their lives and their fate at the outset – but this is illusory, for there are no navigators on the railroad. The destiny of labour is as rigidly laid out as are the routes that the rudderless trains traverse. How they take their fate to be their own to define or at least to negotiate evaporates – much more quickly than they could have anticipated. Their good humour peels away bit by bit and then disappears. The opening scene of the film depicts how attentive they are to elaborate safety procedures and how quick they are to look out for when any of their members puts himself carelessly at risk. The story concludes with an understaffed crew suffering serious injury to one man because there weren't enough men assigned to the job to post a man on the lookout for on-coming train traffic. After tortuous debate, the three men carry the injured man away from the site by the tracks and place him by the side of the highway nearby, even though they know moving him will risk him succumbing to his injuries. They will claim that they found him there, ostensibly hit by road traffic, rather than risk taking blame for insufficient worksite safety, which would jeopardise their getting subsequent work from the job contractors. The argument for doing this pits their own risks against their obligation to look out for his. As with Dobbs in *The Treasure of the Sierra Madre*, their obligation to one another dissipates once their collective endeavour is undermined, and it has nothing to do with how they feel about each other.

Pointless work, impossible labour, inventive job actions

In *Il Posto*, 20 sombre applicants for a few open clerical positions in a large corporate office follow an official who leads them along an oddly circuitous route through hallways and stairways in alternatively old and modern structures. They follow him through large, opulently decorated ballrooms, down sterile corridors and finally into an unadorned, purely functional room equipped with booths where they will sit and complete intelligence tests. The corporate world envelops incongruously adjoined historical facades interchangeably, showing the legacy of its emergence with the industrial age and continuous prominence since. The applicants are given an hour to solve a simple story problem in algebra, which, however, has no clear relevance to any task that they would do. One applicant completes the problem quickly, in no more time than the few seconds it ought to take; others seemingly solve it easily but remain nervously where they are until the time allotted expires; and some obviously haven't a clue. They are summarily tested for basic ambulatory and balance abilities. Individually, they are interrogated with a set of yes/no character questions: Are you comfortable eating meals away from home? Are you repulsed by the opposite sex? Are you defiant towards authority? Do you drown your sorrows in drink? One of the applicants is a young man whose shy equanimity gradually erodes with this pointed interrogation rife with implicit inducements to conformism to a corporate culture. He pauses quizzically at the absurd questions, ponders how to answer and why anyone should care to ask him these questions. He toys with why he should want to answer one way or another. Irresistibly, he offers a playfully ironic retort, but ever so softly. Seeing that the interrogator is humourless, though, he quickly retreats from this stroke of being familiar and funny and answers instead just as he suspects he is expected to answer if he is to be found fit for working in a corporate environment. That impulse to humour and his contented equanimity fade away as he assimilates inexorably into the corporate culture without ever the occasion to ponder what is happening to him.

The young man's *entrée* into the big city workaday world also shows him what attractions there are in having money and spending it. Maybe even someday he could court and marry the young girl hired at the same time, and they could buy everything they could want: all the new household appliances and a fancy sports car, too, which they admire in the window displays along the nearby shopping street during their lunch break. Wanting now to acquire what they hadn't previously imagined they would ever want demonstrates how

> The less you *are*, the less you express your life, the more you *have*, the greater is your *alienated* life and greater is the saving of your alienated being. Everything which the economist takes from you in the way of life and humanity, he restores to you in the form of *money* and *wealth*. (Marx 1964: 171)

The work environment is one of strict silence otherwise found in Carthusian monasteries, more to inculcate that the work is serious in spite of its triviality than for what is actually conducive to work. Workers' private monastic cells are collapsed into the perimeters of their desks, where they tend to their personal neurotic habits cultivated over years in a cramped but nevertheless isolating work environment, where they do tedious and pointless tasks. The only outlet for freely inventive human endeavour lies in petty competition for the smallest of perquisites. These odd marks of status gain esteem because there are no real prizes, no real gratification in the work, and no real purpose that they can comprehend as their own. As the young man's propensity for naturally humorous reaction to absurd corporate behaviour withers without him having the chance to notice, the humour of the film rests in how the absurd and inhumane environment nevertheless prevails unopposed by any sort of challenge, much less the liberating challenge of humour. Its absurdities are nakedly palpable, but no one makes fun of it. Our young protagonist never has a chance to win the heart of the girl. And he is far from ever having the chance to laugh about it.

Omicron shows us how an alien with superhuman physical and intellectual powers proves that the worker most ideally suited for alienated labour is genuinely alien to planet earth. The film's humour lies in this comparison, how we can see the reflected absurdity of the conditions of labour. The humour in *The Old School of Capitalism* (2009) arises not so much as the explicit humour of a group of workers, but in their attempts to resolve their plight subsequent to investors having liquidated the machinery where they had worked, thus eliminating their employment or any possible future resumption of their employment. They resolve – somewhat on a whim – to occupy the foyer in the factory owner's home. His wife tries her best to persuade them to leave, insisting that her husband is not home and not expected soon. They continue their occupation, standing together, silently, patiently and impassively. The wife matches their impromptu benign tactics by asking her young daughter, who has been practising violin, to come and stand in front of the workers and practise scales. The girl doesn't need to play out of tune for the monotony of scales to wear upon the men's tolerance. The workerist humour lies in how the workers' inventive but absurd tactics skewer presumptions of normality, and how the wife is forced into an impromptu tactical reaction in kind confirms the workerist point of taking action, against which the forces of control need to react. The workers also seize property belonging to the factory owner, even though it's useless to them, and dismantle one of his storage buildings and use the bricks for minor improvements in their own homes. Eventually they will collaborate with, but then betray, a group of anarchist journalists. Once they reach compromise with the factory owner, they return the bricks.

Workerism and immanence

In a brief essay on literature, Gilles Deleuze explains that the writer creates a possible people (Deleuze 1997). We might say that this is the common nature of creation for the genuinely inventive writer, and not the writer who recapitulates recognisable cultural stereotypes that proliferate in popular literature and in the visual media as well. But a possible people will *not* mean an abstractly conceivable structure of human behaviour, feelings and thoughts, which is to say, *not* utopian. Instead, a possible people will be understandable as possible though not common or even extant in the prevalent affect of literature and cinema. We understand Howard as a possible man, and perhaps in contrast to the more likely men, Curtain and Dobbs. But we also understand Howard as understandable to men like Curtain and Dobbs. Moreover, we understand Howard's culminating laughter as the laughter that witnesses that possible glee that one can take in a reality that negates the alienating conditions of labour. That moment of humour renders a glimpse into what Deleuze and Félix Guattari call *a line of flight* (Deleuze and Guattari 1987: 3–4). A line of flight finds a way out of the stultifying structures that fill a congealed cultural territory. A line of flight seeks a de-territorialisation. De-territorialisation does not alone guarantee an escape from subjectification, or avoidance of retrenchment (Deleuze and Guattari 1987: 133–134). De-territorialisation invariably invokes volatility. It is an explosive volatility for an open set of fates that Howard and Curtain find at the end of *The Treasure of the Sierra Madre*. It turned out happily for them, but the exuberant joy and the laughter that expresses it could hardly have the intensity Howard and Curtain enjoy without the volatility of fate that has been visited upon them. The *banditos* who murder Dobbs for his burros and hides, not knowing about the worth of the sacks of sand, represent a different outcome from that same volatility. Indeed, when the prospectors had encountered the *banditos* before, near their diggings in the mountains, the *banditos* claimed at first to be Federales. They abandon that immediately upon being challenged, delivering a line of dialogue that everyone remembers from the film:

> Badges? We have no badges. We don't need badges. We don't have to show you any stinking badges!

And so both the pretence and any real difference between authority and force are non-existent in the desolate realm of the mountain wilderness. It is an unterritorialised realm.

Workerist film humour provides the moment of elevating glee that rests upon understanding the immediacy of the environment that conditions labour, even if there isn't much more than a glimmer of humour. In *The Treasure of the Sierra Madre* the three prospectors pursue a narrow opportunity for a precarious line of flight in collecting gold, but then the two that survive stumble onto alternative roads away from the territorialised realm of exploited labour, roads that don't require the gold. In *The Navigators* the railway workers have initially little need to contemplate a line of flight, and gradually find opportunities for finding a way out already closed by the politicised environment of privatisation before they come to have the inspiration for escape. In *Il Posto* the imagination of the young applicant for a menial clerical career in the corporate world would entertain lines of flight at every turn, but inexorably he closes those off himself in order to fit into that environment. In *Omicron* the line of flight appears in negative reflection – the alien super-worker who is singularly apt for the physical and spiritual demands of labour and hence *not* conditioned by those demands, but whose traits are all exactly *in*human, whereby re-territorialisation into the mould of the perfect worker is exactly alienating even if it were possible. Accordingly, the workerist humour arises in the reflective laughter of Howard in *The Treasure of the Sierra Madre*, in the railway workers as something lost in *The Navigators*, as something that becomes repressed in the young applicant in *Il Posto*, and in the satirical model of the alien super-worker in *Omicron*. In *The Old School of Capitalism* it appears in the revelatory moment when the workers put on the odd equipment of American football, which they found among the useless acquisitions in the factory owner's shed, and play around at being football players. They would have little reason to know anything about the rampant militarism and severe violence of the sport that exemplifies how capitalist competition uses up those who labour at the endeavour – the professional players – until they are maimed beyond use, when they are discarded and replaced (Culverhouse 2011).

Particularly in collaborations with Guattari, Deleuze's writings on the social world are Marxian through and through. But, as is also typical of how Deleuze exhibits a strong indebtedness to Kant, Leibniz, Spinoza, Nietzsche, Bergson and Sartre, that influence is selective and transformative – so that there is little that counts as recognisable elements of essential doctrine, terminology or structures. De-territorialisation, for example, encompasses proletariat revolution, but hardly so specifically to enumerate familiar Marxian issues such as class-consciousness, the unequal exchange of wages for labour-power, the socialisation of the proletariat through the collective definition of labour under industrial capitalisation, the crises of over-production, or the intractable opposition of the political-economic base of the bourgeoisie and the purposes of the proletariat. Dialectics takes no hold in Deleuzean thought for the simple reason that its intractable adherence to binarisms constrains how philosophical conceptualisation can yield efficacious insights about the world we live in. Deleuze and Guattari present the long sequence of innovative conceptualisations in *A Thousand Plateaus*, including de-territorialisation, as practical conceptual tools for use in understanding the world (Deleuze and Guattari 1987: 22). The relevance of these tools is open-ended, which one can see as an extension of how Marx employed Hegel's *Science of Logic* (Levine 2002; Marx 1992b). Hegel's dialectics were practically useful to Marx, and one can see that as especially important in face of theories of political economy that were (and still are) built upon rigid structuralisms, structuralisms that deftly obscure the availability of a compelling anti-capitalist critique.

Antonio Negri attended Deleuze's lectures in the late 1970s, and then absorbed Deleuze and Guattari's *A Thousand Plateaus*. At about the same time, Negri was incarcerated in Italy for dubious charges that were eventually dropped several years later. Deleuze published a defence. Guattari and Negri carried on a theoretical and personal correspondence (Dosse 2010: 298–301). The outcome of that collaboration was a co-authored text that saw the further expansion of the notion of the active source of potential revolutionary action, with this elaboration of the object: 'community and singularity are not in opposition' (quoted in Dosse 2010: 299). This synthesis incorporates Deleuze's 'possible people' as well as the essential insight of how choosing a day spent hunting, fishing, herding and criticising offers a glimmer – but not a model – of how labour could be other than as determined immutably by the unequal exchange of wages for labour-power. Negri then explicates how workerism takes on the new definition of the struggle in the battleground in which technology is more than just instrumental. It becomes a means of conducting the opposition: 'Not only do the movements employ technologies [...] they also begin to adopt these technologies as models for their own organisational structures' (Hardt and Negri 2004: 82). Technology has the potential for revolutionary action in a particular locale: 'this mobility of the labor force and this political exodus have a thousand threads that are interwoven – old traditions and new needs are mixed together' (Hardt and Negri 2002b: 214).

Deleuzean thought dispels philosophical obscurantisms that derive from structuralist analysis. But Deleuze will take it further – these binarisms proliferated by Marxist dialectics create nearly as much potential for obscurantism as either Hegel or Adam Smith. So, the particular advantage of Deleuzean thought directed towards radical change lies first in the more supple capacity to capture the particularities of historical conditions, and also better to facilitate imaginative responses, better to devise actions, indeed workerist actions and not reactions. One can see a model for this focused attention to the particularities of historical conditions in the ten measures that Marx and Engels recommend in *The Communist Manifesto* (Marx and Engels 1988). Some of these measures have been accomplished at least partially and variously in different nations, and some have never been contemplated outside of communist societies. But of course these are recommendations from the standpoint of contemporary historical conditions – in 1848. In effect, what Marx and Engels urge in that segment of the text is how the organisation of the proletariat could push measures that will effectively pressure capital into crisis or reaction, but at any rate for workers to take on an active agenda. Those ten measures hardly add up to a utopian vision or even encompass all that could be essential to a communist society. They lie somewhere between foundational principles and situational tactics, but informed by comprehension of particular historical conditions. These ten measures, though, are hardly overtly derived from dialectics. One could give them an account in terms of dialectics applied to historical conditions, befitting Marx's assurance that the 'method of presentation must differ in form from that of inquiry' (Marx 1992b: 102). It will also be the case, however, that what may be amenable to dialectics can also come from observations about the conditions of labour, such as nevertheless grasps things by the root. Such observations will thus be something akin to the glimmer of how it could be different that we can find in workerist humour.

Workerist film humour provides moments of inspiration derived from keen insights devoid of theoretical edification. The advantage of the Deleuzean-Guattarian critical discourse is precisely in the orientation from immanence, from the molecular, which also aligns with what is workerist (Tynan 2009). Formulation in terms of dialectics or essential principles of Marxism are beside the point relative to these insights and glimmers. Hence the Deleuzean-Guattarian conceptualisation holds the advantage of exploring such insights and glimmers in their open-ended variety, especially since formulaic thinking is invariably grey and humourless – as Marx was sure to remind his collaborator and best friend. As much as we can see Marx's utilisation of Hegelian thought for the sake of its conceptual practicality, we can see a glimmer in Marxian thought of the anti-structuralism for which Deleuze is alone in the legacy of Marxist thought, in which otherwise rigid structuralism predominates.

Possible people and possible cinema

The thoughts that B. Traven had about a possible cinema in which plot would fall away as unimportant and concept and thought would rise instead approximates what Deleuze says about a crystalline narrative in cinema (Deleuze 1989: 127–129). It may well be the case that workerist humour finds its best expression in film. For that reason, as much as a Marxist orientation should look for certain themes and principles in films that would warrant being called Marxist, there will be something wanting in a set of such recommendations if not one of them has anything to do with cinema or with any form of the moving image. The one minute and 20 seconds of Howard's laughter vitally anchors the

144 Marx at the Movies

impact of *The Treasure of the Sierra Madre*. One has to see the fumbling incompetence of the supervisor in *The Navigators*, particularly in contrast to the slick but ruthless management types we see later. One has to see Omicron's irrepressible fast-motion dance of ultimate mechanisation, which is an order of magnitude more callisthenic than Charlie Chaplin's lithe ballet in *Modern Times* (1936). One has to see the workers putting on pads and helmets and playing at football, or standing calmly trying to be unfazed by the little girl practising scales on her violin. One has to see the young job aspirant coyly trying out ironic humour and then quickly suppressing it, and to see the established clerical workers jealously protecting their private space within the small perimeters of the tops of their desks. Indeed, the first thing one needs to recognise about cinema that could be Marxist is that it is far from being an adequate vehicle for any of the usual content of theoretical treatises. But humour works well in cinema.

It is in how workerist humour is situated in the context of the immediacy of the conditions of labour that it shows its exuberant glee. That may be a context in which it will be difficult to corroborate nuances of the legacy of Marxist theory in the contemporary tradition of that theory. Deleuze's open-ended conceptualisations, such as a 'possible people' and the 'line of flight', are particularly apt for capturing the inventiveness of workerist humour. We might think of films as exemplary to demonstrate structural analyses derivative of Louis Althusser, Jacques Derrida, Ernst Bloch, Henri Lefebvre, Frederic Jameson, Theodor Adorno *et al.*, and thus think of a film as if it were to be anointed worthy of *a badge of significance* in the name of Althusser or Adorno or Jameson and so on. But structuralist approaches will miss the inventive humour and tend to force structural categories onto the subject matter in a way that obscures nuances of difference. So the focus on workerist humour will abstain from finding relevance in any of these alternatives, and thus not earn any of those badges. One might respond on behalf of the workerist humorist protagonist, invoking a rather famous bit of dialogue from *The Treasure of the Sierra Madre*,

> Badges? We have no badges. We don't need badges. We don't have to show you any stinking badges!

Bibliography

Agee, James. 1958. *Agee on Film: Reviews and Comments*. Boston: The Beacon Press.
Avineri, Shlomo. 1970. *The Social and Political Thought of Karl Marx*. Cambridge: Cambridge University Press.

Berlin, Isaiah. 1978. *Karl Marx*. Oxford: Oxford University Press; 4th edition.
Bimbach, Martin. 1987. 'The Angry Marx', *American Imago*, 44, 3–4.
Brill, Lesley. 1997. *John Huston's Filmmaking*. Cambridge: Cambridge University Press.
Crowther, Bosley. 1948. '"Treasure of Sierra Madre," Film of gold Mining in Mexico, New Feature at Strand'. *The New York Times*, January 24, 1948.
Culverhouse, Gay. 2011. *Throwaway Players: Concussion Crisis from Pee Wee Football to the NFL*. North Fayette, Pennsylvania: Behler Publications.
Deleuze, Gilles. 1997. 'Literature and Life'. In *Essays Critical and Clinical*, translated by Daniel W. Smith and Michael A. Greco, 1–6. Minneapolis: University of Minnesota Press.
Deleuze, Gilles. 1989. *Cinema 2: The Time-Image*, translated by Hugh Tomlinson and Robert Galeta. Minneapolis: University of Minnesota Press.
Ebert, Roger. 2003. 'Reviews'. *Chicago Sun Times*, October 12, 2003.
Deleuze, Gilles and Guattari, Félix. 1987. *A Thousand Plateaus: Capitalism and Schizophrenia*, translated by Brian Massumi. Minneapolis: University of Minnesota Press.
Dosse, François. 2010. *Gilles Deleuze and Félix Guattari: Intersecting Lives*, translated by Deborah Glassman. New York: Columbia University Press.
Engell, John. 1993. 'Traven, Huston, and the Textual Treasures of the Sierra Madre'. In *Reflections in a Male Eye: John Huston and the American Experience*, edited by Gaylyn Studlar and David Desser, 79–95. Washington and London: Smithsonian Institution Press.
Grobel, Lawrence. 1989. The Hustons. New York: Charles Scribner's and Sons.
Guthke, Karl Siegried. 1991. *B. Traven: the Life Behind the Legends*, translated by Robert Sprung. Chicago, Illinois: Lawrence Hill Books.
Hardt, Michael and Antonio Negri. 2002a. 'Marx's Mole is Dead! Globalisation and Communication'.*Eurozine*.http://www.eurozine.com/articles/2002-02-13-hardtnegri-en.html.
Hardt, Michael and Antonio Negri. 2002b. *Empire*. Cambridge, London: Harvard University Press.
Hardt, Michael and Negri, Antonio. 2004. *Multitude: War and Democracy in the Age of Empire*. New York: The Penguin Press.
Harvey, David. 2010. *A Companion to Marx's Capital*. London and New York: Verso.
Huston, John. 1979. *The Treasure of the Sierra Madre*, edited by James Naremore. Madison: University of Wisconsin Press.
Levine, Norman. 2002. 'Hegel and the 1861–1863 Manuscripts of Das Kapital', *Rethinking Marxism: A Journal of Economics, Culture & Society*, 14(4), 47–58.
Long, Robert Emmett, ed. 2001. *John Huston: Interviews*. Jackson: University of Mississippi Press.
Marx, Karl. 1992a. *Capital: Volume 1: A Critique of Political Economy*, translated by Ben Fowkes. London: Penguin Classics.
Marx, Karl. 1992b. 'Postface to Second German [1873]'. In *Capital: Volume 1*, 94–103.
Marx, Karl. 1978. 'Contributions to the Critique of Hegel's *Philosophy of Right*: Introduction'. In *The Marx-Engels Reader*, edited by Robert C. Tucker. New York and London: W. W. Norton & Company; 2nd edition.
Marx, Karl. 1977a. 'Critique of the Gotha Program'. In *Karl Marx: Selected Writings*, edited by David McLellan, 564–570. Oxford: Oxford University Press.

Marx, Karl. 1977b. 'Theses on Feuerbach'. In *Karl Marx: Selected Writings*, edited by David McLellan, 156–158. Oxford: Oxford University Press.

Marx, Karl. 1977c. 'The Holy Family'. In *Karl Marx: Selected Writings*, edited by David McLellan, 131–155. Oxford: Oxford University Press.

Marx, Karl. 1975. *Early Writings*, translated by Rodney Livingstone and Gregor Benton. New York: Vintage Books.

Marx, Karl. 1964. *Early Writings*, translated and edited by T. B. Bottomore. New York: McGraw-Hill Book Company.

Marx, Karl and Engels, Friedrich. 1988. *The Communist Manifesto*, edited by Frederic L. Bender. New York: W. W. Norton & Co.

Marx, Karl and Engels, Friedrich. 1987. *Heiteresun Bissiges von Marx and Engels*, edited by Käte Schubert. Berlin: Dietz Verlag.

Marx, Karl and Engels, Friedrich. 1970. *The German Ideology*. New York: International Publishers.

Naremore, James. 1979. 'Introduction: A Likely Project', In John Huston, *The Treasure of the Sierra Madre*, edited by James Naremore, 9–44. Madison: University of Wisconsin Press.

Rawls, John. 1999. *A Theory of Justice*. Cambridge: Harvard University Press; 2nd edition.

Steedman, Ian. 1985. 'Heterogeneous labour, money wages, and Marx's theory', *History of Political Economy*, 17(4), Winter, 551–574.

Traven, B. 2010. *The Treasure of the Sierra Madre*. Farrar, Strauss and Giroux.

Tynan, Aidan. 2009. 'The Marx of Anti-Oedipus', *Deleuze and Marx. Deleuze Studies* Volume 3 (2009, Supplement), 28–52.

Wolff, Jonathan, 'Karl Marx', *The Stanford Encyclopedia of Philosophy* (Summer 2011 Edition), Edward N. Zalta (ed.), URL = <http://plato.stanford.edu/archives/sum2011/entries/marx/>. Last accessed November 29, 2013.

Wright, Steve. 2002. *Storming Heaven: Class Composition and Struggle in Italian Autonomist Marxism*. London: Pluto Press.

7
Alienated Heroes: Marxism and the Czechoslovak New Wave

Peter Hames

In 1965, the Italian critic Lino Micciche argued that the Czechoslovak New Wave of the 1960s was a phenomenon of international significance with an importance reaching well beyond cinema (Micciche, quoted in Sviták 1968: 52). In the final years of the 1960s, its progression continued – arguably until 1969, since many products of the Prague Spring of 1968 continued to appear in the months following the Soviet invasion of August 1968. By this time, Czechoslovak films had won extensive festival awards (including two Oscars for Best Foreign Film), and had attracted worldwide critical attention. However, in 1969, the 'normalised' regime of Gustav Husák, installed in the wake of the invasion, clamped down on the film industry and, by mid-1970, ten films, many unreleased, had been banned and several stopped in mid-production. In 1973, a list of banned films was issued, eventually extending to over 100 features. The figures included four banned 'forever'. What had originally been described as the Czechoslovak film 'miracle' was at an end and the Western critical world lapsed into silence.

The Austrian Marxist, Ernst Fischer, once described Czechoslovakia 1968 as 'the freest land ever known' (Fischer, quoted in Pelikán 1971: 320) and the surrealist filmmaker, Jan Švankmajer, stated in a recent television interview that the 1960s was a time when art had a tangible effect on social and political development (Hames 2013: 226).

It is difficult to retrieve the mindset of the 1960s but Western observers of the Communist Eastern bloc placed considerable emphasis on the prospect of 'polycentrism' – the notion that countries might develop their own roads towards socialism. The non-bloc country of Yugoslavia, with its trade links to the West, and development of workers' councils, provided a positive model even before the reform movement began in Czechoslovakia. The Action Programme of the Czechoslovak

Communist Party, launched in 1968, envisaged 'the widest possible democratisation of the entire socio-political system' (Dubček, quoted in Ello 1969: 20) as well as the introduction of workers' councils. This attempt to 'square the circle', it was argued at the time and subsequently, was doomed to failure.

Since the success of such a development would undoubtedly have led to the fragmentation of the Soviet 'Empire', the Russian reaction was predictable. Given US opposition to the threat of socialism in Latin America (the fall of the Allende government took place only a few years later), the notion of a successful democratic evolution in the Eastern bloc would not have been all that appealing to the West either. As Karel Kosík put it, 'Humanistic socialism is the negation of both capitalism and Stalinism' (Kosík 1995: 55).

When the Soviet system collapsed in 1989–1990, it could be argued that the roots lay in its own corruption and contradictions. In Czechoslovakia, it was a matter, noted Václav Havel in a British television interview, of what would light the touch paper. However, the democratic path adopted by Mikhail Gorbachev also played its role, with the Prague Spring reforms often considered an explicit forerunner of what happened in the USSR 20 years later (see the discussions between the Prague Spring reformer Zdeněk Mlynář and Gorbachev: Gorbachev-Mlynář 2002).

When the communist system in Czechoslovakia finally collapsed in 1989, the Communist Party leader from 1968, Alexander Dubček, became Chairman of the Federal Assembly but the reformers of 1968 were not, in general, welcomed back. Tainted by the years of 'normalisation', communism – or rather 'socialism' – was seen as the enemy. Democratic freedoms – at least in theory – were linked to the orthodoxies of neoliberal economics.

Although 1990 saw liberated festivals of the banned films in both Karlovy Vary and Bratislava, interest cannot be said to have been maintained. Directors of the New Wave who had sustained a level of creativity in the 'normalisation' years – Jiří Menzel, Věra Chytilová, Juraj Jakubisko and others – did not find it easy to gain funding for their films. As Chytilová once said, they stood condemned as giving credence to the regime when their films were, in reality, critical and avant-garde (Chytilová, interviewed in Gott 1994). Like the Prague Spring itself, the New Wave and its films were seen as part of a discredited socialism. It was not until 2002 that a substantive study (Přádna *et al.* 2002) was published, and 20 years before the achievements were recognised by Martin Šulík and Jan Lukeš in their 26-part television documentary series, *Zlatá šedesátá (The Golden Sixties*, 2009), featuring hour-long interviews with many of the surviving participants (see Hames 2013: 215–230).

In their relationship to socialism and Marxism, a number of questions arise in considering the films of the 1960s. Were they a product of socialism? To what extent did they reflect socialist beliefs? In what ways were they critical of the socialist system? Whether, to adopt Francis Fukuyama, the end of history is presented as socialism or neo-liberalism, there will be varied reactions. There are those who believe in the ideology, those who go along with it, those who reflect on the possibilities for change and evolution, those who use the system for personal gain, those who adjust for the sake of survival and, of course, those who are actively opposed. As history progresses, many will change their positions through conviction or circumstance. Thus it is not really possible to argue that a member of the Communist Party automatically represents the rule of ideology and the *status quo* or that a non-member will represent some kind of significant opposition. In other words, a filmmaker or writer who remained a member of the Communist Party would not necessarily be less critical than one who was not. The Marxist philosopher and film critic, Ivan Sviták, defined socialist art as 'art produced in the socialist epoch' (Sviták 1996: 80), with the most significant forms demonstrating a serious responsibility toward social questions, the dynamics of historical change, and the 'movement of ideas' in society. This socialist art could not be equated with particular novelties in style or form, art produced in any one territory, or a particular ideological stance. Thus, by extension, one would not have to be a Party member or committed to the Party line in order to produce it. The kind of profound analyses present in the films of a Miloš Forman or Evald Schorm could, in theory, make a more significant contribution to a progressive socialist art than art conforming to any political directive.

It is not without significance that Sviták considered cinema to be the most important agent of change. While the reform movement of the 1960s occurred both inside and outside of the Party, it was largely and perhaps inevitably a development within an intellectual elite. It should also be recognised that it was communists who would be in a position to authorise change and that no film could be passed for production without prior approval. Somewhere there would have to be a commitment to the 'movement of ideas', and also some facility for freedom of expression.

The origins of the Prague Spring reforms are frequently related to Czechoslovakia's democratic heritage between the wars. Thus, the role of the intelligentsia was seen as more significant than in many other countries. Writers, in particular, had played an important role in the national revival of the 19th century and intellectual activity had continued at a significant level after 1918. The Soviet system installed after 1948 was consequently viewed as something alien, frequently described as 'Asiatic', something imposed from a quite different tradition.

Czechoslovakia had a legal Communist Party before the war, a developed industrial working class and a democratic form of government. Before 1948, the Communist Party leader, Klement Gottwald, had spoken of a specific Czechoslovak road to socialism (and had also given assurances that the arts would not be required to follow the Soviet model). The notion that communism could be combined with traditions of democracy and nationalism was promoted. Although events did not bear him out, the British ambassador to Czechoslovakia, Sir Cecil Parrott, once remarked that the Czech communists, unlike the Russians, took democracy for granted (Parrott 1977: 29). According to the wartime head of Czech intelligence, František Moravec, however, post-war democracy was little more than a façade, and President Beneš became a 'prisoner of the Soviet government, unable to make decisions' (see Moravec 1981: 228–233).

At the Writers Conference of 1956, the poet Jaroslav Seifert (winner of the Nobel Prize in 1984), referred to writers as 'the conscience of the nation'. In 1965, at a conference on 'The Czechoslovak Road to Socialism', where most of the participants were protagonists of the Prague Spring, Karel Bartošek argued that it was a long-term process dating back to 1918 (Kusin 1972: 116). Thus, Ivan Sviták's argument that there was a humanist and democratic tradition of Marxism that had been abandoned in favour of a Leninism emerging from strictly Russian circumstances was not as radical as it might seem.

In his important study *The Intellectual Origins of the Prague Spring*, Vladimír Kusin points out the significance of the criticism of Stalinism and neo-Stalinism, which he dates from the second half of the 1950s and the emergence in particular, of two Marxist philosophers, Sviták and Kosík, in 1956–1957. Sviták argued for 'a renaissance of Marxist philosophy' as opposed to 'the exchange of one dogmatism for another' (quoted in Kusin 1971: 38). They were not the only ones (see 38–48).

The challenges presented by the philosophical exchanges in the journal *Literární noviny* in 1956–1957 did not go unnoticed, and a 'Report on the Current Situation in Philosophy' was published in March 1959 attacking 'revisionist tendencies', the overestimation of Hegel, and including criticism of Kosík and Sviták. The report noted: 'Philosophy is not only an effective instrument of Communist theory but also one of the important means of implementing in a Communist way the policies of the Party' (quoted in Kusin 1971: 44). The tasks of philosophy were defined as the elaboration of the Leninist philosophical legacy and the fundamental laws and categories of dialectical and historical materialism. However, the philosophers' shift away from dogma was reflected in a move towards 'authentic Marxism' and, in particular, the views of the young Marx.

If the challenge to Stalinism was already evident, the publication of Kosík's *Dialektika konkrétního* (*Dialectics of the Concrete*) in 1963 was to be of key significance. A distillation of ideas first developed in 1960, his concept of 'concrete totality' was 'reality understood as a structured (not chaotic) whole, constantly evolving and forming itself. It is not given once and for all, it is not given *in toto* and mutable only in parts. As concrete totality, reality is at the same time a totality of nature and a totality of history. Man is always simultaneously in both, and he constantly reproduces his union with the world through practice' (Kusin 1971: 50).

As Paul Piccone has suggested, Kosík interpreted the dialectic to apply not merely to wage labour but to teleological human activity and argued that bureaucratic rule led to a 'false totalisation' in which 'pseudo-concreteness' was not restricted to any one group or class. This readily converted into a political project in which manipulation could be eliminated through the action of 'hitherto privatised individuals' (Piccone 1977: 48–49).

Kosík argues that praxis transcends the moment of labour and also involves a moment of 'recognition'. It is 'the struggle for recognition', notes James Schmidt, 'the "process of realizing human freedom" that gives the interchange between man and nature a significance which goes beyond natural necessity' (Schmidt 1977: 76–77). Art, notes Kosík, like all human praxis, 'has an indivisible two-fold character: it expresses reality but it also forms it' (Kosík 1976: 71). Praxis is man's way of living in the world, a human reality in which man is both subject and object.

In a later essay, he argues that the dialectic is both a destructive and a totalising process. First, it destroys the pseudo-concrete by revealing all reified forms of material and spiritual reality as historical forms of human praxis. Second, it unveils contradictions, emphasising them rather than suppressing them. Third, it expresses the movement of human praxis. 'Once again, we return to the problem of morality, understood by Marxism as the problems of overcoming *reified* and *fetishised* praxis. The morality of the dialectic is *revolutionary praxis*' (Kosík 1977: 92). This is a fairly clear reference to the frozen reality of bureaucratic socialism, which the New Wave films were to challenge in its essence.

Dialectics of the Concrete was published in several editions (1963, 1965, 1968) and, according to Kusin, was always sold out. Translated into German, French, Spanish, Italian and English, Kosík's ideas aimed wider than the specifically Czechoslovak situation. Similarly, when his writings from the 1968 period were published in English in 1995, Kosík remarked: 'If it is true that the crisis of the countries of Central and Eastern Europe is merely a manifestation of the crisis of the entire modern age [...] then conclusions about the situation in Central Europe apply to other countries as well, and affect them equally' (Kosík 1995: x).

Leading members of the philosophical community refused to be brought into line. Given the close links between philosophy and the wider culture, many writers, artists and filmmakers accepted Kosík's concepts as their own. Confronted with the question of who to believe in, Sviták argued, 'Above all, we must believe in ourselves, in our experience of what life around us is like' (Sviták 1968, quoted in Kusin 1971: 48).

In a British or West European context, it is difficult to believe that a work of philosophy or the views of philosophers could have such a wide-ranging impact. When Czech philosophers complained of official persecution, Jürgen Habermas once said: 'Your situation is much better than ours [...] Here, we philosophers and sociologists are completely ignored both by the government and the general public and so we play no public or social role whatever' (quoted in Liehm 1973: 399).

It is also important to bear in mind the relative size of the Czech intellectual community, a degree of interaction arguably greater than elsewhere, and the time honoured cliché that Prague is a city that is also a village. Vera Blackwell observed in 1966 that, as a result of the isolation imposed by the Nazi occupation and the experience of the 1950s, Czechoslovakia became a closed society, 'manageable in size, like a Greek *polis*. Thus, poets, novelists, dramatists, producers, actors, can communicate directly with their public. They know each other [...] In order that serious and basic questions about human existence may become a moving force for a whole society, they must be presented in intimately familiar terms, based on common experiences, fears, hopes, and aims' (Blackwell 1966: 42). While few may have mastered the intricacies of Kosík's text, the notion that reality could be changed through praxis, that it could and should be examined and subject to change, fell on receptive ears. As Věra Chytilová once said, it should be unacceptable not to tell the truth. 'One always reflected one's own vision on the problems of that period. Topics always had a moral component' (Chytilová, interviewed in Buchar 2004: 54). Sviták began his book on *The Czechoslovak Experiment 1968–1969* with a quotation from Marx: 'The philosopher asks, What is truth? He does not ask, What is currently accepted [...] Truth does not know the frontiers of political geography' (quoted in Sviták 1971: 3).

In his essay '*Hrdinové odcizení*' (The Heroes of Alienation) Sviták favoured a cinema that exhibited 'a serious responsibility toward social questions' (Sviták 1996: 80). This would not, of course, be in theoretical opposition to the views of the Party save that, in the case of socialist realism, with its focus on class struggle and socialist 'construction', the answers to the analysis would be given in advance. In discussing the political development of the New Wave, I shall refer to those films that offer a direct analysis or criticism of the building of socialism, and those that mirrored the existential crisis – in Sviták's terms, the fragmented and alienated being – an approach that was ultimately responsible for giving the cinema its revolutionary content. However, it will be apparent that the one does not exclude the other.

Within ten years, critical films began to emerge – although not without bureaucratic opposition. The work of Ladislav Helge, himself a Party member, was of particular significance. His first two features, *Škola otců* (*School for Fathers*, 1957) and *Velká samota* (*Great Seclusion*, 1959), dealt respectively with the problems of a teacher confronting a school life corrupted by ideology, and a committed communist confronting the less-than-perfect reality of his village co-operative. Other filmmakers committed to communism, who challenged the system in the years prior to the New Wave, included the writer-director-producer team of Ján Kadár and Elmar Klos. Best known for their Oscar-winning *Obchod na korze* (*A Shop on the High Street* aka *The Shop on Main Street*, 1965), they had already made a number of films with a strong critical edge. These included *Hudba z marzu* (*Music from Mars*, 1955) and *Tři přání* (*Three Wishes*, 1958), both adapted from scripts by the satirical writer Vratislav Blažek, *Smrt si říká Engelchen* (*Death is Called Engelchen*, 1963), a highly unorthodox take on the partisan war against the Nazis, and *Obžalovany* (*The Accused*, 1964), about a worker-director wrongly accused of fraud. A third figure important in the development of internal criticism was the writer and producer Jan Procházka, who wrote a whole range of critical screenplays, became a candidate member of the Party's Central Committee, and was later denounced by the KGB as a leader of counter-revolution.

One of the most controversial films to reflect on the role of the Party and alienation under state socialism was Evald Schorm's *Každý den odvahu* (*Everyday Courage*, 1964), the first film by a New Wave director to approach the subject. It told the story of a Party worker, Jarda (Jan Kačer), who finds that the world he is trying to create is collapsing around him. The lack of morale, everyday materialism and the failure of the socialist dream is everywhere apparent. In the 1950s, Jarda had been an enthusiastic shock worker, inspired by the idea of working for the good of the people. But the factory workers are now only motivated by the need to feed their families, seeing that ideas of brotherhood merely mask the rule of a self-serving bureaucracy. Perhaps it was this perception that got the film banned – the workers were no longer presented in positive terms and the deficiencies of the system could no longer be attributed to the failings of individuals. Schorm's intensely moral approach was relatively conventional in technique, emphasising his work with actors – amplified by his documentary approach to factory life, and with Jan Klusák's modernist score the only concession to 60s innovation. The film was banned.

The communist self-examination came to a head in 1968–1969 when a whole sequence of films confronted the realities of the 1950s and 1960s with a detail that could probably not have been sanctioned any earlier. All of them were subsequently banned. Perhaps the two most significant films were Vojtěch Jasný's *Všichni dobří rodáci* (*All My Good Countrymen*, 1968) and Jaromil Jireš's *Žert* (*The Joke*, 1968). Both were Party members but had been previously identified with a more poetic brand of cinema.

Jasný's film had been in preparation since the mid-1950s and was personally given the go-ahead by Dubček. Based on his mother's recollections of village life, it chronicles events in a Moravian village between 1945 and 1958, with an epilogue set in 1968. It charts the changing relationships between seven friends as they experience post-war liberation, the introduction of Communism and collectivisation, and the resultant deterioration and political oppression, but ending with the promise of 1968. However, the film reaches well beyond politics, recording the changing lives and moralities of its characters and paying homage to the beauties of the landscape and seasons. The film ends with the voice-over 'Farewell my good fellow countrymen, what could we have done, and what not?'.

Jireš's *The Joke* was based on Milan Kundera's novel, which had first been published in 1967. However, the adaptation had been prepared prior to publication. Kundera once criticised the political interpretation of his book, arguing that it was primarily a love story, but the film version omits the love story, making it directly political. The hero, Ludvík Jahn, a former communist, comes from a small town in southern Moravia. In the 1950s, he decided to outrage his militant girlfriend, Markéta, with a postcard stating: 'A healthy spirit reeks of idiocy. Long live Trotsky!' As a result of this 'joke', he is expelled from both the Party and university, spends three years in forced labour, two in the army and one in military prison. These events are told in flashback as he revisits his home town following his release. He plans to get revenge on his former friend, Pavel, who was responsible for his condemnation, by seducing his wife. This he does, only to discover that they are now separated and that Pavel has become a reform communist, now opposed to the values that he had previously upheld. Jireš's use of flashback constructs an almost literal dialogue between past and present that begins in the year 1949. The film not only exposes the injustices of the 1950s but also remains true to Kundera's spirit of scepticism. Pavel's reformist zeal is little more than accommodation to the times and, since filming overlapped the Soviet invasion in 1968, the political realities were already becoming apparent.

In discussing these explicit criticisms of communist practice, it is clear that there were attempts at criticism within the Party from Khrushchev's secret speech denouncing Stalin in 1956 through to 1968. There were, of course, continuing swings of the pendulum as different film projects were approved or condemned – but there were obviously those within the Party who believed in constructive criticism. However, as Helge remarked in 1968, the bureaucrats who evaluated politically committed work nonetheless saw it as an interference: 'They forget that the people who create that kind of politically committed art must go through agony. They suffer because they see something fundamentally wrong with the society that they want to call their own' (Helge, interviewed in Liehm 1974: 117).

It is no doubt significant that all these direct criticisms of the system – with the exception of Evald Schorm – came from within the Party. The filmmakers were, at any rate in theory, people who could be trusted because they would be seen as sharing ultimate objectives. Significantly, many had moved from an early acceptance of and commitment to the regime to progressive disillusion and were motivated by the 'last chance' offered by the changes culminating in the Prague Spring.

In his *Intellectual Origins*, Kusin follows his chapter on the importance of culture with one specifically titled 'Alienation', dating many significant developments from the conference on Franz Kafka held at

Liblice in 1963. The 'rehabilitation' of Kafka's standing and reputation was to become the springboard for wider considerations. According to Liehm, the trigger for the conference was Jean-Paul Sartre's address at the Moscow Conference for Peace and Disarmament in July 1962 (Liehm 1975: 54–57), in which he effectively argued for the universality of Kafka and the need for a critical Marxist study. The Czech discussions began in 1962 and continued into 1963, the year that would have marked the 80th birthdays of both Kafka and Jaroslav Hašek, the author of *The Good Soldier Švejk*.

Kusin points out that many of the contributions focused on the subject of alienation. According to Alexej Kusák, Kafka was 'a poet of our absurdities', and Kafkaesque situations were 'models of certain situations well known in the socialist countries at the time of the personality cult'. He spoke of the process that 'has made social relations untransparent and institutional power absolute'. Kafka was 'a poet of his time' (capitalism) just as he was 'a poet of our time' (neo-Stalinism) (quoted in Kusin, 1971: 66).

For Ivan Sviták, Kafka presented a philosophical and artistic image of 'man's predicament as such' (Kusin, 1971: 67). He also shared elements with existentialism, including the subjective nature of his truth and experience of an extreme situation. 'The open-ended philosophy underlying Kafka's work relates to states of human awareness and bears little resemblance to any rigid philosophical doctrine. Concerned with modes of actually experienced existence, it does not fit any closed conceptual system' (Sviták 1966: 36).

In his essay 'Theories of Alienation' (1970), Sviták identifies several theories and sources of alienation, speaking of 'the impoverishment of human personalities and their alienation from society'. While alienation can, from one perspective, be seen as the essence of the human condition, alienation can also exist within industrial and class societies, within totalitarian regimes or in individual psychology as 'psychological or moral failure' (he identifies seven sources of alienation). 'But the decisive fact is that the "forces of alienation", which have always existed, today predominate, that they determine the temper of the times, actually threaten the existence of man as a species and jeopardise the freedom of entire societies'. It is 'the most urgent problem facing the industrial societies of West and East alike' (Sviták 1970: 123–141). He concludes: 'Broadly speaking we can say that the basic trend of modern society is the growing scope of manipulation, using technological means to control not only production and labor, but also man and his history' (140).

Sviták argues that Marx presented the most profound and far-reaching analysis of the alienated society 'because it integrates the various individual aspects of alienation in one coherent intellectual construction' (1970: 131). 'His emphasis on the practical way out of alienation, through social activity, through personal practice, through man's participation in history, through his sharing in the revolutionary process that transforms social relations, of course remains unnoticed, so that the meaning of Marx's effort to change the world is substantially distorted' (131).

Here, of course, Sviták is referring primarily to what he calls the dogmatic school and the system of levers and transmission belts where man is merely a recipient of directives from a Party acting on his behalf. It is clearly significant that Kosík quotes Rosa Luxemburg's notes on the Russian Revolution: 'Freedom only for supporters of the government, only for members of a political party, is no freedom at all. Freedom is always freedom for those who think differently' (quoted in Kosík 1995: 90).

According to Sviták, the problems of alienation existed within the context of two power blocs that were striving for world hegemony, a struggle between the managerial elites of monopoly capitalism and state capitalism. Open opposition was impossible but opposition could occur within 'the sphere of thought' (and by extension, also through culture) (Sviták 1970: 141). One is struck here by the similarities between this perspective and those expressed later, in the normalisation years, by Václav Havel in his essay 'The Power of the Powerless', where he describes the 'post-totalitarian' system as 'an extreme version of the global automatism of technological civilization' (Havel, 1987: 115) – indeed, it is a debate that continues to be relevant.

Karel Kosík's contribution to the conference focused on Hašek rather than Kafka, beginning with an imaginary meeting between Švejk and Josef K. He suggested that both the Kafkaesque and Švejkism were worldwide phenomena, existing independently of their authors.

> What is the Kafkaesque world? It is the world of absurdity of human thoughts and action, of human dreams, a world of a monstrous and unintelligible labyrinth, a world of human powerlessness in the network of bureaucratic machines, mechanisms, reified creations. Švejkism is a way of reacting to this world of absurd omnipotence of the machine and of reified relations. (Kosík, 1975: 87–88).

The conference was to have considerable repercussions. It was attended by the leading Western Marxists Roger Garaudy and Ernst Fischer, both of whom had worked for a positive approach to Kafka. There was no representative from the Soviet Union. Fritz Kurella, head of the ideological section of the East German Party, subsequently attacked the conference in the cultural weekly *Sonntag*. This gave the editors of the Czech literary weekly *Literární noviny* an unparalleled opportunity, and the German attack was published in Czech with subsequent replies by Garaudy, Fischer and others. Since *Literární noviny* had a circulation of 140,000, the nature of the debates reached a significant audience. According to Liehm (1975: 73), Kafka became the most popular author and his novels were published in tens of thousands of copies.

Despite the importance and resonance of the Kafka conference, attempts by post-invasion apologists to blame it for the reformist movement were clearly wide of the mark (the notion of 'alienation' as a concept that could be applied to 'socialist' societies came in for particular criticism). The Kafka conference was part of a process, and the relevance of Kafka's vision to everyday reality was already apparent. Kusin lists eight plays, novels and films that could be said to be analogous to Kafka (including Schorm's *Návrat ztraceného syna/Return of the Prodigal Son* and Němec's *O slavnosti a hostech/The Party and the Guests* [both 1966]): 'Consonance between them and Kafka existed in the widest sense as a certain awareness of man-to-man and man-to-world relations being not only social but *also* existential' (Kusin, 1971: 67–68).

It is not without interest that the films of the 'New Wave' proper (Forman's *Černý Petr/Black Peter*, Chytilová's *O něčem jiném/Something Different* and Jireš's *Křik/The Cry*) are conventionally dated from the same year (1963), that the most explicitly Kafkaesque or alienated hero appeared in Pavel Juráček's and Jan Schmidt's *Postava k podpírání/Josef Kilian*, also produced that year, or that the flood of New Wave films began two years later. But it would be naive to posit a causal relationship. It is much more sensible to regard them as part of the same 'movement of ideas'. On the other hand, as Kusin suggests, for the New Wave, 'overt and covert criticism of the prevailing human condition was typical' (Kusin 1972: 69).

In discussing the cross-fertilisation between culture and philosophy, Kosík noted that 'there was a particular cultural "common denominator" which emerged during the last four years and which manifested itself especially clearly in our cinema [...] Czechoslovak culture focused its attention on existential human problems, and the "common denominator" was the question: What is Man?' (Kosík interviewed in Liehm 1973: 397–398). 'In contrast to the regime's official or implicit assumptions, Czech culture emphasised Man as a complex creature, continually

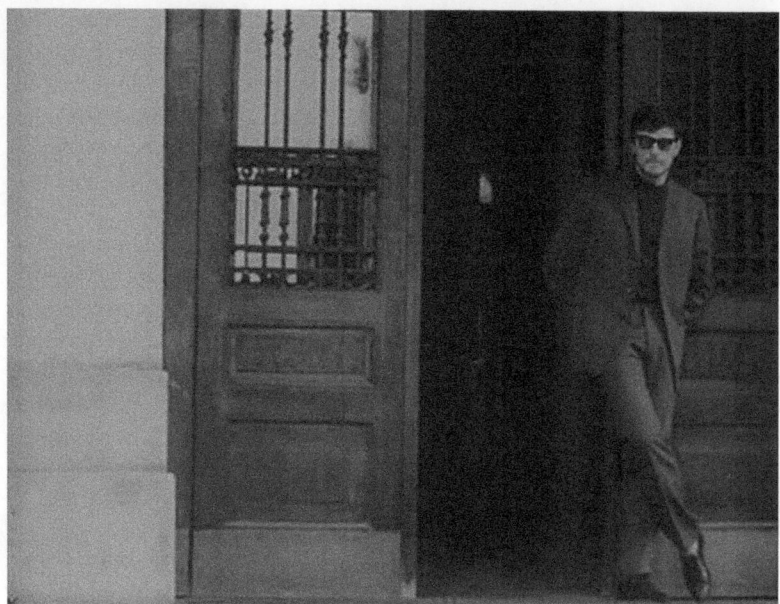

Figure 7.1 Jan Kačer as Jan Šebek
Source: Screen capture from *Return of the Prodigal Son* (1966), dir. Evald Schorm, Barrandov Studios

active, elastic, striving to overcome conflicts, a being irreducible to a single dimension' (Liehm 1973: 398–399).

In his essay 'The Genius and the Apparatus' Sviták argues: 'Marx relies on man, on the working class, on the people as the motive force of history, not on the manipulation of people. For him, man is the subject of the historical process, not an object to be manipulated by apparatuses' (Sviták 1970: 169). The meaning of human life 'lay in the development of man as a many-sided personality, in people's participation in the historical process and the growth of human freedom' (172).

Clearly, the situation of the New Wave was one of 'free' creation, in which the filmmakers identified with the pressure for reform. Any hidden desire to reinstate 'bourgeois democracy' would not have been stated and, in any case, a multi-party system was not in principle seen as incompatible with socialism. Also as Jacques Rancière has suggested in another context, it is also the *political* situation that may determine whether or not a particular work will be likely to perform a radical function.[1]

If one is to turn to the more overt Kafkaesque influences, the films of Pavel Juráček would perhaps lay claim to first place. In *Josef Kilián,* co-directed by Jan Schmidt, the story tells of Jan Herold, a man who decides to borrow a cat from a cat loan shop for the weekend. When he attempts to return it, he discovers that the shop has disappeared (it appears never to have existed) and he embarks on a journey through bureaucracy in order to return the cat. His search leads him in a quest for the elusive Josef Kilián, who appears to be at the centre of the system. His quest ends with an empty room and a ringing telephone. As a portrait of an absurd world ruled by an uncomprehending bureaucracy, it is unrivalled and the Czech film most close to Kafka's vision. However, the film is explicitly linked to Stalinism in a number of ways – the opening scene has its hero pass through a corridor of discarded Cold War posters ending with a portrait of Stalin and, in its conclusion, he walks towards camera from the site that had once boasted the largest statue of Stalin in Eastern Europe. Its hero is adrift, or alienated, in a society in which he searches for an illusory meaning, but also suffers from the existential alienation of the Kafkaesque. As a medium-length film (40 minutes), it was easy for the authorities to 'bury' it during distribution.

With his second film, *Každý mladý muž* (*Every Young Man*, 1965), made during national service in the army and financed by the Czechoslovak Army Film Unit, he told two stories, which could be said to reflect both Kafka and Hašek. In *Případ pro začínajícího kata* (*A Case for the Young Hangman*, 1969), adapted from the third book of Jonathan Swift's *Gulliver's Travels*, he revisits similar themes, but cast in a wider framework. After a car crash, Gulliver is transported to the land of Balnibarbi, where he is required to account to a variety of 'authority' figures. At the Academy of Letters, he is introduced to 'thinking machines' that will remove the necessity for unnecessary thought and, later on, to execution machines which fail to work. While revisiting the world of political absurdism, the hero is always obsessed with memories of his drowned love, Markéta, representing an eternal longing and absence. In these films, perhaps, the existential overwhelms the political. Like Kafka, Juráček's films can be said to demonstrate 'the poetics of absurdity'.

The most powerful portrait of an alienated hero is probably that of Jan (Jan Kačer) in Schorm's *Return of the Prodigal Son*. He plays an architect who attempts suicide and finds himself confined to an asylum. He escapes several times and is eventually released, each time failing to adjust to the world he finds outside. In the search for the cause of his alienation and moral conviction, we are taken on a journey through a society that requires constant adjustment. The hypocrisies of personal relations (both wife and family) are matched by those of the workplace, explicit injustice and the overall threat of war. Jan regards the asylum

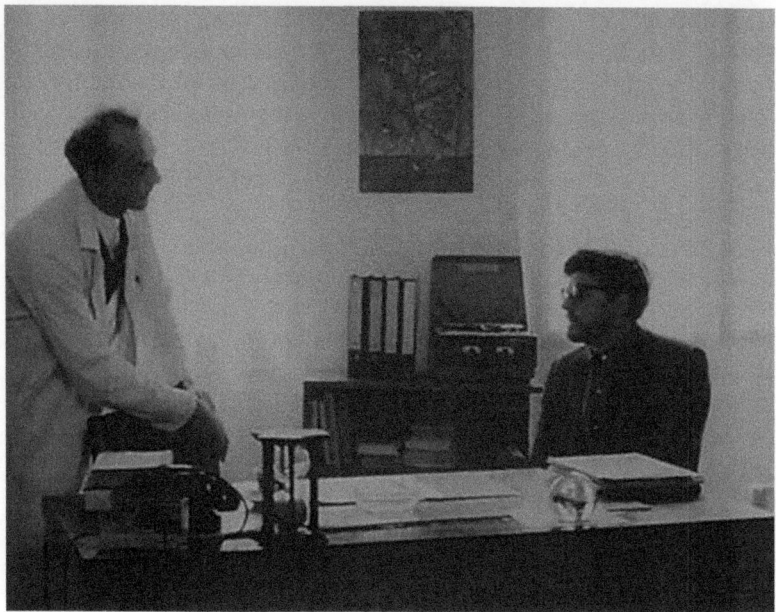

Figure 7.2 Milan Morávek as the doctor and Jan Kačer as Jan Šebek
Source: Screen capture from *Return of the Prodigal Son* (1966), dir. Evald Schorm, Barrandov Studios

doctor's advice that he should adopt an attitude of 'humble indifference' as a recipe for its own brand of continuous suicide. Besides continuing the moral quest that he had already begun in *Everyday Courage*, Schorm's film provides part of an overall oeuvre, in both features and documentaries, that attempts to penetrate society's overall malaise. In documentaries such as *Proč?* (*Why?*, 1964) and *Zrcadleni* (*Reflections*, 1965), he reflected on the fundamental issues of life and death, people's real values and experiences, and 'long forgotten moral and philosophical questions' (Škvorecký 1971: 143).

Jan Němec's 'allegorical' *The Party and the Guests*, is a film that, even today, its director denies was intended as direct criticism of the system. The film opens with a group of well-dressed people enjoying a picnic in the countryside. Without warning, they find themselves escorted by a bunch of sinister-looking thugs to what appears to be an interrogation. They seem to have been accused of something but it is unclear what. After the intervention of a political leader, they are invited to his open-air birthday party. The reaction of the guests varies. Most try to curry favour, one allies himself with the authorities, one protests but is easily bought off, and one remains silent throughout and eventually escapes. A search party with a dog is soon organised for the recalcitrant (played by Evald Schorm), who does not want to be at the party and sees through the false allegiance to democracy. While Němec tried to pass it off as a statement about the exercise of power under capitalism, the more immediate targets were readily apparent.

Of course, on one level Němec is correct – the film is an analysis of how people adapt to power as such, but the Kafkaesque interrogation scene where the characters are not allowed to step outside a circle drawn in the gravel is a little closer to home. Influenced by 'the theatre of the absurd', especially Ionesco, Němec himself drew parallels with Albert Camus' *L'Étranger* (*The Outsider*), where the hero is arrested for failing to cry at his mother's funeral – the politicised absurd was very much part of the 1960s climate.

The search for new means of expression logically led to a revisiting of Czechoslovakia's own pre-war avant-garde, leading to a resurrection of Surrealist influences, with a number of sources permitted because of 'respectable' communist roots. Here one can also identify such varied international influences as Antonioni, Godard, and the American 'underground'. In a Czechoslovak context, such formal dissent already implied a 'political' position and was furthermore used in an analytical and polemical manner.

The director most committed to experiment and the avant-garde was Věra Chytilová, an experiment that has outlasted the New Wave and continues to inspire feminist debate. There is little doubt of her importance in the development of feminist perspectives, but her inter-active approach also bears a clear relation to the subject of alienation. In *Something Different* she told two stories, one documentary and one fiction. The first is a '*cinéma-vérité*' account of the life and achievements of a woman gymnast, while the second is a fictional story of an ordinary housewife and her love affair. The two stories are inter-cut, a technique that not only queries their claim to realism but questions the two worlds presented. As the gymnast, Eva Bosáková, comments off-camera in a recorded interview, she had been searching for 'something different'. The implication is that this refers to her athletic fame and achievements but, in the context of the film (and its title), it suggests something apart from life as currently lived. In *Sedmikrásky* (*Daisies*, 1966), Chytilová focuses on two teenage girls who seem to live in a kind of vacuum and decide that since the world has been spoiled, they will be spoiled as well. Neither is given any developed psychology and the two are basically interchangeable. The film resembles a fragmented collage of short episodes in which they engage in destructive activities – they get drunk, disrupt a nightclub, exploit old men who try to seduce them, cut up their sheets and clothes, destroy an enormous official banquet by turning it into a food fight, and make token gestures of remorse. While enormously invigorating as an aesthetic exercise, we are well and truly looking at alienated youth (and alienated females), who have no access to the world of power and, in one sequence, march past a montage of padlocks chanting 'we are'. While there has been much debate about the role of the heroines (Chytilová says she intended to criticise them), and the film is open to many interpretations, it makes sense to see their behaviour in the wider social framework – the emptiness of a world with false values. The film, after all, ends with a nuclear explosion.

The film is one of two discussed in some detail in Sviták's essay 'The Heroes of Alienation'. The other, rather surprisingly, is Menzel's *Ostře sledované vlaky* (*Closely Observed Trains*, 1966), winner of the second Czech Oscar in 1967. One of the most popular Czech films ever, it's an adaptation of Bohumil Hrabal's novella and, effectively, the beginning of Menzel's long-term collaboration with Hrabal. Hrabal's work became enormously influential in intellectual circles in the mid-1960s and was considered pretty much a breakthrough. Apart from the fact that he was influenced by avant-garde sources, his main significance lay in the fact that he portrayed the authentic speech and lives of the working class – frequently people on the edge of normal society. The direct life experience, he argued, could become a poetic act, and his work seemed to evoke the suppressed consciousness of the whole era. He opened up a space that was inaccessible to official literature.

In *Closely Observed Trains*, set during the Second World War, Menzel provides a portrait of life at a provincial railway station during the Nazi occupation. The young hero, Miloš Hrma, has begun his adult career as an apprentice and is mainly concerned with the problems of his relations with the opposite gender. At the end of the film, by a trick of fate, he ends up planting the bomb that blows up a Nazi munitions train, losing his life in the process. Somehow, the people of the village continue their everyday lives, loves and concerns, and this obstinate commitment to the mundane provides its own defence against enemy occupation. When the time comes, a focus on the everyday, laughing at life, and a Švejk-like rejection of ideology in themselves constitute a kind of defence. Sviták suggests that it is the most accurate portrait of the Czech character (Sviták, 1996). It also, of course, marked a radical break with the narrative and character stereotypes of the resistance film.

In 1969, Menzel and Hrabal completed work on their second feature collaboration *Skřivánci na niti* (*Larks on a String* aka *Skylarks on a String*), which was banned before release but won the Golden Bear at the Berlin Film Festival some 20 years later in 1990. The action takes place in a steel reprocessing plant in the 1950s (when the stories were written), where 'remnants of the "bourgeoisie" are being re-educated and introduced to the benefits of a new utopia via forced labour. They appear to pay little attention to work since they are, ironically, on strike against the imposition of increased work norms. While based on Hrabal's own experiences, the film closely identifies and pillories the realities of the period. The record smeltdown (leading to unusable product) warrants a celebratory polka, the supervisor talks about his working-class origins (almost certainly remote), and the union representative arrives in a chauffeur-driven car. Constant references to labour and 'the glorious future' are no more than meaningless slogans, young pioneers come on a visit to look at 'faces soaked in imperialism', denunciation and police arrests are routine. The 'prisoner-workers' are clearly alienated from this reality (as are its administrators). It is individuality, idiosyncrasy and shared experience that enables them to distance themselves from a frozen and imposed ideology. Enacted with Menzel's typically human touch and taste for comedy, many felt that the subject was too grim for such treatment (as did the post-invasion regime).

I have not so far discussed the role of Slovak cinema in these developments, mainly because it followed a slightly different trajectory. Criticisms of the Party were rather less overt although it should be noted that the Slovak actor Július Pántik played the main role in Helge's *Great Seclusion*. However, one film that incorporated all the themes of the opposition was Štefan Uher's *Slnko v sieti* (*The Sun in a Net* aka *Sunshine in a Net*, 1962), the film which. in fact, opened the doors to the Czech New Wave in the following year. One of the key films of the decade, it was highly significant on a formal level but also on that of subject matter. It focuses on the character of Fajolo and his thwarted relationship with his girlfriend, Bela. Leaving aside its fragmented structure and striking imagery, the film also touches on a number of forbidden topics. Martin Votruba points out that a number of the film's themes would previously have been seen as unacceptable – teenagers changing partners, remote parents, a philandering husband and attempted suicide (Votruba 2005). When Fajolo goes to a voluntary work camp at a collective farm at the insistence of his father, it is in order to impress the authorities on behalf of his parents, who have clearly been found wanting. The collective farm is run badly and inefficiently despite the

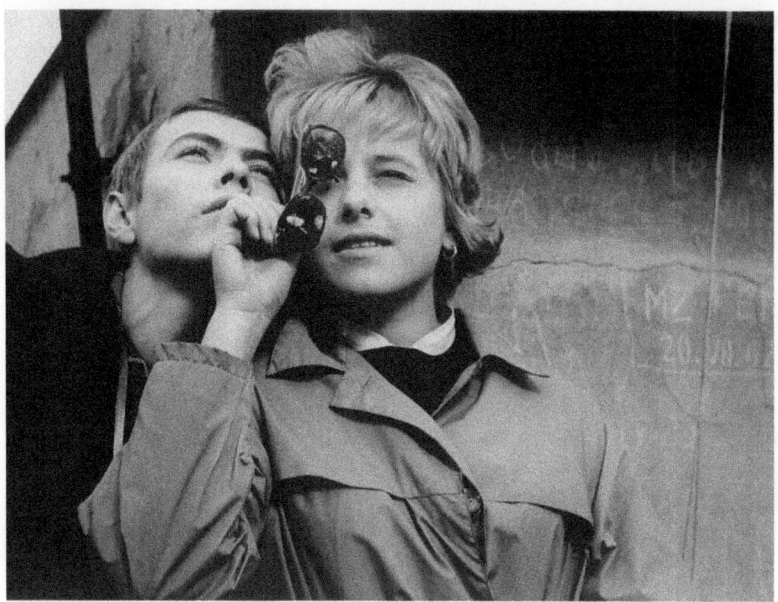

Figure 7.3 Marián Bielik as Fajolo and Jana Beláková as Bela in *Slnko v sieti* (*The Sun in a Net*, dir. Štefan Uher, Czechoslovakia, 1962)
Source: Zuzana Mináčová © Slovenský filmový ústav-Fotoarchiv [© Slovak Film Institute-Photoarchive]

usual positive slogans. All of the characters are 'alienated' in most of the categories offered by Sviták, although the film provides a kind of poetic reconciliation with life's disappointments. The film was perceived as an attack on communism.

The promotion of radical approaches in Slovakia was closely linked to the work of the first production group of Slovak film, headed by Albert Marenčin and Karol Bakoš. Marenčin, who was also a screenwriter, had lived in Paris in the immediate post-war period and had strong links with the French avant-garde. The fact that he wrote an essay on Apollinaire, translated Alfred Jarry, Ingmar Bergman and Alain Robbe-Grillet in the 1960s gives an indication of his tastes. Continuous support for Uher during the 1960s culminated in the group's support for a new generation in 1968–1969 – Juraj Jakubisko, Dušan Hanák and Elo Havetta. Marenčin was sacked from his position in 1972, by which time he had joined the Prague Surrealist Group.

The film closest to the theme of alienation is Hanák's *322* (1969), in which a communist functionary reviews the meaning of his life after learning that he has suspected cancer. The real subject is the society around him that he has helped to build – with its generalised lack of belief overseen by an omnipresent police. The subject, notes Václav Macek, was 'the central theme of his generation [...] what lies beneath the concept of "an authentic life"' (Macek 2005). Highly inventive and poetic, it is perhaps the most bleak of all the New Wave films, with its short scenes preceded by titles, quotations and lines of dialogue. Completed after the Soviet invasion, it won an award at Mannheim but was never released.

The Slovak films were arguably more radical in their formal experimentation than those of the Czechs (excepting Chytilová), with both Jakubisko and Havetta adopting a liberated style influenced equally by folk art and the French *nouvelle vague*. Jakubisko's were also explicitly political but never reached audiences. In *Zbehovia a pútnici* (*the Deserter and the Nomads*, 1968), he presented three stories about war – the First World War, the Second World War (the Soviet liberation of Slovakia presented as a grotesque and bloody farce) and the aftermath of a nuclear holocaust. Absurd, farcical, violent and featuring the personification of Death, it is a shocking and visceral work. In *Vtáčkovia, siroty a blázni* (*Birds, Orphans and Fools*, 1969), he told a story about two friends who live together with a young Jewish woman. Recalling the *ménage à trois* in Truffaut's *Jules et Jim* (1961), Jakubisko tells the absurd and tragic story of three orphans that ends in murder and suicide. Constantly inventive, its political references include Milan Štefánik, the Slovak co-founder of Czechoslovakia, the Slovak National Uprising against the Nazis, and 'Uncle Mao'. Both films were, of course, banned.

There are many other films that could be considered within the aesthetic onslaught of the New Wave – among them Jan Schmidt's adaptation of Pavel Juráček's script *Konec srpna v hotelu Ozón* (*The End of August at the Hotel Ozone*, 1967), another film set after nuclear war, Drahomíra Vihanová's banned debut film *Zabitá neděle* (*Deadly Sunday*, 1969), a study of its central character's mental alienation, and Zdenek Sirový's similarly banned *Smuteční slavnost* (*Funeral Rites*, 1969), a further journey into the moral and political realities of collectivisation. Suffice it to say that we are looking at a unique critical and aesthetic movement that is probably unequalled. Robert Buchar suggests some 60 outstanding films (Buchar 2004: 9).

It is fairly clear that many films produced in the 1960s provided a profound and analytical account of the Czechoslovak experience of the Soviet model of the road to socialism and that an even broader range of films indicated a profound social malaise and state of crisis. Many were banned, often for short periods, while others were subject to an inconspicuous or token release. Others, such as the films of Němec, were almost by definition designed for the world of the film society although Němec correctly states that the significance (or indeed, the influence) of a film cannot be determined by the size of audience.

The films produced in 1968–1969 were an expression of the spirit and freedoms of the Prague Spring, while the films produced in 1963–1967 could be argued to form part of its foundation. If one considers the relatively large numbers of critical films produced, each with differing degrees of influence, together with their interaction with other media and the realities of everyday life, we are nonetheless looking at a general 'movement of ideas'.

Was that movement of ideas socialist or Marxist? This is much more difficult to determine without a prescriptive definition of form or content. Sviták clearly denies such an essentialism, considering art to be an independent sphere. Kosík suggests that the revolutionary nature of cinema lay not in political allusions but in its emphasis 'on such basic aspects of human existence as the grotesque, the tragic, the absurd, death, laughter, conscience and responsibility' (Kosík, in Liehm, 1973: 399). These themes are characteristic of both the 'political' and 'existential' wings of the New Wave as well as the 'avant-garde'.

Cinema certainly reflected the desire for justice and morality that one would expect to associate with socialism, and also the aims and objectives of reformist Marxists such as Kosík and Sviták. If, as Kosík suggests, Kafka is as effective at exposing the 'pseudo-concrete' as Brecht, then the Kafkaesque and (perhaps superficially) existential films of the New Wave can be perceived as politically radical. Like the small theatres of the 1960s, they were an invitation to dialogue, to action and interaction. Furthermore, unlike the avant-garde 'theory' films inspired by the May Events in Paris in 1968, their revolutionary qualities derived from a variety of forms and were not linked to any preconceived aesthetic norms or agenda.

As Brecht himself once suggested: 'Reality alters; to represent it the means of representation must alter too [...] The oppressors do not always wear the same mask' (quoted in Harvey 1978: 73). If one accepts the existing rule of the bureaucracy as representing at best a system of state capitalism, at worst the country's colonial status, it can be argued that it was the government that was 'anti-socialist' while the films represented the free critical and moral reflection characteristic of true socialism (and Marxism).

From an institutional perspective, it can be said that the economic structures permitted the production and distribution of critical or dissident work which would not have been possible under capitalism, where the 'demands' of the market would inevitably have prevailed. Also, as Švankmajer said in his television interview, much became possible because the system was in crisis. From these perspectives, the situation in Czechoslovakia can be said to have been unique. While critical films have been produced elsewhere, it has been rare for them to occur in such quantity or with such resonance.

It is, of course, possible to conceive of a social democratic structure permitting a range of active criticism. In the past, BBC television and Channel Four television have fulfilled this role in the UK. However, it is noticeable that opposition to Thatcherism produced few political repercussions either then or subsequently. Clearly, culture cannot operate in a vacuum independently of other social, political and economic forces. As Sviták wrote after the invasion, the Czech reforms ultimately failed because the most important phenomena of democratisation remained within the control of the bureaucratic power elite (Sviták, 1974–1975, 118–130). The revolution in culture, he notes, almost succeeded. But, of course, it was ultimately international power politics that was the dominant factor.

Culture can serve to keep alive ideas, traditions and alternative possibilities, but it is noticeable that in Czechoslovakia the cinema (and culture) was never able to recapture the role that it played in the 1960s. Under 'normalisation' it was effectively silenced and, since that time, the rule of the market has prevailed. However, this does not mean that the tradition of criticism is dead. In the normalisation period, Chytilová did make some films with political force –*Hra o jablko* (*The Apple Game*, 1976), *Panelstory* (*Prefab Story*, 1979), *Kalamita* (*Calamity*, 1981) – and challenged the new system after 1989.

While the contemporary Czech and Slovak cinemas have prioritised commercial objectives, critical films have also re-emerged. Here, one can mention the absurdist comedies of Petr Zelenka, the work of directors such as Bohdan Sláma and Marek Najbrt, and, in Slovakia, Mira Fornay, Zuzana Liová, and Iveta Grofová. But the universal resonance of cinema has been lost, and it is in the area of documentary that the critical legacy of the New Wave continues to reveal itself. Here the influence of the former New Wave director Karel Vachek has been important, arguing that there must be a revolution in expression and that 'films are about nothing else than the philosophical awakening of the people who make them and those who watch them' (Vachek, interviewed in Buchar 2004: 154–155). Above all, documentary seems to have provided the framework for the reflection, authenticity, tragedy, humour and sense of the absurd that once characterised the films of the 1960s. The 'crisis of modernity' and the problems of alienation have hardly been transcended.

Note

1. It is worth noting that, during the 'normalisation' years, a production of Molière led to 'irresponsible' reactions – as did the popular success of Miloš Forman's *Amadeus* (1984).

Bibliography

Blackwell, Vera (1966). 'Literature and the Drama', *Survey*, 59 (April), 41–47.

Buchar, Robert (2004). *Czech New Wave Filmmakers in Interviews* (Jefferson and London: McFarland).

Ello, Paul (ed.) (1969). *Dubček's Blueprint for Freedom* (London: Kimber).

Gorbachev, Mikhail and Zdeněk Mlynář (2002). *Conversations with Gorbachev: On Perestroika, the Prague Spring, and the Crossroads of Socialism*, trans. George Shriver (New York: Columbia University Press).

Gott, Richard (1994). 'Making Money, Not Movies' (interview with Věra Chytilová), *The Guardian*, 4 June.

Hames, Peter (2013). '*The Golden Sixties*: The Czechoslovak New Wave Revisited', *Studies in Eastern European Cinema*, 4, 2, 215–230.

Harvey, Sylvia (ed.) (1978). *May '68 and Film Culture* (London: British Film Institute).

Havel, Václav (1987 [1978]). 'The Power of the Powerless', in Jan Vladislav (ed.) *Václav Havel or Living in Truth* (London: Faber).

Kosík, Karel (1975 [1963]). 'Hašek and Kafka', trans. Karel Kovanda. *Telos*, 23 (Spring), 84–88.

Kosík, Karel (1976 [1963]). *Dialectics of the Concrete: A Study of Problems on Man and World*, trans. Karel Kovanda and James Schmidt (Dordrecht and Boston: Reidel).

Kosík, Karel (1977 [1964]). 'The Dialectic of Morality and the Morality of the Dialectic', *Telos*, 33 (Fall), 85–92.

Kosík, Karel (1995). *The Crisis of Modernity: Essays and Observations from the 1968 Era*, edited by James H. Satterwhite (Lanham and London: Rowman and Littlefield).

Kusin, Vladimír V. (1971). *The Intellectual Origins of the Prague Spring: The Development of Reformist Ideas in Czechoslovakia 1956–1967* (Cambridge: Cambridge University Press).

Kusin, Vladimír V. (1972). *Political Grouping in the Czechoslovak Reform Movement* (London: Macmillan)

Liehm, Antonín J. (1973) [1968]. *The Politics of Culture,* trans. Peter Kussi (New York: Grove Press).

Liehm, Antonín J. (1974). *Closely Watched Films: The Czechoslovak Experience* (New York: International Arts and Sciences Press).

Liehm, Antonín J. (1975). 'Franz Kafka in Eastern Europe', *Telos*, 23 (Spring), 53–88.

Macek, Václav (2005). 'From Czechoslovak to Slovak and Czech Film', special issue of *Kino Kultura*, December. http://www.kinokultura.com/specials/3/macek/shtml.

Moravec, František (1981 [1975]). *Master of Spies: The Memoirs of General František Moravec* (London: Sphere Books).

Parrott, Cecil (1977). *The Serpent and the Nightingale* (London: Faber)

Pelikán, Jiří (ed.) (1971). *The Czechoslovak Political Trials, 1950–1954* (London: Macdonald).

Piccone, Paul (1977). 'Czech Marxism: Karel Kosík', *Critique*, 8 (Summer 1977), 43–52.

Přádna, Stanislava, Zdena Škapová, and Jiří Cieslar (2002). *Démanty všednosti: Český a Slovenský film 60. let* (Prague: Pražská scéna).

Schmidt, James (1977). 'Praxis and Temporality: Karel Kosík's Political Theory', *Telos*, 33 (Fall), 71–84.

Škvorecký, Josef (1971). *All the Bright Young Men and Women: A Personal History of the Czech Cinema*, trans. Michael Schonberg (Toronto: Peter Martin Associates).

Sviták, Ivan (1966). 'Kafka as a Philosopher', *Survey*, 59 (April), 36–40.

Sviták, Ivan (1968 [1967]). 'Les héros de l'aliénation'. *Image et Son*, 221 (November), 51–69.

Sviták, Ivan (1970). *Man and his World: A Marxian View*, trans. Jarmila Veltruský (New York: Dell).

Sviták, Ivan (1971). *The Czechoslovak Experiment 1968–1969* (New York: Columbia University Press).

Sviták, Ivan (1974). 'Illusions of Czech Socialist Democracy', *Telos*, 22 (Winter 1974–1975), 118–130.

Sviták, Ivan (1996 [1967]). 'Hrdinové odcizení', in Stanislav Ulver (ed.) *Film a doba: Antologie textů z let 1962–1970* (Prague: Sdružení přátel odborného filmového tisku), 76–91.

Votruba, Martin (2005). 'Historical and National Background of Slovak Filmmaking', special issue of *Kino Kultura*, December. http://www.kinokultura.com/specials/3/votruba.shtml.

8
The Work and the Rights of the Documentary Protagonist

Silke Panse

> Searching for a distant land,
> Kant and Fichte into the ether soar,
> While I simply want to understand,
> That – which in the street I saw.
>
> (Marx 1966 [1837]: 28)

Introduction

This chapter looks at the work of the documentary protagonist as the raw material of images taken and owned by others. It develops thought by Marx and post-Marxists on the relation between the material, the worker and the capitalist in order to explore the work of the documentary protagonist. The chapter takes the stance that affective immaterial labour is also material, since it requires physical presence. The material in question is that of the documentary protagonist in the image. The work of the protagonist for the documentary image cannot be acknowledged as work since this would threaten the status of the image as documentary; so the protagonist is denied any appreciation of her contribution as either artistic knowledge work or affective labour and generally cannot claim any rights to the image of herself if it has been taken by others. The images are the property of those who took them and who, in a reading of documentary through Marx, can be regarded as capitalists appropriating the wealth that the documentary protagonist produces. The lack of rights of the documentary protagonist, in contrast to who took her image, is comparable to the lack of rights of the worker whom Marx observed in comparison to the capitalist. In order to emphasise the potential exploitation of the material, affective and creative contribution of the human and non-human protagonists to their image, those who take the product of the work of the documentary protagonists are referred to as image-takers. Further counting against the documentary protagonist is that, according to human rights law, the protagonist has no right to her image if she is working in the image. In addition, this skews the balance towards the image-takers who are privileged in art and law.

Depictions of work in documentary have tended to centre on the representation of manual labour. But situating work strongly in the realm of material labour for an employer other than the filmmaker sets up the work of the protagonist as separate from her work for the documentary. The implication that the worker works for someone other than the documentarian entrenches as well as distracts from the division between the protagonist's work for employment as observed in the documentary and their work for the documentary.

The absence of documentary images of workers working has frequently been criticised (Comolli 1996; O'Shaughnessy 2012), most notably by Harun Farocki in his film *Workers Leaving the Factory* (1995) and his installation *Workers Leaving the Factory in Eleven Decades* (2006). For Jean-Louis Comolli, the focus on the outside of the factory served to distract from the workers' manual labour inside (2005): 'work itself has still tended to remain invisible, not least because the employer controls entry to the workplace and can exclude cameras from it' (O'Shaughnessy 2012: 156). By contrast, theorists of immaterial labour have argued that the emphasis on 'material production had "hidden" that labour produces not only commodities' (Lazzarato 1996: 138), but relations. This applies to documentary film too: the emphasis on the processes of material production as the labour for someone other than the filmmaker has hidden the work of the protagonist for the documentary. The focus on manual labour producing goods for the owner of the means of production distracts from any immaterial labour for the owner of the images. Documentary is positioned as external to the work of its protagonists. But workers in a documentary also provide the material for the work of the filmmaker. The working protagonist is materially immanent to the documentary image.

For Marx, in the 19th century, the worker was 'at home, when he is not working, and not at home when he is working' (1975: 326). The worker knew when she was in or out of the factory, if she was at work or in life. Today, many workers cannot leave the factory because the workplace is everywhere (Hardt and Negri 2000: 332). We are not workers any more, even though we work most of the time.[1] Life has become inseparable from work (Lazzarato 1996: 138) and the factory diffuse (136). The dissolving boundaries between work and life are further permeated by the commanding of space and behaviour through a proliferation of digital image-takers everywhere. It is nearly impossible to resist the imposed work of being oneself in other people's images. To refuse to have one's image taken is often presented as a sign of the protagonist's guilt and is exhibited as part of the documentary. While the material index of the documentary protagonist is infinitely multiplied, she usually has no rights to her image. When work cannot be separated from leisure and the product of the work cannot easily be distinguished from the worker – what is the work of the documentary protagonist?

Documentary relies on the premise that the protagonist is not supposed to work for it, since that would be acting. Because the protagonists in documentary are not meant to act – for which they would have to be paid and acknowledged like in a fiction film – their work is much less clarified. The question of labour thus directly affects the question of documentary: if the protagonists were paid for a change in their behaviour, this work would make the film a fiction: 'the lack of payment to the participant is, in some way, a mark of news or documentary difference from fiction' (Winston 2008: 238). Therefore, to call the documentary protagonist a 'social actor' (Nichols 1991: 42) also distracts from the fact that her affective labour, by definition, cannot be acknowledged as such. The documentary protagonist is supposed to go about what she does anyway. But if we know that a camera is looking right at us, we often act differently than if we were not being filmed. Even continuing with what we thought we would be doing anyway, in the face of a film team staring at us, is an effort. That some documentary protagonists get paid is a moot point. If a protagonist performs the affective labour of acting for a wage, the film is not a documentary. Most often she does not have any rights to her material image, which is ostensibly produced without any labour on her part. The documentary protagonist is hence doubly exploited since she has to work, often without pay, in a situation which is not seen as work, not even as immaterial labour, and without acknowledgment of authorship or rights. Because documentary protagonists by definition do not work, they cannot form a union. This might also be the reason why documentary and what is called 'factual' television have become so prevalent as a cheap mode of production (Hearn 2010: 63). Perhaps, then, less highly regarded documentary formats, such as scripted reality shows, are less exploitative, since the protagonists voluntarily enter into a contract for playing 'themselves'.[2] But in unscripted documentary images, the involuntary protagonist still changes whatever they are doing for somebody else's camera in someone else's decisive moment.

Is this change (or continuation) of behaviour work? Professional actors would think so.

The materiality of immaterial labour

The term 'immaterial labour' is elusive since it still requires the materiality of the worker. Immaterial labour can be abstract knowledge work (Hardt and Negri 2000: 292), or affective labour, such as acting. 'The creation and manipulation of affect', such as in the entertainment industry, Michael Hardt and Antonio Negri maintain, is still 'immaterial, even if it is corporeal and affective, in the sense that its products are intangible, a feeling of ease, well-being, satisfaction, excitement, or passion' (292–293). Passion, for Hardt and Negri, is intangible: 'the affects it [immaterial labour] produces are immaterial' (293). The most salient example of affective labour is the smile of the coffee shop employee towards the customer. Since the product has to be separate from the worker, the smile cannot be a material product. The barrista is physically disconnected from the coffee, but not from her smile – so the reasoning goes. Because this kind of immaterial labour cannot exist outside of the materiality of the protagonist, it cannot be singled out as a product, and is therefore paradoxically classified as immaterial. While affective changes are expected as a part of labour, they are not distinct as a product. The terminology of immateriality makes it harder to acknowledge that work is actually done, which many employers use to their advantage. Immaterial labour is often taken for granted and financially not well rewarded, if at all, in part because it is not easy to determine what is work and what is not. Being enthusiastic frequently is part of a job, but we do not get paid more for producing more units of passion. The statements that 'immaterial labour almost always mixes with material forms of labour' (Hardt and Negri 2004: 109) and that 'instances of affective production too involve material products' (Hardt 2009: 24) rely on the materiality of the making of the coffee and the immateriality of smiling being fundamentally different. This division between immaterial and material labour externalises materiality in objects, and separates material products from the apparent immateriality of protagonists. Affect is regarded as immaterial, as though it is separate from a material, physical body.

But the apparently immaterial smile still needs the materiality of the face. There is no smile without a protagonist. Affective labour is immanent and material. With respect to the authenticity of affective labour demanded, for example, by fast food chain managers (Myerscough

2013), the product that is *being* constitutes a material change of affect. The material affect of the protagonist is a product immanent to the worker. While today 'there is no more outside' (Hardt and Negri 2000: 186), for the early Marx the problem was that the product of labour was external and therefore alienating. The worker is estranged because 'labour is *external* to the worker' (Marx 1975: 326). Marx's smile would have been outside the face:

> What the product of his labour is, he is not. Therefore, the greater this product, the less is he himself. The externalization of the worker in his product means not only that his labour becomes an object, an *external* existence, but that it exists *outside him*, independently of him and alien to him, and begins to confront him as an autonomous power. (324)

Marx described how the feudal aristocratic landowner related to the land as an extension of his body. In feudalism, land was regarded 'as the inorganic body of its lord' (318). After feudalism, the relation between the land and its owner became abstract and reduced to 'the economic relationship between exploiter and exploited' (319). The feudal landowners, who regarded their land as if it was their body, then became capitalists who dealt in abstract relations. Land and man, wrote Marx, then sank 'to the level of a venal object' (319). Even though Marx distinguished his historical materialism from Feuerbach's idealistic materialism and determined that change has to be generated materially through practice (1969), he found that capital is material and 'dead matter' (1975: 319): 'Capital is dead labour, that, vampire-like, only lives by sucking living labour, and lives the more, the more labour it sucks' (1999: 149). Property is 'purely material wealth' (Marx 1975: 319) and 'the material process of private property' (322) is abstract. In this understanding of materiality as external, albeit being kept alive through living human labour, lies the difference between Marx's reading of materialism as capitalist abstraction and conceptions of vital materialism as living matter (Bennett 2010). While the emphasis of vital materialism on every *thing*, including workers, as vibrant matter leads beyond abstractions of ownership, for Marx, capital was material, and what is material is external to the worker: 'the object that labour produces, its product, stands opposed to it as something alien, as a power independent of the producer' (Marx 1975: 324). Raw material is the object of labour and the 'objectification of living labour' (360). But this raw material is still external and not immanent to the labourer even though, according to later Marx, the worker shapes the raw material (1973: 360) in a dialectic relationship to it. Living labour is realised in the material (360). The product of labour is preserved by 'making it into the raw material of new labour' (362). The worker reanimates dead form through living labour. Raw material is kept from being a dead form by 'the simple process of coming into contact with labour' (360). The use value of the unfinished product is refreshed by becoming the material object of living labour, for instance, the 'raw material' of yarn is kept alive through the living labour of weaving (362):

> It is living labour which preserves the use value of the incomplete product of labour by making it the material of further labour. It preserves it, however, i.e. protects it from uselessness and decay by making it the object of new living labour. (362)

The way Marx uses 'object' and 'material' interchangeably in this passage indicates the living, albeit still external, nature of what would be a dead object were it not kept alive by living labour. Because of the invested labour, the externalised object 'ceases to exist in a one-sided, objective form, in which as a mere thing, it is at the prey of processes of chemical decay etc.' (360). Positing human labour against non-human material objects, Marx equates form with decay and in effect maintains that living labour halts entropy. In contrast to vital materialists, who find that *objects* are made by human subjects, and *things* are what, or who, escapes human direction (Bennett 2010: 2; Mitchell 2005: 156–157), Marx equates *things* with formal objects. For Marx, an object-thing decomposes 'in a one-sided, objective form, in which, as a mere thing, it is at the prey of processes of chemical decay etc.' (Marx 1973: 360). Its substance is only kept alive through human labour. Despite Marx finding that it is human activity that changes 'the thing, reality', not just 'in the form of the object of contemplation' (Marx 1969: 13), 'reality' is still external to the worker.

According to Marx, the 'shaping of the raw material, adds to the value of the raw material' (1973: 360), but the value of documentary images is supposed to lie in the fact that their protagonists do *not* shape themselves, since they are not supposed to work as such. Marx could at least write about the worker that 'the time during which the labourer works, is the time during which the capitalist consumes the labour-power he has purchased of him' (1999: 149). About the documentary protagonist as worker it can only be said that the time during which the protagonist is in the image is the time during which the image-taker consumes the power of life he has not purchased of her. With respect to the production process 'in each of these subsequent processes, the material has obtained a more useful form, a form making it more appropriate to consumption' (361). There is of course not the same difference of easier consumption between the documentary protagonist and the actor, nor indeed between the object and the art object. The documentary protagonist counts neither as the artistic worker nor as raw material. Living labour would be working with the material *of* the image, a work that is then accredited to the filmmaker. But the material of who or what is *in* the image is not an object.

While for Marx, 'the realization of labour is its objectification' and the worker experiences a 'loss of reality' (324), the documentary protagonists are always already realised and objectified in the images of themselves. Their work is appropriated as the object of the image-taker. It is inevitable, writes Marx, that 'the idle enjoyment of the products of the sweat and blood of other people should become a brisk commerce in the same [monopoly]' (319). Whereas today, abstract corporations are legally treated as people (Parramore 2012), in documentary, the sweat and blood of the multitude (Virno 2004), indexed in images, is the product. We are not merely participants in our documentary image; we are vital for it.

If immaterial labour 'results in no material and durable good' and only 'produces an immaterial good, such as a service, a cultural product, knowledge or communication' (Hardt and Negri 2000: 290), then documentary protagonists are not regarded as material. Materiality is determined in objects made by subjects through manual labour. This is not dissimilar to Marx's positioning of materiality as external and separate from – albeit brought to life by – the worker. The notion that affect is immaterial is at odds with a vital materialism that acknowledges agency in all kinds of materials and matter. The new materialist world of matter, which images are a part of, goes beyond the abstract materialist world created by human capitalism. While capital directs some affect, it does not create or control everything in the world. To emphasise the diversity of material agencies, the use of entities such as *things* (Bennett 2010) and *actants* (Latour 2009: 75) raises the question as to how 'authored' our actions are, when we also consist of things that are not human. Forces have traditionally been subsumed under the category of labour (Lazzarato 2002: 130). Forces cannot claim wages or rights. Waged labour is remunerated in symbolic currency and bound to human discourse. The notion of payment or reward is linked to an individual human or non-human rather than an impersonal actant. Forces, matter, actants and things can be materially rewarded, but they cannot be paid.[3] Although this fact needs to be acknowledged as shaping the image, it would not be in the human category of waged labour. The difference between these two kinds of materialisms poses the question, whether work constitutes human labour, which can be for wages, or, for example, non-human energy, which cannot be paid for in symbolic currency. Vital materialism bypasses the individual and does not deal with the issue of human labour. Lazzarato too finds that 'the "author" must lose its individual dimension' (1996: 144). But if agency is not attached to a singular protagonist and assigned rights, she cannot be acknowledged through wages and in the law as an agent in the image of her. The human documentary protagonist as material agent is neither accounted for by Marx's waged human living labour nor by the unpaid things of vital materialism.

Cinema 'in its incorporation and coordination of bodies in movement' has been described as 'a key site of biopolitical production' and immaterial labour (Goddard and Halligan 2012: 174), since 'it directly incorporates living processes by means of a technical apparatus that records and then later projects them' (171). But the concept of immaterial labour cannot be applied to documentary and fiction moving images in the same way, for it involves 'a series of activities that are not normally recognised as "work"' (Lazzarato 1996: 134). If 'capitalism seeks to involve even the worker's personality and subjectivity within the production of value' (136), then this is the case much more so for documentary protagonists than for fiction film acting, which is acknowledged as affective labour.

Hardt and Negri praise the actor not only for playing for the amusement of many, but for taking their place: 'how remarkable is the actor! When he performs, he is acting for at least three sets of people: himself, the author and above all, the public – he is the multitude!' (2000: 211). But in Hollywood feudalism, it is often the same actors who are paid to embody everybody else: Leonardo DiCaprio as King Louis XIV, as Howard Hughes, as J. Edgar Hoover – more a *multidude* than the multitude. Moreover, with offspring inheriting their ancestors' jobs, a few actors have become an entitled elite, further reducing the multitude of affects and corporeal materialities to the same features and expressions in a dynasticism of human matter. Given that some chosen few represent and transcend the many, the idea that one transcending actor can be 'the multitude' runs counter to

Hardt and Negri's rendering of the multitude in terms of immanence: a feudalism of affect in the land of the face by the landowners of expressions.

It is much more rewarding to be an actor in a fiction film than to be 'yourself' in someone else's images. There is perhaps a reason why the word 'actor' is part of the word 'factory': an actor is acknowledged, credited and remunerated for their affective labour. In capitalism and in fiction film, affective labour is waged and has an exchange value (Hochschild 1983: 7) even though it is distinct from the worker. Because the image of the documentary protagonist is presented as being unrehearsed and unchanged, there naturally cannot have been any immaterial labour or artistic process. Hardt and Negri acknowledge that the term 'immaterial labour' is ambiguous since even abstract knowledge work still needs the material brain, and especially affective labour requires 'labour in the bodily mode' (2000: 293). But even though they find that immaterial production 'remains material – it involves our bodies and brains as all labour does' (Hardt and Negri 2004: 109), they determine that affect is immaterial. The product is immaterial: the worker cannot be the product. This is where it gets complicated for the documentary protagonist, who is vital as the living material for the product that is their image.

When Lazzarato, who introduced the term 'immaterial labour', explains it in sociological terms as an 'interface' activity between different functions, teams or levels (1996: 134), that is, as knowledge work, the work of the documentary protagonist slips through the epistemological gaps since her affective labour does not consist in being an *interface*, but in *being a face* (and body). When Lazzarato writes about film, he sees only the 'matter of images' (2008: 284), or to use a term from art theory, their medium specificity, not the connection to the world they are inscribed by. Counterproductively comparing the electronic image to a painting, he writes that the video image 'is a constantly reshaping profile painted by an electronic paintbrush' (284). The image is a 'result of lines and intertwining' (285) of itself. The 'many vectors of nonhuman subjectivisation' (284) are the flows of the medium, unconnected to the world. The flows of image-matter override those of the world connected to the image. There are no documentary protagonists, only 'pure oscillations' (285). 'Pure perception as image-matter' (286), a notion Lazzarato takes from Bergson and Deleuze, cannot be about any protagonist-whatever – to appropriate the Deleuzean term 'any-space-whatever', which acknowledges the autonomy and singularity of a space. The image is merely of the medium, self-reflexive of human-made technology, even if it is an image 'unseen by the human eye' (2008: 286). Lazzarato writes that 'flows cannot be represented' (285), but a documentary image of someone or something is not the same as representing them. If 'the world is always already an image' (286), where is the world in relation to the image? The emphasis on the 'matter of images' (284) and especially the 'pure perception beyond the image' (286) are why Lazzarato cannot see his theory of immaterial labour in terms of the material and immaterial labour of the documentary protagonist. But in documentary images, there is a material link between the raw material of the protagonists and the aesthetics of the image. The image is an effect of the lines of the world, not just of the medium. Documentary images are not merely pure flows, but their singular elements are connected with differences in forces and referential statuses. The documentary image has a material connection to the world, even if the index of the world is translated into code.

Although the theorists of immaterial labour see the concept as a move beyond the 'old dichotomy between "mental and manual labour"', and even, curiously, beyond that 'between "material labour and immaterial labour"' (Lazzarato 1996: 134), the term nevertheless suggests a negation of materiality. It still sustains the distinction between the material processes of manual labour with 'raw materials (including labour)' (1996: 141) and the '"aesthetic/ideological" model of production' (144) of 'intellectual activity' (144) in which aesthetics are dematerialised and intellectualised. The notion of immaterial labour relies upon the separation between materials and aesthetics, between body and mind, and between the filmed protagonists as raw material and the directing, thinking artist.

Lazzarato suggests to use 'rather than the "material" model of production, the "aesthetic" model that involves author, reproduction, and reception' (144). But in the division between the 'old' materials *in* the image and the 'new' aesthetics *of* the image, the materiality of who and what constitutes an image is not accounted for. There is only the author, the reproduction, and the reception, but there are no protagonists. The processes of the '"aesthetic/ideological" model of production' are 'characterized by their social form' (144) and are 'within the economy of intellectual activity' (144). Having moved beyond Marx, for whom the worker was not paid to think (1973: 358), when Lazzarato describes immaterial labour as a 'synthesis of different types of know-how: intellectual skills, manual skills and entrepreneurial skills' (1996: 145), this emphasis on the conceptual know-how is akin to the traditional notion of authorship with the artist as the conceptual creator of the dematerialised or material art work, even if many were involved in the actual making of a painting or a sculpture. The immaterial labour of the idea – the knowledge work of the artist or image-taker – has always been valued more than the material labour of making and being, which could be outsourced. Claire Bishop refers to the delegating of being to the participants in an art work as 'outsourcing authenticity' (2012: 91). Symptomatically, the intellectual work of the artist, who can be absent in the production, is valued higher than the material, affective labour of the worker, who has to be present to constitute the work of the artist. So within the category of 'immaterial labour', the hierarchy of mind over matter is evident in the relation of immaterial knowledge work to affective labour. But whereas in the difference between ennobling work and physical labour (Arendt 1958: 79–174) usually 'labour is measurable, most importantly in money, hence can be abstracted, while work does not need to be' (Mazierska 2013: 4), the material and immaterial labour of the protagonist for the documentary is not accounted for – neither as work nor as labour.

Immaterial labour involves acting, or, rather, even *being* (Noah 2013) with a positive affective disposition as though there is perceivably no labour involved. It 'is not obviously apparent to the eye, because it is not defined by the four walls of the factory' (Lazzarato 1996: 137). When immaterial labour is successful, we cannot see it. If the means of production of affective labour become visible as mechanics and the smile appears as forced, the worker has failed to deliver. While material labour can be observed and phenomenologically experienced, the notion that labour is immaterial raises the question of how this invisible work can be documented. Immaterial labour, whether distanced and intellectual or immanent and affective, is difficult to capture merely visually through observation and also hard to describe in language. But what is documentary realism, if we can only see either an alienated and unrealised Marxian subject engrossed in material labour, or if we cannot see the immaterial labour of its protagonists at all?

Unfortunately, Marx's thoughts about alienation have been adopted by management strategists (Boltanski and Chiapello 2005). *Work Hard, Play Hard* (2012), a dry documentary about management in the German service industry, shows how large companies try to avoid alienating their employees. Workers should not feel alienated, so that they can be more productive and generate more profit. If they are alienated, they are not supposed to show it. The company checks on the psychology of their employees. There is no room or need for resistance since employers and employees want the same: a happy worker in the flow. Surveillance has become immaterial, but it still controls the materialities of being; or as one management trainer for the Deutsche Post (the German postal service) suggests metaphorically: the leadership vision should be planted in the DNA of each single employee. The language of leadership training is couched in terms of utopian relations: what is good for the company is good for the worker and the world. Hierarchies must be dismantled, cooperation should be optimised and everyone should connect, so that workers can work better and the performance of the company is maximised. It is about 'securing the collaboration of wage-earners in the realization of capitalist profits', as Boltanski and Chiapello describe it (2005: 217). The employee should be an entrepreneur for their company. The stronger the individual worker, the bigger the success of the company, 'concealing the fact that the individual and collective interests of workers and those of the company are not identical' (Lazzarato 1996: 96). This could be rephrased in terms of documentary or participatory art as such: participation conceals the fact that the individual and collective interests of the protagonist or participant and those of the image-taker or artist are not identical.

Even if a documentary observes its protagonists involved in immaterial labour, like *Work Hard, Play Hard* does, the focus is on their immaterial work for their employers, not on their additional immaterial labour for the documentary. Despite the documentary showing, through sanitised and business-like observation with astute ambient sound, the insidious extent to which managers and employees have to adapt themselves to the corporation's ideology and interests, the scope of the observation is confined to the thorough grasp of immaterial labour by the companies depicted in the documentary. Often the leaders come across better than the workers, because the managers are in control and can afford to be human since their posts are secure, while the employees are seen struggling to say the right things and be liked by their superiors in order to keep their jobs. The viewer identifies with the employers and adopts their judging position.

With respect to the worker, the once celebrated ability of the documentary protagonist to performatively subvert the film they are in, or to 'fake it' (Roscoe and Hight 2001), has long become controlled by their employers. The responsibility of subversion cannot just be placed on the unacknowledged, affective labour of the individual working documentary protagonist who has no rights to their image. If work cannot be separated from the worker, it becomes impossible for the realist documentary image to show the work.

The rights of the documentary protagonist

We have little to no right to our documentary image. Images are constantly taken from us legally without our knowledge and explicit consent. We do not have a right to privacy and to our image, for instance, when we are in a public space, where our consent is implicitly presumed and no permission is necessary to publish the image: 'In principle, a picture taken of an ordinary person in a public space can be published without that person's permission' (Brüggemeier *et al.* 2010: 282). According to the European Convention of Human Rights Article 8.1. 'everyone has the right to respect for his private and family life, his home and his correspondence' (Human Rights Act 1988) and 'all persons have an exclusive right to their image' (Brüggemeier *et al.* 2010: 284). But whatever exclusive rights to our own image there are in principle for ordinary people – 'The right to one's image ensures protection not only against publication, but also against merely taking that image without the consent of the person portrayed' (284) – these are practically invalid once we enter into a public space. Then we lose our right to privacy to a public we are part of. For instance, our right is lost, if we are in a

> landscape, a street scene, a group or some other public event. In such a situation the use of an image is legal even without the consent of the person represented because of the difficulty of obtaining the otherwise necessary consent in practice. (285)

So in any group protest, say, a rally for the rights of the protagonist to their own image, the protagonist would lose any rights *because* they are in a group. While a single individual in a shot will usually be asked for permission, particularly if the documentary might depend on them, once the protagonists are several and add up to a group or a 'crowd', especially if they are in public, the need for a permission is forfeited. Only recently, and reported with much protest by the British press, has the Hungarian Court acknowledged the right for consent of protagonists of an image taken in a public place (Nolan 2014).

In his essay 'People Exposed, People as Extras', Georges Didi-Huberman deliberated whether exposing the workers on film when they were leaving the filmmakers' factory in *Workers Leaving the Factory* (1895) had an alienating or liberating effect on them (2013: 35). But it did not really matter what the workers felt when they left the Lumière factory since they had no choice. Regardless of their disposition, the workers had no say over their images, which were owned by their employers like the factory they worked in. Didi-Huberman endorses the screening of these images by the employers who owned the footage to their 'wonderstruck bourgeois spectators' (35) because this would engender a *'political meeting*, created by the image and not cut off from the real' (35) and thus create a collective 'social being of cinema' (36). But this idealistic reading obscures the fact that the workers were safely contained in the images owned by their employers and observed by viewers who were of the same class as the owners. The only material contact was the trace of the workers on the celluloid. Because the workers were *only* in the images in that 'meeting', they posed no threat.

Farocki, too, likes to see workers shown as a collective rather than as individuals, a separation that has usually been implemented in fiction film. He makes this point explicit with respect to *Workers Leaving the Factory*:

> The appearance of community does not last long. Immediately after the workers hurry past the gate, they disperse to become individual persons, and it is this aspect of their existence which is taken up by most narrative films. If, after leaving the factory the workers don't remain together for a rally, their image as workers disintegrates. (Farocki 2002)

But by being collectively in the image – what Didi-Huberman elusively alludes to as the 'social being of cinema' (2013: 36) – the protagonists lose the right to their image.

The right to our private life is dependent on the ownership of the space around us, like a home. If we are homeless and thus have to exist in the public space, our life is not private and we cannot claim any rights to our image. If we own lots of property and move around in transportation we own, we have plenty of private space for which we can claim image rights. The apparent public space in which we lose our right to privacy has become more and more privatised, and the interests of the private owners of the so-called public space overrule the right to privacy of the protagonists who do not own the space they are moving through. And we are not all equal in the public space. Unpaid affective labour is asked especially of women outside of work and in public: 'Just ask any woman if she's ever been told to "smile" by a strange man on the street' (Jaffe 2013).

Immaterial production has been defined through relationships and has been attributed the key words of collaboration, community, cooperation and the common. Hardt and Negri cite Marx's observation that production does not take place in isolation: 'production by an isolated individual outside society [...] is as much as an absurdity as is the development of language without individuals living *together* and talking to each other' (Marx 1973: 84). They define the common as 'communication among singularities' (Hardt and Negri 2004: 204). But by finding that 'our existing affective relationships ground all productions of affect' (148), they undermine the generation and the singularities of new affects, protagonists and images which are not based on the communication of what already exists and is agreed upon. While the reaction of the documentary protagonist to the camera constitutes a relationship, according to Deleuze, affect is exactly that which exceeds communication (1986: 98). Affective labour is not merely communication or language. When Hardt and Negri list abstract ideas, material images and abstract knowledge in the same breath (2004: 147), the difference between the potentially absent image-taker and artistic knowledge worker behind the camera and the material labour in front of the camera is obfuscated. Hardt and Negri find that immaterial production is 'common and shared' in 'our common social image bank': 'A theory of the relation between labor and value today must be based on the common' (2004: 148). The value of the image is arrived at in a common market, but this is not the site of collectivity Hardt and Negri mean. Their suggestion of an appreciation of 'the common' in which value is assigned does not concern the documentary protagonist who provides the raw material of the image since the ownership belongs to the image-taker. The production of the documentary image and the attribution of the image rights to its taker rest on the loss of the rights of the protagonist because she is in a group. The common of the image prevents the right of the protagonist to her image. Perhaps the documentary protagonist in the image could be seen more in terms of the autonomous substances independent of relations of object-oriented philosophy (Bryant 2011: x).

If someone's image is taken in the public space of a market, European law finds that 'the publication of the picture does not necessarily infringe X's privacy. If, for example, the picture is published for the purpose of drawing attention to the opening of the market or that season's fresh produce, X's privacy interests are not violated' (Brüggemeier *et al.* 2010: 277). The protagonist's privacy is said not to be infringed upon by an image of her, because the property she is surrounded by is being advertised – as if that would be of any benefit for the protagonist. The public's right to know and the right of private enterprise to make known override the rights of the protagonist in the image. The rights of the owners of private property to publicity here take precedence over the privacy right of the protagonist not to be seen. Even though recently the right to be forgotten has been acknowledged by the European Court of Justice, this refers only to search engines, not to media websites (Arthur 2014).

Nearly 30 years ago, Brian Winston argued that, by filming the powerless, documentarians avoid looking at those who are in power and are powerful in contrast (1988: 276). Today, there are still professional documentary filmmakers with access to better broadcasting and theatrical distribution of their images, but we also all make documentary images and often distribute them through social media. While Marx found that, ultimately, 'the whole society must split into the two classes of *property owners* and propertyless *workers*' (1975: 322), today we all own images we took of others and we all are protagonists in documentary images which are the property of others. We are all image-takers and we are all in images as we increasingly surveil each other and ourselves. It depends on our actions and temporary positions rather than our permanent status. Nearly 40 years ago, Susan Sontag found that 'the industrialization of camera technology' would 'democratize all experiences by turning them into images' (1977: 7), a sentiment which is repeated more recently in statements such as 'the participatory camera can be understood as a symbol of the democratization of media production' (Tarrant 2009: 150). But unless we regard a democracy as being inherently inegalitarian, the reverse is the case today: by being turned into images owned by others, we lose our agency as we become the material of their images of us. On the other hand, through the potentially endless distribution of images, we also lose our agency as image-takers. In the infinite distribution of documentary images by many, the connection to an owner and responsibility for the work vanishes (Brazil and Migliorin 2014).

Merely by us working in the image, we have no rights to it. In Belgian law, if we are 'photographed as a *professional*, the photograph will be regarded as topical and no consent is necessary' (Brüggemeier et al. 2010: 279). In most national jurisdictions, the protagonist loses her status as a person *because* she is working: 'A picture taken of a policeman directing traffic or a bus driver constitutes a photograph of a profession, not of a person' (279). In Germany, the law presumes consent of 'a person who is photographed during his or her work' (288) and also when a protagonist 'regularly carries out a professional activity' (289) in a public space. In Austrian law, the more the protagonist is depicted working in her professional context, the less she can claim the right to privacy, even if she is doing something private. Because we are working, we have no rights to the image of us doing so. Marx observed that in capitalism the worker loses the right to control the value and the product of her labour. This lack of rights extends to the working documentary protagonist in the image. By working materially and immaterially in images, we not only produce a product that we do not own, or generate a smile we would otherwise not have, but our image is also exploitable as a product we do not own. Because we have 'been photographed while exercising a profession' (284) and our image is used to represent a worker, we have no right to our image.

Knowing that we are filmed makes us work more, and more conscientiously. We keep our expressions in check because we are being filmed. If we were to exercise our freedom of expression to make an expression that illustrates the alienation between our being and the work we are employed to do – which would not be possible with affective labour – we have even less right to claim the image of us expressing our alienation than if we were not working. Such images are then available to our employers through social media, even if they did not take them. The legally taken index of the worker working contributes to her being the object of her employer's gaze, and to her surveillance. The working protagonist does not only experience a psychological feeling of *to-be-looked-at-ness*, the term Laura Mulvey coined for the female objects of the male gaze in fiction films (1990: 33). Images of us working are even more likely to be owned by others than if we were not working, so the working documentary protagonist is doubly captured: first by her employer and then by the documentarist.

Marx wrote 'Estranged Labour' (1975: 322–334) in 1844–1845, just before manual labour started to be depicted in French realist paintings in the late 1840s in Millet's *The Haymakers Resting* (1848) and *Harvesters* (1849), and Courbet's *The Stone Breakers* (1849–1850). But if the realist 19th-century paintings of peasants labouring in the landscape would be documentary images, they would not be liberational by showing workers working. The land workers would have no right to their image, first because they are in a landscape and second because they are working. Filming work might 'force hidden oppressions into visibility' (O'Shaughnessy 2012: 155), but it can also draw upon and create invisible and immaterial labour. Farocki understandably laments how 'over the last century virtually none of the communication which took place in factories, whether through words, glances, or gestures, was recorded on film' (2002). But while it is lamentable that the history of cinema is full of images of workers leaving the factory, and not of them working, workers would have had even less right to their image had they been filmed working, or merely been doing something private in the factory. Their labour is owned by the factory owner and their image by the filmmaker, who are one and the same in the case of the Lumière workers leaving the factory.

Underscoring the visible excludes the invisible processes of work. In documentary, the reification of manual labour *in* the image has distracted from the immaterial labour of the protagonist *for* the documentary. This took place under the banner of realism. While the visibility of material labour constituted the realism of a painting or a film, immaterial labour is imperceptible. The invisibility of the processes of material, as well as immaterial labour is what makes documentary realism insufficient when filming work.

The freedom to express someone else

The assignment of image rights to the image-taker and not to the documentary protagonist is supported by the law. The freedom of speech and expression of the image-taker prevails over the protagonist's image rights for her own expressions. Article 10.1 of the European Convention of Human Rights states that 'everyone has the right to freedom of expression'. But freedom of expression primarily protects the communication of information and already formed opinions and ideas: 'The "expression" protected under Article 10 is not limited to words, written or spoken, but it extends to pictures, images and actions intended to express an idea or to present information' (Macovei 2004: 15). This right is not about the expression of affect and mutable life, but about representing a content that is considered as separate from the forms of its expression. As a representation of what has already been formed, the right to freedom of expression thus falls within the purview of semiotics. An expression registers only if it can also be articulated in language, which is the form of expression of the law. The right to freedom of expression thus reveals its origin in the freedom of speech act, which has been expanded to include symbolic expressions (Winston 2012: 269). Only if expressions are of something that can also be articulated through other semiotic means, such as the refusal to salute the American flag (270), are they deemed in need of protection. Here a speech is seen as a deed and the action makes a statement that could be expressed in another form.

In the US, the power of the speech act, speech as deed (273), is inscribed in law. The US is also where speech act theory initially gained prominence through the notion of performativity and where Judith Butler applied speech act theory to the liberation of biological determined sex through the performative acts of gender. Imported from gender studies, documentary studies have celebrated performativity (Bruzzi 2006, 2013; Nichols 1994, 2001), attributing the power to change the 'body' of the film through performative acts to the documentary protagonist, whose 'agendas exceed and transform those of the filmmaker' (Marks 2000: 68): 'There are many instances in documentary of the physical and spiritual being of a person seemingly to overflow the film that sets out to contain it' (MacDougal 1998: 157). But this overflow does not translate into an acknowledgment of authorship or image rights. Moreover, when Peter Wollen writes that 'protagonists appropriate the places they are "in"' (1980: 25), this appropriation is only in the reading of the scene, not in terms of the law. The notion of performativity masks the actual lack of rights of the documentary protagonist. Despite the material connection, the relationship between the performative act of the documentary protagonist and the images of her is not the same as that between performed gender and biological sex. The film is not the body of the protagonist. The documentary protagonist is in the 'body' of someone else's images. In human rights law, the rights to the images of performativity as deed belong to the image-taker, not to the performative protagonist.

Within a legal framework that regards expression as translatable into deed and knowledge, being filmed merely pursuing an ordinary activity such as walking does not count as an act the image of which should be protected as private. Only if there is a negative referential meaning attached to it, such as when the supermodel Naomi Campbell is photographed coming out of a Narcotics Anonymous meeting (Winston 2012: 317), can the right of privacy be claimed. Only if the documentary image 'is taken in a public space in humiliating or in awkward circumstances, [can] the photographing [...] constitute a defamatory act' (Brüggemeier *et al.* 2010: 282), and only then does publication constitute a crime. An ordinary person has to be asked for consent for an image taken of them in a public space, only if it constitutes defamation. 'Photographing a drunken, non-famous person sleeping in the street' is 'a possible defamatory act' [...] 'which can lead to sanctions and consequently to damages' (282). We can only claim the right to privacy in a public space by doing acts that are usually done in private. We have to be offensive or offended, despondent, humiliated or indecent, that is, doing something the publication of which can be interpreted as defamatory, in order to claim the right to our image and to privacy. We need to prove damage on grounds of distress if we want to prevent publication. In this way privacy only registers in terms of a negative semiotics. Even if we were to be upset about images of us, say, being upset, it used to be the case that we could only claim the right to privacy if we had endured great material, that is financial, damage (Kilkelly 2003: 21): 'Non-economic loss is only compensated in cases involving particularly serious intrusions' (Brüggemeier *et al.* 2010: 277), for instance in Austrian law. But whereas in 1995 being upset was not enough – as Winston put it (1995: 224) – more recently the law also takes mental damage into account (Winston 2008: 241).

So, it is not merely the case that because a protagonist is seen as a victim, she is represented in a documentary, as Winston observed in 'The Tradition of the Victim in Griersonian Documentary' (1988), but that because she is in a documentary, she becomes a victim. By making the rights of the documentary protagonist dependent on a negative image, the law reinforces her victim status. The documentary protagonist has to prove that she has suffered defamation with material effects in order to claim any rights to her image. Because the law reads lives in terms of a semiotics of knowledge, it does not protect unstructured, inadvertent and possibly positive expressions of affect that do not refer to something else, thereby allowing for the right to know to overrule the right to privacy. The disclosure of 'non-defamatory details of private life' (Kilkelly 2003: 14) is not protected. The right to shock with 'information or ideas that [...] offend, shock or disturb',[4] as has frequently been utilised in art and film, is given; the right to just be affective, and not to offend, is not. Expressions that do not refer to anything other than themselves are not protected. Only if our expressions can be isolated as being different from us, like in acting, and if they have been isolated through a discriminate, temporally limited act in what could be called an immaterial object, then the work of production is acknowledged. Immanence of expression prevents image rights and generates affective labour. Instead of expression being based *on* life, expression is set *against* life in the phrasing of the European Convention of Human Rights, as in the stated need for 'balancing the protection of private life *against* [italics added] the freedom of expression.'[5] Although Article 10 states that 'the freedom to hold opinions includes the negative freedom of not being compelled to communicate one's own opinions',[6] the right *not* to express is read in terms of communicating the content of an opinion, not as an expression of affect.

The right for the freedom of expression constitutes the condition 'for each individual's self-fulfillment'.[7] The notion of fulfilment of the self excludes the minor and singular expressions that we have without consciously seeking fulfilment. We cannot then exercise the freedom of expression merely through affect, and, therefore, we cannot claim it in the images someone else takes of us to express themselves. The freedom of expression of the image-takers trumps the freedom of expression of those who are the objects of their expression. The right for freedom of expression belongs to the image-takers, not to the protagonists.

So if you want to have the best shot at the rights to your documentary image, avoid the public space, avoid private property, don't work, don't lend yourself to be an illustration for a topic, don't be in a group, don't be in an event or in a historical situation, don't be incidentally anywhere, and don't know anyone! Instead, humiliate yourself, be drunk and indecent. Engage in intimate activities in a public space unless you work as a prostitute, in which case you probably have no right to privacy even if you are intimate, if prostitution is legally regarded as work. That said, even if we are intimate in a public space and this is not our work, we often have no rights to the image of our affection, as was the case for the couple who wanted to prevent Henri Cartier-Bresson from publishing his photo of their kiss and lost the case.[8] If you are happy, decent and not intimate in public, you have no rights to the image of you.

It is only when we have been turned into an image or an object, which is to say, into property, that there are rights of ownership. We do not hold the copyright to ourselves since we are not a product. The copy of us is more protected than the original because the copy can be sold as a commodity. Owning something external to oneself is more protected than material being: 'the law looks for property to protect' (Winston 2008: 239). Only if we are a brand and if the image of us is used to economically benefit a publication because we are famous, then we might claim violation of our privacy.

Not only has the factory been replaced by the corporation (Deleuze 1992: 4), *we* have: 'the company does not exist outside the producers and consumers who express it' (Lazzarato 2004: 188). The corporatisation of the worker is accompanied by the legal anthrophormisation of the corporation. While especially migrant labour in the global market increasingly operates outside of human rights, corporations appropriate the rights of people when convenient: 'funny how a corporation is a person until it breaks the law', when it is 'too big to jail' (Parramore 2012). Because abstract owning is valued higher than material being, corporations can claim the image rights of people. Public property can have restrictions on its image being taken, while people generally have no rights to their image if it is taken in a public space.

Conclusions

The indexical documentary image owes its status to the fact that the image '*is* the model' (1967: 14), as André Bazin famously phrased it. The documentary image of us is constituted through our index. But while we provide the raw material for the image of us, 'the ownership (as it were) of the thing imaged (e.g. the person photographed) is not legally significant; the ownership of the image is' (Winston 2008: 239). The law follows the dominance of the appropriator, who took the image, over the original, who is in it (238). The expression 'to take one's image' does not imply without reason that something is being taken, as already Sontag questioned: 'to photograph is to appropriate the thing photographed' (1977: 4), and 'it turns people into objects that can be symbolically possessed' (14). But it is not (only) the soul that is stolen. To take an image and thereby acquire ownership is also to take the value generated by who or what is depicted. Authorship, wages and rights are taken in a very materialistic way from the protagonist despite the material dependence of the documentary image upon the world and its protagonists: 'photographed images do not seem to be statements about the world so much as pieces of it' (4). But this dependence of the image on what it shows remains legally unacknowledged: 'physical film exists in the law almost without reference to the pre-existing physical objects captured by the exposure [...] the physical storage medium is what is owned' (Winston 2008: 238). Franco 'Bifo' Berardi finds that it is this separation of 'value production from the physical interaction of things' that fuels capitalism: 'the abstraction process at the core of the capitalist capture (subsumption) of work implies abstraction from the need for the concreteness of products: the referent is erased' (2012). In this vein, the acknowledgment of the contribution of the referent that is the documentary protagonist – the acknowledgment of the contribution of life to the product that is the image – remains likewise wiped out.

Little has changed in terms of the rights of the protagonists, since Winston raised concern that any consideration of the rights of the subjects of documentary to their image is seen as an infringement of the documentarists' freedom of speech (1988: 270). The privileging of the freedom of expression, Article 10, over the right to privacy, Article 8, and the slant of human rights law towards the takers of images, at the expense of those who make up the material of the images, has again been confirmed in the response to the Leveson report in the UK, the country with the weakest privacy laws in Europe: 'English common law has not yet formally recognised a tort of violation of privacy' (Brüggemeier *et al.* 2010: 9). When the report criticised the invasive intrusion of the UK press into private lives and recommended more statutory privacy rights, they were opposed by human rights and civil liberties campaigners because it would be in breach of the freedom of expression.[9] Only image-takers have human rights. The material that the artist uses is regarded as non-human and therefore without rights. Human rights law enshrines the rights of the artist and the filmmaker over their human and non-human materials. The right of others to express themselves through images of us takes precedence over our right *not* to be the material of their freedom of expression. Our lives are the raw material for images, and raw material usually counts less than what has been processed and selected, be that of human or other matter, in art or in law. The human exploitation of resources extends to human resources as the material of other humans' images.

The generative work and the affective labour of the documentary protagonist slip through the gaps of Marx's conception of living labour as working with external materials, of post-Marxist thought that only sees the material of the image, and of human rights which assign the freedom of expression of the worker only to the image-taker. It remains to be the case that the owner of the site of labour controls the generated product, be that with respect to the factory or the image.

Notes

My translation of 'Kant und Fichte gern zum Äther schweifen, suchten dort ein fernes Land, doch ich such nur tüchtig zu begreifen, was ich — auf der Strasse fand!' (Marx 1966 [1837]: 28).

1. Workers are not even employed anymore even though they are available all the time for work on zero-hours contracts in '21st century serfdom' (Milne 2013). Zero-hours contracts are used by universities, cinemas and art institutions. Universities are now the largest providers of zero-hours contracts (Butler 2013).

2. Even though the protagonists in scripted reality shows earn relatively little, due to the serial format, the protagonists often derive additional sources of income as they become celebrities. The cast of scripted reality show *The Only Way is Essex* received a pay rise from £50 a day in 2011 to £120 a day in 2013 (Mediamonkey 2013). The *Daily Mail* reported in 2011 that "they're only making 32p more than the National Minimum Wage hourly rate of £5.93, if their wage is split over an eight hour day" (Daily Mail Reporter 2011).

3. There is a not yet articulated space between the immanent materialism of non-human actants on the one hand and a political analysis with declared demands of equal rights for the human subject of historical materialism on the other. This gap became apparent at the very interesting conference *Matter, Life and Resistance*, which featured proponents from either proclivity (Canterbury: University of Kent, 1 June 2013–2 June 2013).
4. Handyside v. the United Kingdom, 1976; *Sunday Times* v. the United Kingdom, 1979; Lingens v. Austria, 1986; Oberschlick v. Austria, 1991; Thorgeir Thorgeirson v. Iceland, 1992; Jersild v. Denmark, 1994; Goodwin v. the United Kingdom, 1996; De Haes and Gijsels v. Belgium, 1997; Dalban v. Romania,1999; Arslan v. Turkey, 1999; Thoma v. Luxembourg, 2001; Jerusalem v. Austria, 2001; Maronek v. Slovakia, 2001; Dichand and Others v. Austria, 2002, cited in Macovei (2004:6).
5. Von Hannover v. Germany, 2005, cited in Winston (2012: 318).
6. Vogt v. Germany, 1995, cited in Macovei (2004: 8).
7. Lingens v. Austria, 1986; Sener v. Turkey, 2000; Thoma v. Luxembourg, 2001; Maronek v. Slovakia, 2001; Dichand and Others v. Austria, 2002, cited in Macovei (2004: 6).
8. Gill v. Hearst, 1953, cited in Winston (1988: 280).
9. Shami Chakrabarti from *Liberty* about statutory regulation recommended by the Leveson Enquiry: 'It is this alternative that *Liberty* cannot support and which would in our view, breach article 10 of the ECHR [European Convention on Human Rights] and Human Rights Act' (Wintour 2012). Chakrabarti was herself an assessor who assisted with the Leveson Enquiry. Her defence of the freedom of expression over the right to privacy was then opposed by the UN special rapporteur on human rights, Ben Emmerson: 'Leveson isn't a threat to human rights – not adopting his proposals would be. Comments attributed to Shami Chakrabarti of Liberty are the kind of nonsense that gives human rights a bad name' (2012).

Bibliography

Arendt, Hannah (1958). *The Human Condition* (Chicago: The University of Chicago Press).

Arthur, Charles (2014). 'Explaining the Right to be Forgotten', *The Guardian* (14 May 2014) http://www.theguardian.com/technology/2014/may/14/explainer-right-to-be-forgotten-the-newest-cultural-shibboleth (accessed 20/5/2014).

Bazin, André (1967). *What is Cinema? Volume I*, ed. and trans. by H. Gray (Berkeley, Los Angeles and London: University of California Press).

Bennett, Jane (2010). *Vibrant Matter: A Political Ecology of Things* (Durham, NC: Duke University Press).

Berardi, Franco (2012). 'Emancipation of the Sign: Poetry and Finance During the Twentieth Century' *e-flux*, 39, November, http://www.e-flux.com/journal/emancipation-of-the-sign-poetry-and-finance-during-the-twentieth-century/ (accessed 1/11/2014).

Bishop, Claire (2012). 'Delegated Performance: Outsourcing Authenticity', *October*, 140, Spring, pp. 101–112.

Boltanski, Luc and Eve Chiapello (2005). *The New Spirit of Capitalism* (London: Verso).

Brazil, André and Cezar Migliorin (2014). 'Amateur Biopolitics: Generalization of a Practice, Limits of a Concept', in Silke Panse and Dennis Rothermel (eds.), *A Critique of Judgment in Film and Television* (New York and Basingstoke: Palgrave Macmillan).

Brüggemeier, Gert, Aurelia Colombi Ciacchi and Patrick O'Callaghan (2010). *Personality Rights in European Tort Law* (Cambridge: Cambridge University Press).

Bruzzi, Stella (2006). *New Documentary* (New York and London: Routledge).

Bruzzi, Stella (2013). 'The Performing Film-maker and the Acting Subject', in Brian Winston (ed.) *The Documentary Film Book* (London: The British Film Institute), pp. 48–58.

Butler, Sarah (2013). 'Universities Twice as Likely as other Employers to use Zero-hours Contracts', *The Guardian* (5 September 2013), http://www.theguardian.com/uk-news/2013/sep/05/universities-colleges-zero-hours-contracts (accessed 1/11/2014).

Bryant, Levi R. (2011). *Democracy of Objects* (Ann Arbor: Open Humanities Press).

Comolli, Jean-Louis (1996) 'Corps mécaniques de plus en plus célestes', *Images Documentaires*, 24, pp. 39–48.

Daily Mail Reporter (2011). '*The Only Way is Essex* Cast Struggle to Make Ends Meet on £50 a Day Wage', *Daily Mail* (23 March 2011), http://www.dailymail.co.uk/tvshowbiz/article-1368696/The-Only-Way-Is-Essex-cast-struggle-make-ends-meet-50-day-wage.html#ixzz2q0gdxyL9 (accessed 1/11/2014).

Deleuze, Gilles (1986). *Cinema 1: The Movement-Image* (Minneapolis: University of Minnesota Press).

Deleuze, Gilles (1992). 'Postscript on the Societies of Control', *October*, 59, Winter, pp. 3–7.

Didi-Huberman, Georges (2013). 'People Exposed, People as Extras', in Peter Osborne and Éric Alliez (eds) *Spheres of Action: Art and Politics* (London: Tate Publishing), pp. 33–44.

Emmerson, Ben (2012). 'Leveson isn't a threat to human rights – not adopting his proposals would be', *The Guardian* (3 December 2012), http://www.theguardian.com/commentisfree/2012/dec/03/leveson-human-rights-shami-chakrabarti (accessed 6/6/2014).

Farocki, Harun (2002). 'Workers Leaving the Factory', trans. by L. Faasch-Ibrahim, *Senses of Cinema*, 21, July, http://sensesofcinema.com/2002/21/farocki_workers/ (accessed 1/11/2014).

Goddard, Michael and Benjamin Halligan (2012). 'Cinema, the Post-Fordist Worker, and Immaterial Labour: From Post-Hollywood to the European Art Film', *Framework*, 53 (1), Spring, pp. 172–189.

Hardt, Michael (2009). 'Production and Distribution of the Common. A Few Questions for the Artist', *Open*, 16, pp. 20–28.

Hardt, Michael and Antonio Negri (2000). *Empire* (Cambridge MA: Harvard University Press).

Hardt, Michael and Antonio Negri (2004). *Multitude. War and Democracy in the Age of Empire* (New York: Penguin Press).

Hearn, Allison (2010). 'Reality Television, *The Hills*, and the Limits of the Immaterial Labour Thesis', *tripleC*, 8 (1), pp. 60–76.

Hochschild, Arlie Russell (1983). *The Managed Heart: Commercialization of Human Feeling* (Berkeley and Los Angeles: University of California Press).

Human Rights Act (1988). http://www.legislation.gov.uk/ukpga/1998/42/schedule/ 1 (accessed 12/1/2014)

Jaffe, Sarah (2013). 'Grin and Abhor It: The Truth Behind "Service with a Smile"', *In These Times* (4 February 2013), http://inthesetimes.com/working/entry/14535/grin_and_abhor_it_the_truth_behind_service_with_a_smile/ (accessed 1/11/2014).

Kilkelly, Ursula (2003). *The Guide to Respect for Private and Family Life. A Guide to the Implementation of Article 8 of the European Convention of Human Rights. Human Rights Handbooks, No. 1* (Strasbourg Cedex: Directorate General of Human Rights. Council of Europe).

Latour, Bruno (2009). *Politics of Nature. How to Bring the Sciences into Democracy* (Cambridge, MA: Harvard University Press).

Lazzarato, Maurizio (1996). 'Immaterial Labour', in Paulo Virno and Michael Hardt (eds.), *Radical Thought in Italy* (Minneapolis: Minnesota University Press).

Lazzarato, Maurizio (2002). *Videophilosophie. Zeitwahrnehmung im Postfordismus* (Berlin: b-books).

Lazzarato, Maurizio (2004). 'From Capital-Labour to Capital-Life', *Ephemera*, 4 (3), pp. 187–208.

Lazzarato, Maurizio (2008). 'Video, Flows and Real Time', in Tanya Leighton (ed.), *Art and the Moving Image: A Critical Reader* (London: Tate Publishing and Afterall), pp. 283–291.

MacDougal, David (1998). *Transcultural Cinema*, ed. by Lucien Taylor (Princeton: Princeton University Press).

Macovei, Monica (2004). *Freedom of Expression: A Guide to the Implementation of Article 10 of the European Convention of Human Rights', Human Rights Handbooks No. 2* (Strasbourg Cedex: Directorate General of Human Rights. Council of Europe).

Marks, Laura U. (2000). *The Skin of the Film. Intercultural Cinema, Embodiment, and the Senses* (Durham: Duke University Press).

Marx, Karl (1966) [1837]. *Texte zur Methode und Praxis I. Jugendschriften 1835–1841*, edited by Ernesto Grassi with Walter Hess (Reinback bei Hamburg: Rowohlt).

Marx, Karl (1969). 'Theses on Feuerbach', *Marx/Engels Selected Works, Volume One*, trans. by W. Lough (Moscow: Progress Publishers), pp. 13–15, http://www.marxists.org/archive/marx/works/1845/theses/theses.htm (accessed 1/11/2014).

Marx, Karl (1973). *Grundrisse* (Harmondsworth and London: Penguin Books and New Left Review).

Marx, Karl (1975). *Early Writings*, trans. by Rodney Livingstone and Gregor Benton (London and New York: Penguin Books).

Marx, Karl (1999). *Capital*, ed. by David McLellan (Oxford: Oxford University Press).

Mazierska, Ewa (2013). *Work in Cinema: Labor and the Human Condition* (New York and Basingstoke: Palgrave Macmillan).

Mediamonkey (2013). 'Towie Pay Rise Won't Buy Much Extra Bling', *The Guardian* (11 March 2013), http://www.theguardian.com/media/mediamonkeyblog/2013/mar/11/towie-pay-rise.

Milne, Seumas (2013). 'Zero-hours Contracts: in Cameron's Britain, the Dockers' Line-up is Back', *The Guardian* (6 August 2013), http://www.theguardian.

com/commentisfree/2013/aug/06/david-cameron-britain-dockers-line-up-back (accessed 1/11/2014).

Mitchell, W. J. T. (2005). *What do Pictures Want?* (Chicago: University of Chicago Press).

Mulvey, Laura (1990). 'Visual Pleasure and Narrative Cinema', ed. by Patricia Erens. *Issues in Feminist Film Criticism* (Bloomington and Indianapolis: Indiana University Press).

Myerscough, Paul (2013). 'Short Cuts', *London Review of Books*, 35 (1), (3 January 2013), p. 25, http://www.lrb.co.uk/v35/n01/paul-myerscough/short-cuts (accessed 1/11/2014).

Nichols, Bill (1991). *Representing Reality Issues and Concepts in Documentary* (Bloomington and Indianapolis: Indiana University Press).

Nichols, Bill (1994). *Blurred Boundaries. Questions of Meaning in Contemporary Culture* (Bloomington and Indianapolis: Indiana University Press).

Nichols, Bill (2001). *Introduction to Documentary* (Bloomington and Indianapolis: Indiana University Press).

Noah, Timothy (2013). 'Labour of Love. The Enforced Happiness of *Pret A Manger*', *New Republic* (1 February 2013), http://www.newrepublic.com/article/112204/pret-manger-when-corporations-enforce-happiness (accessed 1/11/2014).

Nolan, Daniel (2014). 'Hungary law requires photographers to ask permission to take pictures', *The Guardian* (14 March 2014), http://www.theguardian.com/world/2014/mar/14/hungary-law-photography-permission-take-pictures (accessed 20/3/2014).

O'Shaughnessy, Martin (2012). 'French Film and Work: The Work Done by Work-Centered Films', *Framework*, 53 (1), Spring, pp. 155-171.

Virno, Paolo (2004). *A Grammar of the Multitude* (Los Angeles: Semiontext(e)).

Parramore, Laura (2012). 'HSBC: Too Big to Jail; After being Charged with Money Laundering, HSBC Gets a Monopoly-style Get-out-of-jail Card', *Salon* (13 December 2012), http://www.salon.com/2012/12/13/hsbc_too_big_to_jail/?source=newsletter (accessed 11/19/2013).

Roscoe, Jane and Craig Hight (2001). *Faking It. Mock-documentary and the Subversion of Factuality* (Manchester: Manchester University Press).

Sontag, Susan (1977). *On Photography* (London: Penguin Books).

Tarrant, Patrick (2009). 'Camera Movies: *Awesome, I Fuckin' Shot Them!*', *Journal of Media Practice*, 10 (2&3), pp. 149–165.

Winston, Brian (1988). 'The Tradition of the Victim in Griersonian Documentary', in Alan Rosenthal (ed.), *New Challenges for Documentary* (Berkeley, Los Angeles and London: University of California Press).

Winston, Brian (1995). *Claiming the Real. The Documentary Film Revisited.* London: British Film Institute.

Winston, Brian (2008). *Claiming the Real II. Documentary, Grierson and Beyond* (London: British Film Institute).

Winston, Brian (2012). *A Right to Offend* (London, New Delhi, New York and Sydney: Bloomsbury).

Wintour, Patrick (2012). 'Shami Chakrabarti Clarifies Liberty Backing for Leveson Report', *The Guardian* (2 December 2012), http://www.guardian.co.uk/media/2012/dec/02/shami-chakrabarti-clarifies-liberty-leveson-backing (accessed 4 December 2012).

Wollen, Peter (1980). 'Introduction: Place in the Cinema', *Framework*, 13 (3), Autumn.

9

Amateur Digital Filmmaking and Capitalism

William Brown

In the digital age, cameras that can record moving images and sounds have become ubiquitous; they exist not only in the form of cheap, stand-alone moving image cameras, but also on various devices such as mobile phones, tablets and still image cameras. Practices such as machinima (the making of films using footage recorded in videogames and/or virtual environments), or using footage found from online archives to create edited works (some of which might be referred to as 'mash-ups'), mean that one does not even need a physical moving image camera to make a film (although the digital era is of course preceded by a history of found footage films, scratch films, painted films and films made with still images that similarly did not necessitate a physical camera). Furthermore, many computers now come with editing software pre-installed on them, while one can also download editing freeware from the internet in order to put films together. Simultaneous to the increased ease of producing films is the increased ease of getting those films 'out there'. For the internet has, of course, put in the hands of anyone with online access the ability to upload, and thus in some senses to distribute, their films – popularly via sites such as Vimeo and YouTube.

In other words, while there is a whole history of amateur filmmaking, as explored most prominently by Patricia R. Zimmermann (1995), it seems that the digital era has seen amateur filmmaking take on a new lease of life – with 48 hours of footage allegedly being uploaded every minute to YouTube alone (Burgess 2013: 53). Not all of those 48 hours will be uploaded to YouTube by amateur filmmakers. Indeed, many films uploaded to YouTube are professional films that are made with the intention of creating revenue for their makers. Nonetheless, much material uploaded to YouTube is created by amateurs – filmmakers who are not paid at all for their efforts.

Now, many online filmmakers do move from an amateur to a professional status as a result of their popularity, such that the distinction between amateur and professional often becomes blurred (Salvato 2009). The blurring of these two is not simply a case of online films having institutional support (productions for YouTube uploaded to the channel of a corporation, for example); nor is it a case necessarily of image quality and production values (as the supposed six-figure income generated by *Charlie Bit My Finger* (Howard Davies-Carr, UK, 2007) would suggest – since the film (see Figure 9.1) is simply a 56-second amateur movie of a one-year-old boy, Charlie (Charlie Davies-Carr), biting the finger of his three-year-old brother (Harry Davies-Carr); (see Burgess 2013: 54). One might argue that this blurring of the distinction between amateur and professional is, with regard to YouTube, as a result of a shared aesthetic that, loosely put, might best be understood in light of the 'cinema of attraction(s)' (Gunning 1986), in that most films that receive many hits – and thus which gain income via advertising – are short films that downplay narrative in favour of the 'simple' spectacle of life – with *Charlie Bit My Finger* mirroring Lumière actualities like *Le Repas de Bébé/Baby's Dinner* (Auguste and Louis Lumière, France, 1895) in duration and in terms of theme, even if the more recent *Charlie* film has a handheld, as opposed

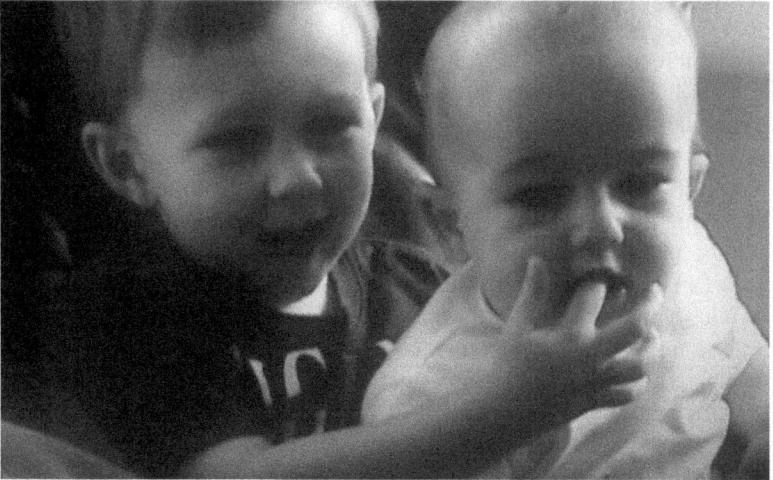

Figure 9.1   Charlie biting the finger of his three-year-old brother
Source: Screen capture from YouTube (10 March 2014)

to fixed camera, aesthetic, and even if it is shot from a closer distance to its subject than the Lumières' film. However, while an 'attraction(s)' aesthetic might describe many YouTube and other online films, it by no means defines all of them. Many successful YouTube and other online films do have narrative content, and not all are limited in duration to one or a small number of minutes. *Dr Horrible's Singalong Blog* (Joss Whedon, USA, 2008), is, for example, a musical narrative that lasts 40 minutes and which tells the story of an aspiring supervillain, Dr Horrible (Neil Patrick Harris), whose attempts both to join the Evil League of Evil and to win the favours of a local charity worker, Penny (Felicia Day), are continually stymied by superhero Captain Hammer (Nathan Fillion). The film was initially released online via Hulu, with releases via iTunes, Amazon Video on Demand and Netflix soon following – with the film also being easily found on YouTube to watch in parts or in whole. In other words, there is no simple explanation for why internet films in general achieve success: many unlikely amateur films receive numerous hits (*Charlie*), while many professional films garner nothing like the same attention.

Providing an authoritative guide to online filmmaking, be it amateur or professional, is not, however, the aim of this essay. Nor, indeed, is the aim of this essay to offer anything like a definitive guide to only amateur (as opposed to professional) filmmaking in the digital era, be it distributed online, via other means (for example, via DVD), or not distributed at all, but instead kept on discs or computer drives in the domestic home. To do either of those tasks would be quite impossible in a single essay – or even in a multitude of essays, since there is just far too much content for any one human to see or even to know about in several lifetimes. Instead, the aim of this essay is to ask what amateur filmmaking *means* in the contemporary, digital era, in particular in relation to capital. In order to do this, I shall consider amateur filmmaking in light of the work of Karl Marx and, more pertinently, in light of subsequent thinkers who have themselves been inspired by Marx. There will be an aesthetic dimension to this argument, by which I mean to say that I shall consider closely amateur films, including my own, that aim explicitly to be 'artistic' films made by amateur, not professional, artists.

It is important to bear in mind that not all amateur films aim to achieve the same results. Some/many amateur films are made with the specific hope/intention of replicating professional works in a bid for their makers to become professionalised/monetised themselves – a key example being Fede Alvarez's *¡Ataque de Pánico!/Panic Attack!* (Uruguay, 2009), a micro-budget short film featuring giant robots destroying Montevideo, and which led to Alvarez being invited to direct the

Hollywood remake of *The Evil Dead* (USA, 2013). However, some, perhaps most, amateur filmmakers do not aim – and do not even aspire – to be professionalised. Nonetheless, some amateur filmmakers do on occasion engage specifically with what it means to be an amateur filmmaker in the contemporary age, thereby drawing attention to how amateur films as a whole potentially subvert rather than reaffirm the ongoing and globalised hegemony of capitalism.

Digital Marxism and immaterial labour

Interest in the work of Karl Marx has been reinvigorated in the digital age, as I have explained elsewhere (Brown 2013: 50–54). To recap this argument in a different manner, the renewed interest in Marx potentially comes about as a result of the seemingly relentless privatisation of industry since the 1980s, typified in the UK by the policies of Margaret Thatcher. According to sociologist Göran Therborn, 'Marx foresaw a historical tendency of development – that the productive forces would acquire a more social character and would thus come into increasing contradiction with the private ownership of the means of production' (Therborn 2008: 16). However, since the rise of Thatcherism and other drives towards not social but privatised capital, Marx's foretold trajectory seems to have changed. And this change of direction has paradoxically reinvigorated interest in Marx, and perhaps more pertinently in Marxism, in a bid to put the world 'back on track' towards a social(ist), global economy (or social(ist) local, national and/or regional economies at the very least). As Therborn says: '[n]ew compasses of the Left have to be made' (Therborn 2008: 116).

Although wary that political engagement in the age of the internet, or what he terms 'cyber-politics', is 'primarily young middle-class politics', Therborn nonetheless still believes that 'the cyber-enthusiasts who created the internet were not wrong in pointing to its participatory democratic potential' (22).[1] In other words, the digital age, with the internet as its chief medium, offers the potential not just for critique, but also for change. And capital may yet evolve into socialism because the infrastructure required for such an evolution is beginning to be put into place. To return to Marx himself, under socialism – or, more specifically, communism – 'where nobody has one exclusive sphere of activity but each can be accomplished in any branch he wishes, society regulates the general production and thus makes it possible for me to do one thing today and another tomorrow, to hunt in the morning, fish in the afternoon, rear cattle in the evening, criticise after dinner, just as

202 Marx at the Movies

I have a mind, without ever becoming hunter, fisherman, shepherd or critic' (Marx and Engels 2004: 53). In other words, communism would in some senses signal the age of the amateur, carrying out Facebook in the morning, YouTube video production in the afternoon, and maybe even some fleshworld fishing in the evening, as humans come to do what they want when they want, without the need for specialised work routines.

For all of Therborn's guarded optimism, then, and for all of Marx's belief in moving beyond a capitalist division of labour, in which workers are alienated as a result of the specialised nature of their travails, others are less sure about the internet's potential for change. For example, a common argument that is made in relation to the internet age is that work done by amateurs constitutes a form of exploitation. In the context of what is referred to commonly as 'Web 2.0' (the development from the web as a space for consumption to the web as a space for participation, with the advent of social networking sites being a principle example of this development), '[t]he amateur's voluntary participation is [...] being transformed into (surplus) value for the administrators of the aforementioned social networks and services' (Kostakis 2009: 458). In other words, it is the participants in social networks that create their value: I am an entertaining user of Facebook, posting funny and/or profound thoughts, as well as links to popular and cute cat videos, meaning that people stay on Facebook as a whole (and on my Facebook profile perhaps in particular), because they are entertained. While they are on my Facebook page in particular and on Facebook more generally, they see advertisements that bring in revenue for Facebook (while Facebook at the same time monitors, and keeps, information regarding the kind of things that interest both them and me). In short, then, I am making money for Facebook, but I am not being paid for it. The same argument applies to sites like YouTube; although YouTube does pay some of its more prominent participants, the vast majority of users – and thus of workers – do not get paid.

Toby Miller makes a similar argument when he says of clips from American TV shows uploaded to YouTube that 'far from undermining the mainstream media, [such] YouTube videos are the greatest boon imaginable to mainstream US television' (Miller 2009: 427). For, such clips are among the most watched on YouTube, and they constitute free advertising for the makers of those shows – many of whom might also advertise on YouTube. Conversely, '[w]hile amateur content may form the majority of content on YouTube, it is barely watched by contrast with the vastly more-popular texts that come from the culture industries; fifteen of its top twenty search terms are for US TV programs' (Miller 2009: 427). In other words, ripping clips and uploading them is not subversive, but in fact a reinforcement of the hegemonic power of movie studios and television companies; those who carry out such practices in effect 'work' for those studios. In Miller's terms, the 'prosumer' is in fact a performer of casual, flexible labour (Miller 2009: 433) – and the same may also be true of the (signally less successful) amateur making their own films.

A similar argument has been mounted in regard to MySpace by Mark Coté and Jennifer Pybus, who relate the notion of such labour for social networks to the concept of 'immaterial labour' devised by Italian Autonomist thinker Maurizio Lazzarato (Coté and Pybus 2007). For Lazzarato, 'immaterial labour involves a series of activities that are not normally recognized as "work" – in other words, the kinds of activities involved in defining and fixing cultural and artistic standards, fashions, tastes, consumer norms, and, more strategically, public opinion' (Lazzarato 2006: 132). He goes on to list the 'classic forms of "immaterial" production: audiovisual production, advertising, fashion, the production of software, photography, cultural activities, and so forth' (136). Perhaps all of these are united by the production of information, although Lazzarato also argues that 'the "raw material" of immaterial labour is subjectivity and the "ideological" environment in which this subjectivity lives and reproduces' (142). In other words, if historically 'subjectivity' has been a means of social control (in that I identify myself as X, and this is my job, such that who I am, or what I could be/become, is thus delimited/controlled), now subjectivity is not just a means to retain control, but it is itself put to work. Let us think about it thus: I work in advertising and I need to get people to look at my adverts, something that people do typically in their leisure time. The more people look at the adverts, the more likely the product being advertised will sell, which in turn means more advertising for my company. What is more, people actually want adverts and they want the consumer products being advertised. For this reason, '[i]mmaterial workers [...] satisfy a demand by the consumer and at the same time establish that demand' (142). And because, in short, looking at adverts involves making money for advertising companies, then '[r]eception is thus, from this point of view, a creative act and an integrative part of the product' of immaterial labour (144; original emphasis).[2] For this reason, since many of our leisure activities also involve the creation of capital for the industries of immaterial labour, the distinction between work and leisure time becomes increasingly eroded.

Now, Lazzarato does not write specifically about the digital age or the internet in his founding essay on immaterial labour – even if he does mention software development as a core 'immaterial' industry. So perhaps it is worth translating, briefly, the concept of immaterial labour into the internet age and the context of Web 2.0 – and also to relate this to the foregoing discussion of the amateur. We can think about it thus: In the pre-digital era I had an identity and a job, and then during my leisure time I spent my money on leisure items (say, alcohol), such that what money I earned from my employers in part went back to them, particularly if the owners of the factory in which I worked also owned the bar in which I drank (which is not to mention paying rent for the accommodation that the factory bosses also owned). Nowadays in the digital era, however, I spend my leisure time not just drinking alcohol but also on the internet posting cat videos that keep other people on the internet such that I am making money for the social network companies. My subjectivity is no longer developed as a means of control such that I work (I am happy because I have an identity, as affirmed on Facebook by my profile page), but it is now also doing work, since producing capital becomes a part not just of my working day, but also of my leisure time (I don't just 'have' an identity on Facebook; my Facebook page is also a site for re-posting adverts, getting people to see adverts, and so on). In other words, my status as an amateur using social networking sites is a key part of immaterial labour, benefitting those who are employed in those industries, while also constituting a form of exploitation, in that I am not paid for my (often creative) contribution to those industries. Speaking of 'free time,' Theodor W. Adorno writes: '[during their free time] people are at least subjectively convinced that they are acting of their own free will, this will itself shaped by the very same forces which they are seeking to escape in their hours without work' (Adorno 2002: 188). That is, the fact that people believe that they are willingly and willfully using their free time in their own, chosen way, when in fact they are making money for the very same 'forces' for which they make money during their working hours, only redoubles the exploitation that is taking place.

A brief history of amateur filmmaking

Let us turn our attention more specifically to amateur filmmaking in order subsequently to relate it to the elaboration of the amateur and immaterial labour given above. As mentioned, Patricia R. Zimmermann

(1995) has provided the most comprehensive history of amateur film-making, particularly in the USA. It is a history that depends on techno-logical developments and the availability of filmmaking equipment to the general public. More particularly, it is also a history that involves both amateur filmmakers and those who have defended the amateur in relation to the professional in writing; that is, amateur filmmaking requires not just amateur filmmakers, but a discourse of the amateur as well. Key figures in creating such a discourse of the amateur in rela-tion to cinema include Bertolt Brecht, Maya Deren and Harry Alan Potamkin. Writing on the theatre, Brecht figured the amateur as equally important to culture as the professional, saying that 'it mustn't be imag-ined that there is no point in discussing amateur efforts in the arts if nothing of benefit to the arts results' (Brecht 1964: 150). Zimmermann furthermore explains how Brecht saw the 'popular' as 'the active par-ticipation of people in the development of culture' (Zimmermann 1995: 85). In other words, culture is not something handed down to citizens, but something that the people help to create, with the amateur there-fore being an expression of the creation of culture. To relate this to film history, it is perhaps no surprise that many of the amateur filmmakers celebrated by Zimmermann are defined as 'avant-garde' – in that they work 'ahead' of popular culture, shaping and informing it, meaning that amateur cinema is, in this sense, also an integral part of film culture (and necessary for/to professional filmmaking). Conversely, the label 'amateur' – together with all of the negative connotations that it often carries – is used by professionals in order to legitimise their own work and to exert power over the amateurs, who, in being non-professionals threaten to undermine their business (for if someone can do for free what the professional is doing at great expense, then there is no longer any need for the professional).[3]

Meanwhile, Maya Deren asserts the superiority of the amateur film-maker, because she has 'one great advantage which all professionals envy [...] namely, freedom – both artistic and physical' (Deren n.d.). Zimmermann elaborates on Deren's words:

> Deren postulated a definition of amateur film embodying two separate economic relationships: first, as individual artisanal work is removed from market relations, amateur filmmaking is peripheral to the social hierarchy of specialisation. Second, its privatised mar-ginalised status preserves the mythicised ideals of democracy – risk, freedom, participation, personally meaningful work – ideas no longer expedient in more rationalised work situations. (130)

Participation is again here emphasised as a key aspect of amateur film-making, with participation also helping to achieve 'democracy' and a move away from the production of capital at every turn ('rationalised work situations').

Finally, Potamkin, a well-known critic in the 1920s and early 1930s, decried what we might in the language of Marxist film criticism term the ideological indoctrination of mainstream cinema: 'His conception of the American film-going experience as one giant ritual in which we go to worship the on-screen icons in the modern cathedral of the movie palace gives rise to his description of uncritical cults in which the validity of the object of veneration is never questioned' (Schenker 2010). To combat this, Potamkin encouraged amateur filmmakers to take up amateur cameras and to make films that conformed little to the perceived realism of the continuity system of mainstream Hollywood – through techniques such as slow, fast and stop action. As Zimmermann says, such films would constitute 'small, discursive acts of resistance to the dominant ideology of Hollywood narrative' (Zimmermann 1995: 89).

Ryan Shand is correct to point out that Zimmermann, in discussing figures like Brecht, Deren and Potamkin, is not so much offering up a history of amateur filmmaking as a history of discourses surrounding amateur filmmaking (Shand 2007: 44). Nonetheless, Zimmermann does also name in the course of her monograph a good many amateur filmmakers, in particular from pre-war America, including Deren, Robert Florey and, at least in passing, post-war filmmakers such as Jonas Mekas, George Kuchar and more. However, Shand perhaps does gain some ground on Zimmermann when he argues that the latter's conception of amateur cinema as 'oppositional' does not necessarily take into account much amateur filmmaking, which aims precisely to reproduce and – *contra* Potamkin – not to subvert mainstream (read, Hollywood) aesthetics (see 42–46). In looking at the films themselves, argues Shand, we might come up with a different conception of amateur filmmaking, particularly amateur fiction filmmaking, which 'drew on and adapted recognisable genres such as fantasy, comedy, and action films' (55).

I shall argue that amateur filmmaking as a whole may nonetheless constitute something like an oppositional, or subversive, practice, contrary to Shand's suggestion that ultimately it does not – drawing in particular on the term 'adapted' used by Shand above. However, I should like first briefly to weave together the considerations of amateurism, immaterial labour, amateur filmmaking and the digital era in order to set up the means to mount such an argument.

Amateur filmmaking: the return

In an essay originally published in 2003, Chinese filmmaker Jia Zhangke proclaimed that 'the age of amateur filmmaking will return' (if it ever went away, that is). In a fashion that recalls Shand's words above regarding the majority of amateur filmmakers, Jia argues that many filmmakers indeed try to reproduce professional aesthetics making their films. Nonetheless, Jia believes that 'real film enthusiasts who have an unquenchable passion for film' will come to take centre stage in film history – and that these will be filmmakers who 'ignore the so-called professional methods', and the 'standardisation' of film practice, and who instead are innovative and freed from 'conventional customs and restraints' (Jia 2003).

However, such filmmaking will not happen in a bubble; noting the increasing homogenisation of global culture ('the trend of globalisation will make this world tedious'), Jia suggests that 'only independent films that remain committed to the depiction of local culture can provide some cultural diversity' (2003). We might take Alvarez's *Panic Attack!* as a useful example here (see Figure 9.2), since it simultaneously demonstrates both tendencies that Jia mentions – tedious globalisation and local diversity. For, it is the 'local' Montevideo setting of the film, and not the 'tedious' reproduction of Hollywood-style special effects, that makes interesting its

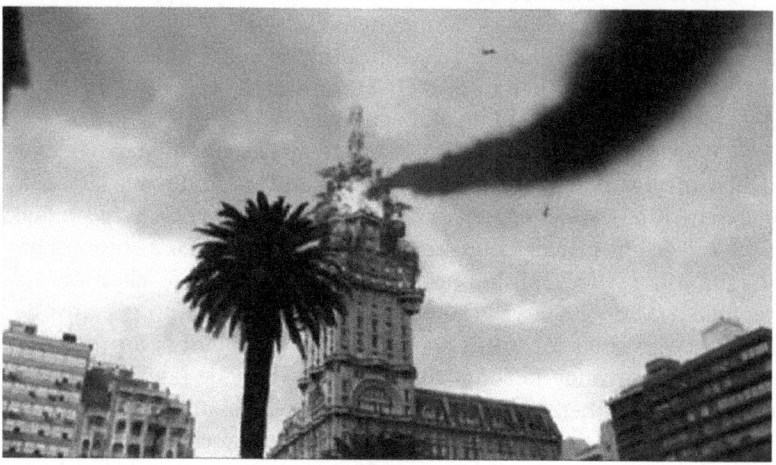

Figure 9.2 Montevideo and Hollywood-style special effects
Source: Screen capture from YouTube (10 March 2014)

otherwise clichéd tale of alien invasion. Even if Alvarez has overtly sought to become a professional – going to Hollywood and directing an unimaginative and humourless (and, if I may judge, an equally 'tedious') remake of *The Evil Dead*, the original version of which was relatively independent, irreverent and therefore noteworthy – *Panic Attack!*, perhaps in spite of its actual creator's intentions (Alvarez was actually trying to make a clichéd film), shows innovation via its local/diverse elements (Montevideo). In short, then, the amateur film will always demonstrate some diversity and originality because, as per *Panic Attack!*, it cannot but document in part the amateur status of its production (Montevideo is the interesting aspect of the film, not the special effects).

However, while amateur films such as *Panic Attack!* may be noteworthy for their diverse elements (and not so much for their replication of professional standards), do these films have any 'Marxist' value when read in the context of immaterial labour? That is, are films like *Panic Attack!* in fact simply adding to, and perhaps even legitimising, exploitation in the film industry, since such films – as well as viewing them on internet sites such as YouTube – constitute an immaterial form of unpaid labour? Michael Chanan (2014) takes up this question in relation to his own filmmaking practice as a video blogger. Chanan suggests that the digital age produces 'not just the instant flow of free expression across borders but also a propensity for causing ideological upset by breaking down social and cultural barriers, and discovering new socio-political constituencies' (Chanan 2014: n.p.). However, he also recognises that Web 2.0 seems also to lead to 'immaterial labour 2.0', which he deems a 'new form of exploitation' (n.p.). In other words, Chanan is wary of the contradictions inherent in Web 2.0, in that it seems to further the possibilities for both freedom and exploitation.

In constructing his argument, Chanan draws upon Marx, in particular his distinction between productive and unproductive labour as elaborated in *Theories of Surplus Value*. For Marx, a writer is 'a productive worker not insofar as he produces ideas, but insofar as he enriches the publisher who publishes his works, or if he is a wage labourer for a capitalist' (Marx 2000: 124; quoted in Chanan 2014: n.p.). Meanwhile, a singer who sings for free is an 'unproductive labourer', for they produce only use value (a song) that makes no money (and thus is not capitalist). In other words, Marx, too, is aware of the contradictions involved in artistic production, in that art can subvert capital, while also often being profitable (with a further contradiction being highlighted by Chanan, now drawing from *Grundrisse*, when he says that '[r]eally free labour, the composing of music for example, is at the same time damned serious and demands the greatest effort' (Marx 1993: 611; quoted in Chanan 2014: n.p.). But where Chanan compares productive with unproductive labour, perhaps a different line of thought can be drawn out by comparing productive labour with spiritual labour.

There is an oft-cited passage in *Theories of Surplus Value* where Marx argues that 'capitalist production is hostile to certain branches of spiritual production, for example, art and poetry' (Marx 2000: 251).[4] What Marx means by spiritual production here is not the development of any religious sentiment; rather, spiritual production refers more to the 'spirit' of the times: material production leads to 'a specific structure of society [...] [and to] a specific relation of men to nature' – and it is the structure of society and the relation of men to nature that is the 'spirit' produced (251). In other words, capitalist/material production and spiritual production are not antithetical, but closely linked; at the risk of simply repeating Marx, it is only 'certain branches' of spiritual production to which capitalist production is hostile, with art and poetry being key examples. In the context of contemporary cinema, it is worth remembering that all cinema thus involves spiritual production, but that only certain branches of cinema involve the type of spiritual production to which capitalist production is hostile. For not all cinema tries to qualify itself as art, and industrial cinema is not hostile to, but an embrace of, capitalist production; such films are the industrial results of the immaterial, as well as affective, labour that goes into them. Nonetheless, perhaps another 'branch' of film results in a more oppositional/subversive form of spiritual production – and this, I wish to argue, is the artistic amateur film that embraces the amateur rather than pursuing a would-be professional aesthetic. This is a different contradiction to the one identified by Chanan. For, the immaterial and spiritual labour of amateur, artistic productions subverts capitalist production; indeed, mainstream cinema considers it an enemy and is hostile to it because it does not try to replicate its aesthetics (thereby reaffirming the mainstream's centrality and power), but instead it deliberately seeks *not* to replicate such work.

In my own film, *En Attendant Godard* (UK, 2009), the opening shot features the pages of a cheque book being signed one after the other by a disembodied hand. Each cheque is made out for £0.00 – the amount invested for this film in lighting, casting, stars and the other aspects of the production (see Figure 9.3).

On the soundtrack, a man and a woman discuss why one would make a film for free, with the male voice (my own) suggesting that an amateur film is made for free out of love for cinema, and that this enriches such

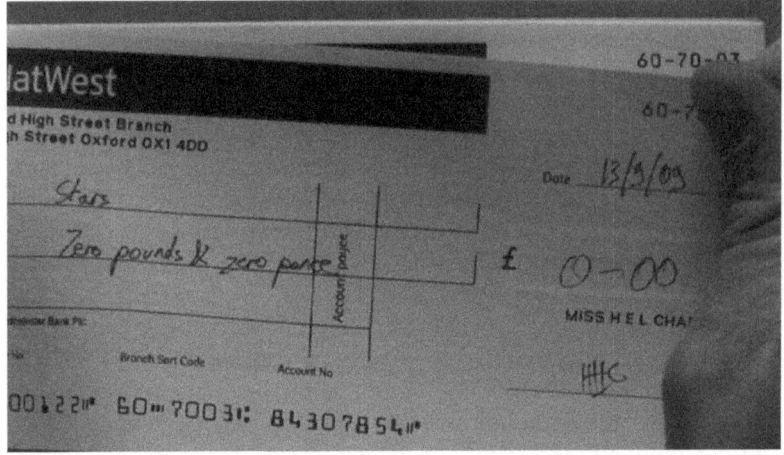

Figure 9.3   Cheque book signing for £0.00
Source: Screen capture from *En Attendant Godard* (2010), dir. William Brown, Beg Steal Borrow Films

a film over a professional production. Nonetheless, the female voice (Anne-Laure Berdugo) reminds us that people are not often interested in free films, and will not watch them because they prefer to see films that obviously cost a lot of money. The sequence is an overt homage to Jean-Luc Godard and Jean-Pierre Gorin's *Tout Va Bien* (France/Italy, 1972), except that where Godard/Gorin point to the industrial nature of film by having a cheque sign off large sums of money, here the zero-budget nature of the film is affirmed (although, alas, in a slightly disingenuous fashion, in that the film did cost some money to make). By being free, *En Attendant Godard* runs the risk, and openly admits to the likelihood, of being unpopular in the sense that not many people know or will like the film, even if it retains elements of the 'popular' in Brecht's sense of the term outlined above, since my fellow collaborators and I are people who, in making a film, try to enrich culture from without the official institutions. In being 'unpopular', the hostility of capitalist production to the spiritual production of art and poetry (if my film can lay claim to such a status) is potentially revealed.

Never forget the historical context

If anything, Marx's argument in his discussion of spiritual labour is that one can never forget the changing historical context in which capital operates. Indeed, the passage cited above comes from a section in which

Marx upbraids political economist Friedrich Storch for believing capital to outwith with a historical context (as such, the latter's theory of civilisation does not get beyond 'trivial phrases'; Marx 2000: 250). Marx reaffirms the same idea when, in another much-quoted passage from *The German Ideology*, he and Friedrich Engels ask the following: '[i]s the conception of nature and of social relations which underlies Greek imagination and therefore Greek [art] possible when there are self-acting mules, railways, locomotive and electric telegraphs?' (Marx and Engels 2004: 150). The point here is that art does not exist on some immaterial and ideal plane, but that its production is linked to the world in which it is created; Greek art can only be the product of ancient Greece, even if such work still has resonance today. Bearing this in mind, then, it is key to reiterate that films like *En Attendant Godard* and *Panic Attack!* can only exist as a result of their being embedded into a specific historical moment (and geographical place), as the technological aspect of the production of each film makes clear. That is, both films are specifically the product of digital technology, and could not have existed prior to that technology's advent.

That said, even in the age of YouTube, when it is supposedly easy to distribute one's films, the chances of people watching a film even online and for free (especially one that lasts 96 minutes, as opposed to 56 seconds) are slim. Michael Chanan has pointed to the difficulty of achieving 'viral' success in his work on video blogging, with Ryan Shand also acknowledging how '[b]oth the domestic and oppositional perspectives assume that amateur ciné production is an activity pursued by isolated individuals for *a very small audience*' (Shand 2007: 52; emphasis added). While very small audiences might be assumed for amateur films, however, they are not necessarily the case – and what stands between amateur films and a large audience remains access to meaningful distribution.

As Broderick Fox argues, 'whatever technological advances have been made in the realm of media *production*, access to viable modes of *distribution* still arguably remains the greatest hurdle between amateur and professional valuation' (Fox 2004: 15; original emphasis). YouTube does indeed present a supposedly 'viable' mode of distribution – but YouTube is owned by Google, a major (capitalist) corporation. Furthermore, how to get one's work seen amidst the other 48 hours of footage being uploaded every minute? Publicity becomes again the key, together with possible help from various types of gatekeeper such as journalists, bloggers, tweeters and more. That is, one needs large sums of capital in order to (pay Google to) promote the film and/or the unpredictable luck of going 'viral' via a large network of supportive contacts in order for people to see the work.[5] In a related fashion, an online-only release runs the risk of being considered 'amateur' in the negative sense of the word (i.e. not very good) because it has not had the validation of a cinema release, or some festival screenings. For, even if most people now watch films at home (or what Gabriele Pedullà terms 'in broad daylight'; see Pedullà 2012) rather than at the cinema (or in the 'black box'), the theatrical run of a film, or the fact that it has played at theatres in a number of metropolitan film festivals, is a sign of 'quality', thereby improving a film's chances of finding a significant audience via other media. There are occasional amateur films that get picked up by distributors, though they tend to be would-be professional productions, not those that embrace a deliberately amateur aesthetic. But on the whole, the professional film industry is hostile to deliberately amateur productions – arguably because they challenge too greatly the norms of professional filmmaking. As such, perhaps amateur filmmaking is not just exploitation via immaterial labour, but it does constitute a form of opposition/subversion in the face of a highly capitalised film industry. And even if would-be professional films stand a greater (if still extremely slim) chance of achieving monetisation, and thus a professional status, they also subvert mainstream filmmaking practice because they always demonstrate some 'amateur' or original elements (Montevideo in *Panic Attack!*). To return to Shand, then, his use of the term 'adapted' becomes telling, for it opens up a gap between would-be and 'truly' professional productions; amateur films are not from recognisable genres, but *adaptations* therefrom, and as such they never fully replicate that which they are trying to copy, instead always allowing into their aesthetic something of the amateur, and subsequently also of the oppositional/subversive.

What is subversion? (*Dissensus*)

A few issues remain. First, while I have discussed distribution as a key barrier between amateur films' success and failure, the fact remains that 'success' is only a relative term. As Chanan argues, many amateur filmmakers might dream of their work 'going viral' or being successful. However, such success is not, ultimately, the goal of the amateur film or filmmaker. Maya Deren speaks of how the word amateur comes from the Latin for 'lover', or 'one who does something for the love of the thing rather than for economic reasons or necessity' (Deren n.d.). Meanwhile, Vasilis Kostakis reminds readers that the Greek for 'amateur' is ερασιτεχνης, which comes from the synthesis of 'lover' εραστης and 'art' τεχνη' (Kostakis 2009: 458). This definition lends a specifically artistic aspect to the term amateur. In other words, to be an amateur filmmaker is always to be an artistic filmmaker, and to be an amateur filmmaker is not to desire success, or to make a film in order to maximise its chances of success (for example, by replicating a professional aesthetic). Rather, amateur filmmaking cares not for success or popularity; if above I have suggested that my own films court being unpopular – in the sense of not much viewed or liked – perhaps the term 'apopular' is better for demonstrating that popularity does not matter that much to/for the films.

And yet, if this is the case (and if I am not being disingenuous), then what power do amateur films really have? That is, what do they really subvert? Surely they just exist alongside professional films, being overlooked by the general public, with mainstream cinema hostile somewhat to amateur films, while at the same time profiting from the immaterial labour that goes into the consumption thereof on websites like YouTube and Facebook. But perhaps the problem is not that these films ultimately 'reaffirm' capitalism or exploitation. Rather the problem is in expecting any film overnight to revolutionise cinema from outside: an amateur film that storms the professional film industry and explodes it into fragments such that it can never be built again. Such an incendiary film would surely only and very quickly be monetised, for it is the 'event' of such a revolutionary film that the professional film industry craves in its desire always to expand into new markets. In this sense, an 'anticapitalist' film might only ever reaffirm capitalism.

Jacques Rancière makes a similar claim in his work on 'dissensus'. While expressing some scepticism towards 'political art', Rancière nonetheless suggests that all 'fiction'

> involves the re-framing of the 'real,' or the framing of a dissensus. Fiction is a way of changing existing modes of sensory presentations and forms of enunciation; of varying frames, scales and rhythms; and of building new relationships between reality and appearance, the individual and the collective. (Rancière 2010: 141)

All fiction, then, in a certain sense modifies the world in which we live, and thus serves a 'progressive' function, whether or not that fiction qualifies as 'art' (and I would suggest, in the context of cinema, whether or not it qualifies as a fiction film or a documentary, in that all documentaries cannot but in part 'fictionalise' the world – hence my use of quotation marks around the word fiction above). Nonetheless, 'critical art' especially aims to 'produce a sensory clash *and* to mobilise bodies through the presentation of a strangeness, of an encounter between heterogeneous elements' (Rancière 2010: 143). In other words, while all fiction might make us see the world 'anew' (we see a 'strangeness'), critical art does so intentionally. 'Doing art means displacing art's borders,' continues Rancière, 'just as doing politics means displacing the borders of what is acknowledged as *the* political' (149). With regard to cinema, Rancière seems to be suggesting that all films expand what cinema is/can do, but that those films that seek deliberately not to replicate cinema's (professional) standards, but instead to 'displace its borders', are perhaps the most progressive. In this way, amateur filmmaking may well, as per Maya Deren, be an 'avant-garde' movement, one that subverts the 'consensus' of the mainstream by enacting what Rancière terms *dissensus*.

We would do well to note that Rancière is sceptical about the power of deliberately 'political cinema' because to create such a cinema is to try in advance to produce specific effects in audiences (I am now really angry about capitalist exploitation) – when the real power of cinema, or of any art form, is for it to produce an effect that cannot be foretold, and that has not yet been experienced by that viewer. 'Truly political' art, then, does not set out to be specifically political; instead it sets out to be specifically artistic. As Rancière says, a film 'cannot sidestep the fact that a film remains a film and a spectator remains a spectator' (151). To try to be otherwise is perhaps pointless.

There is a contradiction in Rancière's work, in that cinema must forever be pushing into the 'non-' or the 'super-' cinematic if its affects are to be at any point in time, let alone always, 'new' (or 'strange'). As such, to say a 'film remains a film' is paradoxical, if what defines film is its evolution into new forms. Furthermore, if film forever expands, then this is as true of mainstream and professional filmmaking as it is of amateur filmmaking. But amateur filmmaking, specifically amateur filmmaking that does not seek to replicate the norms of mainstream cinema, perhaps is 'truly political' in Rancière's terms; perhaps it is 'Marxist', in that it subverts mainstream cinema by being free and by being 'apopular'.

Amateur cinema should perhaps not have as its intention a deliberate politicisation of cinema as a whole, nor a deliberate opposition to the mainstream. Instead, amateur filmmaking must work on a 'quieter' level. Amateur filmmakers must just simply carry on making amateur films. This will not generate the (capitalist) spectacle of revolution that many (especially capitalists) dream of. But it may well take cinema and, by extension, society towards a socialist future in a slow but definite fashion.

Little is new in making such an assertion; Marx foresaw this as the very destiny of capitalism, and filmmakers have been making amateur productions in territory both charted and uncharted by academia since long before the digital 'revolution'. However, the contemporary era, with the digital means put in place to restore hope for such a (slow) revolution, renews the significance of the amateur film production. *Panic Attack!* cannot help but demonstrate its amateur status, even if it aspires to hide it; *En Attendant Godard*, meanwhile, aspires only to be an amateur film. Even within the context of a society in which immaterial labour is increasingly common – and even in a world where access to digital media may well be the preserve predominantly of Westerners and the rest of the world's bourgeoisie – both would-be professional and deliberately amateur films take us slowly in the direction of our socialist future.[6]

Notes

1. In addition to Therborn's suspicion that the internet is primarily young and middle class in nature, Toby Miller points out how '87 per cent of US YouTube visitors are white, and just 0.2 per cent of visits involve posting videos [...] The vast majority of YouTube vloggers are men, and women who produce vlogs are sometimes subject to harassment by viewers. Is this new technology producing new social relations – or a rerun of old-style social relations with which we are all too familiar?' (Miller 2009: 427).
2. Although he does not refer specifically to Lazzarato, Miller might remind us that arguments concerning how reception is a creative act are not new, but that they in fact date back to at least the 1950s; Dallas Smythe, Herbert I. Schiller and Armand Mattelart, Miller reminds us, have all made similar claims (Miller 2009: 433–434).
3. Ewa Mazierska makes a similar point in her consideration of Krzysztof Kieślowski's film *Amator/Camera Buff* (Poland, 1979): referring to Marx's comparison of the alienated specialist under capitalism with the more free-roaming worker under communism, Mazierska suggests that the amateur might subvert the capitalist system – even though in *Camera Buff* the amateur filmmaker becomes increasingly professionalised (Mazierska: forthcoming).
4. Perhaps it is worth remembering that Marx himself harboured ambitions to be a poet.
5. Miller also makes a similar point when he says that 'YouTube is a digital distributor, and as such may appear to undermine this crucial part of conventional media power [the uploading by the general public of copyrighted materials onto the site]. But it doesn't do anything of the sort' (Miller 2009: 429).
6. I am indebted to Ewa Mazierska and to Lars Kristensen for their help in writing this chapter. *En Attendant Godard* is available online at http://vimeo.com/86769855.

Bibliography

Adorno, Theodor W. (2002) *The Culture Industry: Selected Essays on Mass Culture* (trans. various), London: Routledge.

Brecht, Bertolt (1964) *Brecht on Theatre: The Development of an Aesthetic,* (ed. and trans. John Willett), New York: Hill and Wang.

Brown, William (2013) 'Becoming Cinema: *The Social Network*, Exploitation in the Digital Age, and the Film Industry,' in Ewa Mazierska (ed.), *Work in Cinema: Labor and the Human Condition*, New York: Palgrave Macmillan, pp. 50–67.

Burgess, Jean E. (2013) 'YouTube and the Formalisation of Amateur Media', in Dan Hunter, Ramon Lobato, Megan Richardson and Julian Thomas (eds), *Amateur Media: Social, Cultural and Legal Perspectives*, London: Routledge, pp. 53–58.

Chanan, Michael (2014) 'On the Immaterial Labour of the Video Blogger', in Ewa Mazierska and Lars Kristensen (eds), *Marxism and Film Activism*, London and New York: Berghahn Books, 2015 (forthcoming)

Coté, Mark and Pybus, Jennifer (2007) 'Learning to Immaterial Labour 2.0: MySpace and Social Networks', *Ephemera: Theory & Politics in Organization*, 7:1, pp. 88–106.

Deren, Maya (n.d.) 'Amateur versus Professional,' reproduced online at http://museopath.tumblr.com/post/2873621823/amateur-versus-professional-by-maya-deren. Last accessed on 22 January 2014.

Fox, Broderick (2004) 'Rethinking the Amateur: Editor's Introduction', *Spectator*, 24:1 (Spring), pp. 5–16.

Gunning, Tom (1986) 'The Cinema of Attraction: Early Film, Its Spectators and the Avant-Garde', *Wide Angle*, 8:3–4, pp. 63–70.

Jia, Zhangke (2003) 'The Age of the Amateur Will Return' (trans. Yuqian Yan),http://dgeneratefilms.com/critical-essays/jia-zhangke-the-age-of-amateur-cinema-will-return.Last accessed: 22 January 2014.

Kostakis, Vasilis (2009) 'The Amateur Class, or, the Reserve Army of the Web', *Rethinking Marxism: A Journal of Economics, Culture and Society*, 21:3, pp. 457–461.

Lazzarato, Maurizio (2006) 'Immaterial Labour' (trans. Paul Colilli and Ed Emory), in Paolo Virno and Michael Hardt (eds), *Radical Thought in Italy: A Potential Politics*, Minneapolis: University of Minnesota Press, pp. 132–146.

Marx, Karl (1993) *Grundrisse* (trans. Martin Nicolaus), London: Penguin.

Marx, Karl (2000) *Theories of Surplus Value*, New York: Prometheus Books.

Marx, Karl and Engels, Friedrich (2004) *The German Ideology*, London: Lawrence &Wishart.

Mazierska, Ewa (Forthcoming) 'The Portrayal of Workers in the 1970s Films of WojciechWiszniewski and Krzysztof Kieślowski'.

Miller, Toby (2009) 'Cybertarians of the World Unite: You Have Nothing to Lose but Your Tubes!' in Pelle Snickars and Patrick Vondereau (eds), *The YouTube Reader*, Stockholm: National Library of Sweden, pp. 424–440.

Pedullà, Gabriele (2012) *In Broad Daylight: Movies and Spectators After the Cinema* (trans. Patricia Gaborik), London: Verso.

Rancière, Jacques (2010) *Dissensus: On Politics and Aesthetics* (trans. Steven Corcoran), London: Continuum.

Salvato, Nick (2009) 'Out of Hand: YouTube Amateurs and Professionals', *TDR: The Drama Review*, 53:3 (Fall), pp. 67–83.

Schenker, Andrew (2010) 'Marxism Goes to the Movies: On Pioneering Activist Film Critic Harry Alan Potamkin', *Bright Lights Film Journal*, 70, http://brightlightsfilm.com/70/70potamkin_schenker.php. Last accessed 22 January 2014.

Shand, Ryan (2007) 'Theorizing Amateur Cinema: Limitations and Possibilities', *The Moving Image*, 8:2 (Fall), pp. 36–60.

Therborn, Göran (2008) *From Marxism to Post-Marxism?*, London: Verso.

Zimmermann, Patricia R (1995) *Reel Families: A Social History of Amateur Film*, Bloomington: Indiana University Press.

10
Citizen Marx/Kane

John Hutnyk

The cinema hall as a place to sell Eskimo Pie

This chapter addresses the question of how, today, to start reading that rich book that is Marx's *Capital* – of which an immense, even monstrous, accumulation of commentary on the Marxist mode of literary production appears to have already shaped its elementary forms. In reading *Capital*, if anything about beginnings should be considered necessary, it is usual to say it is good to start at the beginning – not always of course, but usually to start with what is immediately at hand. Commentaries, primers, prefaces, intros, first sentences and first chapters start at the beginning and continue on from there. This is itself debated, but my argument is that we can only approach *Capital* through the already existing commentary, even as we would like to start as if the book were new. And the commentary that exists is not only that which is explicitly marked as such, but also includes all the ideas we have already received about so many things – about Marx, capitalism, communism, exchange, commodities and so much more. A vast accumulation of things filter reading, so it would be naive to simply say that materialism might start with things themselves, even if it makes sense to start with commodities, the objects that are the souvenirs or detritus of our lives.

The key to the beginning of volume one is where Marx starts with 'a monstrous accumulation of commodities' ['*ungeheure Warensammlung*' – translation modified by author], but there are many possible starts and many people don't get much further than chapter one, or they take chapter one as the 'proper' beginning. I want to suggest that there is something more here and so want to begin with something else, or even someone else, who might seem the total antithesis of the celebrated critic of the commodity system. A monstrous figure to expose the workings of

218

monstrosity all the more (the monstrous will be explained). My reading is angular, so I choose a character from a parallel history of commerce, although glossed through a film. I have in mind William Randolph Hearst – Moneybags – portrayed by Orson Welles in the classic film *Citizen Kane*. In this chapter, I want to develop this as an introduction to *Capital*, through its incarnation in the figure of Moneybags Kane, and to begin to get at commodities through a focus on the kind of obscure, miniature, almost irrelevant and insignificant objects to hand – those baubles and trinkets that mesmerise Kane, and us all.

When you watch *Citizen Kane*, you will be well aware from the start that Kane collects. Collection itself has a problematic philosophical heritage, chastised even by Nietzsche:

> Witness the repugnant spectacle of a blind lust for collection [...] Man envelops himself in the odour of decay [...] often he sinks so low as finally to be satisfied with any fare and devours with pleasure even the dust of bibliographical quisquilia. (Nietzsche 1980: 21)

I have been reading Marx in the cinema. Reading in the dark, to emphasise sensitivities. To read this way is to tamper with another accumulation that seems a dull dead half-life of narrative: the spectral forms of celluloid, politics and critique that surround the film *Citizen Kane*. Orson Welles might be a good choice for an illustration in *Marx at the Movies* because like that other famous old beard, Welles insists on being both actor and director, at the same time working to a script and writing that script. Marx is famous for saying something similar in the *Eighteenth Brumaire* – we make our own history but not in conditions that we have chosen (Marx 2002: 19). Perhaps this is like rewriting a script as a means to combat studio control. In the making of *Citizen Kane* Welles started out shooting 'screen tests' so the studio would not interfere with his shooting schedule, and in the first weeks he had already begun, started before the start, so to speak. A feint. Later, there will be reason for dress-ups and farcical returns aplenty when we ask after the status of allegories about those who are (mis)represented by opportunists with pretentions to power.

I will suggest that the idea of Marx at the movies has something of prophecy about it. In the preface and in the main text of *Capital*, Marx twice quotes Horace: '*Mutato nomine de te fabula narratur*' (Marx 1970: 267). This translates as 'the names are changed but the joke is told of you'. In the preface this is a message to the German workers, warning that this story of Capital in England presages coming events in Germany. In the main text the reference is wider: 'For slave-trade read Labour market' (Marx 1970: 267). Of course, Marx did not see the cinema, but even more thought provoking than discovering optical metaphors in his text – the *camera obscura*, for example – I want to argue that the mode of presentation that Marx offers for his dialectical analysis is already proto-cinematic. As recognised but not realised in the house of Eisenstein, as realised but not recognised through the prism of Kluge (see Mazierska, this volume). I want to suggest that the cinematic embodiment of the categories of *Capital* can be found on screen, and the personification of class and economic figures can, in a sense very close to how Marx might present them, be realised, in all places, on celluloid. As an experiment then, I propose to take *Citizen Kane* as the candidate for a comparison that reveals Marx's key arguments in ways that have contemporary resonance.

Orson Welles' career as filmmaker and personality is much examined, and yet he was a self-mystifying figure – famous and notorious in advance. Myths, rumours and smears abound (Leaming 1985: 214). Convenient parallels with the 'reputation' of Marx, and Marxism, need not be spelled out in detail, but it might be possible to establish a reading protocol that notes how a book from the 1860s and a film from 70 years ago both somehow seem to be critically renewed every decade. As John Waters says, we still 'babble on about Orson Welles' (Waters 2005: 192). We also still babble on about Marx. The book *Capital* is read differently in each decade. We could debate leading frames: Lenin for the 1900s; Lukacs the 1920s; Bataille in the 1930s; Adorno for the 1940s and 1950s; Althusser the 1960s (recommending we skip chapter one); the autonomists in the 1970s; world systems theory in the 1980s; deconstruction in the 1990s (only reading chapter one); Jameson in the 2000s (skip chapters 1–3 and section 8). All prefaces have preferences, according to proclivity.

There are simply hundreds of commentaries and guides and introductions on Marx and Marxism. Indeed the history of Marxism is an instructive lesson in how reading is multiple and contested. A fratricidal spectacle even.[1]

Allegory of property

Welles too can dazzle us with intros, but the point is to warn against them. The 'News on the March' sequence at the start of *Citizen Kane* is a jarring synopsis designed to challenge. His opening can be reinterpreted (as I will do below), and just as Welles was maligned for his politics (as we shall see), he was considered a difficult filmmaker and was often attacked for threatening bourgeois norms and complacency (more below). The allegorical mode of presentation is also strong in this one. There is a sense in which his work was effective because it was a coded vehicle for other fears. Japan, Germany, Russia, *not* Mars, for example, in *War of the Worlds* (this was also true for H. G. Wells writing before an earlier war). I will argue that *Citizen Kane* is never more relevant than now – financial crisis, do-gooder philanthropists, special United Nations 'Goodwill Ambassador' celebrity endorsements – all as alibis for business-as-usual capitalism on the march.

The allegorical in *Citizen Kane* deserves a critical response. While Welles' character is possibly usefully seen as semi-autobiographical, it is also a critical biographical portrait and personification of the capitalist turned philanthropic campaigning journalist. It is well-known that many have suggested that *Citizen Kane* is based on the life of William Randolph Hearst (though this was to be Howard Hughes in the initial 'An American' pitch, see *F is for Fake*), and today Hearst could be taken to stand in for any of the personifications of capital that go by the proper names of contemporary oligarchs like Gates, Jobs or Zuckerberg, or even Gordon Gecko or the *Wolf of Wall Street*.

The figure of Kane as embodiment of the capitalist is just a ruse – of course the capitalist is not interested in things as such, but rather in the exchangeability of any old thing – so as to recoup appropriated surplus value for profit – to valorise. Marx did not explicitly name his capitalist, and was careful to insist, for the most part, that any named capitalist was a 'personification' of a class category. Welles' figures are, necessarily, portrayed in advance of categories, and his cinematic-theatrical lead actor staging forces him into another place, even as astute readers will recognise that his 'arguments' are already given stories, pre-presented by interpreters and spruikers, simplified and condensed for inattentive readers – as dozens of biographies attest. The genius of the film was to present at least six different takes on the man. We know this already because the pre-publicity, rehearsed controversies and crafted reputation of Welles precedes any viewing. Perhaps the question to ask is whether it is possible to reclaim a critique of Hearst from the vast accumulations of biography and myth about Welles. We should note at the outset that already in *Citizen Kane* Welles mocked such ambitions. The first image in the film is of a sign on the gate that says 'No Trespassing'. The camera passes directly through the mesh fence.

Marx will have plenty to say about property, but this is not the comparative point I want to make. Rather, consider the ways in which Marxism is always already mystified and characterised, even picturised in advance by all manner of *critics*. A grotesque huge head erected upon a site near – some 50 yards away from – his grave in Highgate. A grotesque representation, or a statue of some secular god. His words, barely heard as they were meant, his words revised over and over – indeed the same words coming to mean different things at different times. Marx is open to interpretation and journalistic cliché. So, might a parallel with the opening of *Citizen Kane* – both the 'no trespassing' warning and the fetish of a single word, 'Rosebud' – tell us something? The first time we see Kane, we see only a giant close-up of his lips, originally planned for the abandoned screenplay 'Heart of Darkness'.

The figure is larger than life, and the movie is the story of an emergent socio-political and scandalous culture feeding off this largesse – starting with the death of its main character and star. What a great opening, this 'maw of a giant in his castle, ready to gobble up the audience, the cinema, the industry' (Walters 2004: 51) ... is no more (Figure 10.1). Of course, Marx too is long dead, and as we discover that the movie about Kane's life begins with Kane's death, we see that it is the journalists who squabble over interpretations of the residue of greatness. The maw eats

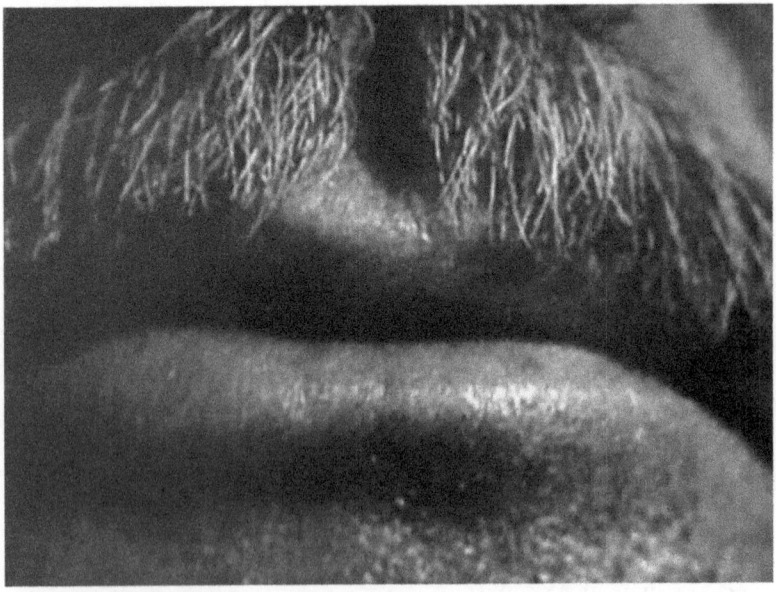

Figure 10.1 Kane's lips
Source: Screen capture from *Citizen Kane* (1941), dir. Orson Welles, Universal Home Entertainment

no more, and Welles himself will be unjustly rejected by Hollywood (as profligate director) unable to raise funds or complete further films.

Whatever the subsequent reputation of the film – and its subsequent critical success – a death at the start is a noteworthy premise for a film. The lips as fetish object, monstrously large, the mouth of a giant prophesising the trajectory of the narrative, trespass or not, and the journalists hunting the true story, itself of little significance, that only the audience will find. The camera draws the eye through the forbidden gate, across various panoramas of the same scene, with the window in the same place on the screen, approaching the citadel of a faded power. This is a detective seduction, for a film in which the mode of presentation is different to the analysis, as Marx will also say of his book. Are those lips a fetish in the same way that a commodity is only the staged opening to *Capital*? Are we to identify the part for the whole, the man, the life, the man's life for that of the capitalist, the capitalist for that of the system – propertied wealth as destructive, greed as alienation – and rosebud, the innocent flower, the mystery?

Philanthropic biography

Citizen Kane might be a way into a particular and contingent reading of *Capital* because as a capitalist figure Kane represents one of the pantomime villains that Marx skewers in his book. The villain takes several forms: he is Moneybags, alongside whom we will see bankers and moneylenders, usurers, factory owners, company managers, vampires, 'agents' of capital, an 'idle stratum', an executive committee, the state, the factory inspectors, the philanthropists and the learned professors of political economy, who may or may not emanate from the same cloth that cut the dons of Haileybury College who trained the officials of the British East India Company. Police, politicians, philanthropists and pranksters may have reason to regret the carbuncles that enraged Marx as he wrote. All populate the staging of the book as personifications of economic categories, each operating a theatrical politics rather than a progressive one. A performative rendering of class that can be analysed as theatre perhaps, yet all the more communicable as rounded, fleshed-out, cinema.

With Welles, the biographers are also on the march, aiming to skewer his theatre. Should we guard against too many retellings that get in the way of reading the 'original', such that it becomes near impossible to see through the hedging? There are dozens of commentaries that cloud the way, and of course Marxists, like commentators on Welles, will be the most complicit in this. Simon Callow begins part one of his multi-volume biography of Welles (1995, 2006) with a quote that might be read as revealing as much about the anxieties of a biographer ready to approach 'the fabulist Orson Welles' as it does about its subject's self-consciousness:

> If you try to probe, I'll lie to you. Seventy-five percent of what I say in interviews is false. I'm like a hen protecting her eggs. I must protect my work. Introspection is bad for me. I'm a medium not an orator. Like certain oriental and Christian mystics, I think the 'self' is a kind of enemy. My work is what enables me to come out of myself. I like what I do, not what I am [...] Do you know the best service anyone could render to art? Destroy all biographies. Only art can explain the life of a man – and not the contrary. (Orson Welles to Jean Clay, 1962, quoted in Callow 1995: xi)

Callow continually takes away Welles' stories about his life – even the place where he was said to be conceived is labelled a fabrication. So much energy devoted to undoing the Welles myth only confirms it, and Welles had already anticipated these moves. In what may be his most admired acting role, as Harry Lime in *The Third Man* (Leaming 1985: 445), Welles plays an elusive mystery figure intent on collecting for gain, a selfish and predatory dissembler, perhaps the embodiment of capitalist deception. Seven years before the interview with Callow, in *Touch of Evil*, Welles had Marlene Dietrich say of his character Quinlan, who had just been found dead: 'He was some kind of a man. What does it matter what you say about people?'.

> The more we know about the men who wrote [*Don Quixote, King Lear* and so on], the bigger chance there is for all the Herr Professors in the academic establishment to befuddle and bemuse. (in Welles and Bogdanovich 1998: 257)

Welles critiques the learned professors too. Among the routine retinue, it has become commonplace to sort commentators into two camps – defenders and opponents – with Pauline Kael, who raised controversy over the co-writing credit given to Herman Jacob Mankiewicz for *Citizen Kane*, in an international brouhaha on the one side, and Peter Bagdonovich, still attempting to finish Welles' final masterpiece, *The Other Side of the Wind* and caught up in legal disputes with its French and Iranian funders, on the other. In between are sects and factions, a host of divergent positions jockeying for favour, and a massive publishing culture industry that has made a commodity, franchise and brand out of the good name of the citizen.

Welles himself deserves some praise for this. In cases where there is so much written, this will always be offered with some perspectival bias. It is well known that Marx too will be first to not be a 'Marxist'. Should it matter then that the following highlights of Welles' 'bio' are only a selection?:

1915: Born. His mother a suffragette who once served time in prison for her radical views (Welles and Bogdanovich 1998: 326); a 'brilliant public speaker', she was the first woman in Kenosha to be elected to political office (Callow 1995: 9).

1936: An all black production of *Macbeth* – admittedly there are issues of exoticisation here in the move of action from Scotland to Haiti, and where Welles contrives a voodoo witches scene (235). Nevertheless, an important production.

1938: Campaigns for and champions various leftwing causes, including speaking against Franco at 'Stars for Spain' – a medical aid benefit. Welles gives a series of talks on the 'People's Front' at the Workers Bookshop and writes for the *Daily Worker*. Plays Sigmund Freud on stage, gets to know Hans Eisler, Count Basie, Vincent Price, Lucille Ball.

30 October 1938: *War of the Worlds* radio play (more on this below).

1941: Welles is 'attacked as subversive and communistic' by leaders of the American Legion and the Californian Sons of the Revolution in Hearst papers (Rosenbaum 1998: 363). The FBI's J. Edgar Hoover writes a memo linking Welles to various 'communist' organisations (Bogdanovich 1998: xxxvi):

FBI director J. Edgar Hoover writes a 'memorandum for the assistant to the attorney general Mr Mathews F. McGuire' stating: 'For your information the Dies Committee has collected data indicating that Orson Welles is associated with the following organizations, which are said to be Communist in character: Negro Cultural Committee, Foster parents' Plan for War Children, Medical Bureau and North American Committee to Aid Spanish Democracy, Theater Arts Committee, Motion Picture Artists Committee to Lift the Embargo, Workers Bookshop, American Youth Congress, New Masses, People's Forum, Workers Bookshop Mural Fund, League of American Writers [and] American Student Union'. (Rosenbaum 1998: 364)

1 May 1941 [released May Day]: *Citizen Kane*. In a scene edited out of the film, Kane's first wife's son was to have been killed 'when he and other members of a fascist organization try to seize an armoury in

Washington', with the son's body shown interred in a mausoleum where a wall inscription from the *1001 Nights* begins 'The drunkenness of youth has passed like a fever' (Carringer 1996: 148).

1946: Welles gives protest speeches against the nuclear tests on Bikini Atoll (Rosenbaum 1998: 397) and uses his ABC programme *Orson Welles Commentaries* to campaign to bring charges against a policeman who had beaten and blinded black war veteran Isaac Woodward. With heavyweight boxing champion Joe Louis, Welles draws 20,000 people to a benefit for Woodward. The culpable policeman is finally identified in mid-August (398–399).

1955: On a television program Welles speaks out against passport control and immigration bureaucracy, a subject later dramatised in Welles' film *Touch of Evil*.

The bureaucrat is really like a blackmailer. You can never pay him off; the more you give him, the more he'll demand. If you fill in one form, he'll give you ten. (Welles and Bogdanovich 1998: 262)

1962: Welles' film of Kafka's *The Trial* in part conceived as a commentary on displaced person camps (281).

1972: Welles reports that he still wants to make a film of Conrad's *Heart of Darkness*, emphasising the contemporary political associations (Rosenbaum 1998: 512). Seven years later Francis Ford Coppola releases *Apocalypse Now*.

1977: 'In 1977 the original Rosebud sled turned up in a prop warehouse at Paramount that used to belong to RKO. Custom-built in the RKO property department, it was thirty-four inches long, made entirely of balsa wood, and fastened together with wood dowels and glue [...] three identical sleds were built; two were burned in the filming' (Carringer 1996: 49–50).

1973: *F is for Fake* – if you haven't seen this, see it now. Welles' knowing commentary on commentaries.

Bogdanovich: Well, do you have a theory about possessions, or just an inability to keep things from getting lost?

Welles: Both. The things you own have a way (a way?) of owning you.

Bogdanovich: How about things like letters and books?

Welles: I'm not laying this down as a law for anybody else. Its just that I feel I have to protect myself against things, so I'm pretty careful to lose most of them. (Welles and Bogdanovich 1998: 183)

Welles began, but did not complete, a made-for-television version of Quixote, in which he appeared as himself (Bazin 1991: 132), setting Quixote in the modern era, sending him and Sancho Panza on a voyage to the moon. Welles was much influenced by the early filmmaker and magician Georges Méliès (Conrad 2003: 92), but was planning to end his version with a (never completed) nuclear explosion killing all but the knight and his companion Sancho. Welles had other unfinished projects, among them *Heart of Darkness* and *The Odyssey*. Eisenstein and Welles were asked by Alexander Korda to collaborate in filming Tolstoy's *War and Peace* (139). The 'explanation' of both Marx and Welles as authors leaving many works incomplete is both merely 'pop psychology' (Leaming 1985: 408) and fuel for myth-making. What if Welles' films *The Magnificent Ambersons* or *Touch of Evil* had not been savagely cut by the studio? What if Frederik Engels had not interpolated great chunks of his own text into *Capital's* later volumes?

War of the Worlds

Welles was a prankster, although his empire takeover expansion story was of a different order to the coming communist chain-rattling revolution. The Mercury Theatre 'War of the Worlds' radio play (1938) was something more than a Halloween gimmick presentation working through the conceit of a radio programme interrupted by progressively more alarmist news reports. Martians had landed in America! A spectre is haunting Europe! It is a matter of record that hundreds of thousands believed the play, leading to all manner of incident, with panic and heart attacks and allegedly one woman in Pittsburgh taking her life rather than risking violation by Martians. As Bazin points out, it should be remembered that this occurred just as the world was preparing for WW2 and 'the day was not far away when an unidentified announcer would interrupt an entertainment broadcast to declare in trembling voice that Pearl Harbour had just been destroyed by the Japanese. But this time, many Americans who had gone along with Welles would believe it was a joke in bad taste' (Bazin 1991: 49). Does it still surprise anyone that many people who saw the images of the twin towers of New York hit by planes in 2001 thought it was just an action movie?

Welles loved a good mystery, and with *War of the Worlds* and later in *Citizen Kane* he innovates in many ways, most effectively in his use of the news flash as a synopsis. His great insight, shared by Kane, the tabloid newspaperman in the film, is that the news is staged entertainment. A fact now central to our culture but then still lost under the illusion that the news report was always about the realist delivery of the facts. Stripping out the reflexive prank in a later version, the 2005 Spielberg *War of the Worlds* filmed with the scientologist Tom Cruise in the lead role is inferior. Imposing an ideology-saturated panic about terrorists attacking America on the audience, there is no sense of irony or distance in allegory. The hero (Cruise) just wants to protect his kids and the pregnant mum in her perfect home, even if it is not quite a perfect home in Brooklyn ('Boston' in the film), while he lives in a dodgy flat in Bayonne, New Jersey (see Worldwide Guide to Movie Locations 2014). Our hero is prepared to, reluctantly, sacrifice his teenage rebel son to the war effort, and to kill a red-neck type marine. The equally heroic soldiers still organise disciplined effort amidst chaos. Subtlety sacrificed for propaganda is a significant loss and tells us more than we need to know about our current climate of fear. Perhaps this is what H. G. Wells had intended? The book, and the radio play, and the film, all begin with the earth being studied 'across an immense ethereal gulf' (*War of the Worlds* 1938) – an anthropological moment that is revealing in itself.

But Welles's radio play was not intentional war propaganda. It was rather an attempt to toy with America's faith in the 'new magic box' of the radio. It was an 'assault on the credibility of that machine' (Conrad 2003: 90). It was almost the destruction of Welles' career, and also that which granted him the opportunity to go to Hollywood to make *Citizen Kane*. Considering the immediate aftermath of the broadcast, with looting in half-abandoned cities and chaos all over, it is hard to imagine it going ahead had Welles known of the extent of this prank's consequences. Was there a plan to create more than a sensational outrage? Perhaps. Welles' radio contract with CBS had been checked by his lawyer and it left him with no responsibility for any consequence of his plays except for questions of plagiarism. CBS had to deal with over 100 law suits as a consequence of the Martian visit (Bazin 1991: 49).

Two brief mentions of 'the Orson Welles broadcast' occur in Theodor Adorno's *Current of Music* (Adorno 2006: 47–48, 373), the first time, along with the suggestion that 'it might be worthwhile to study whether children and naive persons are really thoroughly conscious that radio is a tool' (47). Confronted with authentic 'voices' with which they cannot argue, it is not too difficult to see a contemporary significance here – even as it should also be remembered that Adorno was writing for an audience (the Princeton Radio Project Group, led by Paul Lazarsfeld) that he did not much respect. Adorno denounced the Radio Project for being not dissimilar to market research. Its inquiry into the ways the mass media created effects was, he argued, unable to do anything significantly different to just what the programme owners and advertisers wanted. The Princeton Radio Group had been studying the radio play of *War of the Worlds* in the year before Adorno offered this criticism. They had identified similarities between Welles' radio panic and the demagoguery of the National Socialists in Germany, but Adorno argues that without an examination of production methods, this research remained epiphenomenal.

Today, the dialectical shift of course necessitates recognition that we all very well know that the production process of the media (news, critique, scholarship even) is all 'tool' and that authority is a function of style, carefully calibrated through presenter fashion and product placement. It is Marx who launched a critique of political economy and yet the culture industry as market still works. We shop eagerly, even ironically, for books about Marx, for example.

The snow globe fetish and the structure of beginnings

That amazing first close-up of the lips. But no-one was there to hear what Kane's last words were. This is the great conceit of the film, about which further controversy with writing credits and authorship circulate. Welles seems to have thought the rosebud device somewhat obvious, but it was in Mankiewicz's first draft. Who writes the text? Marx in *Capital* already quotes himself in the first line, as has often been mentioned, and of course there is a silent co-author, Engels, having already written *The Condition of the Working Class in England* (Engels 1845) and who sends Marx reports on the factory practice, production, accounting and much other data. The Blue Books too, the factory inspector reports, are already a pre-text for *Capital*. The first words are not the opening. Indeed, there are four prefaces, and the whole thing is rewritten just five years after its first publication. We read the fourth edition, into which Engels interpolates some of the corrections Marx made in his own copy as he was rewriting the text for French serialisation in the years immediately after the Paris Commune – a little complex of intertextuality that deserves its own separate essay (Hutnyk forthcoming).

The snow globe is a way into the start. A snow globe is a trinket collected by many, contemplated, pondered, shaken, smashed. The word is Rosebud and the film moves from ice to fire. According to Adorno, Walter Benjamin collected snow globes (Adorno 1963: 237), but for him a snow globe is not always a frozen moment; its kitsch relevance to the everyday and its souvenir quality make it both domestic and profound, familiar, but also strangely remote. Miniaturised. I am fascinated by these domes, as many have been before.

I want to develop this as condensation of the film. When the film opens, Kane's life is over, the story ends before it begins, as if to flummox any would-be explanations of a man's life, or – since we know the ending – to dissuade us from thinking that Kane's life can be referred back to the primordial scene where he is wrenched from his sled, and from his mother, to be catapulted into corporate education, current affairs, the world ... abundance and loss.

Kane is a collector – and one thing he hangs onto is the snow globe. The first sequence of the film has him dropping it as he dies. It shatters. I like to think of this as *the* cinematic scene. The snow globe shakes up conventional souveniring versions of cinema – stars and cameos – in favour of miniature worlds and *mise-en-scène*. A glass ball into which myriad interpretive occult effects can be projected. The snow globe can be thought of as a miniature TV, a time machine for memory, for second sight. It records and replays the past in newsreel fashion.

Despite the 'No Trespassing' sign, Freud should be called. In case he is busy, we might look into that crystal ball and take the snow globe as a vision machine, not just that which Bazin describes as a 'childish souvenir' which Kane 'grasps before dying', a 'toy that was spared during the destruction of the dolls room belonging to his wife Susan' (Bazin 1991: 65). He also reports that Welles had described the style of Kane as 'bric-a-brac' in comparison to his less famous *Magnificent Ambersons* (59), but Bazin also provides an excellent analysis of the single shot which presents Susan's suicide attempt, contrasted with the six or seven cross-cut shots that 'anyone else' would have used (78).

Melanie Klein wrote extensive notes on *Citizen Kane* but these were not published until 1998, not only, I think, because they were not written up, but also because the film outdoes psychoanalysis before the letter – another Wellesian prank perhaps, like Marx, clearing aside the beloved 'Robinsonades' and origin stories of the professors of economy so that a more fundamental explanatory framework can begin. Whatever the case, Klein notes that the snow globe Kane drops as he dies is 'obviously' a breast, and that Kane, though lonely at the end, is not ill and has always pursued manic progressive goals:

> in his youth, Kane has strong social feelings and purposes. The underprivileged, the poor are to be helped. He is going to devote his powers, his money, his capacities to this purpose, and later, after

failing in politics because of the scandal when he marries Susan the opera singer it is in part to 'control multitudes' through her voice. (Klein, in Mason 1998: 148)

Kane merely collects, oblivious to what this means. He is after all a distorted capitalist, a personification of the wealth he made on the back of an originary accumulation, the Colorado Load. He does not work for his capital, he continually feels he should do something worthy – his patronising charitable impulse is not, we might think today, unlike certain other tycoons, who also collect. But Capital is not just a collection of commodities. Would we want to pursue a psychoanalytic enquiry? The materialist comprehension of the commodity, object, souvenir or trinket is different to that of the psychoanalytic approach, which takes individuals and their drives, desires and motives into first account. The fetish is not just a deviant displacement, not just a sexual misrecognition – mommy–daddy – but a feint or trick that hides a deeper social malaise to do with the ethics of distribution. The point is to do away with the idea that the beginning is the key to the whole. That said, when Klein identifies the snow globe as the maternal breast, there is cause to recall it is the one thing Welles keeps with him after Susan leaves. Like Rosebud, this is perhaps a kind of cheesy memory of a past present made virtual in the object. A cheap trinketisation.

Susan herself ends up a maudlin drunk, but she had spent a good part of the film trying to put the puzzle of trinkets together – literally in the case of her jigsaw puzzles in the great hall of Xanadu.

Rosebud

What is Rosebud? I am not giving anything away here, as from the start the journalists are seeking the meaning of this enigmatic last word. The journalists never find out what the audience gets to know – the 'truth' remains undiscovered within the contrivance of the inner plot of the movie. We achieve, however, only what Kane achieves in the end in the contemplation of the snow globe – the grand overview of the complete collection with no central or final meaning. Within the contrivance of the investigative plot, the journalists amass much about Kane through interviews and records, but they do not discover Rosebud. Listing the trinkets collected by Kane or even narrating Kane's life as a reverse sequence of scenes, would do little more than entertain. Without analysis we get little insight – in the film the collection is on its way to destruction in the furnace. Kane dies lonely, surrounded by the detritus of a decimated European culture, plundered as Europe was destroyed by self-hatred and fascism. This may be the interpretation to which viewers are led, with Kane's nostalgia a metaphor for isolationism in the run-up to the war, as also anticipated by Gore Vidal writing about Roosevelt's trick to get the Japanese to provoke, and thus win support for the war away from the isolationists (Vidal 2000). Welles was close to Roosevelt and – take note Mr Hoover, this was not very communist – he tours South America as a Goodwill Ambassador speaking for the Rockefeller Inter-American Affairs Committee to shore up support for the US war effort there.

What symbolic effects help the interpretation? Perhaps like the illustrative table in the first chapter of *Capital*, the sled should catch your attention as a mystery. In the film, the sled is marked by the haunting vibraphone music. Is this inner plot of the movie an intended distraction, something to also throw the knowing viewers – as critics, after the event – off the trail? Of course, Kane himself has missed the point. At the end, the grand overview of the futility of the collection, the amazing final tracking shot into the fire in the failed fantasy jigsaw empire of Xanadu leaves the media tycoon paralysed and immobile, wasting his days. The audience is led to draw their own conclusions, and it does not seem unimportant that Marx presumed a reader 'willing to learn something new, and therefore think for themselves' (Marx 1970: 8). Rosebud, ultimately, is that insignificant icon of significance – the emblem of an incoherent power, the fantasy of another life, the image of alienation. The immense power of Kane is shown as impotent because of this loss – indeed, in a wheelchair at the end, a paralysed nostalgic alone in his decayed pleasure palace, Xanadu – Kane confusedly mistakes loss of the past as the source of his errors. The moral testimony of his spurned friend, Jedediah (played by Joseph Cotton), suggests a more adequate assessment.

In the end, each narrator in *Citizen Kane* fails to explain him. Even if Kane is a collector, not a creator, there is still interpretive work demanded of spectators. The slow opening scene is interrupted by the crash of the racy newsreel, which some minutes later clutters to an end and is shown as the shadowy construction of journalists in a smoky room. There is much in the film worth noting: its innovations, authorship, controlling genius, lighting, shots, music, structure. The different windows on the story of *Citizen Kane* also offer an allegorical way into reading Marx's *Capital* – the initial newsreel section something like the commodity fetish chapter, a platform that warns, as does the very first sentence, that things are not what they appear, that the wealth of societies in which the capitalist mode of production prevails only presents itself – *erscheint*, see below – as a monstrous accumulation.

Although the film begins and ends with the 'No Trespassing' sign, it is Welles, I think, who does want, and wants us, to trespass. His camera passes through the chain mesh, and again through various windows and signs to examine and inquire. This same metaphoric architecture governs the presentation of *Capital*. The theatrical references to drawing back curtains (long before the *Wizard of Oz*), the ocular vision and *camera obscura* that 'at first look' implies always a second and third, look, the ghost commentary so beloved of Derrida, and much more.

The presentation of *Capital* requires work to comprehend much more than the commodities chapter. Such that, it is worth thinking of Kane as only the personification of a member of the capitalist class at a certain – changing – time in the capital cycle. And the unfolding of the film as a diagrammatic performance of a much wider drama. We see the boom and bust, growth and crisis of the man's career – this we should consider as an allegory of the cycle. We need to read further into *Capital* to see the same, that the commodity chapter is followed by an ever wider analytic purchase.

The implied reader

Marx wrote his analysis of capital not only because he wanted to set down the answers, but so that the working class would have the wherewithal to make their own analyses, to read the world. I follow the work of Gayatri Spivak (Spivak 2012) where she implores us to read and learn and teach a patient non-coercive rearrangement. I think we could learn to read more slowly and watch several times the way the film and the book warn us not to attach too much significance to the items collected – the sled, the wooden table, the snow globe – but to see these suspended in a social world, class relations, with not so straightforward answers. We can have issues with this metaphor, which privileges text as unproblematic transcription, but Marx himself would not have difficulty here.

But what are we to think about *Capital* as an organised book for readers who are willing to learn, but who are starting, like everybody else, like Kane, with commodities? There are no people at the start. Marx warns that 'individuals are dealt with only in so far as they are the personification of economic categories, embodiments of particular class relations and class interests' (Marx 1970: 10). But Capital is a social system – the commodity in this use is a social form, and to examine this Marx sets out a dialectical method – ever so briefly he notes that this is the opposite of the method of Hegel. Here is another personification, I suppose. Yet even as the capitalist class has an interest in the development (and exploitation) of the working class, we share that interest since a developed working class best develops the productive forces – only we think it dialectically, and deploy a model of critique that comes from, yet inverts, reverts, the then out of fashion (today, very much the fashion) Hegel (for example, Žižek 2012), so as to sublate that interest. Marx 'coquettes' – flirts – with Hegel and distinguishes between method and analysis. We should keep this in mind when we ask why Marx starts as he does. In the preface to the second edition of *Capital*, Marx writes: 'Of course the method of presentation must differ from that of inquiry' and 'my dialectical method is not only different from the Hegelian, but its direct opposite' (Marx 1970: 19). I would stress this – the procedure is dialectical. Yet, not exactly the same as Hegel's 'mystified dialectic' (it is always more complicated than thesis, anti-thesis, synthesis etcetera). I am not saying that Welles is dialectical in the same way, but the unfolding of perspective on a 'life' might help us see how Marx offers a procedure that stitches back and forth between complex examples and accumulating understanding.

We need to be able to read dextrously, to have several ways in, and be alert to a dialectical versioning of Marx's thinking. The first sentence announces the basic premise of the book. 'The wealth of societies dominated by the capitalist mode of production, presents itself as a monstrous accumulation of commodities' (translation slightly modified by author). We can read this sentence with the help of Adorno, for example, as a critical Hegelianism that rails against identity. The work of showing that appearances of identity are non-identical. 'Presents itself' is a translation of '*erscheint als*', with *erscheinung* being an important, powerful, spectral Hegelian word (see Hutnyk 2009 – in the Penguin edition 1976 this word is glossed as 'appears'). The non-identity here is that, except in 'presentation', Capital is *not* just that monstrous accumulation. Nor is it exchange, property, circulation, credit or labour. We should also read this sentence according to our time, but of course cannot but be influenced by readers of other times, such that we do not read alone, but we read each time ourselves. Let us try to keep both these things in mind. We are reading a text that is a 'carbuncle' on the complacency of the ruling classes – at the end of the third preface discussion of crisis, unemployment and prospects for revolution leads Engels to insist that 'the voice ought to be heard of a man whose whole theory is the result of a life-long study of economic history'. That this history would lead to social revolution was tempered with the realisation that the ruling classes would not submit 'without a "pro-Slavery rebellion"' (Engels quoting Marx in the preface of Marx 1976: 113), yet another reference to the context of the American Civil War and reason once again for all workers of all lands to unite.

Anti-communist Hearst

Hearst cannot be reclaimed.

The film variously deals with New Deal cultural content, US hegemony 'on the march', the 'battle between intervention and isolationism' (Mulvey 1992: 15). There are some films, and even rumours that get filmed, that seem to say more truthfully what goes on than others. Eisenstein commented on the telegraphic communication between Hearst and a photographer in his employ called Frederic Remington, where Hearst reportedly wrote regarding the 1897 Spanish-American conflict: 'you furnish the pictures, I'll provide the war', as glossed in *Citizen Kane*. Eisenstein called these alleged telegrams 'more truthful as "human" documents than numerous historical documents' (Eisenstein 1987: 309). It is unfortunate, or perhaps appropriate, that Welles' correspondence with Eisenstein was lost when a house fire in Spain destroyed much of the Welles archive.

Fire plays an earlier role too. Hearst the adventure capitalist was interested in photography in the 1890s and had travelled to Luxor in Egypt to photograph in the Valley of the Kings. The British Government ultimately forced him to leave for fear that his explosive flash photography was damaging the tombs (Pizzitola 2002: 23). Undaunted, his stereopticon projections were then taken to Paris to impress people there, but his collection, along with many photographs taken of the San Francisco Bay area, was reportedly destroyed in the great fire of 1906 (29). If it were not for eschewing cheap psychology, I would be tempted to diagnose a poignant career jealousy in the symbiotic relation between the protagonists.

The French film critic André Bazin points out that the controversy over Kane as Hearst was a consequence of the rivalry between Hearst gossip columnist Louella Parsons and Hedda Hopper (Bazin 1991: 57). Was Hearst's hostility to *Citizen Kane* reason for the wider film industry to fear exposure, through Hearst papers, of Hollywood's foibles – sex, payola – or rather its employment of 'aliens at the expense of American labour' (Leaming 1985: 209)? His support for the working man may well have got Hearst called a communist in his youth, but it was always a misnomer.

The importance of rumour in the reception of *Citizen Kane* is clear, but what then of the unspoken exclusions in the Hearst story, the bits of narrative not voiced: Hearst as Moneybags plundering the material culture of the world, the arrogance of his taking photos in Luxor where the flash damages the art of millennia. Hearst thought WW1 a financial venture for Wall Street tycoons, and his defence of regular soldiers, even deserters, and pro-Irish anti-imperialists was impressive – for example, his campaign in support of British diplomat Roger Casement, a man eventually hung for seeking German military support for Irish independence. But such campaigning was, however, not without financial benefit to Hearst's own purse in the form of ever-growing newspaper sales to those who approved of his anti-corruption stance.

Hearst campaigned against pro-Soviet Hollywood films in the early 1940s, for example, *Mission to Moscow* and *North Star* (Pizzitola 2002: 409). Hearst's support for what became the House Un-American Activities Commission (HUAC) meant he rapidly became an advocate of anti-communism in the post-WW2 era. Despite denials by Hearst that he orchestrated it, the film, *Citizen Kane*, was branded communist, only saw restricted release, got bad early press, and took several years before being recognised the 'greatest film of all time' and so on ... the rest is cinema history. Welles was investigated by FBI agent Hoover (398) and his directing career never recovered – he was forever dogged by studio interference and funding troubles.

In order to get his film released, Welles denied Hearst was the model for Kane, though the parallels are several. Hearst approvingly met with Hitler in 1934 (as does Kane), owned newspapers and became a recluse (as does Kane), had a mistress (as does Kane) – and though I will read no significance into this, Hearst's secret name for his mistress Marion Davies' genitalia was Rosebud (Leaming 1985: 205). There is possibly reason to dispute this – Pizzitola reports that Rosebud was the painter and family 'friend' Ocrin Peck's nickname for Hearst's mother (Pizzitola 2002: 181), though Leaming's story that Hearst was incensed that Kane dies with 'Rosebud on his lips' is virtuoso journalism. Welles himself says that the Remington cable story was 'the only purely Hearstian element in *Citizen Kane*' (in Conrad 2003: 144).

Conrad suggests that Hearst papers created both the gossip column and celebrity (145). It was thanks to AT&T (American Telephone and Telegraph Company) and MGM (Metro-Goldwyn-Mayer) that Marion Davies 'became the first film celebrity to have her image transmitted over telephone wires' (Pizzitola 2002: 230). Conrad also notes that Welles had written a foreword to Davies' posthumously published memoir of her time with Hearst at San Simeon. Welles' first wife lived for many years next to Marion Davies near San Francisco, and Welles spent some months living there as well, long after *Citizen Kane*, when Rita Hayworth threw him out of their Los Angeles home (Leaming 1985: 343). When Davies came to dinner, as she sometimes did, Welles was told to hide, but he watched through the window with his coat collar turned up against the snow (a possibly apocryphal story, given the weather).

So let's find that image from the film that encodes it all – a hammer and sickle graffiti on the façade of the Inquirer newspaper office where Kane's news proprietor career starts. If the multiple perspectives of the *Citizen Kane* film can be twisted to do allegorical service for a reading of *Capital*, then the subsequent repetition of shot framings are not inconsequential. In the scene immediately following the newsreel sequence that (re)starts the film after Kane's big-lipped death, the next camera movement echoes the passage through the 'No Trespassing' gateway as the camera moves through a neon sign and down through a glass window to Susan's table and the first of five or six interviews which structure the rest of the film. The sections are not consecutive, temporally concurrent, and can even be contradictory; they warn that these many perspectives do not add up to an explanation of the life of Kane, yet by the end, when the ice of the snow globe has turned to the fire of the furnace that consumes all that collected junk, we do perhaps know a little more than before, can examine things in a more nuanced way, and we maybe even get to know something of Hearst.

Trinketisation

Kane collects, well, Hearst does, but in the film the end of the collection is junk. Excess – all those statues. Freud's interest in statuettes betrays what he would have called an object-choice that 'serves as a substitute for some unattained ego ideal' of his own. Futile. In the end, the trinkets get consumed in the furnace that is not unlike a TV. If the snow globe can be a miniature television, the furnace is the sucking vortex of the carnivorous news machine that *Citizen Kane* sets out to critique. The movement is from inquisitive to acquisitive, and this destroys.

Perhaps though, the snow globe is less relevant today. More important is the 'more or less' cynical valet who is there at the end, orchestrating the destruction of Kane's empire of things, burning the detritus of collecting in the flames of squander (potlatch). It may be relevant to ask just why and where the migrant figure is there at the end of the film? Just as Marx dedicated *Capital* to an exile (Wilhelm Wolff), and was himself, like Welles, also to some extent a refugee (however comfortable in Kentish Town), the position of the migrant in the text is left to one side but always present. Excavation might bring this position out more, as a reading that leverages the text into the politics of global capital today. Think of what Spivak does to Jane Eyre's Bertha, Hegel's Hottentot, and Kant's 'Raw Man' in *Critique of Postcolonial Reason* (1999). Inspired, as ever, by Spivak, I think the figure of the character who does not quite 'fit' the narrative can indeed be used to generate other readings. If the 'cynical valet' is not so readily present in Marx, certainly there is a host of other figures that might invite speculation. I would nominate Leonard Horner, the factory inspector, who provides so much useful data through the Blue Books that Marx uses, as someone deserving closer attention. Another figure might be Wilhelm Wolff, since his involvement in the 1848 revolution alongside Marx and Engels might remind us that *Capital* is also still an activist's text, and that Marx never really lets go of his early revolutionary formation. And at the end of *Capital* another 'embodiment' of the class system on a wider scale might bring in the colonial theatre in ways that also emphasise that the book has a wider scope – here the tragic-comic experience of a certain Mr Peel, mentioned by E. G. Wakefield, who imports workers and means of production to the Swann River in Western Australia. But since Capital is a social relation, mediated through things, not just the things themselves, once Mr Peel 'arrived at his destination [...] [he] [...] "was left without a servant to make his bed or fetch him water from the river." Unhappy Mr Peel, who provided for everything except the export of English relations of production to the Swann River' (Marx 1976: 933).[2]

But what does Kane do that makes him a tragic figure, alone in Xanadu at the end, lost and lamenting, writing lonely memos to aides who hardly care? All the problems of the present day capitalist (Moneybags) are figured in Welles' oligarch. A super wealthy tycoon dedicates himself to the uplift of the common man, setting himself against the trusts (banks), 'Boss Bill Geddes' (corrupt power) and elitist conventions (celebrity culture), only in each case to miss his target, compromise his ideals, and realise these are wayward. The patron of the arts cannot disrupt the money-making schemes of capital – Jedediah is the only one to speak truth to Kane, and he points out a warning that goes unheeded within the film (but not for us?). Kane's well-meaning liberalism will count for nothing if those who are downtrodden stand up and claim their rights. How is this not a picture for today, an indictment of the patronising philanthropy of a capitalist that would try to impress with charitable works, with green credentials, with fiscal restraint? Let us not overlook the ways in which Kane participates behind the scenes so to speak. As with today's Capital-with-restraint ideology, the structural underbelly of exploitation and oppression must be ignored for Kane's philanthropic fantasy to be more than philandering.

What is Kane's crime? Yellow journalism or self-aggrandising ambition? Searching for a love that could not be bought for money? He wants desperately to be loved, but his isolation within millions makes him a sad and impotent figure. He fails because the populist cult of personality – targeted as fascism in the film, as noted in the film poster (Figure 10.2) – is not one that can enact real change.

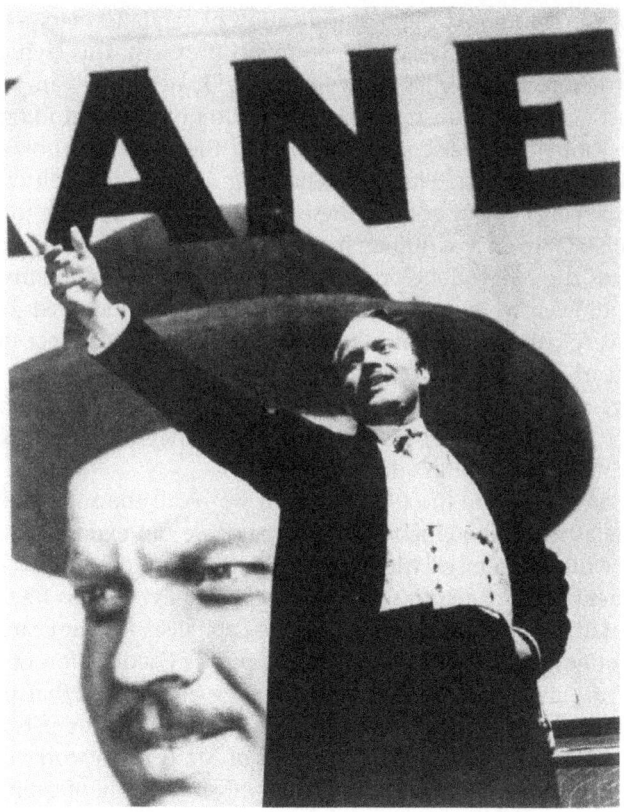

Figure 10.2 Kane on film poster
Source: Screen capture from *Citizen Kane* (1941), dir. Orson Welles, Universal Home Entertainment

Kane collects objects, but as an industrial capitalist. This is a ruse, a trick – his fascination with objects is the inverse image of his interest in the immaterial exchangeability of objects. Stallybrass notes that entrepreneurs 'were interested in objects only to the extent that they could be transformed into commodities and exchanged for profit on the market' (Stallybrass 1998: 186). We should be careful here not to think that profit comes directly from exchange, but certainly the interests of the individual collector are different to the social power and interest of capitalists as a class, which is in the valorisation (recoupment of surplus value as profit through circulation) of profit through sales.

The philanthropic charitable connoisseur collector-as-capitalist cares not one jot about things or about people, but collects and gives as a public relations alibi to excuse extortionate remuneration. The central figure of *Citizen Kane* is the personification of capitalist class relations, and to see this otherwise would be to deny exactly this hypocritical social structure that Welles seeks to expose. Kane as the campaigning journalist against the trusts, with a declaration of high-sounding 'principles' is not simply false consciousness in the film, but shown to be the embodiment of the fetish-like character of the commodity system. Sure, Kane collects, but none of these trinkets mean anything to him as a capitalist. Or even as a human being – as Melanie Klein points out, he only saves the snow globe/breast of lost nostalgia. The remains of his collection, even when he is alive, is stored in boxes, hoarded – and in a way every collector of knick-knacks is rehearsing the abject mystery at the heart of capitalism as alienated social system. Bill Gates collects paintings, Gordon Gecko has a fine eye. The objects and attachment to them are little lies, personalised mementoes – they belie the frisson of transformation at Capital's dead heart.

Kane is dead before the film begins, if we recall the suggestion that has Kane as the embodiment of Moneybags, we can expose the curiosity that while he himself tries to fight for the 'common man' and has a sentimental attachment to things (Rosebud), nevertheless he is still a representative of his class, a class who – as capitalists – do not care about things, only the possibility of recouping profits (valorisation of appropriated surplus value) through the exchange of things. What perhaps we see in the film that is not in the book – *Capital* – is the personification of a class relation, and the naming of Moneybags works both to obscure the systemic character of the oppressive regime of capital, and to, most deceptively, provide named capitalists with alibis via philanthropic personality for their acquisitive plunder. To collect is not as monstrous as to profit, but both are intrinsic to the day-to-day activity of a Kane, a Gates, a Jobs, a Gecko or the allegorical-oligarchical Wolves. In this respect *Citizen Kane* serves as a warning for how to continue to read Marx's *Capital* – it is not pop psychology and it is not a one-shot scene. 'No Trespassing' is a more complex property claim than even Welles may have realised.

Notes

1. The Marxism-Leninism of the Bolsheviks, the varieties of Stalinism, Council communism, Luxemburg and Liebknecht, the Maoists, Heidegger even, of course the well-meaning existentialists, Sartre, the Eurocommunists, Trotskyists and autonomes, in a certain sense Foucault, and, with flying vaginas and speeding penises our favourite two-headed beast Deleuze-Guattari, which is a strange echo of the Marx-Engels head-birth, repeated again as farce as Hardt-Negri, then as Badiou-Žižek. These revenants would include a call to a return to reading Marx by Jacques Derrida in the 1990s – 'When was it time to have ever left off reading Marx', quipped Spivak, who 'so desperately wanted Derrida to get Marx rightish' (Spivak, 1995: 72). After that, implosion of communism in Eastern Europe, but before long declarations that Marx was relevant again. Re-releases of *The Communist Manifesto* on the 150th anniversary, and recently, Harvey's lectures on *Capital* – which reorders the book (Harvey 2010) and is very dry compared to Jameson's provocative volume on unemployment (2011). See also Michael Lebowitz's *Following Marx* (2006), Jacques Bidet's *Exploring Marx's Capital* (2005), Peter Osborne's *How to Read Marx* (2005), Stephen Shapiro on *How to Read Marx's Capital* (2008), Ben Fine and Alfredo Saad-Filho's 'expert guide' (2010), the excellent Simon Clarke (available online, 2011) and from the publishing house of Continuum: *Marx for the Perplexed* (Seed 2010). More and more texts to read on how to read Marx. It is as if we can never be done with prefaces.
2. This moment of mirth which has Marx quoting Wakefield quoting Mr Peel is the basis of Simon Barber's PhD work at Goldsmiths College and subject of many discussions for which I am thankful.

Bibliography

Adorno, Theodor (1963) *Prismen: Kulturkritik und Gesellschaft*, Munich: Deutscher Taschenbuch Verlag.
Adorno, Theodor (1993) [2006] *Current of Music*, Cambridge: Polity Press.
Bazin, André (1991) [1958] *Orson Welles: A Critical View*, Los Angeles: Acrobat Books.
Bogdanovich, Peter (1998) 'My Orson: New Introduction', in *This is Orson Welles*, Perseus: Da Capo Press, pp. vii–xxxix.
Bidet, Jacques (2005) *Exploring Marx's Capital*, Chicago: Haymarket Books.
Callow, Simon (1995) *Orson Welles: The Road to Xanadu*, London: Jonathan Cape.
Callow, Simon (2006) *Orson Welles: Hello Americans*, London: Jonathan Cape.
Carringer, Robert L. (1996) *The Making of Citizen Kane*, Berkeley: University of California Press.

Carringer, Robert L. (1978) The Scripts of 'Citizen Kane', *Critical Inquiry*, 5(2) (Winter), pp. 369–400.

Carringer, Robert L. (1975) '"Citizen Kane", "The Great Gatsby", and Some Conventions of American Narrative', *Critical Inquiry*, 2(2) (Winter), pp. 307–325.

Clarke, Simon (2011) 'Reading Guide to Capital' [online] – available online at http://homepages.warwick.ac.uk/~syrbe/, last accessed 14 Jan 2014.

Conrad, Peter (2003) *Orson Welles: The Stories of His Life*, London: Faber and Faber.

Derrida, Jacques (1994) [1993] *Spectres of Marx: The State of the Debt, the Work of Mourning and the New International*, London: Routledge.

Eisenstein, Serge (1987) [1946] *Nonindifferent Nature*, Cambridge: Cambridge University Press.

Engels, Frederik (1845) 'The Condition of the Working Class in England' – available online at http://www.marxists.org/archive/marx/works/1845/condition-working-class/, last accessed January 3 2014.

Fine, Ben and Alfredo Saad-Filho (2010) *Marx's 'Capital'*, London: Pluto Press.

Freud, Sigmund (1985) 'Group Psychology and the Analysis of the Ego', in *Civilization, Society and Religion*, PFL 12, pp. 65–143

Harvey, David (2010) *A Companion to Marx's Capital*, London: Verso.

Jameson, Frederic (2011) *Representing 'Capital': A Reading of Volume One*, London & New York: Verso.

Leaming, Barbara (1985) *Orson Welles*, London: Weidenfeld and Nicholson.

Marx, Karl (2002) [1852] 'The Eighteenth Brumaire of Louis Boneparte', in Cowling, Mark and James Martin (eds) *Marx's 'Eighteenth Brumaire': Postmodern Interpretations*, London: Pluto Press, pp. 19–109.

Marx, Karl (1970) [1867] *Capital Volume 1*, London: Lawrence and Wishhart.

Marx, Karl (1975) [1867] *Das Kapital*, Berlin, Dietz Verlag.

Marx, Karl (1976) [1867] *Capital Volume 1*, London: Penguin.

Mason, Albert (1998) 'Melanie Klein's Notes on *Citizen Kane*, with Commentary', *Psychoanalytic Inquiry*, 18, pp. 147–153.

Mulvey, Laura (1992) *Citizen Kane*, London: British Film Institute.

Nietzsche, Friedrich (1980) [1874] *On the Advantage and Disadvantage of History for Life*, Indianapolis, Cambridge, Hacking Publishing [accessed via http://archive.org/stream/Nietzsche-AdvantageDisadvantageOfHistoryForLife/Nietzsche-AdvantageDisadvantageHistoryForLife_djvu.txt 14 January 2014].

Osborne, Peter (2005) *How to Read Marx*, London: Granta.

Pizzitola, Louis (2002) *Hearst over Hollywood: Power, Passion and Propaganda in the Movies*, New York: Columbia University Press.

Rosenbaum, Jonathan (1998) '"Welles" Career: A Chronology', in Welles, Orson and Peter Bogdanovich (1998) *This is Orson Welles*, London: De Capo Press, pp 323–453.

Seed, John (2010) *Marx for the Perplexed*, London: Continuum.

Shapiro, Stephen (2008) *How to Read Marx's Capital*, London: Pluto Press.

Spivak, Gayatri Chakravorty (1995) 'Ghostwriting', *Diacritics*, 25(2), pp. 65–84.

Spivak, Gayatri Chakravorty (1999) *A Critique of Postcolonial Reason: Toward a History of the Vanishing Present*, Cambridge, Mass: Harvard University Press.

Spivak, Gayatri Chakravorty (2012) *An Aesthetic Education in the Era of Globalization*, Cambridge, Massachusetts: Harvard University Press.

Stallybrass, Peter (1998) 'Marx's Coat', in Speyer, Patricia (ed.) *Border Fetishisms: Material Objects in Unstable Spaces*, London: Routledge, pp. 183–207.

Vidal, Gore (2000) *The Golden Age*, New York: Doubleday.

Walters, Ben (2004) *Orson Welles*, London, Haut Publishing

Waters, John (2005) *Shock Value: A Tasteful Book about Bad Taste*, New York: Thunder Mouth Press.

Welles, Orsen and Peter Bogdanovich (1998) *This is Orsen Welles*, New York: De Capo Press.

Worldwide Guide to Movie Locations (2014) 'War of the Worlds Film Location', [online] available at http://www.movie-locations.com/movies/w/War_Of_The_Worlds_2005.html#.UtZ0NWRdWJU, last accessed 2 January 2014,

Žižek, Slavoj (2012) *Less than Nothing Hegel and the Shadow of Dialectical Materialism*, London: Verso.

11

The Meaning of History and the Uses of Translation in *News from Ideological Antiquity – Marx/Eisenstein/The Capital* (Video 2008) by Alexander Kluge

Ewa Mazierska

With a length of 570 minutes, divided into three parts, Alexander Kluge's *Nachrichten aus der ideologischen Antike – Marx/Eisenstein/Das Kapital* (*News from Ideological Antiquity – Marx/Eisenstein/Capital*, 2008) (hereafter *MEC*), is stylistically one of the most heterogeneous and complex films ever made, where 'film' is understood widely, including also other forms of moving image, such as video. It is also one of the most complex political works on account of the subjects discussed, such as class relations, and its form, which emphasises discursive activity, making us aware that the reality which unfolds in front of us when we watch a film is never natural, but mediated. As a complex and heterogeneous film, *MEC* lends itself to a comparison with *Histoire(s) du Cinéma* (1988–1998) by Jean-Luc Godard; as a complex and heterogeneous political work, to Marx's *Das Kapital*, which can be described, to use Gérard Genette's terminology, as its principal hypotext, which the hypertext transforms, modifies, elaborates or extends (Stam 2000: 65–66).

However, the research devoted to this monumental work in comparison with *Histoire(s) du Cinéma*, is very limited, perhaps reflecting the fact that, unlike Godard's work, which firmly belongs to the domain of cinema, as conveyed by its title, Kluge's *MEC*, with its enigmatic title, falls into a no-man's land between politics and cinema, as well as between different media.[1] This is paradoxical, as one of Kluge's objectives is to assess the power of cinema in conveying political programmes, and the role of politics in shaping the history of cinema. This essay is an attempt to grapple with these issues, by locating *MEC* within Kluge's oeuvre, describing his purpose and method of adapting Marx's work for cinema and reflecting on the actuality of *Das Kapital* as seen through Kluge's lens.

Alexander Kluge's struggle for autonomy and relevance

In the majority of studies devoted to Kluge (for example Fiedler 1984; Hansen 1986; Liebman 1988; Lutze 1998; Silberman 1995), Kluge is presented as belonging to a certain tradition in German philosophy and study of culture, epitomised by the works of Walter Benjamin, Bertolt Brecht, Jürgen Habermas and Theodor Adorno, even being the last author in this lineage. His connection with Adorno comes across as especially close due to the fact that this philosopher acted as his mentor in Kluge's youth. As Miriam Hansen maintains, 'having just published his doctoral dissertation in law and dreading the prospect of a legal career, Kluge discussed his interest in filmmaking with Adorno, a philosopher not exactly known as a champion of the mass media. Adorno in turn wrote a letter to Fritz Lang, a Los Angeles acquaintance, suggesting that Kluge be hired as an assistant in the production of the two part spectacle, *The Tiger of Eschnapur/The Indian Tomb* (*Der Tiger von Eschnapur/Der indische Grabmal*, 1958–1959), for which the director had returned to Germany' (Hansen 1986: 193).

For Adorno, art should be overtly political by criticising the existing, popular art, which hides its political agenda by presenting itself as merely representing 'things as they are' and in this way advocating and normalising the dominant ideology. Adorno described such art as the 'culture industry' and criticised both its regressive political agenda and its low artistic quality, due to offering the audience standardised, formulaic products, at best infused with 'pseudo-innovations' (Adorno 1991, especially 85–92). For Adorno, to counteract the culture industry, artists should divert from a formulaic realism. In such art, and cinema especially, non-linear montage plays a crucial role, because the assembling of shots belonging to different realities allows for breaking the illusion of continuity of human experience and creates meanings which the individual shots would not have on their own, and therefore is capable of presenting a world that has no referent in empirical reality.

According to this approach, rather than furthering the narrative, montage should allow the viewer to think and to act by presenting him with possible scenarios worth pursuing or avoiding. As Stuart Liebman claims, 'linear narratives, which according to Kluge embody the quantifying abstract logic of instrumental reason, must be abandoned, although narrative elements, punctuated by leaps and reversals of time and circumscribed by reflection-inducing montage sequences, could still be retained. Instead, the filmmaker should use quotations, shifts in the mode of representation, interruptions calculated to break routinised, passive responses, and so forth' (Liebman 1988: 14). Liebman attributes to Kluge a view that montage could be used to produce a self-conscious construction, a kind of 'writing' in images, music and sounds which would be actively 'read' by spectators. 'Such spectatorial engagement was essential if film was ever to constitute a Kosmos, an autonomous world of art not wholly isolated from social experience and potentially available to all' (11). Because films require imaginative engagement and debate, they become training grounds for enlightenment as well as assembly points for the broadly based, spontaneous coalitions which are the ideal vehicle of progress towards it.

In Kluge's film, written material, most importantly in the form of intertitles, plays an especially important function. On the one hand, it summarises the main points made by the director and divides his complex and often long works into smaller units, making them more manageable for the viewer. On the other hand, intertitles, on which the camera often lingers for a considerable time, allow the viewer some rest from the dense visual text and to think about something else. Kluge claims that for him such functions are played by intertitles in silent cinema; they do not explain what one sees as this is obvious from watching the visual part, but help the viewer's thoughts to drift away (13). Intertitles, together with music inserts, especially piano tunes played by a single pianist placed in front of the screen, act as a link to a 'cinema antiquity'. Kluge's films are thus self-conscious and complex 'memory works', encouraging the viewer to dig in his/her own memory and unconscious.

Much connects Kluge and Adorno, but also much divides them, reflecting their different temperaments and the media they use. Adorno's tone is always categorical; it appears as if he offers us the only possible take on a specific idea or situation. Although he advocates thinking 'outside the box', he does not allow his readers to develop independent opinions, but like a stern teacher patronises his readers. Furthermore, his categorisations lack sensitivity to the richness of human experience. In particular, for Adorno there is only the despicable 'culture industry' on the one hand and 'true art' on the other, with nothing in between. Moreover, due to using words as his principal means of expression as well as his life trajectory, Adorno either could not or did not need to compromise with his principal 'enemies': representatives of the culture industry establishment.

Kluge, when addressing the audience, often in interviews with his guests, uses a different tone from Adorno. Rather than presenting himself as the 'one who knows' and wants to illuminate the ignorant reader or viewer, he adopts the tone of an ignorant and humble pupil who wants to learn something from his interlocutor. This attitude is particularly remarkable when his discussants are much younger than him, as is the case with many guests in *MEC*. The talks often come across as unstructured, allowing the other person to drift from the main question and dominate the discussion. In his attitude to his guests Kluge comes across as close to the position taken and discussed by Jacques Rancière, an author of the books *The Ignorant Schoolmaster* (1991) and *The Emancipated Spectator* (2009). In these works Rancière develops a distinctly anti-Adornian position, arguing that spectating is by its very nature active and the 'ignorant schoolmaster', who for Rancière is the preferred type of teacher, should learn from his pupils as much as the pupil learns from him (Rancière 1991). For Kluge, as for Rancière, the spectator is always active, because, as Rancière puts it, 'she observes, selects, compares, interprets. She links what she sees to a host of other things that she has seen on other stages, in other kinds of place. She composes her own poem with the elements of the poem before her' (Rancière 2009: 13). The position Kluge adopts in his films adds to the sense of liminality of his works, especially their being between documentary and fiction, as we are never sure if he is a 'real' journalist or only plays one, if he is truly ignorant and searches for 'enlightenment' or rather, like Socrates, uses dialogue as a means to better present his thoughts.

Unlike Adorno, who thanks to 'working in words' and in academia, where commercial pressure tends to be smaller than in the culture industry, Kluge, due to being chiefly a filmmaker, appears to be always able and willing to compromise with the 'big capitalist beast': the film producers, the state and commercial television. Such an attitude can be attributed to both pragmatic and essential reasons. Kluge is aware that a film director, who wants to be as independent as a poet or philosopher, is practically sentenced to non-existence, because filmmaking, unlike writing poetry, requires significant financial resources, which filmmakers normally do not possess. Further, only by infiltrating spaces colonised by the products of the culture industry, to some extent by compromising with it, does an artist have a chance to change the spectator's mindset and the culture in which he operates. Such a pragmatic attitude, yet informed by high Marxist ideals, most importantly his *Eleventh Thesis on Feuerbach*, which demands that philosophers not only explain the world, but also change it (Marx and Engels 1947: 199), is reflected in the numerous roles Kluge performed in his working life, as listed by Theodore Fiedler: 'filmmaker and film educator, attorney and adjunct professor of law at the University of Frankfurt, author of docufiction, theorist and critic of film, the media, contemporary culture and the public sphere, and since 1962 chief spokesman in the arena of cultural politics and policy making for the economic needs and public significance of an indigenous and revitalized German cinema' (Fiedler 1984: 195).

No doubt in all these roles Kluge had to compromise with his partners and 'enemies' (especially those who put profit before art), which, however, in my opinion had the advantage of adding depth and subtlety to his assessment of reality. From this perspective he can be compared to Marx himself, who was not only a writer (in the widest possible sense of this word) but also a political activist, and in order to survive materially had to rely on the financial help of Engels, who worked in a mill owned by his father. Both Kluge and Marx, while attacking capitalism, had to accept that without using its fruit, they could not survive. It is worth returning here to Kluge's encounter with Fritz Lang. Kluge was admitted as an observer on the set of Lang's Indian epic, *The Tiger of Eschnapur* and *The Indian Tomb*, where he witnessed an ongoing struggle between the director and his producer, foreshadowing the trouble of 'Fritz Lang' to preserve his artistic autonomy in Godard's *Le Mépris* (1963). Although he noticed an immense pressure exerted by the producer on Lang, he also observed that even in such circumstances the director was able to retain much of his vision, and the final film has Lang's personal stamp (Fiedler 1984: 198). At the same time, Lang's struggle with the film industry (international, but mostly West German) demonstrated to Kluge the need to change this industry.

Kluge's effort to understand the complex world and retain artistic and moral integrity while using a medium, which seemingly does not allow for much freedom, is inscribed in the form and narratives of his films, such as *Die Artisten in der Zirkuskuppel: ratlos* (*The Artists in the Circus Dome: Clueless* or *The Artists in the Circus Dome: Perplexed*, 1968) and *Gelegenheitsarbeit einer Sklavin* (*Part-Time Work of a Domestic Slave*, 1973). Liebman argues that *The Artists* perfectly represents Kluge's method of a 'cinematic variety show' by using a very heterogeneous material, such as reports about a fire in a circus, which becomes even more heterogeneous in the process of film production, due to placing it in unexpected contexts (Liebman 1988: 14–17). As Marc Silberman observes in relation to the same film, 'Causality and the relation of the parts to the whole no longer depend on mimetic representation but rather on a highly developed sense of playful contrast and association ... The use of all available cinematic means – image, dialogue, voice-over, music, noise, silence, printed titles, portrait photos, trick shots – suggests a relativity of word and image; both are necessary for the narrative rationale but they are not redundant' (Silberman 1995: 186). Peter Lutze regards Kluge's use of a 'variety show' as an attempt to 'resolve the high culture/low culture split by utilizing the media of mass culture to create "autonomous" art' (Lutze 1998: 18).

Due to its heterogeneity Kluge's cinema has much in common with that of the previously mentioned Jean-Luc Godard and the Yugoslav director Dušan Makavejev. Kluge, like Godard and to a much lesser extent Makavejev, is interested in 'grand moments', such as the Black Friday in the case of *MEC* and great personalities, such as Marx. But like Makavejev and to a lesser extent Godard, he has a 'magpie' personality: he likes to collect what was discarded by grand histories: the quirky, the unusual, the eccentric, the embarrassing and the private. In this way he bears comparison with Walter Benjamin, the creator of 'magic encyclopaedia', whose methods were compared to a 19th-century collector of antiquities and curiosities or ragpicker, rather than a modern historian (Eiland and McLaughlin 1999: ix–x). Although he links these private treasures or pieces of rubbish with grand history, his usual point is to show that these private histories do not match the grand narratives. The authors discussing Kluge's films describe his works as 'essay films'. The director himself, in his typical manner, emphasising the imperfect character of his work, claims that an 'essay film' is a compromise between his desire to shoot a fiction film and a need to account for the richness and heterogeneity of human experience and to do it in an economical way. As he puts it, 'I know of no other possibility to supply so much material so quickly' (Kluge 1990: 13).

Kluge's film, especially *The Artists* and *Part-Time Work of a Domestic Slave*, are also noticeable for representing characters who are idealistic, yet somewhat confused, perplexed and by the same token perplexing the viewers. They want to learn about the reality which surrounds them and change the world along the lines advocated by Adorno, but usually fail or succeed only partially. Leni Peickert wants to create a reformed, revolutionary circus, but fails in her ambition and ends up getting an internship in commercial television. However, we are to believe that what she learnt in the meantime and, especially, her refusal to take the world for granted, but see it in its contradictions, will prepare her to operate in different environments without losing integrity. Roswitha

Bronski in *Part-Time Work of a Domestic Slave* is also forced to move from one occupation to another; she begins her cinematic life as an abortionist and finishes as a political activist saving a chemical plant where her husband works from being relocated to Portugal. During the film we see her studying politics and ending up surrounded by piles of books and newspaper cuttings. Her husband regards her unstructured study as a waste of time and proof that she is good at nothing. And yet, contrary to his assessment, Roswitha's study allows her to gain good insight into the workings of the capitalist society and achieve a political victory – saving a German factory from outsourcing.

Thanks to his unrelenting curiosity and lack of dogmatism, sensitivity to a concrete situation and attention to detail, Kluge, in my opinion, comes across as a more complex and contemporary thinker than Adorno, while sharing with his mentor his wide interests. For this reason, unlike Lutze, who describes Kluge as 'the last modernist' (Lutze 1998), I will describe Kluge as a postmodernist, belonging to the strand which Hans Bertens, after Charles Jencks and Linda Hutcheon, labels 'postmodernism of resistance' (Bertens 1995: 103), on account of being impure, yet radical.

Das Kapital in the works of Marx and Kluge

Even before Kluge embarked on *MEC*, he was compared to Marx. For example, Thomas Elsaesser describes one of Kluge's books, *Geschichte und Eigensinn* (*History and Obstinacy*, 1981) as 'an extended historical meditation on human productivity and human labour power, a kind of third volume to Karl Marx's *Das Kapital* (Elsaesser 2002: 186), and observes that in its size, binding, lettering and colour-scheme, the book mimics the East-German edition of *MEGA*, the Marx-Engels *Gesamtausgabe* (Collected Works) (191). The unofficial names given to Kluge, such as the 'Father of the New German Cinema' or 'Marathon Man', point to his importance in German culture and the vastness of his work, lending itself to comparison with Marx. But it is with Kluge's completion of *MEC* that this comparison gained currency.

There are many parallels between the structure, style and the place *Das Kapital* and *MEC* occupy in the works of their respective authors. They are their *magna opera*, being the longest works they ever produced and summarising and developing many themes they presented in their earlier works, as well as many 'borrowed' from other authors. Both consist of three parts or volumes. The three parts of Kluge's works are: I. 'Marx and Eisenstein in the Same House' (199 minutes); II. 'All

Things are Bewitched People' (200 minutes); III. 'Paradoxes of Exchange Society' (183 minutes). We cannot map the three parts of *MEC* exactly into the three volumes of Marx's *Capital*, but there are parallels between these two grand works. The first part of MEC acts as a kind of introduction to his work by discussing the intentions of his predecessor, Sergei Eisenstein, similarly to the first volume of Marx's *Das Kapital* acting as an introduction to the remaining volumes by explaining the meaning of a commodity (Marx 1965). *MEC's* Part II, 'All Things are Bewitched People', in part deals with the character of a commodity; hence it parallels the first volume of Marx's opus, but also addresses such issues as the circulation of capital and the working of ideology, which is the focus of Volume II of *Das Kapital*: *The Process of Circulation of Capital* (Marx 1967). Finally, 'Paradoxes of Exchange Society' remind me of Volume III of Marx's opus, subtitled *The Process of Capitalist Production as a Whole*, due to Kluge delving into the most philosophical issues, such as the meaning of history (Marx 1966). It can be argued that in these parts both authors attempt to deal with 'the world as a whole', although Marx's 'world' means primarily the world as seen through the lens of economy, while for Kluge it is seen through political and cultural history.

Marx worked on *Das Kapital* for many years and he died before managing to complete it, leaving many issues unresolved, including the question of the character of social class, giving rise to speculation by subsequent generations of philosophers, historians and economists. Kluge's *MEC* was also made by the mature Kluge; he embarked on it when he was over 70 years of age. It is finished in the first sense; the production was released on DVD and subsequently Kluge embarked on new projects. However, it comes across as a purposefully unfinished work, or rather an open work, without a clear beginning and middle, and with an end which is an anti-climax as opposed to a summary or conclusion to this opus.

Das Kapital and *MEC* do not adhere to any established genre and even diverge from what is normally described as literature or economic treatise, in the case of Marx, or cinema, in the case of Kluge. This is consistent with both authors' take on what constitutes literature and cinema. S. S. Prawer claims: 'Literature is not, for Marx, a separate, self-contained region. Poems like those of Heine and the song of Silesian weavers, novels like those of Gustave Beaumont, Étienne Cabet, and George Sand, plays by Gustave Beaumont, Étienne Cabet, and George Sand, plays like Gustav Freytag's *The Journalist* ... are clearly related to other, more utilitarian forms of writing, and may profitably be discussed alongside these (Prawer 1976: 141). Prawer also points to, mostly in relation to *The Communist Manifesto*, but also to *Das Kapital*, the poetic qualities of Marx's work, such as its rhythm and the extensive use of metaphors. What is thus regarded as a political pamphlet or a philosophical work can be seen as an accomplished work of poetry. *Das Kapital*, which is normally regarded as an economic work, contains a distinct vision of the world; hence again it belongs to the realm of philosophy and argues for a new world order; hence it is also a political work. However, it is full of digressions, in the style of early novels such as *Tom Jones* (1749) by Henry Fielding, as demonstrated by the extensive use of footnotes, and has a versatile style, with some parts coming across as a heavy treaty, requiring specialist knowledge, others being easier to read thanks to being illustrated by examples. Furthermore, it is akin to a detective novel, with each chapter providing us with more clues as to the behaviour to the main 'culprit', *'das Kapital'* and to a *Bildungsroman*, describing the pathway of capital from infancy to its maturity and beyond.

As already mentioned, Kluge's films tend to be described as essay films, and he himself endorses this label. However, *MEC* bursts the boundaries of an essay film, due to its length and the use of techniques which are more reminiscent of television and video art than a cine-film. As Julia Vassilieva argues, *MEC* is 'forcefully and deliberately geared towards the conditions of new media. This refers to the range of technologies that rely on digitisation, encompassing, besides digital cinema and television, the genesis of broadband, virtual and immersive technologies, and the development of Artificial Intelligence' (Vassilieva 2011). It can fill a special day devoted in television to the anniversary of Marx or Eisenstein, due to the versatile material devoted to the thinker – such as memories of him – offered by specialists, and fragments of relevant films. The excessive length encourages watching it in parts, rather than all at once, in a way that users of YouTube and other platforms of this kind tend to watch films. Moreover, different parts of the production can stand alone, such as the film on commodities, *Der Mensch in Ding* by Tom Tykwer, which is included in Part II, or discussions with various Marx specialists in the form of a 'talking heads' documentary. Such a structure forces the viewer to take an active part in the construction of the film's meaning. Although there is a certain logic to the way Kluge structured his work, this logic can easily be subverted, which is very difficult to do when dealing with a traditional film.

The main subject of *Das Kapital* is the birth and development of capitalist society, from the production of commodities to the creation of surplus value and capital, colonial expansion, crises and possibly creating an egalitarian, communist society. Being an adaptation of Marx's work, *MEC* inevitably concerns the same subjects as *Das Kapital*, such as the character of commodities and the development of capitalism. However, due to being produced many years after *Das Kapital* and using a different medium, it focuses on different periods (which I will discuss in due course) and approaches it differently than Marx. Two themes feature prominently in *MEC*: the uses of history and the possibility of translation, most importantly translating complex philosophical ideas and theories, such as those presented in Marx's *Das Kapital*, on screen.

The importance of history is transmitted by the title of the film: *News from Ideological Antiquity – Marx/Eisenstein/The Capital*. Each part of the title sends us back to the past, as Marx and Eisenstein are historical figures, but the most historical is the term 'news from ideological antiquity'. The title is explained only in the third part of the work, when Kluge, evoking Hegel and Marx, but also Jürgen Habermas, claims that we can learn a lot about our own time from the past when it has no reference to our own experience. We know that we live in the present not so much by checking our watches and calendars, but by noticing that what once was, no longer exists. Kluge exemplifies this idea by referring to child labour as a practice belonging to the past, illustrating it with images of a boy aged nine or ten, standing on a high bench and working on the production of silk. According to this rule, we still live in the past if the images, descriptions and theories created in the past apply to our current situation. This, to a large extent, is the past described in Marx's *Das Kapital*. Various guests invited by Kluge, especially Oskar Negt, evoking authors such as David Harvey, Alan Badiou and Hardt and Negri, argue that Marx's description of the world is still valid or is even more pertinent to contemporary times than the period when Marx wrote his book because the world under the neoliberal regime resembles more the model created by Marx than the one in which he lived himself. Under neoliberalism many obstacles preventing the capitalist order from prevailing, such as religion, tradition and the law, are removed. It is only now that 'Capital' is free to conquer the world. This idea is excellently captured by Alain Badiou, who wrote: 'Basically, today's world is exactly the one which, in a brilliant anticipation, a kind of true science fiction, Marx heralded as the full unfolding of the irrational and, in truth, monstrous potentialities of capitalism' (Badiou 2012: 12). Kluge also, in a way reminiscent of Freud, talks about the past buried in our consciousness and unconscious; about the experience passed to us by our biological and cultural forefathers. This means that in order to get self-knowledge, to get identity, we need to learn about the past, we have to reach to antiquity.

Such an idea informed many, if not all of Kluge's earlier works, making them look both historical and contemporary. In this respect Kluge counteracts the German problem described in the well-known book by Alexander Mitscherlich and Margarete Mitscherlich as 'inability to mourn' (Mitscherlich and Mitscherlich 1975). On this occasion, however, he is less interested in German history and more in world history, understood as synchrony of different events whose connections need deciphering. This idea is proposed at the beginning of *MEC*, when Kluge refers in the intertitles to events from different parts of the world, mentioning in less than five minutes the Dreyfus affair, abuse of workers in Shanghai and the ordinary life of Soviet workers. Not only does he compare events in different places but of different scale, micro- with macro-history, as exemplified by the theme of making and wearing a silk stocking. For Kluge this motif represents the complexity of seemingly simple objects and events. Production of silk requires heavy exploitation of workers; in different moments of his film Kluge mentions children being employed in the textile industry and silk being produced in the armpits of female workers. Its result, however, is a beautiful and highly seductive object. A silk stocking thus perfectly illustrates the Marxist concept of the fetishism of commodities as a product which hides an ugly reality behind its perfect surface.

The question of history is also a question of representation, understood by Kluge as a problem of applying a specific 'lens', a particular conceptual framework and presenting it in a specific medium. He mentions that the stocking provides an opportunity to engage in discussions about (sexual) morality, art, commerce and personal histories. Equally, the stocking can be presented 'historically', as a stocking from an old newsreel and one used by a contemporary woman, immortalised thanks to digital techniques. Kluge oscillates between the old and new techniques, faded newsreels and the most up-to-date video images, full and split screen, colour and black and white image. There is no apparent hierarchy of these representations; it is as if the author wanted to tell us that all of them are justifiable if they make us feel, think and understand, when 'understanding' is regarded as a process rather than its result (Figure 11.1).

By embarking on the task of making a film about Marx's book, Kluge inevitably brings about the question of adapting to screen 'unadaptable' books due to their length or intellectual complexity, as epitomised by *Remembrance of Things Past* by Marcel Proust or *Ulysses* by James Joyce.

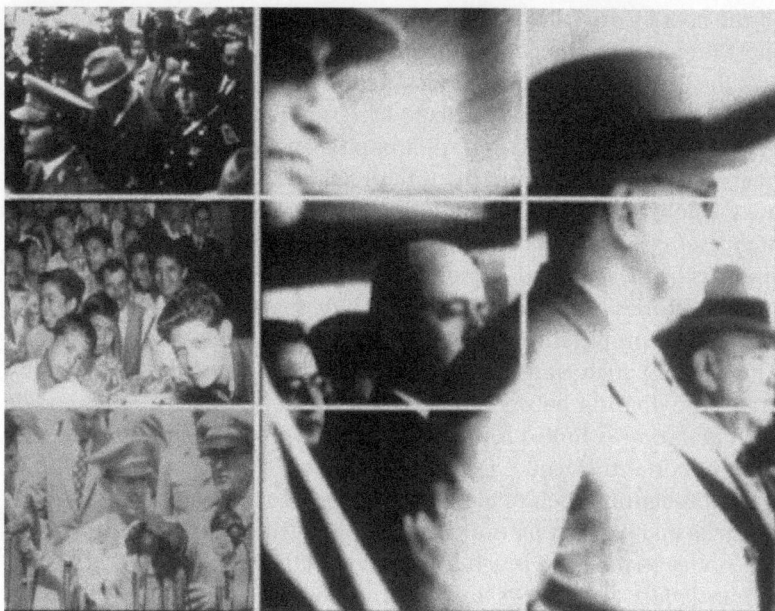

Figure 11.1   Layers of history in *News from Ideological Antiquity*
Source: Screen shot from *News from Ideological Antiquity – Marx/Eisenstein/Capital* (2008), dir.
Alexander Kluge, Suhrkamp Verlag

The director admits that it is impossible to offer their full equivalent in a cinematic form, but adequate translation is nevertheless possible. Overtly and covertly he refers to two or perhaps three uses of translation. One consists of bringing something from the original text to people who cannot understand it. This use can be described as explanatory or educational. Kluge refers to this aspect in his discussions with professional translators, when he asks them to say how a certain phrase sounds in Russian and explain what it means, and how it is different from the German version. By discussing with them what was changed on the way from the original to the translated version, he shows that through commenting about a specific translation, it is possible to overcome the limitation of the new language and inform the reader with a high degree of accuracy about what is contained in the original and how it was understood at the time of its early readings.

The method used by Kluge can be compared to that of Vladimir Nabokov in translating Pushkin's *Onegin*, in which the translator was not concerned with emulating the original form of Pushkin's masterpiece, but only in explaining, as much as possible, the content and context of the poet's work (Nabokov 1955). In his conversations with his guests, most importantly the poet and broadcaster Hans Magnus Ensensberger, and the East German poet and historian of poetry Durs Grünbein, Kluge points to a long lineage of artistic literature which transmitted to the general public the works of philosophy and economy, such as the poetry of Plutarch (in ancient times), Schiller (in the period immediately before Marx) and Bertolt Brecht's poem based on *The Communist Manifesto* (after Marx). The very fact that these adaptations survived the passage of time and on some occasions occupy a distinctive place in the histories of literature or philosophy, suggests that the respective attempts at propagating and enriching 'hard' theories were successful. The value of such translating work is that it bridges the gap or obliterates the division between poetry and theory, art and science. Today such ambition is linked to postmodern and post-structuralist thought, most importantly Jacques Derrida and Michel Foucault. Although Kluge does not mention their names or any other French post-structuralist, for practical and perhaps patriotic reasons privileging German authors, one can notice that he has much in common with them.

Translation also allows us to learn how language and culture in which a specific language is embedded has changed over the years, as presented in a slightly humorous episode showing two actors, playing STASI students, reading *Das Kapital* for their exam. They discuss the meaning of some crucial words in the Marxist discourse, such as 'humanism' and 'materialism'. These discussions illuminate different meanings these words have in the current usage in comparison with the times when Marx used them (for example, materialism is now associated with greed, rather than rejecting any teleological positions). Meaning, as Kluge suggests, is thus unstable not only in the sense that words change their meanings when they travel in time and space, but also the old meanings cannot be accurately retrieved because the new meanings affect the old ones.

The educational value of translation is also revealed in Kluge's discussion with the film historians, who ponder on Eisenstein's rationale for screening Marx's work. In this way we learn about Marx's and Eisenstein's approach to their subject and about problems of screen adaptation at large, resulting, for example, from the different speed involved in reading books and watching films. Kluge proposes the idea that while filmmakers create their own speed, writers cannot do so. In this sense the moving image is better attuned to representing capital than words, as capital moves in time and space with a different speed, which cannot be rendered adequately in literature.

Film can be seen as a superior tool for representing capital and, by the same token, Marx's thought also because, as Peter Sloterdijk mentions, capital is about constant transformation and appearance which is different from reality. Such an idea is excellently put forward in the film by Tom Tykwer which, by means such as freezing image, close-up and voice-over, presents a history of various things used by a man, demonstrating that, as the title suggests, 'things are bewitched people', an idea widely known as 'fetishism of the commodities'. Sloterdijk describes Marx as belonging to a generation of post-philosophic philosophers, who merge the seriousness of Hegel with the assumption pertaining to sophists that things are not what they appear, they cannot be taken at face value; representations are always deceptive or perhaps the world is just a representation.

The second use of translation consists of enriching the original. Kluge uses a metaphor of prism, which changes the object whenever it is refracted. This prism might be seen as reflecting a particular moment when the original is read, in this case after Eisenstein's aborted attempt to screen *Das Kapital* and the world economic crisis following the crash of 1929. In this case, enriching the original means bringing insights which were unavailable to the author of the 'hypotext': for example, Eisenstein's knowledge about the stock market crash and Kluge's knowledge about the Second World War, Stalinism and neoliberalism. Enriching the original makes it alive; it is because Marx can be put in ever-changing contexts that he became one of the most important philosophers of all times.

Kluge also shows that translating leads to multilingualism. First, only authors who know more than one language are able to translate, and the best translators are fluent in several languages. Second, the act of translation requires leaving traces of the original language and sometimes adding a third and further languages to reflect the complexity of the new 'space' in which the translated text functions. Kluge points to this fact when discussing the case of Eisenstein with the film historian Oksana Bulgakova, who claims that in order to express himself well, Eisenstein sometimes wrote a sentence in five different languages. Kluge is not a polyglot in this sense; he does not even know Russian or English, but he is one of the most multilingual filmmakers in the world (next to Godard and Makavejev), able to write one 'cinematic sentence' in the language of a silent film, a classical film and in most advanced digital video, as already noticed. Bulgakova also recalls an anecdote about a meeting between Joyce and Eisenstein when the blind Joyce put on a record with Joyce's book, so that Eisenstein could hear it. Eisenstein, however, remembered that Joyce himself read the book for him. This episode demonstrates that when translation is satisfactory, the change of the medium does not matter; we imagine the translated version rendering the original perfectly.

All these above-mentioned uses are of importance for Kluge: he wants to inform us what Marx's *Das Kapital* was about, enrich it by adding contemporary insights and present it in a new medium or even operating between the media, and read it in a sympathetic yet, on occasions, also polemical way. In this way Kluge follows in the footsteps of Marx, who, as S. S. Prawer and Terrell Carver argue, was himself an accomplished translator and a multilingual writer, both in the sense of using many languages in his works, translating from French to German and back, showing sensitivity to different audiences (as conveyed by writing numerous introductions to his *Manifesto*) and operating between different genres. Carver describes Marx as a 'German, living in England, writing for an international German-speaking audience, and expecting to be translated' (Carver 1998: 150). Carver, who himself embarked on translating Marx, says that he did not want to 're-write Marx as a rap artist' (150), but in this way he suggests that the author of *Das Kapital* can be compared to contemporary rappers.

To demonstrate that Marx was aware of what is gained and what is lost in the process of translation, Prawer refers to Marx's concept of the 'world literature' and the passage from *The Communist Manifesto* where Marx argues that upon its transition/translation to Germany, French socialist and communist writings lost their political power (Prawer 1976: 138–165) because 'French social conditions had not immigrated with them. In contact with German social conditions, this French literature lost all its immediate practical significance, and assumed *a purely literary aspect*' (Marx, quoted in Prawer 1976: 142). This passage also points to the fact that in order to save Marx from the fate of these socialist writers, we have a duty to put him in the ever-changing context, keep translating his works.

Eisenstein versus Kluge

After Marx's *Das Kapital*, the principal context of Kluge's work is Eisenstein's aborted project of filming *Das Kapital*; the first part of *MEC* is devoted specifically to this subject. Overtly, Kluge presents himself as Eisenstein's follower, who wants to retrace Eisenstein's footsteps, find out about his political and aesthetic agenda and continue the work he started. At the same time, however, the character of *MEC* suggests that his approach to Marx's opus magnum and the medium of the moving image is different from his esteemed predecessor.

Eisenstein attempted to film Marx's work by presenting one day in the life of a worker. This day, however, was meant to allow him to reveal all economic, political and social forces which affect the worker's situation, as if being able to show the whole world reflected in a drop of water. Such an approach Eisenstein borrowed from James Joyce, who used it in his *Ulysses*, which chronicles one ordinary day in the life of Leopold Bloom (Michelson 1976). *Ulysses* is regarded as one of the masterpieces of modernist literature. One reason for this status is Joyce's ambition to say everything in one, albeit long, book. Equally, Eisenstein, from the early part of his career, attempted to provide a comprehensive take on a specific subject or idea. Eisenstein's films are always coherent, even if complex. Yet, we also observe a certain trajectory in Eisenstein's works, marked on embarking on increasingly complex and abstract topics. While his *Stachka* (*Strike*, 1925) is thus a simple film about a strike in a factory as a response to capitalist injustice, *Bronenosets Potyomkin* (*Battleship Potemkin*, 1925) refers to the same topic, but also shows how strike spreads, leading to politicisation of the masses. *Oktyabr* (*October*, 1928) covers all these subjects but also delves into the complexity of revolutionary politics. Although ultimately Eisenstein succeeded, or at least this is the opinion prevailing today, he was on the verge of failure. Oksana Bulgakova mentions his grave difficulties in editing the immense amount of material, which left him physically and mentally exhausted, even blind as a consequence of taking performance-enhancing drugs. This story suggests that there is a limit to Eisenstein's method of translating complex text, be it a literary work, a theory or a historical event, in a coherent, well-organised text. At a certain point, the consequence is either chaos or a work which greatly simplifies the original.

Oskar Negt, who collaborated with Kluge on earlier occasions, argues that Eisenstein was destined to failure, because it is impossible to show what he wanted to show; both capital and *Das Kapital* are too complex to be adapted for screen. However, to this argument Kluge replies that although Eisenstein's ambition might be impossible to fulfil by one director, it can be done by a succession of filmmakers, with each picking up where the other finished. In line with this idea, Godard could follow Eisenstein and, presumably, Kluge Godard and so on. Kluge also shows fragments of Werner Schroeter's theatrical production loosely based on Eisenstein's *Battleship Potemkin*, as a means to open up Eisenstein's work on capitalism and *Das Kapital* to a different medium and different audience.

Yet, the idea that many directors might screen *Das Kapital*, hence in principle it can be a never ending and polyvalent project, with each new director adding to, as well as contradicting what his/her predecessor has done, does not fit comfortably with Eisenstein's concept of intellectual cinema, which Eisenstein's screening of *Das Kapital* was meant to crown. Kluge's use of Eisenstein in *Das Kapital* can thus be compared to what he offered in *The Artists in the Circus Dome: Clueless*. Discussing *The Artists*, Liebman claims that Eisenstein attempted to create a specific reaction in his audience. He quotes from 'The Montage of Film Attractions': 'The method of agitation through spectacle consists in the creation of a new chain of conditioned reflexes by associating selected phenomena with the unconditioned reflexes they produce [...] It is then possible to envisage in both theory and practice a construction, with no linking plot logic, which provokes a chain of the necessary unconditioned reflexes that are, at the editor's will, associated with (compared with) predetermined phenomena and by this means to create the chain of new conditioned reflexes that these phenomena constitute. This signifies a realization of the orientation towards thematic effect, i.e. a fulfillment of the agitational purpose'. Elsewhere, Eisenstein compared the hold such sequences have over the audience to a lecturer's 'steely embrace', in which 'the breathing of the entire electrified audience suddenly becomes rhythmic'. Finally, Eisenstein celebrated cinema's ability 'to penetrate the mind of the great masses with new ideas and new perceptions. Such a cinema alone will dominate, by its form, the summit of modern industrial technique' (Eisenstein, quoted in Liebman 1988: 18–19). Eisenstein's unwillingness to grant his viewers much freedom of interpretation is also discussed in *MEC*.

Kluge, by contrast to Eisenstein, in *MEC* wants to free the viewer from the 'steely embrace' of cinema and allow him to make his own film in the head. He claims that such film will encourage people to think, and not only educated people, but also ordinary ones. This might be as true about Eisenstein as about Kluge, but for Eisenstein every viewer should think the same film based on the fragment s/he was allowed to watch; for Kluge each viewer should create his/her own film. For this reason he offers in *MEC* disparate fragments, which need a significant mental work to be put together, unlike Eisenstein, whose principles of montage are much more limited.

Eisenstein's approach to Marx does not suit Kluge also because they have different views on how cinema should behave when faced with *Das Kapital*, as well as what *Das Kapital* is about. According to Eisenstein, the film should adjust to Marx's opus magnum by becoming as abstract as

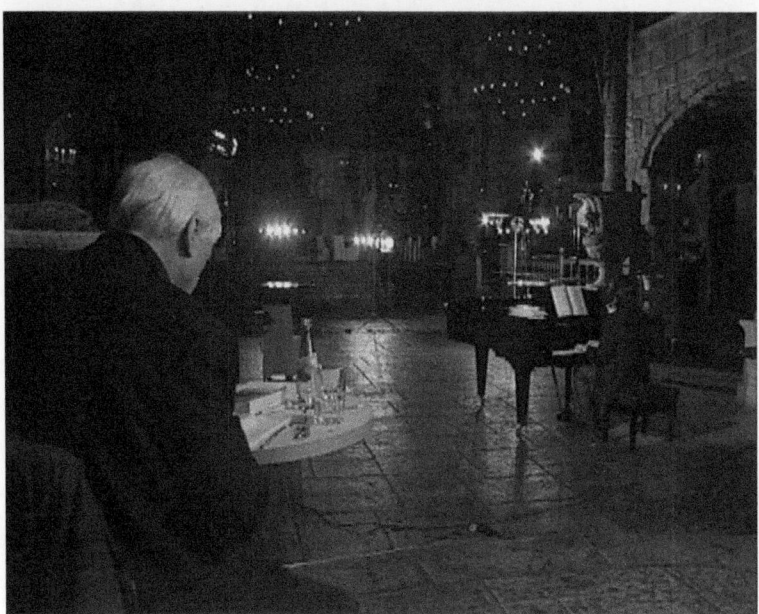

Figure 11.2   Alexander Kluge in his film
Source: Screen shot from *News from Ideological Antiquity – Marx/Eisenstein/Capital (2008)*, dir.
Alexander Kluge, Suhrkamp Verlag

possible. He believed that shooting this film in a sense would put cinema
into a crisis, even destroy it, allowing for creating a new, purely abstract
or intellectual one. Kluge, in contrast, wants *Das Kapital* to adjust to the
already existing medium of moving image, which is very rich. In particular, discarding the power of cinema to awaken emotions equals for
him amputating one of its most important and best-developed organs.
Furthermore, Kluge differs from Eisenstein by regarding *Das Kapital* not
only as a story about ideas, or at least not exclusively so, but as a story
of real people and 'enchanted' things. He singles out 'The Working Day'
from the first volume of *Das Kapital* as the most concrete, accessible and
dramatic part of *Das Kapital*. Consequently, in order to screen Marx's work
in a satisfactory way, one has to transmit its concreteness and show real
people with their emotions and unique histories. In the discussion with
his interlocutors and through the choice of visual material, which is full of
references to whimsical and idiosyncratic events as well as to some whose
very occurrence is problematic, and editing them in a way which adds to
their irrationality, Kluge conjures up for us a 'Benjaminian Marx', namely
a Marx who does not discard any 'crumbs of history', but interweaves

them into a rich texture. Moreover, in place of the utterly rational Marx, he proposes, especially in his dialogue with Peter Sloterdijk, an 'enchanted Marx', similar to Ovid, who sees the flow of commodities and capital as a magical passage which cannot be fully grasped and explained.

Non-idealistic Marx

As already mentioned, in his famous Thesis 11 on Feuerbach, Marx says: 'Philosophers have hitherto only interpreted the world in various ways; the point is to change it'. This sentence can be regarded as a demand to create philosophy relevant to the current experience – philosophy which does not deal merely with theoretical issues but also with practical questions and which inspires people to act in a certain way. Marx thus demanded that his philosophy will be constantly updated. Kluge responds to this demand in two ways. The first is to imagine what Marx would have done if he had lived later and by the same token witnessed later historical events. The second consists of accounting for certain gaps in Marx's theory or even correcting Marx.

There are three periods which keep reappearing in Kluge's film. One is the year 1929, when a great economic crisis started in the world, eventually leading to the Second World War. It is also the year when Eisenstein was meant to make his film. This moment illustrates Marx's point from *Das Kapital* that capitalism leads to crises. The second period is the Second World War, again supporting Marx's idea that the war is a natural consequence of the development of capitalism. Finally, Kluge and his interlocutors, especially Durs Grünbein, echoing such Marxist thinkers as David Harvey, argue that the neoliberal reality in which we live has more in common with the world governed by capitalist rules, as described by Marx, than the one in which Marx lived.

The question arises as to why capitalism always wins, despite such despicable consequences for humanity and whether it is possible to resist it, on the level of both communal and personal life. Such questions can be placed against an idealistic or non-idealistic (materialistic) reading of Marx. As Simon Choat argues, 'Idealism searches for order, giving everything an Origin and an End: everything has a place, a *telos* inscribed at birth' (Choat 2010: 24). In the materialistic interpretation, the course of things can be changed by human intervention. Kluge leans towards the second view, as revealed in his interviews with his guests and the previously mentioned freewheeling form of his film, which suggests that things can always go different ways, unlike Eisenstein, who appears to favour the idealistic Marx.

One such moment when Kluge presents himself as a non-idealistic Marxist takes place when he discusses with Hans Magnus Enzensberger

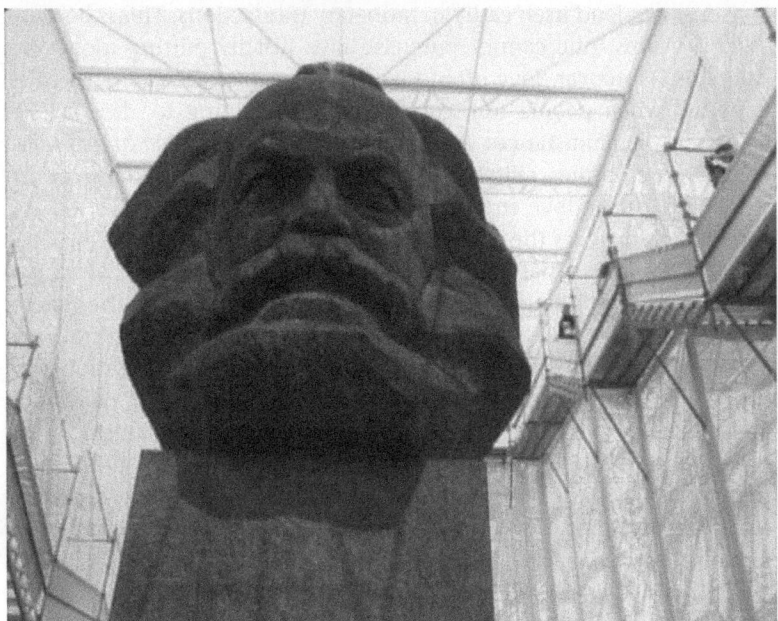

Figure 11.3 Marx reshaped
Source: Screen shot from *News from Ideological Antiquity – Marx/Eisenstein/Capital* (2008), dir. Alexander Kluge, Suhrkamp Verlag

the role of great personalities on the course of history, in the context of a view, widely attributed to Marx, that such personalities are of little importance: it is masses and deeper historical rules which affect history. Enzensberger, by contrast, believes that the role of great personalities should not be underestimated: without Napoleon the history of France and the entire world would be different from what it is now. But if individual people matter, then we cannot and should not allow history to take its course, but try to shape it. This is not only a more rational but also a more moral approach. Leaving history to 'do the work for us', as Kluge and Enzensberger agree, is a 'lesson in depression'.

Another example of where Kluge departs from reading of Marx as an idealistic/deterministic thinker is in his discussion about love with an actress Sophie Rois. To begin with, they both concede that money can assist in purchasing somebody's love and, conversely, its lack can be a factor in rejecting love, as described in *Father Goriot* by Balzac (who was one of Marx's favourite writers). Money, then, can act as a pimp, making people behave in the erotic sphere in a way which otherwise they would not behave. Ultimately, however, money is not a perfect pimp or love does not lend itself easily to monetary transactions. This is because, as Rois claims, one cannot purchase love just by putting money on the table. Moreover, love often takes place against the capitalist rules; it occurs when people transcend barriers pertaining to class, age or other social circumstances, as shown in Shakespeare's *Romeo and Juliet*. Furthermore, while capitalist exchange enriches the capitalist at the worker's expense, love enriches both sides. Love is thus presented as a force which opposes the allegedly 'natural' rules of economy. Yet, Kluge and Rois also agree that love is not a solution to the problems of capitalism; it cannot replace socialism understood as overthrowing the system. However, socialism without love degenerates into totalitarianism. Such a view can be compared to the ideas of Wilhelm Reich, mentioned in Kluge's film, who advocated combining socialist with sexual revolution as a means to overcome capitalism and prevent totalitarianism, in his times ruling both in Germany and Soviet Russia (Reich 1972), and, more recently, Alain Badiou, who in his book *In Praise of Love*, objects to reducing love to finding the best partner from an economic/class point of view (Badiou 2012b).

Kluge, unlike Marx, who argues for the society developing in an antagonistic way, leading to the situation when only two classes remain: the rich capitalists and the proletariat, by his choice of examples suggests that reality remains more complex than Marx envisaged. He points, for example, to the role of foremen as a link between proletariat and capitalists and machines as being below the workers, but in a future world being able to develop intelligence and rebel against the capitalist *status quo*, alongside the workers or perhaps against them.

However, rather than discarding the idealistic Marx *tout court*, Kluge suggests that neither of the Marxes should be rejected. Such an idea is proposed when discussing the meaning of 'spectre' in *The Communist Manifesto* with Durs Grünbein. For Grünbein it means that Marx himself felt uneasy about the idea of communism. For him it was something intangible, a chimera, an entity impossible to define, even less to predict when it becomes a proper reality. At this point Grünbein compares Marx to Hegel, the idealistic philosopher *par excellence*, from whom Marx distanced himself in order to become a historical materialist. He says that Hegel introduced metaphors to philosophical and political discourse, putting them in place when things became uncertain, difficult to express or not clear to the author himself. On this occasion it points to Marx's uncertainty about communism and by the same token about his entire political vision. Communism, according to this interpretation, might or might not happen. History is not a closed book, but a dynamic process with many possible outcomes. This also means that Marx, even in his most persuasive work, comes across as uncertain of himself; he does not know where his theory will take him. Perhaps in the same vein, Kluge was not certain what would turn out from his notes on Marx and Eisenstein.

Dietmar Dath argues that more than one Marx can be identified in Marx's writings, most importantly the fatalistic Marx and the rebellious Marx – Marx who analyses the *status quo* and Marx who is outraged by it and projects the future. We need both of those Marxes to be able to understand our reality and to change it. Our duty (those 'believing in Marx') is to put Marx into motion, keep presenting his work in new forms and adapting it to new generations of readers, including those whose visual literacy greatly exceeds their reading skills. A duty of Marxists towards Marx is also to test his views against new events, treating *Das Kapital* as 'news from ideological antiquity': belonging to the past, yet influencing the present in a profound way.

Notes

1. Exceptions are texts by Fredric Jameson (2009), Julia Vassilieva (2011) and Christian Schulte (2012), all rather short and sketchy, as suggested even by their titles, including words such as 'remarks'.

Bibliography

Adorno, Theodor W. (1991). *The Culture Industry: Selected Essays on Mass Culture* (London: Routledge).
Badiou, Alain (2012b). *In Praise of Love*, trans. Peter Bush (London: Serpent's Tail).
Badiou, Alain (2012). *The Rebirth of History: Times of Riots and Uprisings* (London: Verso).
Bertens, Hans (1995). *The Idea of the Postmodern: A History* (London: Routledge).
Carver, Terrell (1998). *The Postmodern Marx* (Pennsylvania: The Pennsylvania State University Press).
Choat, Simon (2010). *Marx through Post-Structuralism: Lyotard, Derrida, Foucault, Deleuze* (London: Continuum).
Eiland, Howard and Kevin McLaughlin (1999). 'Translators' Foreword' to Walter Benjamin, *The Arcades Project* (Cambridge, Massachusetts: Harvard University Press), pp. ix–xiv.
Elsaesser, Thomas (2002). 'New German Cinema and History: The Case of Alexander Kluge', in Tim Bergfelder, Erica Carter and Deniz Göktürk (eds), *The German Cinema Book* (London: British Film Institute), pp. 182–91.
Fiedler, Theodore (1984). 'Mediating History and Consciousness', in Klaus Phillips (ed.), *New German Filmmakers: From Oberhausen Through the 1970s* (New York: Frederick Ungar Publishing), pp. 195–229.

Hansen, Miriam (1986). 'Space of History, Language of Time: Kluge's *Yesterday Girl* (1966)', in Eric Rentschler (ed.), *German Film and Literature: Adaptations and Transformations* (New York: Methuen), pp. 193–216. 31.

Hansen, Miriam Bratu (2004). 'Room-for-Play: Benjamin's Gamble with Cinema', *October*, 109, Summer, pp. 3–45.

Jameson, Fredric (2009). 'Marx and Montage', *New Left Review*, July–August, http://newleftreview.org/II/58/fredric-jameson-marx-and-montage, accessed 15/02/2013.

Kluge, Alexander (1990). 'The Assault of the Present on the Rest of Time', trans. Tamara Evans and Stuart Liebman, *New German Critique*, 49, (Special Issue on Alexander Kluge), pp. 11–22.

Liebman, Stuart (1988). 'Why Kluge?', *October*, 46, pp. 4–22.

Lutze, Peter C. (1998). *The Last Modernist: The Film and Television Work of Alexander Kluge* (Detroit: Wayne State University Press).

Marx, Karl (1965) [1887]. *Capital: A Critical Analysis of Capitalist Production*, vol. 1 (Moscow: Progress Publishers).

Marx, Karl (1967) [1885]. *Capital: A Critique of Political Economy*, vol. 2: *The Process of Circulation of Capital* (Moscow: Progress Publishers).

Marx, Karl (1966) [1894]. *Capital: A Critique of Political Economy*, vol. 3: *The Process of Capitalist Production as a Whole* (Moscow: Progress Publishers).

Marx, Karl and Frederick Engels (1947). *The German Ideology, Parts I and III* (New York: International Publishers).

Michelson, Annette (1976 and 1977). 'Reading Eisenstein Reading *Capital*', *October*, 2 (Summer 1976), pp. 27–38 and 3 (Spring 1977), pp. 82–89.

Mitscherlich, Alexander and Mitscherlich, Margarete (1975). *The Inability to Mourn: Principles of Collective Behavior*, trans. Beverly Placzek (New York: Grove Press).

Nabokov, Vladimir (1955). 'Problems of Translation: "Onegin" in English', *Partisan Review*, 22, pp. 486–512.

Prawer, S. S. (1976). *Karl Marx and World Literature* (Oxford: Clarendon Press).

Rancière, Jacques (1991). *The Ignorant Schoolmaster: Five Lessons in Intellectual Emancipation*, trans. Kristin Ross (Stanford: Stanford University Press).

Rancière, Jacques (2009) [2008]. *The Emancipated Spectator*, trans. Gregory Elliott (London: Verso).

Reich, Wilhelm (1972) [1951]. *The Sexual Revolution: Toward a Self-Governing Character Structure*, trans. Theodore P. Wolfe (London: Vision). pp. 409–415.

Schulte, Christian (2012). '"All Things Are Enchanted Human Beings": Remarks on Alexander Kluge's News From Ideological Antiquity', in Tara Forest (ed.), *Alexander Kluge: Raw Materials for the Imagination* (Amsterdam: Amsterdam University Press).

Silberman, Marc (1995). *German Cinema: Texts in Context* (Detroit: Wayne State University Press).

Stam, Robert (2000). 'Beyond Fidelity: The Dialogics of Adaptation', in James Naremore (ed.), *Film Adaptation* (London: The Athlone Press), pp. 54–76.

Vassilieva, Julia (2011). 'Capital and Co.: Kluge/Eisenstein/Marx', *Screening the Past*, http://www.screeningthepast.com/2011/08/capital-and-co-klugeeisen-steinmarx/, accessed 12/05/2013.

12
Marx for Children: *Moor and the Ravens of London* and *Hans Röckle and the Devil*

Martin Brady

Children's film between vagueness and vulgar materialism

Between 1946 and 1990 DEFA (Deutsche Film-Aktiengesellschaft), the state film studio of the German Democratic Republic (GDR), produced a diverse corpus of around 180 feature-length films for children (*Kinderfilme*). Despite the success of these films with audiences and, for the most part at least, with critics and functionaries, the East German filmmaker Heiner Carow – later director of *Die Legende von Paul und Paula* (*The Legend of Paul and Paula*, 1973), the GDR's most successful film, and *Coming Out* (1989), its first explicitly gay movie – identified as early as 1958 an ideological crisis in the industry. He summarised the problems facing children's films as a deficit of realism, a tendency towards 'vagueness and vulgar materialism', either they were too fantastical (the fairy-tale narratives) or too negative in their portrayal of contemporary society (the gritty, neorealist 'every-day' stories): 'We can thus only conclude that the directors of films for children and young people [...] are lagging behind the developments in society' (König *et al.* 1996: 23).[1] Whilst self-criticism of this kind was an obligatory ritual amongst GDR artists at this time, Dziuba does neatly identify a schism in films for young people in the wake of the success in the previous year of the most iconic of all GDR children's films, the whimsical, faintly psyche-delic fairy-tale *Das singende klingende Bäumchen* (*The Singing Ringing Tree*, Francesco Stefani, 1957),[2] and official disapproval of the candid portrayal of teenage disillusionment with GDR society in Gerhard Klein's *Berlin – Ecke Schönhauser* (*Berlin – Down Schönhauser Way*, 1957).

The two films that I wish to examine in this essay, one from each of the decades following Carow's diagnosis, attempt to bridge the afore-mentioned schism by bringing Marx to the screen, the first in the form

267

of a biopic of his life in Victorian London, the second by adapting the Faustian fairy-tales that he dreamt up for his own family's entertainment. Surprisingly, they are the only two films of any genre to have brought Marx to the film screen in the GDR. More surprisingly still, the first of these, *Mohr und die Raben von London* (*Moor and the Ravens of London*, Helmut Dziuba, 1969), has remained, through to the present day, one of only a handful of Marx biopics worldwide.[3] Perhaps the commonly held view that Marx's life, especially in London, lacked drama – was 'uneventful' (Samuelson and Nordhaus 2012: 694) or even 'boring' (Kalder 2013) – may go some way to explaining the notable absence of the man himself from cinema screens.

The only other GDR film with Marx in its title is, perhaps not surprisingly, also a film about England: *These Britons, These Germans* (*Diese Briten, diese Deutschen*, 1989), a documentary co-production between the GDR directors Barbara and Winfried Junge and Amber Films in Newcastle: when shown on Channel 4 in May 1989, its two parts were given punning English titles, *From Marx and Engels to Marks and Spencer* (for the trip to Britain) and *From Marks and Spencer to Marx and Engels* (for the return trip). The former presents a remarkably old-fashioned view of English working-class life on Tyneside shortly before the unexpected demise of the GDR, complete with Elgar's 'Pomp and Circumstance', rampant Thatcherism and dole queues, crumbling social housing, Brown Ale and buttock cleavage.

In revelling, mordantly and perhaps a little lazily, in clichés of Englishness in general, and class culture in particular, the Junge/Amber documentary of 1989 has more than a little in common with the first GDR 'Marx film' I wish to examine in this essay, the aforementioned *Moor and the Ravens of London*, made in 1968 to coincide with the 150th anniversary of the philosopher's birth, but not actually released until March of the following year. It was the first major film by the filmmaker who was to become the most celebrated East German director of children's films, Helmut Dziuba (1933–2012), and whose *Sabine Kleist, 7 Jahre...* (*Sabine Kleist Aged 7...*) of 1982 is one of the most frank portraits of everyday life the GDR produced, and one of its finest films. Three of his features, the two already mentioned and *Als Unku Edes Freundin war...* (*When Unku was Ede's Friend...*, 1981) – a story set during the period of mass unemployment in late Weimar Germany which addresses many of the issues tackled by Bertolt Brecht and Slatan Dudow in *Kuhle Wampe oder Wem gehört die Welt?* (*Kuhle Wampe or Who Owns the World?*, 1932) – have remained in circulation through DVD releases, although only *Sabine Kleist Aged 7...* has been seen more widely abroad, thanks to the availability of an English subtitled version for cinema screenings.[4]

Clichés of Englishness

Moor and the Ravens of London is a feature-length historical costume drama, spectacularly shot in black and white by Helmut Bergmann and based on the successful children's book of the same name (Korn and Korn 1963). It was aimed at an audience of eight years and above. Set in 1856, it tells the story of Marx's efforts to improve the working conditions of children labouring in a Dickensian cotton mill:

> Set in proletarian London in the middle of the last century, the film not only narrates a chapter of the history of the workers' movement, but also explains the role of the philosopher and his beliefs. (König *et al.* 1996: 170)

From its opening shot of a horse-drawn omnibus racing down improbably rural country lanes from North London to Charing Cross, Dziuba's film abounds with clichés about England and its class system: in the wealthier districts of London the men sport military regalia and every woman seems to twirl a fluffy parasol; the slums are populated by deranged, drunken men (figure 12.1, Marx compassionately draws the

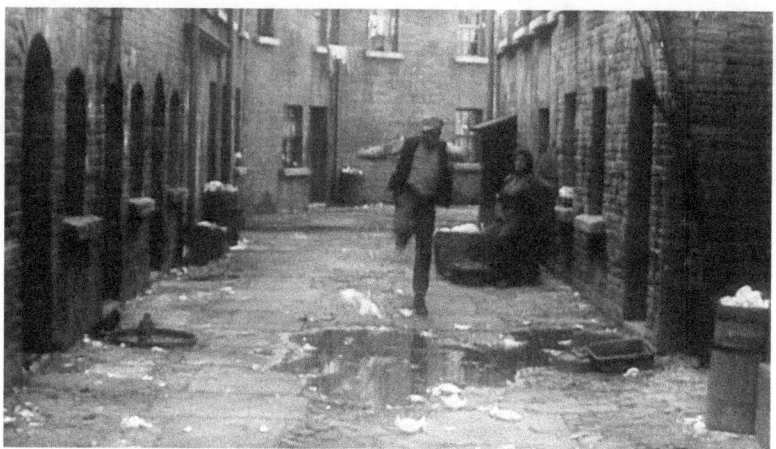

Figure 12.1 Drunken man in the London slums
Source: Screen capture from *Moor and the Ravens of London* (1969), dir. Helmut Dziuba, ICESTORM Entertainment GmbH

local children's attention to the social causes of their alcoholism); a mad hag strikingly similar to the one who haunts London's docklands in Walt Disney's *Mary Poppins* (Robert Stevenson, 1964), made only four years earlier; a strange faceless ghost vaguely reminiscent of an extra in a Jack-the-Ripper B-Movie. The shops betray Britain's Imperialism and exploitation of the colonies – an antique shop has a chubby Buddha in its window, another sells colonial haberdashery. The only representative of law and order comes in the form of a lonely bobby on the beat beside a Thames seemingly lifted from G. W. Pabst's *Die Dreigroschenoper* (*The Threepenny Opera*, 1931) and charity comes, as in Pabst's *Die Büchse der Pandora* (*Pandora's Box*, 1929) and many an Expressionist drama, in the form of the Salvation Army. And, of course, the English weather is a problem. As Marx puts it, when his entire family has gone down with flu:

> I'm tired Joe. It's the wretched climate here in England, that's why we've all got coughs. In Germany the air is dry. The spring there is warm.

Accuracy is not always the film's strong point, either: it unpromisingly opens with Big Ben chiming in 1856, three years before the bell was actually installed, and there is rolling, open country as far as the eye can see between Islington and Charing Cross, which looks suspiciously like the March of Brandenburg on the outskirts of Berlin rather than Camden or Hackney.

Yet, despite its anachronisms, clichés and the *longueurs* and verbosity lamented even by contemporary critics,[5] at least two things make this film worthy of our attention here. First, the aforementioned accolade of being one of cinema's very rare Karl Marx biopics. Second, it is visually spectacular: the neo-Expressionist depiction of the shadowy world of the 'dark Satanic mills' and Dickensian London, largely thanks to the outstanding cinematography of Dziuba's regular cameraman, Bergmann, and some bravura set-designs, gives the film an unexpected grandeur, solemnity and beauty which initially seem rather at odds with the story's depiction of the uglier sides of wage slavery. I shall suggest a possible explanation for this in what follows.

Genre and intertext

Whilst the rather magnificent factory in which the children slave for 12 hours a day recalls the dystopian underground world of Fritz Lang's *Metropolis* (1926), there is a stark, *chiaroscuro* realism to the domestic interiors in the film which owes a palpable debt to 'proletarian cinema' of the Weimar Republic and its post-war legacy in the GDR films of Dudow and others. One is frequently reminded not only of Dudow's *Kuhle Wampe or Who Owns the World?* and Piel Jutzi's *Mutter Krausen's Fahrt ins Glück* (*Mother Krause's Journey to Happiness*, 1929), but also of classic Weimar chamber and street films such as Murnau's *Der letzte Mann* (*The Last Laugh*, 1925) and Joe May's *Asphalt* (1929).

Cinematographer Helmut Bergmann, it should be noted, worked with Dudow in the late 1950s, shooting not only the Bulgarian's most famous GDR film, *Die Verwirrung der Liebe* (*The Confusion of Love*, 1959), a 'big-budget, colour(ful) Shakespearean romp',[6] but also his much darker, unfinished final film *Christine* of 1964, shot, like the Marx film, in stark black and white (and starring a very young Armin Müller-Stahl). It is Bergmann's arresting, at times almost materialist cinematography, with echoes of Dreyer and even Bresson, with its ability to embrace the grand and the quotidian (the factory bosses on an incongruously modernist spiral staircase addressing the child labourers on the factory floor (Figure 12.2), Marx peeling onions at home), which distinguishes this film from other, more famous GDR biopics, including Kurt Maetzig's gargantuan two-part homage to Ernst Thälmann: *Ernst Thälmann – Sohn seiner Klasse; Ernst Thälmann – Führer seiner Klasse* (*Ernst Thälmann – Son of his Class; Ernst Thälmann – Leader of his Class*, 1955).

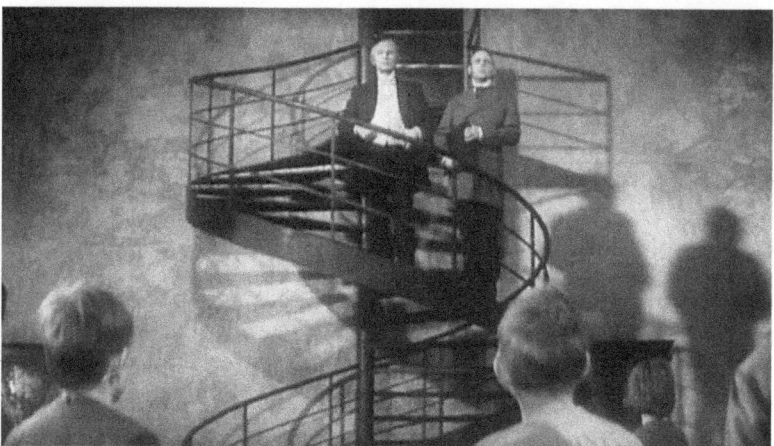

Figure 12.2 The spiral staircase and the child labourers
Source: Screen capture from *Moor and the Ravens of London* (1969), dir. Helmut Dziuba, ICESTORM Entertainment GmbH

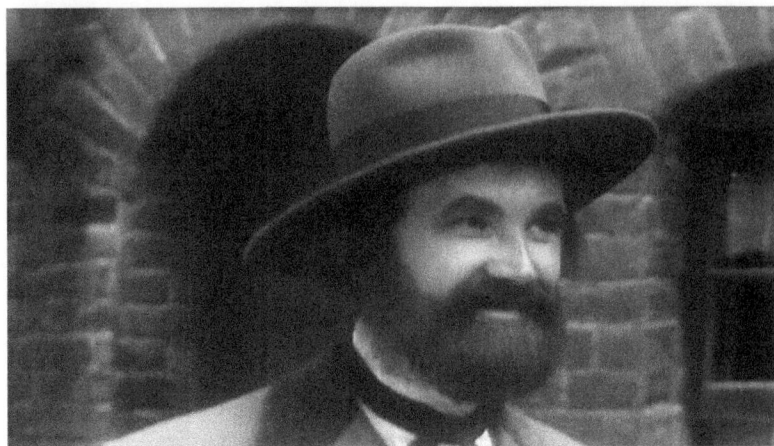

Figure 12.3   Alfred Müller as Karl Marx
Source: Screen capture from *Moor and the Ravens of London* (1969), dir. Helmut Dziuba, ICESTORM Entertainment GmbH

In terms of genre, however, Maetzig's epic hagiography is undoubtedly an important precedent for Dziuba's film, as it doubtless also was for the 1974 children's film about Thälmann's early years, *Aus meiner Kindheit* (*From My Childhood*, Bernhard Stephan). Interestingly, however, Bergmann not only provides a direct link to Germany's first Marxist feature film, *Kuhle Wampe or Who Owns the World*, but also to another, more mainstream genre within the GDR children's film itself. In 1962 he had shot Götz Friedrich's adaptation of the Grimms' tale *Rotkäppchen* (*Little Red Riding Hood*, 1962), as retold by Soviet author Yevgeny Schwartz (Evgeny Shvarts), a contribution to the very genre which Heiner Carow had deemed 'damaging to children' on account of its 'unrealistic view of the world', the *Märchenfilm* (fairy-tale film).

Contemporary films and neorealism

Fairy-tale films and so called 'contemporary films', *Gegenwartsfilme*, constitute the main body of GDR children's cinema, along with a handful of anti-fascist (*Antifa*) historical films. The 'contemporary film', depicting positive aspects of contemporary GDR society, represented the principal programme for GDR feature filmmaking from the early 1950s. At a state-organised Film Conference in 1952, Hermann Axen, later a member of the Politbüro, delivered a speech to an audience of 250 'On the Question of Progressive German Film Art':

Show in your films the new democratic face and democratic character of our new state apparatus and its closeness to the people!
Reflect the progressive nature and powerful impact of our new
democratic laws in your films! Ridicule bureaucracy and laziness with
good humour and a satirical edge in your films. Create films which
enhance the political awareness of the workers and their willingness
to defend our country! Rejoice in the great revolutionary fact that we
have created strategic defence forces, that we have a police force and
security organisations led by fighters who have proved their worth
and who serve only the greater good of the people. Above all, show
the new consciousness, the new ideological and moral complexion
of our people. [...] Capture the rising sun of socialist labour, of socialist consciousness with your spotlights and camera lenses! (Schenk
1994: 73–74)

Whilst official demands had the desired effect of directing filmmakers'
attention towards the progress made in attaining the 'all-round developed socialist personality', rather than focusing on the fascist past, there
were, by the mid-to-late 1950s, undesirable side-effects of the call for
'progressive film art'. Not least amongst these was the emergence of what
was diagnosed as an unhealthy fascination with Italian neorealism. In
1958 Alexander Abusch, the newly elected Minister of Culture, delivered
a coruscating speech at the Second GDR Film Conference on the malevo-
lent influence of bourgeois realism on the GDR feature film entitled
'Contemporary Problems and Goals for our Socialist Film Art':

A film artist in the German Democratic Republic must understand
that the creative method of Italian neorealism [...] cannot be
adopted for the creation of film works set in a workers' and peasants'
state in which the working class under the leadership of its party is
constructing socialism [and in which] the simple man on the street
is not in opposition to the state because this emerging socialist state
is his own. To capture the dialectical nature of this development
in an artistic manner, the creative tools of socialist realism must
be employed. The method of critical realism can only result in a
superficial pseudo-truth in the context of our new reality. (Schenk
1994: 134)

Tellingly, the attack was directed, in part at least, at the enormously
successful films of director Gerhard Klein and his scriptwriter Wolfgang
Kohlhaase, including the aforementioned *Berlin – Down Schönhauser*

Way of the previous year, which were aimed at a young, largely teenage audience. The recipe offered the delegates by Abusch consisted of:

> the uplifting, exciting, politically motivated depiction of positive heroes of the working class, [...] the fate of the socialist warrior, the sufferings and triumphs, defeats and victories in his historically inevitable, triumphant victory over the doomed forces of the old capitalist society [...] all this is and remains our main task. (Schenk 1994: 134)

Moor and the Ravens of London is a (very) belated response to this call for action, motivated by the desire to mark the 150th anniversary of Marx's birth. Its aesthetic, as we have seen, is more Weimar Republic or even August Sander than Italian New Wave, and its source material equally weighty and affirmative: a hefty hardcover tome that had already found its place in the curriculum of GDR schools and received official approval, the 448-page fictionalised biography of Marx, *Mohr und die Raben von London* of Ilse and Vilmos Korn, which in 1963 had been awarded the Theodor-Fontane prize and in the following year received a special prize from the Ministry of Culture for its contribution to the propagation of socialist children's literature in the GDR. As Stefan Wolle puts it in his book on everyday life in the GDR from 1961 to 1971, the first decade after the erection of the Wall: 'the book was much liked by the SED [Socialist Unity Party] authorities on account of its child-friendly popularization of Karl Marx, who here mutates into a nice family man and friend to all children' (Wolle 2011: 282). According to its colophon, the Korns' novel (Korn and Korn 1963) is aimed at children 'of 13 and above'.[7]

Adaptation and intermediality: Kurt Zimmermann

Although the film has only taken the bare bones of the novel's narrative, it is remarkably faithful to it on at least two levels: first, much of the dialogue is lifted verbatim from the text and, second, there seems to have been a considerable effort on the part of the casting director, costume and make-up departments, and possibly the director himself, to follow very precisely the illustrations in the book, a series of fine ink drawings by the established GDR graphic artist Kurt Zimmermann. In certain scenes, notably the opening episode in which the children are refused a seat on the horse-drawn omnibus, it is as if these ink drawings have been used as a storyboard. The novel contains 34 one- and two-page illustrations (along with a colour drawing on the dust jacket and bust of Marx in brown on the linen cover), predominantly of figures, but also of London scenes (including Dean Street and the docks). Although occasionally verging on the melodramatic, notably in the scenes of children in distress, these illustrations are for the most part naturalistic and surprisingly free in execution, more so indeed than the majority of Zimmermann's drawings illustrated (and celebrated) in a collection of his work published in 1958 by the GDR Ministry for National Defence, *Kurt Zimmermann: Sozialistische Grafik: 'Kämpfende Kunst'* (*Kurt Zimmermann: Socialist Drawings: 'Combative Art'*) which indefatigably, and at times quite repetitively, illustrate the claim made in the introduction that he 'takes part with all his strength in the construction of a society organised on socialist lines' (Brockdorff 1958: 5). The introduction informs us that he understood at an early point in his career that modernism and 'other isms' were a thing of the past and that 'the main problem facing realist art is the representation of reality' (8). Zimmermann, we are told, turned his back on Picasso and formalism in favour of proletarian artistic traditions, most notably the work of 'the greatest artistic genius of the German workers' movement, Käthe Kollwitz' (9). His approach, the author explains, is grounded in empathy, pathos and class consciousness (10–11). In this, Zimmermann's method is comparable to that of Marx portrayed in *Moor and the Ravens of London*, and indeed of its authors: one of benevolent pedagogy.

Zimmerman's drawings for the novel are fluid, often quite sketchy – a little in the manner of Rembrandt, also cited as an influence in the 1958 publication (12) – and dynamic. In a number of cases where the drawings cover two pages, for example in the depiction of Marx and Engels playing piggy-back with the children, there is a sense of animated movement reminiscent of cartoon films. In general the film is, if anything, more static than Zimmermann's illustrations, although they concur in their adoption of the conventional view of Marx as a dignified and statuesque figure.

Marx and education

Dziuba's film, unlike much of his own later work, but in accord with the novel on which it is based, is uncompromisingly didactic. In lengthy discussions Marx explains to the children, for example, the value of solidarity and of the withdrawal of labour. His principal aim throughout is to enlighten them politically and dissuade them from stealing from the rich in the manner of Robin Hood. Thanks largely to a comparatively restrained performance from the ever-jovial Marx-lookalike Alfred Müller (Figure 12.3) – who won a somewhat meagre Third Class National Prize for his performance[8] – the film does, for all its wordiness and earnestness of purpose, refrain from the excesses of hagiography demonstrated, for example, in Maetzig's *Ernst Thälmann* films, in certain films depicting Lenin and Liebknecht, and documentaries of the famous *Du und mancher Kamerad* (*The German Story*, 1956) variety.[9] The latter, a Stalinist history of the birth of the GDR from the ruins of fascism by Andrew and Annelie Thorndike, interestingly also concludes its story with a paean to education in the form of a GDR primer for younger children, *Lesen und Lernen* (*Read and Learn*) by Robert Alt, Hans Balzer and Johannes Feuer, from which a young girl reads a passage beginning 'Germany is our Fatherland. Everyone is working to make it a beautiful country'.[10]

One particularly astute film reviewer in the state newspaper *Neues Deutschland* identified an anti-anarchic subtext to Dziuba's film, shot, after all, in the year of Europe-wide youth unrest in the West, 1968, to which the Eastern Bloc authorities responded with palpable fear and outspoken condemnation:

> Key passages in the film are devoted to an 'outsider' in the Kling family, the rebellious Billy, the 'King' of the Raven Gang. He decides to tackle the wretched factory owner on his own. Anarchic tendencies, evident today amongst the youth of many capitalist countries, are present in this character. This is why it is worth paying careful attention to the friendly lessons which Karl Marx offers Billy without preaching to him. It could well be that one day one might need Marx's arguments when faced with a latter-day 'Billy'.[11]

The appearance of a few too many Billies on GDR cinema screens had significantly contributed to the banning of an entire year's production of GDR feature films in 1965 – the so-called 'Forbidden Films', the *Verbotsfilme* – foremost amongst them Jürgen Böttcher's *Born in '45* (*Jahrgang '45*, 1965), somewhat reminiscent of the work of Gerhard Klein in its debt to Italian neorealism (here tempered by French *cinéma-vérité*), in which a group of directionless teenagers hangs around on East Berlin street corners. The Ravens in Dziuba's film look and sound like Western teenagers as seen through the lens of GDR ideology: dropouts, criminals and anarchists. It is only the intrepid Marx, who visits them and rolls up his sleeves to get them back on the ideological straight and narrow, who can save them from the kind of lawless revolt portrayed in the films of the Thorndikes and, in the Soviet Union, in Mikhael Romm's *I vsyo-taki ya veryu...* (*And Still I Believe...*, 1976).

The *auteurist* film journal *Filmkritik*, in a rare West German response to the film, summed up its pedagogical purpose in the following, relatively dispassionate terms:

> You have to imagine that this film is like our radio broadcasts for schools: an historical process is made comprehensible and plausible by means of a fictional story. The narrative progresses step-by-step, without ellipses, and the basic concepts of the National Economy and of late Marx are explained and then demonstrated in action. [The] film avoids irritating the audience in any way. (Roth 1969: 539)

Interestingly the film was, moreover, prominently advertised in the GDR's film journal *Deutscher Filmexport* in 1969 as a potential export product, with a brief descriptive text in Russian, French and (strikingly ungrammatical) English. There is no evidence, however, to suggest that it was screened in the United Kingdom. In the GDR itself the film was positively received, although, despite its uplifting message and celebratory tone, at least one critic ventured the opinion that it was somewhat weighed down by its ideological zeal:

> The attempt to achieve clarity in the film's message has undoubtedly on occasion led to a tendency on the part of the film's authors to indulge in rather excessive passages of dialogue, a fact which somewhat undermines the aim of providing a thoroughly convincing interpretation of their material. Didactic intentions may have won out over specifically cinematic techniques on these occasions.[12]

There is anecdotal evidence, over and above the re-release of the film on DVD, to suggest that it made a lasting impression on young audiences. It is referred to, for example, in a number of studies of youth culture in the GDR; in Barbara Felsmann's collection of personal recollections of Young Pioneers (*Jungpioniere*), Corinna Sylvester recalls the impact it made on her:

> A kind of Karl Marx biography for children. The poverty he had to endure, his many children, and despite everything he remained intellectually active and committed to social change. Those were

things with which I could easily identify. He was an ideal, showing how one could live for non-material values, for idealist values. In the GDR what underpinned the whole idea of human life was a contempt for consumption and striving for material prosperity rather than stressing creative, non-material values. (Sylvester 2003: 65)

Machines

What is fascinating about this film, aside from its status as a unique attempt to introduce Marx the man to GDR cinemagoers, and its outstanding cinematography, is the dialectical, or perhaps just plain contradictory, portrayal of labour. The most striking and most beautiful scenes in the film are undoubtedly those in the cotton mill. The faces of the young workers, the brutality of the foreman and the effusive condemnation of Victorian working practices by Marx leave the audience in no doubt as to the film's attitude towards wage slavery. However, it seems torn between condemning capitalist exploitation on the one hand, and celebrating the value of labour itself on the other. This ambiguity is manifest in the portrayal of the machines themselves: they may well have enchained the children in 1856, but in the film they are lovingly recreated and beautifully shot in lingering sequences that have a degree of visual invention and rhythmic complexity which the film otherwise noticeably lacks. The looms in particular with their wheels and myriad threads, also suggest a self-reflexive nod to the technology of film itself (with its spools and strips), which may go some way to explaining the film's ambivalent attitude to technological progress.[13] At times one is reminded in these sequences of the machines in Walter Ruttmann's famous city film *Berlin: Die Sinfonie der Großstadt (Berlin: Symphony of a Great City*, 1927) and the fervent affirmation of industrial and technological progress in Dziga Vertov's *Chelovek s kino-apparatom (Man with a Movie Camera*, 1929); it is perhaps here that Helmut Bergmann's early experience as a cinematographer for documentary films is most keenly felt. As a recent commentary on the film in a volume on GDR children's films neatly, if somewhat contradictorily puts it:

> the extremely successful, seemingly documentary insight into an unknown world reminiscent of the novels of Dickens, means that Helmut Dziuba's debut film remains, as ever, well worth seeing. (König *et al.* 1996: 170–171)

I would suggest that in its salute to the machinery of industrial production in 'the Land of Tomorrow and the Day After', a thinly veiled reference to the GDR within the fairy-tales that Marx tells his children both in the novel and the film, and as an adaptation of a prize-winning contemporary socialist novel, *Moor and the Ravens of London* is a striking, indeed unique, combination of historical biopic, straightforward Marxist pedagogy and the *Gegenwartsfilm*. As the novel concludes, none too cryptically, on its final page:

> The dream of the Land of Tomorrow and the Day After, which our fathers only saw from afar, is for us becoming a reality. (Korn and Korn 1963: 448)

Faustian technology and the Marxist wager with the devil

The success of their novel with audiences and critics, the Marx anniversary, and perhaps the imminent appearance of Dziuba's adaptation, appear to have spurred the Korns into revisiting the subject of Marx once more in 1968, when they published a kind of sequel, or more accurately a follow-up, to *Moor and the Ravens of London*. *Meister Hans Röckle und Mister Flammfuß (Master Hans Röckle and Mister Flamefoot)* is a much more modest volume than its predecessor at a mere 209 pages, and is aimed at a slightly younger audience, 'for readers of 11 and older' according to its colophon (Korn and Korn 1968). As the authors explain in an expansive afterword, their story expands imaginatively on the fairy-tales which Marx narrated in their previous book (and which had made a brief appearance in Dziuba's film):

> The name and character of Hans Röckle were not our invention, but rather of Karl Marx. We discovered them on reading the memoirs of his youngest daughter Eleanor [...]. Few people know that Karl Marx loved fairy-tales, invented his own, and was a master of the imagination. Someone who spent his life scientifically predicting a better future with bold foresight had need of creative fantasy like no other. And how could he have told his children, when they were still young, about his great work for the world more effectively than in the guise of a fairy-tale? [...]. Our own biographical and historical studies demonstrated to us that Moor and his hero Hans Röckle have much in common [...]. Once we had found this thread we were emboldened to recreate the lost fairy-tale figure of Hans Röckle who fights with the devil: in the spirit of Karl Marx and out of the spirit of our own age [...]. The Land of Tomorrow and the Day After is not a magical land in the sense of some fanciful utopia. It is the

future that lies before us and which we conquer with every step. It will make our lives brighter and more beautiful, but can only be reached when the devils are banished from this world for good and all. With Hans Röckle, this figure born of a Marxist spirit, we build a bridge out of the social gloom of the nineteenth century, in which the fairy-tales are themselves rooted, to our own present, which with its bold dreams is able to connect tomorrow with today. In the year of the 150th anniversary of the birth of Karl Marx. (Korn and Korn, 1968: 211–215)

The fairy-tale of Hans Röckle and the devil as envisioned by the Korns is a thinly veiled reworking of the Faust legend. In the second part of Goethe's drama, Faust famously proclaims 'Power will be mine, property!' and Marx himself quoted the scene in Faust's study in part one of Goethe's play when discussing 'The Power of Money' in 1844.[14] Röckle is a carpenter, puppet-maker, inventor and magician, his nemesis a greedy capitalist who opposes technological progress (figure 12.4):

> Now they even want to make fire in a new-fangled way. Very un-devilish. Ec-clec-tric, or whatever they call it. Did I hide away my precious burn-everything-away-stone for that? The flame, big or small, belongs to me! Now they press on some kind of switch or other, it rattles and crackles, and golden snakes dance around the place and light up the darkness. (49)

According to Stefan Wolle, Hans Röckle is nothing less than the 'demiurge of a technological world' and 'visionary of a communist future based on modern technology' (Wolle 2011: 283). In the Korns' expanded version of the Faustian fairy-tale, Röckle signs a contract which states, in its third, distinctly productivist paragraph, that he will relinquish his soul to the devil if he loses the will to produce:

> § 3   Master Röckle may produce whatever he wishes as long as it gives him pleasure. Should it make him miserable, if the fun turns sour, if he utters the word 'enough!', then he is mine, body and soul. And that's that! (Korn and Korn, 1968: 64)

Inevitably, Röckle/Marx outwits the devil with his technological vision, wit and a pair of 'time boots' which send the devil packing in the final pages. In case the young readers should miss the point, the illustrator of this volume, Erich Gürtzig, has the victorious hero look even more

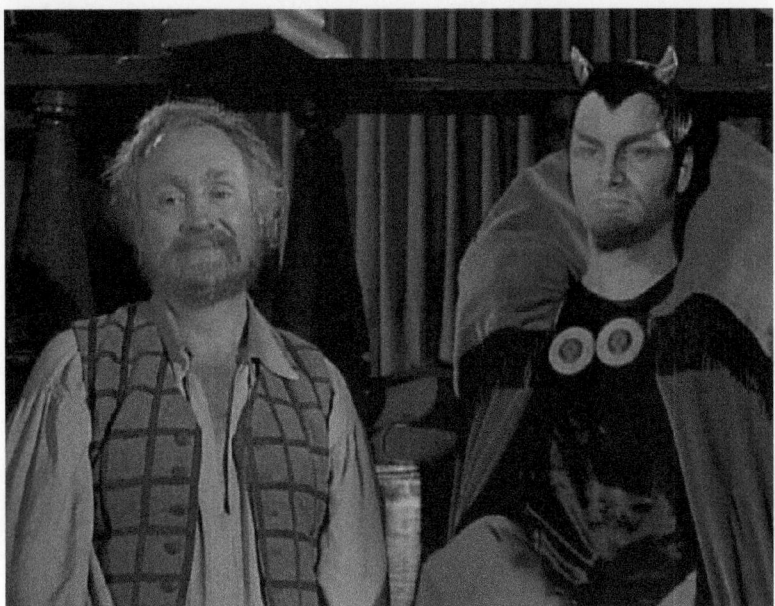

Figure 12.4 Röckle/Marx (Rolf Hoppe) and the devil
Source: Screen capture from *Master Hans Röckle and Mister Flamefoot* (1974), dir. Hans Kratzert, ICESTORM Entertainment GmbH

like Marx than was the case with his progenitor in *Moor and the Ravens of London*. Here, however, the drawings are not only in colour, but also more fantastical (and at times whimsical) than those of Zimmermann, who, unsurprisingly, had not provided any illustrations for the fairy-tale interludes in the 1963 volume.

The Marxist fairy-tale

In 1974 *Master Hans Röckle and Mister Flamefoot* was, like its predecessor, adapted for the screen, this time in the guise of a cheerful, somewhat hallucinogenic colour film, unashamedly situated within the tradition of fairy-tale 'vagueness' denounced by Heiner Carow in 1958. Directed by Hans Kratzert and starring Rolf Hoppe as the Faustian hero, it was given the more explicit title *Hans Röckle und der Teufel* (*Hans Röckle and the Devil*).[15] Ebullient, albeit once again rather wordy, and peppered with slapstick and fairly basic special effects, the film was aimed at a slightly younger audience than its predecessor, this time five years and above. Wolle perceptively identifies in the film, for all its light-hearted fairy-tale trappings, a subtextual Marxist twist here too – in the small print of Flamefoot's contract:

> In the adaptation of 1974 the contract also contains an interesting rider. Hans Röckle loses the wager with the devil if he doesn't invent anything new in seven times seven hours. The loss of pleasure in work implies, entirely in the spirit of Karl Marx, alienation [*Entfremdung*], more precisely alienated labour. Stasis means death, the end of creativity, social entropy. A society unable to invent something new in seven times seven hours falls prey to evil. (Wolle 2011: 284)

Aside from some distinctly atonal music (composed by the jazz musician Günther Fischer and rather conventionally deployed to underscore devilish activities), a magic mirror, which appears to function as a television screen, and some very East German nudity, the film avoids overtly anachronistic references to the GDR as the Land of Tomorrow and the Day After. Moreover, although it proclaims that 'we will tell all the children how to defeat the devil', it does not labour the analogy of Marx as Faust. Unlike Alfred Müller in *Moor and the Ravens of London* and Gürtzig's dignified hero in the book, Hoppe is not a dead ringer for Marx, and his study is more Auerbach's Cellar than Dean Street. The set-designer Klaus Wild, on the other hand, did allow himself a rather baroque flourish in furnishing Röckle's chamber with a massive globe in only two colours: marine blue for the oceans and revolutionary red for all the countries of the world. At one point Röckle is referred to by one of his assistants simply as 'clever and witty', and throughout he is presented as a genial, socialist magician-inventor who avoids sententious political pronouncements, although he doesn't hesitate to inform the devil that he has 'never wanted to work for the rich'.

Unintentionally damning the film with faint praise, a reviewer in the East German *Mitteldeutsche Neueste Nachrichten* concluded that Kratzert's film was 'light-hearted, thought-provoking and slightly serious [...] staged with pedagogical sensitivity'; others were less charitable: in the *Wochenpost* Hans-Dieter Tok deemed the film at times 'too superficial, too didactic', despite its 'wealth of poetic scenes [...] and an arsenal of special effects', whilst Renate Holland-Moritz, In the *Eulenspiegel*, identified a 'strained tweeness which will bore the younger audience (and not only them)'.[16] However, the fact that ICESTORM Entertainment GmbH, the company responsible for re-releasing DEFA films commercially to the unified German market, saw fit to release the film on DVD in 2003, suggests that it may have more lasting appeal than some suggested.

Hans Röckle and the Devil is significant in the present context for a number of reasons. First, it is only the second, and indeed the last, DEFA feature film to portray Marx on screen; second, it remained, until Alexander Kluge's nine-hour compendium *Nachrichten aus der ideologischen Antike: Marx – Eisenstein – Das Kapital* (*News from Ideological Antiquity: Marx – Eisenstein – Capital*, 2008), the only film adaptation of Marx 'texts' (albeit here imaginatively recreated by the Korns);[17] third, it returns Marx to the genre from which he had been exiled in the 1950s, the fairy-tale film, a potentially risky strategy, perhaps, given the unavoidable implication that Marxism is little more than a fantasy or, in Kluge's words, a utopia 'which gets better the longer you wait for it';[18] fourth, it self-reflexively celebrates film itself as the home of progressive, socialist technology.

The children's film: pedagogy and utopia

Whilst *Moor and the Ravens of London* self-reflexively hails the mechanics of cinematography and projection (the spools, wheels and strips) as the legitimate legacy of (de-alienated) industrial labour, *Hans Röckle*

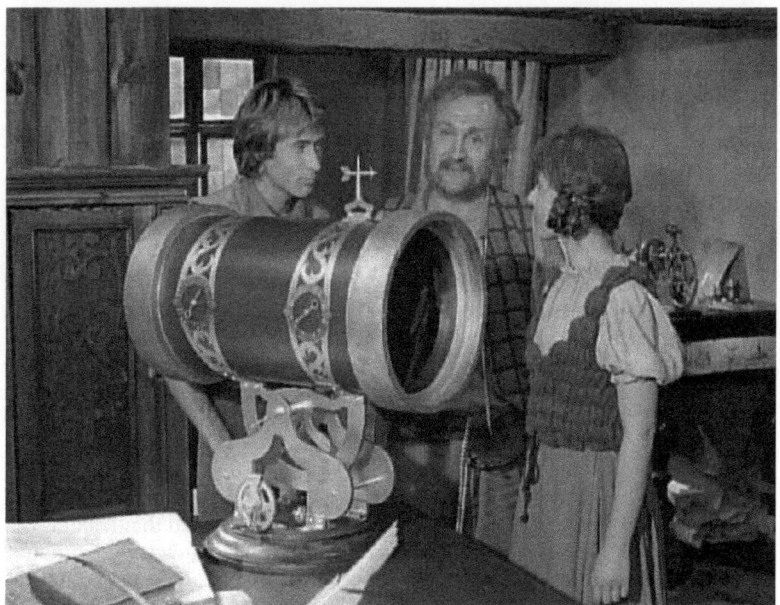

Figure 12.5   Celebration of technology
Source: Screen capture from *Master Hans Röckle and Mister Flamefoot* (1974), dir. Hans Kratzert, ICESTORM Entertainment GmbH

and the Devil rejoices in the ability of technology – the aforementioned 19th-century television, Röckle's magic telescope 'Look Everywhere (*Überallhin*)' (figure 12.5), the film's own special effects (which include stop motion, superimpositions and 'unchained' objects) – to afford good-humoured glimpses of the Land of Tomorrow and the Day After.

Although the two children's films discussed in this essay have very little in common stylistically – the first being a historical costume drama in the style of the pre-war 'proletarian film', the second a colourful fairy-tale film in the post-war DEFA manner – they have much in common ideologically, pedagogically, and in their portrayal of Karl Marx. Strenuously avoiding the bombast of the hagiographic biopic, both portray the philosopher as a benevolent, paternalistic inventor and visionary. Both also present his utopia as a dream yet-to-be-realised, but view education, technological progress, and therefore by analogy the medium of cinema itself, and in particular the *Kinderfilm*, as means of reaching Hans Röckle's Promised Land.

Notes

1. All translations in this chapter are by the author.
2. The cult status of Stefani's film was sufficient to earn it a protracted parody in series three, programme eight of the BBC television comedy series *The Fast Show* first broadcast on 29 December 1997, where it was rechristened 'Ton Swingingen Ringingen Bingingen Plingingen Tingingen Plinkingen Plonkingen Boingingen Triee', which suggests the team may have thought the original was more Scandinavian than German. The characters speak in a mash-up Esperanto-like language with occasional echoes of French and Italian. See: http://www.youtube.com/watch?v=7XqMF5ou7hE (accessed 18 December 2013).
3. Among the very few exceptions are the Soviet feature film *God, kak zhizn* (*A Year is Like a Lifetime*, Grigori Roshal, 1965, music by Dmitri Shostakovich), which focuses on Marx and Engels in the year 1848 to 1849, and the TV mini-series *Karl Marks: Molodye gody/Karl Marx: Die jungen Jahre* (*Karl Marx: The Young* Years, Lev Kulidzhanov and Michael Krause, 1979), a Soviet/GDR co-production consisting of seven one-hour episodes recounting the life of Marx between 1835 and 1848. See also, for example, the Wikipedia entry 'Karl Marx in Film', http://en.wikipedia.org/wiki/Karl_Marx_in_film (accessed 24 September 2013). The entry lists three documentaries, all from the 2000s. In January 2012 the website Cineuropa reported that Raoul Peck's long-awaited feature based on Marx's early years had received funding: 'Seven feature film projects were selected during the last 2012 session for the CNC's second committee for advances on receipts. Raoul Peck's *The Young Karl Marx* (*Le Jeune Karl Marx*) stands out among them. Peck was a member of the jury for the last Cannes competition, and has been well reviewed in the past, notably for *Lumumba* (2000 Directors' Fortnight) and *Moloch Tropical* (Berlinale Special in 2010). Co-scripted by the director with Pascal Bonitzer,

his latest project's screenplay starts just as young Karl Marx finishes his PhD aged 19, then recounts his journey up until the 1848 revolution. Produced by Velvet Film (Peck's production company), the feature film should start shooting in September 2013'. See: http://cineuropa.org/nw.aspx?t=newsdeta il&l=en&did=230871 (accessed 24 September 2013).

4. For a study, in German, of the films Dziuba made in the last decade of the GDR see Röske (2006). The volume also includes an interview with the director.

5. See Section 'Marx and education' below.

6. See: http://en.wikipedia.org/wiki/Slatan_Dudow (accessed 23 September 2013).

7. The volume ends with a fairly extensive index of places and people in London. St Giles, the location of the Rookery of St Giles, one of London's worst Victorian slums, is described as a 'poverty-stricken district in Central London' (Korn and Korn 1963: 456), Bethnal Green 'densely populated with many poverty-stricken quarters' (451). Robin Hood is a 'noble thief who stole to help the poor and save those on the run or stripped of their rights' (454). Substantial entries are reserved for workers' organisations in 19th-century London, the Chartists, Robert Owen and Trade Unions. It is worth noting in passing that Vilmos Korn was actively involved in the production of DEFA documentary films in Dresden immediately after the war and wrote the script for Richard Groschopp's 1946 reconstruction film *Dresden* (Jordan and Schenk 1996: 20).

8. 'Here Marx certainly does not have the aloof grandeur of a monument, but his depiction also avoids descending to the level of mere anecdote. The film captures his full humanity and thus his true greatness. We see a thoroughly down-to-earth Karl Marx. For example when he is forced to cook for his sick family and turns out to be rather inept when it comes to peeling the onions. Alfred Müller understands how to capture the strength of character, the hunger for justice and the clarity of thinking in countless everyday details of this kind. It is a characteristic, but also, despite the inevitable limitations imposed by the episodic form, quite comprehensive picture of Marx that is offered here.' Helmut Ullrich, *Volksstimme* [Vienna], 18 October 1969 (König *et al* 1996: 171).

9. The online *Filmlexikon* at www.zweitausendeins.de characterises the film as 'emotional but not excessively heroic' in its depiction of Marx. See: http://www.zweitausendeins.de/filmlexikon/?sucheNach=titel&wert=57487 (accessed 23 September 2013).

10. This volume appeared in various different editions including Alt, Balzer, Feuer (1955). One of the two narrators of *The German Story*, Gerry Wolff, has a small role (Collins) in *Moor and the Ravens of London*.

11. Elvira Mollenschott, *Neues Deutschland* [GDR], 31 March 1969 (König *et al.* 1996: 171).

12. F. Salow, *Filmspiegel* [GDR], 9, 1969 König *et al* 1996: 171.

13. There are strikingly similar shots, now in colour, in the historical reconstructions which pepper the German television documentary *Karl Marx und der Klassenkampf* (*Karl Marx and the Class Struggle*, ZDF, 2010), the seventh episode of the second series of *Die Deutschen* (*The Germans*). See: http://www .zdf.de/ZDFmediathek/beitrag/video/1187338/#/beitrag/video/1187338/ Karl-Marx-und-der-Klassenkampf- (accessed 23 September 2013).

14. For an online translation of this famous passage from the *Economic and Philosophic Manuscript of 1844* (otherwise known as the *Paris Manuscripts*) see: http://www.marxists.org/archive/marx/works/1844/manuscripts/power.htm (accessed 23 September 2013).
15. Hoppe, a prolific actor in the GDR and subsequently, had also appeared in a minor role, as a banker, in *Moor and the Ravens of London*. The films also share an editor, Bärbel Weigel.
16. These and other responses to the film are gathered in (König *et al* 1996: 195). The editors themselves conclude that 'this long-winded and woodenly staged journey into the land of fantasy would then, as now, only have inspired a handful of children' (König *et al* 1996: 195).
17. 'Strictly speaking this fairy-tale adaptation is the first screen adaptation of a work by Karl Marx, who came up with the story that Ilse und Vilmos Korn later made into a book' (Habel 2000: 231).
18. The famous maxim 'utopia gets better the longer you wait for it' appears in Kluge's 1968 film *Artisten in der Zirkuskuppel: ratlos* (*Artistes at the Top of the Big Top: Disorientated*).

Bibliography

Alt, R., H. Balzer and J. Feuer (1955) *Lesen und Lernen* (Berlin: Volk und Wissen).

Brockdorff, C. (1958) *Kurt Zimmermann: Sozialistische Grafik: 'Kämpfende Kunst'* (Berlin: Verlag des Ministeriums für Nationale Verteidigung).

Habel, F. -B. (2000) *Das große Lexikon der DEFA-Spielfilme* (Berlin: Schwarzkopf & Schwarzkopf).

Jordan, G. and R. Schenk (eds) (1996) *Schwarzweiß und Farbe: DEFA-Dokumentarfilme 1946–1992* (Berlin: Jovis).

Kalder, D. (2013) 'Book Review: "Karl Marx: A Nineteenth-Century Life," by Jonathan Sperber', *Dallas Morning News*, online 13 March 2013, http://www.dallasnews.com/entertainment/books/20130316-book-review-karl-marx-a-nineteenth-century-life-by-jonathan-sperber.ece, date accessed 18 December 2013.

König, I., D. Wiedemann and L. Wolf (eds) (1996) *Zwischen Marx und Muck: DEFA-Filme für Kinder* (Berlin: Henschel).

Korn, V. and I. Korn (1963) *Mohr und die Raben von London* (Berlin: Der Kinderbuchverlag).

Korn, I. and V. Korn (1968) *Meister Hans Röckle und Mister Flammfuß* (Berlin: Der Kinderbuchverlag).

Roth, W. (1969) 'Mohr und die Raben von London', *Filmkritik* [FRG], 13, 539.

Röske, S. (2006) *Der jugendliche Blick* (Berlin: DEFA-Stiftung).

Samuelson, P. A. and W. D. Nordhaus (2012) *Economics*, 19th edition (Indian Adaptation) (New York: Tata McGraw Hill).

Schenk, R. (ed.) (1994) *Das zweite Leben der Filmstadt Babelsberg: DEFA-Spielfilme 1946–1992* (Berlin: Henschel).

Sylvester, C. (2003) 'Da war Ende der Fahnenstange, da warst du der Feind', in B. Felsmann, *Beim Kleinen Trompeter habe ich immer geweint: Kindheit in der DDR – Erinnerungen an die Jungen Pioniere* (Berlin: Lukas Verlag), 63–77.

Wolle, S. (2011) *Aufbruch nach Utopia: Alltag und Herrschaft in der DDR 1961–1971* (Berlin: Christoph Links Verlag).

Index

287

Printed and bound by CPI Group (UK) Ltd, Croydon, CR0 4YY